DATE DUE

PROBLEMS OF BALKAN SECURITY

PROBLEMS OF BALKAN SECURITY

SOUTHEASTERN EUROPE IN THE 1990s

PAUL S. SHOUP, EDITOR
GEORGE W. HOFFMAN, PROJECT DIRECTOR

WW THE WILSON CENTER PRESS   WASHINGTON, DC

The Wilson Center Press
1000 Jefferson Drive, S.W.
Washington, D.C. 20560 U.S.A.

Distributed by arrangement with:
University Press of America, Inc.
4720 Boston Way
Lanham, MD 20706

Printed in the United States of America.
∞ Printed on acid-free paper.

9 8 7 6 5 4 3 2 1

Library of Congress Cataloging-in-Publication Data

Problems of Balkan security : Southeastern Europe in the 1990s / Paul S.
Shoup, editor ; George W. Hoffman, project director.
        p.   cm.
     ISBN 0–943875–22–6 (alk. paper). — ISBN 0–943875–21–8 (pbk. :
alk. paper)
     1. Balkan Peninsula—Politics and government—20th century.
     2. Balkan Peninsula—Foreign relations—20th century.   I. Shoup, Paul.
DR48.5.P74   1990
949.6—dc20   89–77744
                                                                  CIP

The Center is the "living memorial" of the United States of America to the
nation's twenty-eighth president, Woodrow Wilson. The U.S. Congress
established The Woodrow Wilson Center in 1968 as an international
institute for advanced study, "symbolizing and strengthening the fruitful
relationship between the world of learning and the world of public affairs."
The Center opened in 1970 under its own presidentially appointed board of
trustees.

In all its activities, The Woodrow Wilson Center is a nonprofit, nonpartisan
organization, supported financially by annual appropriations from the U.S.
Congress and contributions from foundations, corporations, and
individuals. Conclusions or opinions expressed in Center publications are
those of the authors and do not necessarily reflect the views of the Center
staff, fellows, trustees, advisory groups, or any individuals or organizations
that provide financial support to the Center.

Woodrow Wilson International Center for Scholars
Smithsonian Institution Building
1000 Jefferson Drive, S.W.
Washington, D.C. 20560
(202) 357-2429

Southeastern Europe

CONTENTS

III THE GREAT POWERS AND SOUTHEASTERN EUROPE

MAP, TABLE, AND FIGURES

Map

Table

Figures

ACKNOWLEDGMENTS

As project director, coordinator, and co-initiator of this study, I wish to express my gratitude to Dr. Phillip Petersen of the Defense Department, who not only contributed to the study (with his assistant, Joshua Spero) but also contributed greatly to the planning of this study; to Dr. Nils Wessel of the U.S. Information Agency (USIA) who was a constant source of help during the work of this study; to Professors Carl Linden, Acting Director of the Institute for Sino-Soviet Studies at George Washington University, who helped in the preparation of the project; and to his successor, William R. Johnson, who assisted during the project.

My special appreciation goes to the thirteen authors of this study, and to the editor, Professor Paul S. Shoup, who joined the project only at the meeting in Munich/Tutzing in January 1989. With the constantly changing political and economic situation in the four Balkan Communist countries, it was our job to see that the contributions were up-to-date and to give special attention to avoid duplicating discussions. Dr. Roland Schönfeld, Executive Director of the Südost Gesellschaft in Munich, was kind enough to cosponsor our four-day meeting at the Academy for Political Science in Tutzing, and he, his wife, and his staff ably assisted in making that meeting a success.

I also wish to express my appreciation to the nine commentators of the draft papers who attended the Munich meeting from Turkey, Greece, Yugoslavia, Austria, Hungary, Britain, and the Federal Republic of (West) Germany. All the commentators prepared written comments and made oral presentations, which served as most valuable contributions for the individual papers. John Scanlan, at the time U.S. Ambassador to Yugoslavia, not only made a formal presentation and answered questions at the Munich meeting, but also attended the review meeting in May 1989. In addition, numerous invited guests from West Germany and Radio Free Europe/Radio Liberty participated in the Munich meeting. (Their names are listed in the appendix.)

During our last policy review meeting in Washington in May 1989, which was principally devoted to the papers commissioned after the Tutzing meeting, Jack Seymour and Diane Montgomery of the Office of Eastern European and Yugoslav Affairs, William Stearman of the National Security Council, and Lawrence Orton, Chair, Soviet and

East European Studies, Foreign Service Institute, Department of State, as well as Professors Linden and Johnson participated in the discussions. Numerous colleagues reviewed some of the individual contributions, and they earned the gratitude of both the authors and project director. Special appreciation is extended to Professor Emeritus R. V. Burks and Professor Tadis K. D. Kristof, who contributed to the Munich/Tutzing meeting. My appreciation is also extended for assistance from the staff of the Institute for Sino-Soviet Studies. The project coordinator, the editor, and all the authors are in debt to Nicholas Andrews, who reviewed the manuscript for The Woodrow Wilson Center and whose helpful comments and several specific background statements were incorporated in the final manuscript.

George W. Hoffman
Project Director

INTRODUCTION

George W. Hoffman

The origin of this book goes back several years. No interdisciplinary study of the countries of Southeastern Europe dealing with the contemporary scene from the perspective of national stability and security and superpower interests has appeared in the English language for many years. My contacts with academic and government specialists working on the problems of the region strengthened my conviction in late 1987 that the Communist Balkan states were in deep systemic crisis, which could easily undermine their stability and thus have an important effect on U.S. and Western European policy. This concern also reflected the serious situation in the two non-Communist countries of Southeastern Europe, Greece and Turkey, which could be affected by developments in the Communist Balkan states.

A similar idea was expressed at that time by Dr. Phillip Petersen, Assistant for Europe and the Soviet Union in the Office of the Deputy Under Secretary of Defense for Policy. His interest in a study on Southeastern Europe was shared by Dr. Nils Wessel, Director of Research of the U.S. Information Agency.

This interest by a number of people led me to prepare a project outline for a research study on Balkan security problems, which was supported by the acting director of the Institute for Sino-Soviet Studies of the Elliott School of International Affairs at George Washington University, Professor Carl Linden. All four of us agreed that an in-depth geopolitical analysis of security issues related to the broader region of Southeastern Europe with the participation of American and European specialists would be an important research task and could make an important research contribution to the work of U.S. and Western policymakers. An agreement was signed between the USIA and George Washington University to support such a study. I was appointed project coordinator and director of this project and, in early 1988, began to assemble a group of scholars. Eleven contributors to this study are American; two well-known area specialists of the region came from Europe: the Director of the Southeast Europe

Society of Munich and the East European correspondent of *The Economist* and editor of the monthly journal *The World Today*, published by the Royal Institute of International Affairs in London, England.

A few words are in order concerning the terminology used in the study. The study refers to the region as a whole, which includes Albania, Bulgaria, Greece, Romania, Turkey, and Yugoslavia. The term *Southeastern Europe* applies to the whole region. It includes four Communist countries referred to in this study as the *Communist Balkan countries*; Greece, a member of the twelve-nation European Community (EC); and Turkey, which is an associate member (having applied for full member status). Like Greece, Turkey is a member of the North Atlantic Treaty Organization (NATO) (the Table shows some basic statistics on the countries of Southeastern Europe), whereas Bulgaria and Romania are members of the Warsaw Treaty Organization (Warsaw Pact). The term *Balkan* or *Balkan Peninsula*, which is so often applied to the whole area, is of relatively recent origin. Early in the nineteenth century it replaced the term *European Turkey* and is a Turkish word meaning *mountain*.[1]

A basic assumption of the study is that the issues facing all countries of Southeastern Europe in the coming years are of considerable importance to Western Europe and the United States. Neither the people who initiated this study nor the authors assembled during the spring of 1988 expected the rapid changes in the region and within the Soviet Union. Many of those changes have affected regional developments. For example, Romanian-Hungarian relations have been strained by Romania's treatment of the Hungarian minority in Romania, and Serbia's relations, not only with its Albanian minority in the autonomous province of Kosovo but also with the other nationalities of Yugoslavia, have been affected by renewed Serbian nationalism. And Bulgarian-Turkish relations have been strained by Bulgaria's treatment of its Turkish speaking citizens.

The rapid economic and political changes in the region and the impact of Gorbachev's policies have caused this manuscript to be updated several times between the first meeting of most of the present authors in Washington in May 1988, a critical review meeting when most chapters were submitted to European specialists for an in-depth critique in Munich in January 1989 and the time when final drafts were sent to the editor and project coordinator in April and May 1989. Moreover, three additional chapters were commissioned after the Munich meeting to provide a more complete picture of the political processes in Yugoslavia and an analysis of the U.S. and Soviet positions. These chapters, written by Christopher Cviic, Ronald Lin-

Table
THE COUNTRIES OF SOUTHEASTERN EUROPE

	Total Area (sq. km.)	*Total Land Boun- dary (km.)*	*1988 Popula- tion (in millions)*	*Ethnic Divisions (%)*		*Religions (%)*[a]	
Albania	28,750	768	3.1	Albanians	96%	Muslim	70%
				Greeks	4	Orthodox	20
						Rom. Cath.	10
Bulgaria	110,910	1,881	9.0	Bulgarians	85.5	Orthodox	85
				Turks	8.5	Muslim	13
				Macedonians	2.5	Others	2
				Others	3.5		
Greece	131,940	1,228	10.0	Greeks	97.7	Gr. Orth.	98
				Turks	1.3	Others	2
				Others	2.0		
Romania	237,500	2,904	23.0	Romanians	89.0	Rom. Orth.	80
				Hungarians	7.8	Rom. Cath.	6
				Germans	1.5	Protestant	4
				Others	1.7	Others	10
Turkey	780,580	2,715	54.0	Turks	85	Muslim	98
				Kurds	12	Others	2
				Others	3		
Yugoslavia	225,800	2,961	24.0	Serbs	36.3	East. Orth.	50
				Croats	19.8	Rom. Cath.	30
				Muslim	8.9	Muslim	10
				Slovenians	7.8	Protestant	1
				Albanians	7.7	Others	9
				Macedoninas	6.0		
				Montenegrin	2.6		
				Hungarians	1.9		
				Yugoslavs	5.4		
				Others	2.3		
				Unknown	1.3		
	Total population:		123.1				

Sources: National and various international statistics.

[a]The date of reference for the ethnic and religious divisions of some of these countries, such as Albania, Bulgaria, and Romania, is difficult to set and is not in the official publications of these countries. Also, in the case of Albania it must be pointed out that the country is officially atheist and has suppressed all religious activity. Therefore, these figures are guesses only. In addition, because the number of Gypsies is difficult to ascertain, they are simply not listed in most countries.

den, and Dennison Rusinow, contribute to an understanding of the relations within and among the countries of the region as well as of the future policies of the two superpowers.

All contributors agree that the Communist countries of Southeastern Europe appear to be entering a critical period in which they must reform their economies. This is of special importance in view of their trade relations with the future internal market of the twelve members of the European Community after 1992 and with the six countries of the European Free Trade Association (EFTA). To put their house in order, economically and politically, and to reduce their domestic confrontations constitute the challenge of the 1990s for every Communist country of Southeastern Europe.

As Paul Shoup points out in the concluding chapter, after years of peaceful coexistence due in large part to Soviet efforts to control developments in all the Eastern European countries under its hegemony, decreasing superpower influence in the region, combined with rising nationalism brought about in part by serious economic problems, could easily increase the danger of regional conflicts. The Soviet Union now is concerned primarily with achieving social and political stability at home and avoiding involvement in the internal affairs of other countries. With pressure from the Soviet Union drastically declining, some of the Communist Balkan countries have again started to stir up long-dormant controversies. The impact of these tensions cannot yet be foreseen, but they could easily get out of control and again involve the superpowers. After all these years of peaceful coexistence, the probability exists that the countries of Southeastern Europe could again face rapid change.

An important objective of this study was to develop insights for the future and to make policy recommendations for the United States and the Western European countries giving special attention to the political problems, economic challenges, and security interests of the countries of Southeastern Europe and stressing the Soviet (and Warsaw Pact) dimension.

The study has three parts: the first part is devoted to historical and domestic considerations. The second part addresses the security problems of the region. The third part deals with the superpowers and Southeastern Europe.

The last chapter, which concentrates on future U.S. policy toward the region, is based on existing U.S. policy and is expressed at times as a policy of "differentiation" toward the countries of Eastern Europe. Paul Shoup describes this future policy "as a pragmatic choice of programs that will have some chance of success, will maintain momentum toward reform, and will divert energies to constructive national renewal and away from destructive nationalist vendettas." In addition, he suggests that Western European countries and the United States should help the countries of Southeastern Europe that wish to join the EC or EFTA (Greece is already a member of the EC). Western Europe and the United States should take into account the efforts by the countries of the region to building a market economy (avoiding some of the pitfalls of moving too quickly in this direction) and ending their economic isolation (Albania), strengthening their commitments to human rights, and reducing their national conflicts (the history of such conflicts is especially pronounced in Yugoslavia).

Despite the varied backgrounds of the authors and commentators, they generally agreed on the larger issues affecting all the Communist Balkan countries, for example, the need for greater attention to human rights for minorities and for basic structural changes, including implementation of a competitive market system. The closing of unproductive enterprises will probably lead to increased unemployment. The changes will also pose challenges to U.S. and West European foreign policy decision makers, some of them more serious than any during the past forty years. Increased and rapid confrontations among the countries of the region or internal upheavals could lead to renewed Western and Soviet policy disagreements. Not without reason have the countries of the region been known as "Europe's tinderbox."

NOTE

1. For a more detailed explanation of the use of this term, see George W. Hoffman, *The Balkans in Transition* (1963, reprinted Westport, Conn.: Greenwood Press, 1983), 9–12.

I

HISTORICAL AND DOMESTIC CONSIDERATIONS

1

SOUTHEASTERN EUROPE AND THE LEGACY OF INSECURITY

John R. Lampe

The ongoing evolution of Communist rule everywhere except Greece will, in conjunction with contemporary events, determine much of the direction that Southeastern Europe will take toward the year 2000. But regional security will also depend on how problems left from five hundred years of Balkan insecurity and delayed modernization, from the Ottoman conquest to the shocks of World War II, will be addressed. Greater territorial integrity and political stability since World War II than in the preceding decades or centuries now seem to have removed less of this legacy than we had assumed.

True, Balkan borders remain unchanged, as elsewhere in Europe, obviating the Great Powers' impulse to interfere in the region's affairs. Since the early 1950s, no forced migration across state boundaries has occurred to fan domestic irredentism, nor has actual warfare broken out, despite several threats. Post-World War I pressures from neighboring Italy, Hungary, and Austria vanished with World War II, and the earlier Habsburg and Ottoman empires are long gone. A generally stable international environment has prevailed from the 1960s forward, dominated by the military stalemate between the United States and the Soviet Union and the strategically benign advance of West European economic integration. The USSR has not regarded membership by Greece and eventually Turkey in the European Economic Community (EEC) as the threat to its security posed by their inclusion in NATO a generation earlier. The possibility of Soviet intervention in the region, discussed at length in subsequent chapters, now appears remote.

Within Southeastern Europe itself, nonetheless, there are two serious threats to national and personal security for the 1990s: the same economic crisis that has confronted all of Eastern Europe since the process of rapid modernization stalled painfully at the beginning of the 1980s, and the domestic revival of neighbor-blaming, ethnic nationalism. Assuming that Soviet leader Mikhail Gorbachev continues on his present course, relations with larger, more distant states are unlikely to pose an external threat to the security of Southeastern Europe or even an internal obstacle to reform.

This chapter therefore concentrates on home-grown problems: on pre-1945 barriers to the decentralizing economic reforms that need to be taken in the Communist states of Southeastern Europe, and on the political culture and military traditions that have contributed to enduring ethnic insecurity in the region, Greece and Turkey included. Great-power intervention is often found to be an unsatisfactory explanation for the region's economic failures and insecurities. So is the Western tendency to rely on some ethnocentric theory of Balkan backwardness as an explanation of the region's instability and belated modernization.

Behind the economic and ethnic threats to security lies a deeper threat to the legitimacy of the existing regimes in Southeastern Europe. The Communist leaders that received political credit for postwar economic growth are dead (Tito in Yugoslavia), departing (Zhivkov in Bulgaria), or discredited (Ceausescu in Romania). In Greece, Papandreou's effort to use a charismatic personality to build a ruling, popular party is ending badly. New, more democratic forms of legitimacy may follow. But political legitimacy in Southeastern Europe cannot be built on a broader, more democratic base if it does not begin to overcome long-standing economic and ethnic problems. Otherwise, familiar forms of prewar authoritarianism may reemerge as the only workable guarantee of internal security and territorial integrity.

THE DEMOGRAPHIC AND IMPERIAL LEGACIES

Balkan historians have typically held five hundred years of Ottoman domination responsible for the disabilities with which Southeastern Europe clearly entered the nineteenth century. Broader, still longer-standing demographic and imperial legacies seem more responsible for this premodern institutional backwardness, economic and political. The region's unusually low density of population, previously dated from Ottoman deprivations and disorder during the seventeenth century, seems also to have characterized the pre-Ottoman period. Density of five to six persons per square mile derived in part from the lack of fertile lowlands, adequate rainfall, accessible coastline, and navigable rivers. At the same time mountainous uplands were insufficiently forbidding to bar invading armies from terrain that lay at a strategic crossroads. All this discouraged the emergence of urban markets, bulk trade, or even intensive agriculture, in contrast to the more fortunate West European position as a protected peninsula with ample rainfall and access to the Atlantic. In addition, the uncertainty and relative lack of settlement meant that the subsequent ethnic claims to Kosovo by Serbs and Albanians and to Transylvania by Romanians and Hungarians would be difficult to resist or resolve.[1]

The relatively short-lived Serbian and Bulgarian states of the medieval period, each of them including Macedonia, should be seen as part of region's imperial tradition as well as its national heritage. At the time, these states nurtured imperial aspirations to the widest possible territory, on the model of neighboring Byzantium. By the time that the Ottoman armies confronted them in the fourteenth century, they had largely exhausted their feudal forces in battle with the Byzantine Empire.[2] According to recent research, the demographic damage of these prolonged conflicts, plus losses from the bubonic plague, were barely repaired during the initial relatively favorable period of Ottoman domination, the sixteenth century. Then came further losses from war, disease, and disorder during the seventeenth century. The amazingly low estimates we possess of perhaps 6 million people on the entire Balkan Peninsula by the mid-eighteenth century still stand as testimony to a continuing absence of the critical demographic mass that Eric Jones finds so important in explaining the unequaled advance of early modern Western Europe.[3]

The Ottoman imperial legacy was undoubtedly more powerful than legacy of the Byzantine and native predecessors, although not so different as we used to think. This was a state organized more around military imperatives, successfully when new territory was added and unsuccessfully when existing territory was threatened. The principal armies and their officers, at first more closely controlled from the center than those of the native empires, did eventually become a law unto themselves. The Ottoman command economy, or better, regime of military occupation, worked well enough to supply the army and the imperial capital of Constantinople as long as new territory was available for administration by a relatively small corps of land-based cavalry officers. Western military technology reversed the territorial advance and forced the formation of far larger, town-based infantry units, the famous janissaries. Their numerous officers helped to spread a political culture of urban corruption and contributed to rural disorder.

The corruption of the original Ottoman system did, however, allow market relations to widen surprisingly in the western border areas of Serbia and the Romanian principalities, in southern Greece, and to a lesser extent in Bosnia and Macedonia. The resulting border trade, principally with the Habsburg lands, gave Southeastern Europe some sustained, if still geographically confined, commercial experience with which to enter the modern era.[4]

THE HABSBURG MILITARY AND ADMINISTRATIVE LEGACY

The Habsburg struggle with the Ottoman Empire was the primary vehicle of foreign penetration of Southeastern Europe during the early modern period. West European penetration would never be pervasive, contrary to some early nationalist and recent neo-Marxist scholarship. German and Russian presence would only come later. Even into the nineteenth century, Habsburg military engagement with the Ottoman Balkans was the primary source of war, disease, and migration along a border that ran from Croatia to Transylvania. Here British Marxist Perry Anderson rightly finds at work the same process of "slow, reciprocal exhaustion" that characterized the late Byzantine period.[5]

The wide band of territory designated as the Habsburg Military Border played a more complex role than simply mobilizing troops for this long, fitful struggle against Ottoman forces. Stretching from Croatia in the sixteenth century across the Vojvodina to Transylvania by the eighteenth century, the *Militargrenze* was a principal Habsburg institution in what William McNeill has called the victory of bureaucratic empire.[6] The border's administration attracted a permanently settled militia through land and tax concessions. The settlers' participation and high reputation in Habsburg campaigns over the centuries helped to build the considerable military tradition of the Yugoslav lands, Slovenia significantly excepted.

Although the Habsburg border regime would do little to promote commerce, it did draw many Serbs into the western Yugoslav lands and the Vojvodina. It also created a Romanian counterweight to Hungarian hegemony in Transylvania. Yet little assimilation with Croats and Hungarians, respectively, resulted. In the long run these mixed populations would only add to ethnic insecurity in the region. Habsburg policy at the time was "populationism." Vienna sought simply to secure these relatively empty southern territories by means of settlement and local forces rather than by fortification and a large standing army. Again we see the relevance of the Balkans' unusually low density of population.

Habsburg administrative rule here and elsewhere was driven by fiscal and military imperatives, rather than any strategy for commercial development. These imperatives helped to create a modern, if bureaucratic, tradition of public administration, one that the Balkan states would subsequently draw on to replace the Ottoman reliance on religious law and military power. But the Habsburg tradition of secular civilian government was also hostile to any independent source of private economic power. The anticapitalist, or more precisely, antimarket, disposition that we associate with Austria-Hungary after 1873 owes its origins to this hostility.

At the same time, the market tradition so essential to economic reform in the present day was hardly absent in the southern Habsburg borderlands of the early modern period. In curious contradiction to its presumably mercantilist policy, but consonant with an overriding concern for military security through settlement, the Habsburg bureaucracy allowed relatively free trade to flourish along its Balkan borders. Despite a persistent import surplus, this trade was left primarily to Balkan merchants from the Ottoman lands.[7] Austro-Hungarian attempts to reverse the deficit and to displace or control Balkan traders later in the nineteenth century thus constituted an abrupt change for the new nation-states of Southeastern Europe, culminating in Habsburg tariff wars with Romania between 1886 and 1891 and Serbia between 1906 and 1911. Primarily Hungarian agricultural interests now wished to restrict this traffic. Serbian trade with the Vojvodina and Romanian trade with Transylvania had, however, already begun to provide some economic binding for the enlarged states of Yugoslavia and Romania that were constituted after World War I.

THE POLITICAL-MILITARY CULTURE OF THE PRE-1914 BALKAN STATES

The Balkan states that won independence during the nineteenth century covered less than one-half of Southeastern Europe but became the role models for state building for the entire region. Serbia, Bulgaria, Romania, Greece, and Montenegro have shared traits of political culture and military tradition that contributed to the ethnic insecurities and economic problems still facing the region.

First, these were nation-states, more or less homogeneous, with 85 to 90 percent of their population from the predominant ethnic group and with much of the remainder freely pursuing assimilation into that dominant nationality. Expanding systems of education emphasized a single ethnic identity, while genuine economic and cultural achievements within each of these newly independent states contributed to their political legitimacy. So did Orthodox churches and folk customs that had survived the long Ottoman domination with a specific ethnic identity intact. None of this smoothed the way for the transition to states with new multinational territories or with migrations from lost lands following World War I.

Second, two native military traditions diminished the potential of the independent Balkan states for economic and social modernization. The bandit or rebel tradition of upland bands battling Ottoman, often Albanian, warlords and ignoring or exploiting existing commerce served the Yugoslav resistance well during World War II but proved generally detrimental for postwar Yugoslavia, as we shall see. The other native ingredient in the Balkan military tradition was the professional officer corps that grew up everywhere in the 1880s and assumed a modern appearance, complete with European arms, after 1900. The corps' immense social prestige attracted many able young men, who were given training that included engineering in German-style military academies.[8] At the same time, military careers diverted these able, well-educated young men from political life or private entrepreneurship.

Despite these uniformities, distinctive political cultures took root in the various Balkan states. In Serbia, powerful Habsburg-style ministries and a native monarchy in Belgrade found their inclination to expand state power supported by rising tax revenues but limited by a constitutionally strong parliament, where a real two-party system emerged during the last prewar decade. Before then, peasant traditions of village democracy and suspicion of state power as a ruse for raising taxes somewhat restrained the growing ministerial bureaucracy in Belgrade. The Bulgarian bureaucracy in Sofia had a freer hand. There, the German Prince Ferdinand's monarchy and the same set of Habsburg-style ministries faced less successful resistance to the assertion of state over any private power. The native political spectrum was too much and too bitterly divided. In addition, as I have argued elsewhere, Sofia's isolated location and small commercial interests left the Bulgarian capital with no real alternative to state initiative.[9]

The Romanian and Greek central governments also revolved

around foreign monarchs and powerful ministries established, respectively, on the Russian and Bavarian patterns. Each was, in turn, a variation on Napoleon's French model. But in Romania, the native landowning nobility was a powerful, separate political force. The boyars dominated both the anti-Habsburg Liberal party of Wallachia and the anti-Russian Conservative party of Moldavia, creating sort of a two-party structure that survived until World War I. Their common desire for economic modernization allowed private, often Jewish economic enterprises to prosper. European and U.S. investment in oil extraction was invited under the Conservatives and tolerated under the Liberals. The Greek economy could draw on the return of a number of emigré merchants to carry out or finance the privately based modernization of commerce, if not industry. Agricultural land in Greece was poorer, however, and its ownership less clearly established than elsewhere in the Balkans. Greece's political leaders were in any case generally more concerned with territorial expansion than with stimulating domestic investment in agriculture or industry.[10]

The unfortunate Greek attraction to the *Megali Idea*, a restored Byzantine Empire, intertwined with the legitimate concern for the large number of ethnic Greeks outside the state's borders, to create irredentist, potentially imperialistic ambitions from the nineteenth century forward into World War I. These territorial ambitions differed from those of the other major Balkan states only in extent. Serbia and Bulgaria recalled medieval kingdoms, and Romania an early modern one, to augment their claims to borders that would include all their ethnic fellows. The greatest threats to regional security occurred precisely in unliberated territories where ethnic identities were in dispute, like Ottoman Macedonia, or evenly divided, like Habsburg Bosnia-Hercegovina.[11] The resulting *local* ferment had deeper repercussions in the Balkan states than any great-power initiative. None of these independent states was, however, large or powerful enough, then or now, to impose its hegemony on the others.

What part do we assign to the European Great Powers, presumed by so many native historians to have exerted the decisive influence throughout this period? Their role was admittedly crucial in uniting the Romanian principalities after the Treaty of Paris and in confirming Serbia's independence, expanding Greece and establishing Bulgaria with the Treaty of Berlin, all at Ottoman expense. Afterward, the powers seemed content to hold one another in check and confined their interests to keeping the peace, opposing territorial expansion, and collecting the interest on state loans in overvalued local currencies. Which Great Power, or coalition of powers, can we now say sought political-military hegemony in Southeastern Europe prior to the Balkan wars? None. Which Balkan state fell or placed itself under the sway of a single Great Power or alliance prior to that time? Again, none.

A different sequence of events suggests itself, whereby *all* the independent Balkan states balanced between the Great Powers, seeking loans and diplomatic support wherever possible, but never cutting all ties to any power. Witness the absence of any tangible Franco-Serbian alliance or French military presence despite a Serbian tariff war with Austria-Hungary from 1906 to 1911, which, although bitter, never led Belgrade to break relations with Vienna.[12] The energy expended in navigating among the major European foreign ministries and in dealing with the powers' private commercial representatives was nonetheless considerable. The effort was enough to keep alive the Balkan presumption that some foreign presence was always preparing an intervention.

WORLD WAR I AND ITS CONSEQUENCES

The two Balkan wars that began World War I for Southeastern Europe in 1912–13 upset these small states' balancing act between the Great Powers. Bulgaria, as the loser of the Second Balkan War, was the first to be drawn into a particular orbit, that of Germany and Austria-Hungary.[13] World War I sucked all the Balkan states into defining previously undefined war aims and into choosing sides between the two great-power alliances, both of them promising postwar territorial gains. Romania and Greece delayed and agonized over their choices, finally backing the Entente, to their territorial advantage. The unequivocal Bulgarian and Serbian choices of the Central Powers and the Entente, respectively, first favored Sofia and then Belgrade, as Macedonia came under Bulgarian control but was ceded to the new Yugoslavia in 1918.

For Serbia, Macedonia, and part of Romania, the choices made or made for them brought the experience of military occupation down on the heads of the civilian population. Army restrictions closed down most manufacturing. Rural *centrale* requisitioned food supplies. This regime, plus largely German control of mining operations, introduced more central economic controls than had ever been seen. Where occupation regimes were not in charge, existing governments tried to mobilize all resources for total war in comparable, if less brutal fashion. The western Yugoslav population of Croatia-Slavonia and Slovenia, for instance, did not enrich themselves during the wartime regime of Austria-Hungary, as some Serbian leaders would assume after the war.[14]

The war itself had three principal military legacies: A number of officer corps from the Balkan states acquired training directly from European officers for the first time, and learned more about the use of modern equipment and tactics. The performance of the Balkan armies during World War I nonetheless seemed to rest more on the mass morale of their peasant troops. This frontline experience was a second military legacy, useful to the Yugoslav Communists during World War II. For the interwar period, it was not a stimulus to fascist movements as in Germany or Italy, but did reinforce ethnic animosities. Third, the capture of large numbers of Balkan troops, either by Russia or the Central Powers, helped to radicalize the interwar left, particularly through Communist converts returning from wartime and then revolutionary Russia. Josip Broz Tito was only the most famous of these prisoners of war. The brief Communist regime in Hungary under Bela Kun and other returnees encouraged Yugoslav and Transylvanian Hungarian Communists, but also added to the resolve of Serbian and Romanian government leaders to use military power to consolidate their two newly enlarged states.

The victorious Western powers—France, Britain, and for the first time, the United States—played the decisive role in setting the state boundaries that were retained, with small changes, and recognized as legitimate after World War II. But for the interwar period, the new state of Yugoslavia and an enlarged Romania faced truncated Bulgaria, Austria, and Hungary, generally supported by Italy and joined by dissatisfied ethnic minorities. The resulting struggle over border revision became the *primary* threat to the region's security. Recognition of minority status within the East European states after World War I was real only in Czechoslovakia, despite the specific guarantees for minority rights in the Paris peace treaties. In Southeastern Europe, such attention to minority rights has been paid, with some success in Yugoslavia, only since World War II.

The Western powers turned quickly away from the Southeastern European framework that they had created after World War I. This turn seems far more important than debating, as Balkan and Hungarian scholars do, what President Wilson really thought about alternative postwar settlements, particularly a Danubian federation.[15] American naval presence in the Adriatic probably prevented an Italian assault on Yugoslavia's Dalmatian territory in 1920, and French army officers encouraged Serbian troops to stay in southern Hungary until 1921. After that, there is little evidence of active Western interest, let alone influence, in Southeastern Europe. The prewar Western role of major marketplace and creditor was not revived. High Balkan expectations for trade even with the United States went unfulfilled. Local monetary stabilizations had again, by the mid-1920s, overvalued local currencies, as before World War I, in order to make repayment attractive to foreign lenders. Yet the London and New York capital markets furnished few loans and then at high rates of interest.[16] By 1928, the huge French army had withdrawn behind the Maginot Line, signaling an end to any active French link to the series of alliances with Yugoslavia, Romania, and Czechoslovakia known collectively as the Little Entente.[17] The depression dealt a final blow to the region's capacity to finance its economic modernization through agricultural exports, clearing the way for rising German influence and tentative Russian interest to assert themselves during the 1930s.

THE INTERNAL THREATS TO INTERWAR SECURITY

The new states of Southeastern Europe were thus left largely to their own devices to face the two powers, Germany and Russia, whose revisionist resentments and readiness for revolution were the primary dangers, as Joseph Rothschild has rightly observed, from a Paris peace settlement that punished but did not permanently hobble either power.[18] Unresolved problems of ethnic conflict, Greece excepted after 1922, and of economic modernization throughout the interwar period would make each of the region's small states more vulnerable to revisionist threats or promises.

Their only joint efforts to establish regional security were the weak Little Entente of the 1920s, soon deserted by its French sponsors, and the toothless Balkan Entente of the 1930s. The first was designed to contain Hungarian claims to its lost Habsburg territories, and the second to curb Bulgarian designs on Macedonia and Thrace. But neither addressed the ultimate threat that Germany and then Russia would pose.

Yugoslavia survived its birth pangs in part because of more early idealism about the new multiethnic state than is usually acknowledged. Yet Yugoslavia also survived because the Serbian army and political leadership moved quickly to hold the country's western borders against further Italian advances and to restore public order in Macedonia and Kosovo.[19] In the latter locations, the Serbian hegemony so often presumed to be the bane of the first Yugoslavia did persist. Police powers in "southern Serbia" were sufficiently arbitrary to store up resentment that neighboring Bulgaria and Albania were waiting to exploit. But in western Yugoslav lands, stalemate rather than Serbian hegemony was soon the result.[20]

While grievously wartorn Serbia awaited first German reparations and then Western loans that never came in the anticipated amounts, Slovenia and Croatia recovered quickly and surged ahead, perhaps for the first time, with their transport system in tact. Exports to and capital from the prostrate economies of Austria and Hungary fueled bank-led investment. Strengthened by political parties that did not subdivide like Serbia's, the two western Yugoslav lands ignored the central bank established in Belgrade and refused to agree on a law for industrial encouragement (tariff and tax exemptions) on the prewar Serbian pattern until 1934. Separate cooperative movements and other economic institutions remained ethnically as well as regionally divided throughout the interwar period. By the start of World War II, the security of Yugoslavia still depended too heavily, as it had during the state's creation in 1919, on a Serbian-dominated army and police force.

Romania's interwar insecurity also revolved primarily around an effort, albeit more successful and more expensive, to absorb its new territories, above all, Transylvania. The Romanian National Liberal Party found itself in a far stronger postwar position than did the ruling Serbian Radicals. Rather than subdividing themselves like the Radicals, the Liberals saw their principal rival, the Conservative Party, discredited and dissolved by a fatal wartime alliance with Germany and Austria-Hungary. In Transylvania, the now predominant National Liberals were able to consolidate the territory's economic connection to Romania through the postwar financial weakness of Hungary and by use of a very favorable conversion rate (2:1) for Austro-Hungarian crowns into Romanian lei. The main Bucharest banks enjoyed a leading position in the Transylvanian economy that no Belgrade bank could imagine in Croatia or Slovenia. The Hungarian intelligentsia in Transylvania found the resulting Romanian hegemony hard to accept, and a number of them joined the minority-dominated Romanian Communist Party.

The Liberals' economic policy of *prin noi înşine* ("through ourselves alone") did not, however, much advance modernization or the spread of market relations. The state budget and money supply were, in fact, smaller than the prewar level on a real per capita basis. Yet the Liberal regime of the 1920s pushed ahead not only with its expensive Transylvanian policy but also with a mining law that discouraged Western capital from investing in a Romanian petroleum industry that badly needed new equipment. Financial pressure from the state's Banca

Romaneasca forced the country's most entrepreneurial private bank, the Jewish-owned Banca Marmarosch-Blank, to close by 1929.[21] Behind these tactics was an early inclination toward the strategy of etatist autarkic development that both the fascist Iron Guard of the 1930s and the Ceausescu regime of today have favored for different anti-market reasons. The economic result of the Liberal measures was a poor performance that helped force them from power before the onset of the Depression.

The Bulgarian experience in the interwar period was more promising economically, although not for private enterprise, and less promising politically despite a far smaller fascist movement. A sense of political failure hung over interwar Bulgaria following the imposition of huge reparations and the loss of Macedonia to Yugoslavia and Greece. Aleksandur Stamboliiski's Agrarian regime, popularly elected in 1919 but arbitrary toward its opponents, was brutally overthrown and its leaders murdered in 1923. More than 220,000 refugees from Macedonia and Thrace poured into Bulgaria, adding their frustration to the general malaise. They staffed a revived Macedonian Revolutionary Organization (MRO), which became a law unto itself in southwestern Bulgaria until 1934. Then a small band of military officers, the Zveno, seized power, albeit briefly, under the banner of efficient, nonparty government and disbanded the MRO enclaves.

After 1935 the royal regimes of Tsar Boris, like King Carol's in Romania, attempted to set both party and military rule aside. All of them remained hostage, however, to a revisionist readiness to treat first with Italy and then with Germany for the transfer of Macedonia from Yugoslavia under almost any terms. Economically, the successors to Stamboliiski did not dismantle his constructive cooperative network. They used his labor battalions to build infrastructure, as he had intended, and also to evade peace treaty limits on the size of the Bulgarian army.[22] We shall see shortly what use the post-1945 Communist government made of these established institutions.

Interwar Greece had fewer and weaker public economic institutions with which to modernize. At the same time, this most Mediterranean of the southeast European states had had more experience with private enterprise and international trade than any of its Balkan neighbors. Many emigrant Greek merchants from across Europe and around the Mediterranean had moved to independent Greece during the nineteenth century, bringing with them valuable market skills. By the last prewar decade, Greek enterprises conducted more of the country's foreign trade, and Greek-manufactured or -owned vessels carried far more of Greece's exports and imports than did any other private sector in Southeastern Europe.

The failed military campaign to annex western Anatolia in 1922 brought some 1.3 million Greek refugees from Smyrna and other towns into Greece, primarily to the north. This proved to be a significant infusion of new entrepreneurial energy and talent.[23] The very mass of these refugees sharply reduced the share of Slavic-speaking, that is, Slavophone, Greeks in the northern population and thus defused the Macedonian question for Greece until after World War II. The poverty of the refugee majority also won recruits to the small Greek Communist Party (KKE) that played such a large role in World War II.

The initially successful and then disastrous Anatolian expedition led by King Constantine and his royalist officer corps left the interwar political spectrum bitterly divided between adherents of a republic and those of the existing monarchy. The army's involvement in this split was also greater, forcing most officers to choose sides. Greek political parties also were shorter-lived than parties elsewhere, tied to the personal prestige of the leader and the reach of his client network.[24] Despite these domestic difficulties, interwar Greece expected less from the Western powers in the 1920s and was less prevailed upon by Germany in the 1930s than any other southeast European state. But Italian territorial ambitions continued to threaten Greece, as well as Yugoslavia.

Albania can be mentioned briefly because of its failure to preserve independence, which had been won only on the eve of World War I when Austro-Hungary supported the creation of a separate state to prevent Serbia from absorbing the former Ottoman territory. During the 1920s the new state fell into the Italian economic orbit. Albania's struggle during the 1930s to avoid Mussolini's political grasp failed, in part because no Western power or Balkan neighbor would stand up for its territorial or political integrity.[25] The Balkan neighbors' perception of this largely Muslim population as a threat, born from Albanian military prowess and banditry during the Ottoman era, received encouragement from the interwar and wartime link with Mussolini's Italy. Yugoslav and Greek distrust of Albanian intentions, perpetuated since 1945 by alliances with Stalin's Russia and Mao's China, and the Albanian sense of isolation among hostile Balkan neighbors thus have a long history.

WORLD WAR II AND ITS CONSEQUENCES

Ethnic antagonisms throughout Southeastern Europe were made worse by World War II. The Serb-Croat, Romanian-Hungarian, and

Greek-Albanian animosities come most readily to mind, along with the persecution of Jews and Gypsies by German and local fascists. These were especially deep wounds to the multinational states of Yugoslavia and Romania.

The native populations' sense of responsibility for their own destiny was dealt an unprecedented blow. German and Italian military occupation spread more widely and cut more brutally into civil society than had the occupation regimes of World War I. To the extent that they destroyed or discredited the old order, these regimes cleared political ground for the Communist parties that would seize power or have it handed to them after the war everywhere except Greece, where an attempt was also made.

Ironically, it was native Communist rule that introduced more prolonged great-power leverage in Southeastern Europe than ever before—all the levers of Stalinist power and the Soviet model. Western aid protected first non-Communist Greece and then Communist Yugoslavia from Soviet domination, but otherwise Western influence was minimal. France had vanished as a military or economic presence. The Anglo-American interest in the region during the war had largely been to divert German troops there on what we now know were false promises of an Allied invasion. At the war's end, Anglo-American representatives on the Allied Control Commissions found that they had no effective way of restricting local Communist or Soviet initiatives in Romania or Bulgaria, or of offering territorial or other tangible incentives to non-Communists.[26] Once again, as Prince Paul of Yugoslavia had expressed it to the American ambassador, Arthur Bliss Lane, in 1941, "You big nations . . . speak of honor, but you are far away."[27]

The continuing Soviet military presence in Bulgaria and Romania after the war helped to set them apart from Greece and Yugoslavia. Both had been German allies, rather than occupied territories, during the war. Their state apparatus and professional officer corps were apparently preserved but sufficiently compromised by support for the German war effort to prompt them to switch to the winning Soviet side in late 1944. Both armies were conveniently swept out of the country to join the Red Army's advance into Hungary.

The new Communist-dominated regimes in Bulgaria and Romania were able to purge most prewar officers and civilian employees quickly by 1945–46 and still leave this massive institutional apparatus in place. Such institutions proved invaluable to the consolidation of Communist power along Stalinist lines, and a continuing obstacle to economic reform in more recent times. A further Communist advantage in the immediate postwar period was the non-Communist fear that the Western Allies would use the postwar settlements to impose heavy reparations on Bulgaria and to deny Romania the reacquisition of Transylvania from Hungary. Soviet support was seen to ensure against either imposition, thus meriting more non-Communist concessions on other issues than otherwise would have been the case. Bessarabia, lost to the USSR in 1940, was rightly presumed beyond recovery.

The postwar shocks to Romanian and Bulgarian society were severe, although not readily comparable. Soviet presence was more decisive in Romania, including the imposition of reparations that clearly set back postwar recovery. In Bulgaria, a stonger, larger Communist Party was the major instrument of change. The existing state marketing agency for agricultural goods (*Hranoiznos*) served the Bulgarian Communist Party (BKP) well in preparing the groundwork for collectivization. Had the long-standing cooperative network of Stamboliiski's Agrarians been put to comparable use by the Communist authorities and allowed to survive the relatively early drive for collectivization, current Communist efforts to maintain agricultural production in the face of a shrinking rural population might well have had a better chance of success.[28]

Both the Bulgarian and the Romanian armies survive as respected institutions, although with little significance for the actual defense of the country. Soviet intervention in Romania now seems far less likely, in any case, than it did during the 1970s. The Romanian army's leadership may retain some potential for independent political action, perhaps not during the rest of the Ceausescu era but possibly afterwards in the Polish fashion of General Jaruzelski. The Bulgarian army remains closely tied to Soviet forces in training and at all decisive levels, but it also affords a career that receives popular respect. This is less because of the army's continuing economic service in the tradition of Stamboliiski's labor battalions than because of its still longer standing role as a repository for national self-respect.

The Yugoslav and Greek experiences with World War II began with terrible human losses and the destruction of the prewar state institutional structure. Yugoslavia was literally dismembered. Civil war there and in Greece compounded the tragedy. The areas of German occupation in both countries, the so-called Independent State of Croatia, and the Italian-controlled expansion of Albania into Kosovo were the scenes of the greatest losses and the most destruction. The brutal process of mobilizing local economic resources for the Axis war effort fell far short of the results that German authorities had envisaged, let alone setting any effective pattern for state intervention after the war.[29] The principal German legacy to postwar economic development was not foreign investment but the bilateral clearing agreements that had been the vehicle for Nazi economic penetration of all the Balkan states during the late 1930s.

The strengths and weaknesses of the postwar regimes that emerged must be seen against this black wartime background. Belated Anglo-American material aid to Tito's Partisans and then largely American United Nations Relief and Rehabilitation Administration aid for recovery between 1945 and 1947 did help the new Communist regime in Yugoslavia to establish itself sufficiently to survive the Tito-Stalin split. Similar Western aid to anti-Communist forces in Greece plus Stalin's 1944 agreement with Churchill to cede Greece on a 90-to-10-percent basis, in return for a 90-to-10-percent Soviet predominance in Romania, played a significant part in deciding the ensuing civil war.

For Yugoslavia, the new Partisan army was initially the regime's greatest source of strength. Largely formed from Serbs and Montenegrins in 1941–42, the Partisan forces attracted enough participation from the other major ethnic groups by 1943–44, the Kosovar Albanians perhaps excepted, to substantiate the federal mythos on which the new Yugoslavia was created. The split with the Soviet Union in 1948 was partly occasioned, and more clearly sustained into the 1950s, by the largest army—more than a half-million men—anywhere in Eastern Europe. It remains an essential federal institution and, in Oskar Jaszi's phrase, a centripetal force, despite too large a Serbian percentage in its officer corps and Slovenian dissatisfaction with its high cost and obligatory service. The economic role of this large Partisan force and its successor, the Yugoslav National Army (JNA), has been less fortunate. The elevation of party cadre who genuinely distinguished themselves during the war to postwar positions as enterprise managers or higher economic officials gave crucial economic responsibilities to too many people who apply standards of a rudimentary political-military hierarchy, rather than those of cost-efficiency and market relations.[30]

In Greece, the royalist faction of military officers which had bested their republican rivals by the late 1930s survived wartime exile and the two civil wars of 1944 and 1946–52.[31] The Greek generals, however, proved powerless in 1967 to overturn the populist, antiparty coup of subordinate colonels. The colonels' political failures prompted the surviving old guard to withdraw from politics. A new group of less political officers, outside the old royalist and wartime

Communist cadre, have in the meantime come forward to make Greece, whatever its other problems, more secure from a domestic military coup than is Yugoslavia.

The external security of Greece and Yugoslavia received important American backing after 1948. Although Greece, as a NATO member, has been given somewhat more economic aid and a great deal more military training and support, it is Yugoslavia, ironically, that regards the assistance as having proved more valuable in preserving its territorial integrity and international independence. That assistance stands in any case as the one historical occasion when Western interest in Southeastern Europe endured beyond a wartime, immediate postwar, or treaty period. Now that long period may be past, and the Balkan states again find themselves on their own to face as great a challenge from German (or now Common Market) economic predominance as from perhaps receding Russian political pressure.

THE BALKAN LEGACY AND PROSPECTS FOR THE 1990S

The 1990s will see the states of Southeastern Europe more conscious of being left to their own devices than in any preceding decade of the twentieth century. In the concluding words of the most recent German survey of the region's history, it is the return of "Balkan relations."[32] Rather than celebrating the promise of this independence, analysts West and East are more concerned with the risk of the region's economic irrelevance to an increasingly integrated Western European market and with the danger of political change that promises only nationalist authoritarianism.

Greece, as a member of the European Economic Community, faces neither the danger of economic isolation nor the problem of transforming a politically controlled economy, both of which confront the Communist states of the region. Thus, a distinction must be made between the fate of Southeastern Europe's Communist systems, on the one hand, and Greece and Turkey, when considered part of the region, on the other. Yet common problems remain. Up to this point, we have spoken of their historical origins; now we may speak of their potential resolution, focusing on the Communist states of the region.

The Balkan legacy to economic reform is mixed but fairly clear. A commercial tradition based on market behavior and international trade does exist and has been stronger historically than in Russia, if not in Italy. But something like the Russian dilemma of rolling back the role of the state in favor of autonomous enterprises has confronted the region's effort to industrialize for nearly a century. Before World War I, trade with Western Europe or the rest of the Austro-Hungarian customs union provided the major pressure for free competition. This pressure encouraged agriculture but discouraged local manufacture. World War I broke up the Habsburg monarchy, and its aftermath disrupted the direction and reduced the level of European trade for the entire interwar period. The revival and unparalleled growth of that trade since World War II point the way to wider integration with the West, and perhaps with some of the East European economies, that is the best guarantee of successful, market-oriented reforms. Only such a wider competitive arena can offer sufficient rewards to successful enterprises and sufficient punishment to the inefficient ones, without allowing national governments the chance to intervene. Only such a wider geographic area can overcome the limitations of expanded trade within Southeastern Europe itself. A Balkan customs union would still face too similar a set of comparative advantages to represent a major new stimulus.

Wider economic connections nonetheless require more coordination within the region than now exists. The Balkan foreign ministers' conference in Belgrade in 1988 may represent movement in that direction. Future contacts could realistically follow in the footsteps not of the abortive efforts in the early 1930s to create a Balkan Federation, but in those of the concurrent League of Nations conferences to explore avenues of economic and social cooperation. Such nonpolitical approaches would also be the best way to begin dealing with the minority problems that still trouble relations between Yugoslavia and Bulgaria, Bulgaria and Turkey, Turkey and Greece, Greece and Albania, Albania and Yugoslavia, and Romania and Hungary, simply by making individual movement and cultural communication between these states easier.

How can the governments of Southeastern Europe take any of these positive steps if internal political stability is maintained only through authoritarian regimes whose primary recourse to popular support is narrow nationalism and suspicion of neighboring countries or ethnic groups? The emergence of such regimes now looms as a major threat to long-term regional security. The traditional Western prescription for arbitrary, inward-looking regimes, is of course, a multiparty system. The promising experience of several Balkan states with competing, if not democratically tolerant, political parties before World War I took place within borders that did not include large or intractable numbers of other ethnic groups. Today, not just in Yugoslavia but also in Romania and Bulgaria, the popular appeal of exclusive national identities works against any process of democratization.

Yugoslavia's ethnic divisions are, of course, the greatest and most dangerous in the region. These divisions have provided a long-standing justification for rule by a single Communist party, instead of a multiplicity of presumably ethnic parties. But ethnic divisions within the League of Yugoslav Communists have now become so pronounced that it may require the emergence, or at least the specter, of other parties—with Yugoslav-wide constituencies, it is to be hoped—to keep the country from becoming a permanently unworkable confederation. Strictly ethnic, non-Communist parties will only recall the failures of the first Yugoslavia. The fate of Yugoslavia's inescapable experiment with federalism and its survival as a single state carry implications that seem more portentous for Southeastern Europe, for good or ill, than any other single circumstance.

For the rest of Southeastern Europe as well as Yugoslavia, the simple desire to maintain the territorial status quo may serve to keep irredentism in check. Yet the legacy of ethnic separatism persists, threatening the prospects for economic modernization and political pluralism. Ironically, it is the Communist states of the region that are most squarely confronted with the choice between recourse to narrow nationalism and more fundamental modernization and democratization. The former path can lead no further than the authoritarian politics and etatist economics of the 1930s, guaranteeing the failure of greater integration into the Europe of the 1990s and leaving observers to lament: *Im Balkan nichts Neues.*

NOTES

1. Much of the furor in Romania over the new Hungarian history of Transylvania derives from its persuasive argument that the territory was sparsely settled when the first Magyars migrated there in the eleventh century. (This is not to dispute earlier Romanian presence and subsequent predominance in the area's population.)
2. Eric L. Jones, *The European Miracle* (Cambridge, Eng.: Cambridge University Press, 1981), 175–91. It was Western Europe, rather than the Balkans, that enjoyed the major benefit of being a peninsula—isolation from outside attack on three sides. For a review of recent demographic research that suggests limited Balkan growth from the sixteenth until the eighteenth centuries, see the essay by Maria Todorova, *Revues Balcaniques* (1983), 111–16.
3. John V. Fine, Jr., *The Late Medieval Balkans: A Critical Survey from the Late 12th Century to the Ottoman Conquest* (Ann Arbor: University of Michigan Press, 1987).
4. John R. Lampe and Marvin R. Jackson, *Balkan Economic History, 1550–1950: From Imperial Borderlands to Developing Nations* (Bloomington: Indiana University Press, 1982), 55–61.
5. Perry Anderson, *Passages from Antiquity to Feudalism* (London: New Left Books

(NLB), 1974), 285–93, and his *Lineages of the Absolutist State* (London: NLB, 1974), 370–75.

6. William H. McNeill, *Europe's Steppe Frontier, 1500–1800* (Chicago: University of Chicago Press, 1964), 125–80; Gunther M. Rothenberg, *The Austrian Military Border in Croatia, 1522–1747* (Urbana: University of Illinois Press, 1960); and Carl Gollner, *Die Siebenburgische Militärgrenze* (Munich, 1974).

7. The classic study remains Traian Stoianovich, "The Conquering Balkan Orthodox Merchant," *Journal of Economic History* 20, no. 2 (June 1960): 234–313.

8. See Ljuben Petrov, "The Training of Bulgarian Officers, 1878–1918," and Thomas Verenis, "The Selection and Education of Greek Officers from Independence to the 1920s," in Bela Kiraly and Walter Scott Dillard, eds., *The East European Officer Corps, 1740–1920: Social Origins, Selection, Education and Training* (New York: Columbia University Press, 1988), 107–36.

9. John R. Lampe, "Modernization and Social Structure: The Case of the Pre-1914 Balkan Capitals," *Southeastern Europe* 5, no. 2 (1978): 11–32.

10. A brief overview may be found in Richard Clogg, *Parties and Elections in Greece* (Durham, N.C.: Duke University Press, 1987), 1–7. On the agricultural regime, see William H. McGraw, *Land and Revolution in Modern Greece, 1800–1881: The Transition in Tenure and Exploitation from Ottoman Rule to Independence* (Kent, Ohio: Kent University Press, 1986).

11. See the new study by Duncan Perry, *The Politics of Terror: The Macedonian Revolutionary Movements, 1893–1903* (Durham, N.C.: Duke University Press, 1988).

12. See Alan Palmer, *The Chancelleries of Europe* (London: Allen & Unwin, 1983), 209–30; and John R. Lampe, "Austro-Serbian Antagonism and the Economic Background to The Balkan Wars," in Bela Kiraly and Dimitrije Djordjević, eds., *East Central European Society and the Balkan Wars*, East European Monographs no. CCXV (New York: Columbia University Press, 1987), 338–45.

13. Their two governments would now play active roles in seeking client states and economic access to their territories. See Andrej Mitrović, "Germany's Attitude towards the Balkans," in Kiraly and Djordjević, eds., 295–316; and Milcho Lalkov, *Balkanskata politika na Avstro-Ungariia, 1914–1917* (Sofia, 1983); and R. E. Simmons, *German Balkan Diplomacy, 1906–1913: The Genesis and Implementation of a War-Risk Policy* (Ann Arbor: University of Michigan Press, 1982).

14. John R. Lampe, "Unifying the Yugoslav Economy, 1918–1921: Misery and Early Misunderstandings," in Dimitrije Djordjević, ed., *The Creation of Yugoslavia, 1914–1918* (Santa Barbara, Calif.: ABC Clio Press, 1980), 139–56.

15. Precious little, according to recent American analysis. See Arthur Woolworth, *Wilson and His Peacemakers* (New York: W. W. Norton, 1986), 443–68.

16. Lampe and Jackson, *Balkan Economic History*, 376–94.

17. For a brief summary of these alliances and the still weaker Balkan Entente of the 1930s, see Branimir M. Jankovic, *The Balkans in International Relations* (New York: St. Martin's Press, 1988), pp. 149–57. On the French role in the 1920s, see Piotr Wandycz, *France and Her Eastern Allies, 1919–1925* (Westport, Conn.: Greenwood Press, 1974 reprint). On the regional efforts of the 1930s, see Robert J. Kerner and H. N. Howard, *The Balkan Conferences and the Balkan Entente, 1930–1933* (Berkeley: University of California Press, 1936); and G. Reichert, *Das Scheitern der Kleinen Entente, Internationale Beziehungen im Donauraum von 1933 bis 1938* (Munich, 1971).

18. Joseph Rothschild, *A Return to Diversity: A Political History of East Central Europe Since World War II* (New York: Oxford University Press, 1988), 1–7.

19. On the army's complex role, see Mile Bjelajac, *Vojska Kraljevine SHS, 1918–1921* (*The Army of the Kingdom of Serbs, Croats and Slovenes, 1918–1921*) (Belgrade, 1988).

20. Lampe, "Unifying the Yugoslav Economy, 1918–1921." For a different view, see Ivo Banac, *The National Question in Yugoslavia*, (Ithaca, N.Y.: Cornell University Press, 1984), 379–405.

21. See Maurice Pearton, *Oil and the Romanian State, 1895–1947* (London: Oxford University Press, 1971).
22. John R. Lampe, *The Bulgarian Economy in the Twentieth Century* (New York: St. Martin's Press, 1986), 56–60.
23. Dimitri Pentzopolous, *The Balkan Exchange of Minorities and its Impact on Greece* (Paris and The Hague, 1962).
24. See George Mavrogordatos, *Stillborn Republic: Social Conditions and Party Strategy in Greece, 1922–1936* (Berkeley: University of California Press, 1983).
25. See Dennis Mack Smith, *Mussolini's Roman Empire* (New York: Penguin Books, 1977), 20–21, 149–58.
26. Elizabeth Barker, "British Policy Towards Romania, Bulgaria, and Hungary, 1944–46," in Martin McCauley, ed., *Communist Power in Europe, 1944–1949* (London: Macmillan, 1962), 201–19. Also see Michael M. Boll, *Cold War in the Balkans: American Foreign Policy and the Emergence of Communist Bulgaria, 1943–1947* (Lexington: University of Kentucky Press, 1984).
27. Jacob Hoptner, *Yugoslavia in Crisis, 1935–1941* (New York: Columbia University Press, 1962), 236.
28. The personal plots leased by Bulgarian peasants from the collectives over the past fifteen years at the least had an integrated commercial and credit framework of their own. Lampe, *The Bulgarian Economy*, 210–12.
29. On Yugoslavia, see Holm Sundhausen, *Wirtschaftsgeschichte Kroatiens im national-sozialistischen Grossraum, 1941–1945* (Stuttgart, 1983); on Serbia, Karl-Heinz Schlarp, *Wirtschaft und Besatzung in Serbien, 1941–1944* (Stuttgart, 1986). The best overall view is E. A. Radice, "The German Economic Program in Eastern Europe," in M. C. Kaser and E. A. Radice, eds., *The Economic History of Eastern Europe, 1919–1975*, vol. II (Oxford: Clarendon Press, 1986).
30. David A. Dyker, "Yugoslavia: Unity Out of Diversity," in Archie Brown and Jack Grey, eds., *Political Culture and Political Change in Communist States* (New York: Holmes and Meier, 1979), 70–7.
31. Richard Clogg, "Greece," in McCauley, *Communist Power in Europe*, 184–200.
32. Edgar Hosch, *Geschichte der Balkanlander von der Fruhzeit bis zur Gegenwart* (Munich, 1988), 260–5.

2

U.S.-YUGOSLAV RELATIONS: A HISTORICAL APPRAISAL

Walter R. Roberts

As U.S.-Yugoslav relations enter the 1990s, it is important to reassess them from a historical perspective. Such an exercise should help determine whether this relationship is based on elements that transcend the period of the cold war and should indicate what problems might arise in U.S.-Yugoslav relations in the years ahead.

U.S. interest in Southeastern Europe was minimal before World War I. The United States nevertheless took a direct part in the final settlement of the war through President Wilson's Fourteen Points and thereafter participated in the peace treaties of St. Germain (Austria), Trianon (Hungary), Sevres (Turkey), and Neuilly (Bulgaria).

THE FIRST AND SECOND PHASES

In the years following World War I, the first phase of U.S.-Yugoslav relations, the United States maintained a correct, formal attitude toward countries located on the Balkan Peninsula, but had relatively small interest in the Balkans. Economic matters as well as intellectual and scientific exchanges received some official attention, but, by and large, U.S. policy toward all areas of the world except Latin America lapsed into almost complete isolation.

The Italian invasion of Albania in 1939, the subsequent outbreak of war and victories of the Germans in Europe, and the German efforts to win Hungary, Romania, Bulgaria, and Yugoslavia over to the Tripartite Pact reawakened U.S. interest in the Balkans. This marked the beginning of the second phase of U.S. relations with Yugoslavia—the period of World War II. As early as January 1941, Colonel William J. Donovan, who later headed the U.S. Office of Strategic Services, went on a special mission to Greece, Turkey,

Bulgaria, and Yugoslavia to ascertain for President Franklin D. Roosevelt the situation in those countries. He was in Belgrade from January 23 to 25, 1941, and visited the regent and the prime minister; he explained to them the established U.S. policy of giving every possible assistance short of war to countries willing to fight for their independence.

The British, who were already at war, viewed the Balkan situation with great urgency. They saw that the Germans were reinforcing the struggling Italians in North Africa. Foreign Secretary Anthony Eden and Chief of the Imperial General Staff General Sir John Dill visited Athens on February 22, 1941, and on March 7, 1941, British troops landed in Greece to shore up the Greek defenders against the invading Italians. On March 10, 1941, Prime Minister Winston Churchill sent a telegram to Roosevelt in which he said, "At this juncture the action of Yugoslavia is cardinal. No country ever had such a military chance. If they fall on the Italian rear in Albania, there is no measuring what might happen in a few weeks."[1]

Far from falling on the Italian rear, the Yugoslav government was slowly moving in an opposite direction, toward joining the Tripartite Pact, which it did on March 25, 1941. Four days earlier, on March 21, the American minister to Yugoslavia, Arthur Bliss Lane, was instructed to advise the Yugoslav government that the United States was prepared to offer Yugoslavia all facilities under the recently enacted Lend-Lease Act as long as the country remained free and independent.[2]

Two days after the Yugoslavs signed the Tripartite Pact, Serbian officers of the Yugoslav General Staff organized a coup d'état against the government. Although the new government did not renounce adherence to the Tripartite Pact, Hitler and his allies (Italy, Hungary, Romania, and Bulgaria) attacked Yugoslavia on April 6 and within eleven days the country was conquered.[3] Following Yugoslavia's collapse, Serbian officers and men under Colonel Draza Mihailovic organized a resistance movement in the mountains of Serbia. After Germany attacked the Soviet Union in June 1941, the Yugoslav Communists led by Josip Broz Tito also rose against the invaders.

The news of these resistance movements was slow to reach the West. Late in the summer of 1941, Churchill began to receive word of fighting in Yugoslavia and instructed the Special Operations Executive (a highly secret special warfare group) to find out what was going on inside Yugoslavia. In the following couple of years, British liaison officers were clandestinely dispatched first to Mihailovic's forces and later also to Communist (Partisan) units, who by that time were fighting each other. This was clearly a British area of interest. The United States, while concerned, conceded the primary role to Britain.

Nevertheless, the United States was unwilling to leave the Yugoslav problem entirely to the British.[5] President Roosevelt received King Peter of Yugoslavia in Washington in June 1942; the American minister to the Yugoslav government in London, Anthony J. Drexel Biddle, Jr., kept contact with the Yugoslav cabinet; and, by the summer of 1943, American liaison officers were parachuted to both resistance movements in Yugoslavia. Although these American officers were part of the British liaison teams, they were able to inform their superiors directly about events in Yugoslavia.

As matters evolved, it was the British who were more sympathetic to Tito than the Americans. After all, Tito's forces were fighting while Mihailovic was lying low. The United States, for its part, however, was eager to continue its support of Mihailovic, who represented the government-in-exile that the United States recognized as the legitimate Yugoslav government. Yet, in the end, it was the British position that prevailed, helping Tito to emerge as the dominant military force in Yugoslavia at the end of World War II.

As the war entered its closing phases, Churchill became more disenchanted with Tito, but by then the Partisans had won the civil war. Ruefully, Churchill would recall the controversy with the United States regarding Allied military operations in the Balkans, which the United States steadfastly opposed and which in Churchill's view might have produced a different political constellation in Yugoslavia— indeed, all over Eastern Europe.

The first time Churchill and Roosevelt discussed the question of operations in the Balkans was at the Quebec Conference of August 17–24, 1943. In anticipation of the conference, the American Joint Chiefs of Staff met to discuss strategy. General George C. Marshall, the U.S. Army chief of staff, said that President Roosevelt was opposed to operations in the Balkans.[6] On the same day, the U.S. secretary of war, Henry L. Stimson, who had recently returned from England, handed Roosevelt a letter in which he said that "the British theory is that Germany can be beaten by a series of attrition in Northern Italy, in the eastern Mediterranean, in Greece, in the Balkans. . . . To me that attitude seems terribly dangerous."[7]

At the Quebec Conference, Roosevelt indicated his desire to have the Balkan divisions that the Allies had trained, particularly the Greeks and Yugoslavs, operate in their own countries. Churchill suggested that commando forces could also operate in support of the guerrillas on the Dalmatian coast.[8]

Because neither the British nor the American head of government expressed an interest in offensive land operations by their countries in the Balkans, such a possibility was not pursued in Quebec.

A couple of weeks later, on September 8, 1943, Italy surrendered. Churchill, who was in Washington on that day, became intensely interested in the possibilities that the Italian surrender opened up for operations along the Dalmatian coast. In a memorandum to Roosevelt drafted on the day after Italy's capitulation, Churchill said that "utmost efforts should be put forth to organize the attack upon the Germans throughout the Balkan peninsula and to supply agents, arms, and good direction."[9]

On November 20, 1943, Churchill sent a memorandum to the British Chiefs which suggested that a port or ports on the Dalmatian coast be seized, that bridgeheads be established, and that the resistance forces in Yugoslavia and Albania be activated.[10]

No doubt, Churchill had dreams, but, as Ehrman said, "when faced with the realities he saw well enough the impossibility of a Balkan campaign."[11] His views are perhaps best expressed in a speech he gave to the Dominion prime ministers on May 3, 1944, a month before the cross-channel invasion, in which he said that he was bound to admit that if he had had his own way, the lay-out of the war would have been different. He favored rolling up Europe from the southeast and joining hands with the Russians. However, Churchill noted, it had proved impossible to persuade the United States to accept this approach. Washington had been set at every stage on the invasion of northwest Europe. Later, in the same meeting of Dominion prime ministers, Churchill said that

> there had never been any question of major action in the Balkans. . . . The Americans had all along said that we were leading them up the garden in the Mediterranean. His reply had been that, in return, we had provided them in the garden with nourishing vegetables and refreshing fruits. Nevertheless, the Americans had remained very suspicious and thought he was entertaining designs for dragging them into the Balkans. This he had never contemplated doing.[12]

It should be added here that the possibility of Allied landings had been welcomed by the resistance forces in Yugoslavia under General Mihailovic but had troubled the Partisans under Tito. Indeed, during the German-Partisan negotiations of March 1943, the Partisan representatives, Milovan Djilas and Vladimir Velebit, told the Germans that they would fight the British if they were to land on the Dalmatian coast—a statement undoubtedly well received by the Germans who had been fighting the British for more than three-and-a-half years.[13]

After the Normandy invasion in June 1944, the question of Allied operations in the Balkans arose again. At the time, Allied forces, having just taken Rome, were driving northward toward the Gothic Line between Pisa and Rimini. They had three choices: to pierce the Gothic Line, to withdraw troops from Italy for an invasion of southern France, or to land at the top of the Adriatic and drive through the Ljubljana Gap toward Vienna. General Alexander, who headed the Allied forces in Italy, wanted to pierce the Gothic Line and then veer toward France or preferably toward Yugoslavia. The Allied Combined Chiefs, however, asked him to halt his advance and make divisions available for either France or Yugoslavia. General Marshall, the U.S. Army chief of staff, favored the south of France, but British General Wilson, the Allied Mediterranean commander, favored Yugoslavia.

The final decision to invade the south of France on August 15, 1944, was reached mainly because the cross-channel invasion was stalled by bad weather and stiffening German resistance and needed support on the southern flank. That plan was adopted, however, only after the most outspoken disagreement between the United States and Britain. The U.S. Joint Chiefs favored the invasion of southern France and were against the "commitment of Mediterranean resources to large-scale operations to Northern Italy and into the Balkans," a view with which the British Chiefs did not agree.

Churchill appealed to Roosevelt, reminding him of a statement that the president had made at the Teheran Conference regarding possible Balkan operations.[14] But Roosevelt said flatly that he could not agree to the employment of U.S. troops against Istria and into the Balkans. He added that thirty-five U.S. divisions could be landed in the south of France but no more than six beyond the Ljubljana Gap.[15] In the end, Roosevelt prevailed, but Churchill was furious; privately he said that an "intense impression must be made upon the Americans that we have been ill treated and are furious."[16]

U.S. and British files conclusively demonstrate that Roosevelt looked on military operations almost solely from a military point of view, whereas Churchill balanced military with geopolitical considerations. Roosevelt dismissed Churchill's fears of a Soviet takeover of the Balkans; adding that it was undesirable to base hopes for victory on political imponderables.

The death knell to any introduction of substantial Allied forces into the Balkans came on December 2, 1944, when the Combined (British and American) Chiefs sent a directive to General Wilson to try to reach Bologna in Italy, adding that the introduction of major forces into the Balkans was not favorably considered. In any event, the tough German resistance in Italy made a move toward Vienna impossible. Churchill felt that the Italian campaign would have gone better had not several Allied divisions been withdrawn for the landings in southern France; if the Gothic Line had been breached earlier, he believed, the move through the Ljubljana Gap might have materialized and the map of Europe might have been differently drawn.[17]

As the war drew to a close, the United States only hesitatingly followed the British lead to establish a Tito-led government in Belgrade. Roosevelt continued to believe that events in Yugoslavia were remote from U.S. interests. Nevertheless, a new U.S. ambassador, Richard C. Patterson, who had been accredited to the exile government in London, was sent to Belgrade only two weeks after the British ambassador had arrived.

THE THIRD PHASE

The third phase of U.S.-Yugoslav relations covers the 1945–8 period. During the three years in question, relations deteriorated to such an extent that they were at times at the breaking point. Not only did the Yugoslav regime look to Moscow, despite the many disappointments that the Partisans had experienced throughout the war at the hands of the Soviet Union, but as the cold war grew more intense, Yugoslavia played an important supporting role. Yugoslav delegates at the United Nations, most of the time speaking Russian, often outdid the Soviets in their anti-American rhetoric. The Yugoslavs shot down two American planes flying over Yugoslavia from Italy to Austria in 1946, and in 1947, following the Soviet lead, the Yugoslavs rejected Marshall Plan aid.

Although this is not the place to argue that other options were available to the Allies, it is evident that the British and Americans, each in their own way, had helped Tito to power. Churchill saw to it that the Partisans received military assistance, only to find that once Tito had the upper hand in the civil war, the Partisan leader opposed Allied war aims in Trieste, in Austria, and elsewhere. U.S. policy, for its part, was dictated by the lower priority (compared with Western and Central Europe and the Far East) assigned to the area and by the disinclination of Roosevelt to use military operations for political ends. Once Tito was firmly in control of Yugoslavia, with Soviet backing, he proved to be one of the West's most implacable foes. Until the events of 1948, all consideration of a policy of friendship and cooperation with Yugoslavia, based primarily on the U.S. role in aiding the Yugoslavs' resistance to the Germans, became moot.

THE FOURTH PHASE

A fourth phase in U.S.-Yugoslav relations commenced with the Cominform's denunciation of Yugoslavia in June 1948. The U.S. government quickly understood the importance of the break in the Communist camp. For the first time in its history, the United States became a major player in the Balkans. In what turned out to be one of the true U.S. foreign-policy successes since World War II, President Harry S. Truman seized the opportunity and provided Yugoslavia with desperately needed economic and military help. Despite enormous Russian pressure, Yugoslavia remained independent. More than that, Yugoslavia stopped aiding the Greek Communists, thereby contributing to the collapse of the insurgency; agreed to a Trieste settlement; dropped its territorial claims against Austria, thus facilitating the conclusion of an Austrian treaty; and, of course, did not become a member of the Warsaw Pact—important positive developments for the West.

For a decade after the Tito-Stalin break, U.S.-Yugoslav relations improved steadily. The relationship, nevertheless, was based almost exclusively on a shared interest in neutralizing the Soviet threat to Yugoslavia. The absence of deeper linkages between the two countries became evident in the late 1950s and the early 1960s, as the Soviet threat diminished and Yugoslavia's foreign policy began to focus on creating a coalition of nonaligned nations. American hopes that nonalignment would not predispose Yugoslavia to side with the Soviet Union appeared dashed in September 1961, at the first Conference of Nonaligned Nations, when Tito criticized the United States and defended the Soviet violation of the nuclear test ban agreement. Relations between Yugoslavia and the United States were made more difficult by other actions of the Yugoslavs at that time, including the enactment of a press law that almost forced the closing of the U.S. Information Service in Yugoslavia. Nor did Eisenhower's refusal to invite Tito to Washington on the occasion of Tito's visit to the United Nations in 1960 contribute to an improvement of bilateral relations.

Yet during this fourth phase of U.S.-Yugoslav relations, ties between the two countries took on a broader and more lasting character. A watershed occurred in 1963, after Tito's state visit to the United States. Until then, the Yugoslav leader, although grateful to the United States for economic assistance, nevertheless remained suspicious of

U.S. motives. The atmosphere changed when President John F. Kennedy received Tito warmly. Tito was the last foreign head of state to visit Kennedy before the latter's assassination. The young president's death deeply affected Tito, who was in tears when he signed the condolence book at the American embassy in Belgrade.

Almost overnight, U.S.-Yugoslav relations improved perceptibly. Within a year, a Fulbright agreement for academic exchanges, which had been pending for more than five years, was ready for signature. In several other areas, too, the bilateral relationship was elevated to a higher level than before 1963. Despite subsequent difficulties in U.S.-Yugoslav relations in the 1960s and 1970s (e.g., over U.S. policy in Vietnam), the past two decades have been marked by a level of cooperation between the two countries that has gone beyond the narrow considerations of cold war politics and concerns over the Soviet threat in Southeastern Europe.

THE CURRENT PHASE

U.S. relations with Yugoslavia are now entering into a new phase, one that coincides with rising difficulties on the domestic scene in Yugoslavia and with Yugoslavia's hopes to reform its economy. The challenges that this new era poses to both Yugoslavia and the United States are many. Yet in the past several years, relations between the two countries have continued to be mutually beneficial. There has been an increase in high-level visits in Belgrade and Washington. In 1988, a new consular convention was signed, which solved a long-standing disagreement over the problems of dual nationality and furthered joint efforts against international terrorism. U.S.-Yugoslav trade has been increasing to the extent that the United States is Yugoslavia's fourth-largest trading partner. The United States has helped Yugoslavia's financial situation in various ways, including recently making available an additional $50 million in Commodity Credit Corporation export credits.

Yugoslavia has also contributed to regional stability by arranging an all-Balkan conference in 1988. For the first time in the postwar era, all six Balkan states—Albania, Bulgaria, Greece, Romania, Turkey, and Yugoslavia—participated in a government meeting at the foreign minister level. Possibilities for new and expanded multilateral cooperation were discussed, just as the Yugoslavs had hoped.

Yet in this new phase of U.S.-Yugoslav relations, several factors will test the ties that developed in the period since 1948, and especially since 1963. On the U.S. side, now that the Soviet threat has diminished, there is a danger that U.S.-Yugoslav relations will no longer be seen as vital to U.S. interests. For better or worse, many Americans no longer view Yugoslavia as the asset that it was to the United States when the U.S.-Soviet relationship was strained. Just as Yugoslavia stands on the brink of introducing major reforms, other countries in Eastern Europe, notably Hungary and Poland, have taken the spotlight away from Yugoslavia in their bold moves toward sharing power between the party and the forces of the opposition.

On the Yugoslav side, there are also dangers, especially in the rapid deterioration of the domestic situation and the failure to resolve differences among the republics and nationalities. Yugoslavia may not fully realize that these disputes cannot be isolated from the foreign-policy realm and that growing confrontations among the Yugoslav peoples could make it increasingly difficult for the United States to continue to supply aid to Yugoslavia.

There is a need, therefore, on both the U.S. and the Yugoslav sides to draw on the mutually beneficial ties that have developed between the two countries over the past two decades as a basis for relations in the 1990s. In the coming years, U.S. policy should continue to be geared toward helping Yugoslavia maintain its independence and territorial integrity; it should encourage Yugoslavia to take strong economic measures that will require difficult political decisions, including the introduction of political pluralism as an indispensable component of economic reform. It is to be hoped that once these steps are taken, the ethnic problems that have become more volatile will diminish and the unity of the country will be strengthened.

NOTES

The author is indebted to Paul Shoup for incisive suggestions concerning this chapter and to Ambassador Hans Thalberg for his substantive contribution as commentator.

1. Winston S. Churchill, *The Second World War*, vol. III (Boston: Houghton Mifflin, 1950), 110.
2. *Foreign Relations of the United States*, 1941, vol. II (Washington: Government Printing Office, 1959), 961.
3. The Germans rolled on in Greece, forcing the British to evacuate the Continent once again.
4. The Yugoslav government, which had fled into exile, finally settled in London. The U.S. minister to Yugoslavia who had left Belgrade in May 1941 returned to Washington, but a new U.S. envoy was accredited in London to the exile government.
5. The USSR, despite the fact that the Partisans were led by the general secretary of the Communist Party of Yugoslavia, showed surprisingly little interest in the Yugoslav situation.
6. Maurice Matloff, *Strategic Planning for Coalition Warfare, 1943–44* (Washington: Government Printing Office, 1959), 213.

7. Henry L. Stimson and McGeorge Bundy, *On Active Service in Peace and War* (New York: Harper, 1948), 436f.
8. Matloff, *Strategic Planning*, 225.
9. Churchill, *The Second World War*, vol. V, 136.
10. John Ehrman, *Grand Strategy*, vol. V (London: H. M. Stationary Office, 1956), 555.
11. Ibid., 112.
12. Ibid., 555.
13. Discussed at greater length in Walter R. Roberts, *Tito, Mihailovic and the Allies, 1941–1945* (New Brunswick, N.J.: Rutgers University Press, 1973; reprinted by Duke University Press, 1987), 106ff and 148.
14. Churchill, *The Second World War*, vol. VI, 63.
15. Ibid., 722f.
16. Ehrman, *Grand Strategy*, vol. V, 361.
18. Churchill, *The Second World War*, vol. VI, 126.

3

COMMUNIST SOUTHEASTERN EUROPE: CHALLENGES TO STABILITY AND SECURITY

Trond Gilberg

As Eastern Europe and the Soviet Union experience the full force of rapid change in the twilight of the 1980s, the regimes of this area experience multiple stresses in all areas of societal activity. These stresses are so deep and pervasive that many analysts now talk of "systemic change" and "fundamental threats" to the existing order of "real existing socialism" or communism as a system of rule. Many believe (and some East European and Soviet leaders are among them) that this process of change will fundamentally alter "communism" as we know it; what will take its place is not nearly so clear.[1]

The stresses brought about by the processes now under way in the Communist world have clear security implications, because the entire region faces prolonged instability inside each system, with the concomitant possibility that this instability will spill over into neighboring states and perhaps engulf the entire area. Such a process, in turn, would pose additional challenges to the capability of the regimes of the region to cope with their problems, thus feeding on the domestic troubles already experienced. Domestic and external problems and concerns interact symbiotically.

It is necessary to define concepts carefully. *Instability* as used here refers to a *situation* in which established procedures, processes, behavior patterns, and formal structures of decision making no longer function in the manner expected or previously experienced, thus upsetting the established ways of "doing business" politically. Instability, then, may develop in the general population when attitudes, values, goals and objectives, and actual behavior transcend the boundary of the familiar and known. Furthermore, the stresses produced by such developments may hamper or incapacitate the ability of the regimes in question to deal with such mass instability, thereby creating a crisis in the relationship between ruler and ruled. Instability may also proceed from the political order (infighting, rivalries, factional differences) to societal elites and into the masses of the population, thereby triggering problems at the mass level that may feed back on the strife in the political order. Instability, then, is a *condition* of symbiotic relationships among actors at various levels.

This interaction also ensures that instability is a *process* of interaction, in which activities in one area of the system affects the activities of other areas, other parts of that system. And instability has the potential of producing the same effect in other systems. In other words, instability in one unit (whatever its reason) may trigger similar processes elsewhere. This, then, may constitute a *security* problem.

Problem-solving capability refers to the ability (or lack thereof) of regimes to anticipate the conditions that will lead to instability and to undertake measures to prevent such conditions from producing actual behavior that we can term instability. Alternatively, the regime must be able to deal with such behavior once it has occurred, and to take steps necessary to restore stability while ensuring that such behavior does not occur in the same form or intensity in the future.

Instability as defined does not necessarily imply a security problem; only if the process and condition of instability result in some dislocations of the political order in one or more of the systems examined is there potentially such a problem. And that security problem is real only if troubles in one state of the region have direct implications for others, or for the regional hegemon, which is the Soviet Union. Concretely put, severe political upheavals in Romania, for example, may be contained within that country and may have little effect on Albania or Bulgaria. By the same token, the leaders in the Kremlin may decide that troubles in Romania are not really conducive to *regional* instability and may therefore be ignored. Thus there is no necessary connection between domestic instability and external security. But under certain concrete conditions, such a connection may exist. That is the topic of this chapter as it unfolds.

The area under investigation is *Southeastern Europe.* There is no universally accepted definition of this geographic area. For the purposes of this discussion, I define Southeastern Europe as comprising the states of Romania, Bulgaria, Yugoslavia, Albania, Greece, and the European part of Turkey. Hungary is not a part of the region geographers normally term the Balkans, and the Hungarians do not consider themselves part of the culture, traditions, and history of this area. I have chosen to include Hungary in this discussion, if only peripherally, because *domestic* developments in that country clearly affect the socioeconomic, cultural, and political systems of Southeastern European states, and thereby affect the ability of these states to cope with instability and to solve problems.

The ultimate fate of a political system is in the hands of the regime that controls it. A *regime* is the formal structure of political power in society. This includes those institutions that are responsible for the making and enforcing of *binding decisions*, and the administrative-bureaucratic structures designed to implement such decisions. In Communist-ruled states, the most important such structure is the Communist Party and its auxiliaries.

STABILITY, INSTABILITY, AND STRAIN: EXTERNAL AND INTERNAL FACTORS

The stability or instability of the Communist regimes in Southeastern Europe is influenced by both domestic and external factors; as already discussed, these elements feed on each other more or less symbiotically, creating a dynamic relationship that cannot easily be disaggregated in terms of analytical categories. Nevertheless, it is clear that some of these factors are predominantly domestic, while others are basically external. And among the latter, three are the most important: (1) the policies of the Kremlin toward the region as a whole and individual states therein; (2) shared misfortune (the crisis of "real existing socialism"); and (3) the influence of the West.

Kremlin Policies

Since the establishment of Communist regimes in four of the Balkan states in the late 1940s, Soviet policy toward them has been the dominant external factor in the political life of two of the four (Bulgaria and Romania) and a significant, if not dominant, element for Yugoslavia and Albania. The latter regimes broke with the Soviet Union in well-documented disputes that need no elaboration here; suffice it to say that the Kremlin has had only limited *direct* influence on the domestic and foreign policies of these states since the removal of Belgrade and Tirana from full Soviet control.

Nevertheless, both these regimes (and particularly Albania) remain Communist in the sense that the local Communist Party has attempted to run the polity, economy, cultural sphere, and social order according to some basic principles of Marxism-Leninism. These principles include an autocratic political system in which the Communist Party maintains control over the structures and processes of the political order and allows only limited pluralism, if any (here, Yugoslavia clearly stands at one end of the East European spectrum, and Albania, together with Romania, are located at the other extreme). In the economy, centralized planning, limited private enterprise, heavy state interference in the agricultural sector, and a firm emphasis on industrialization continue to hold sway, despite the well-known efforts of decentralization and workers' management found in Yugoslavia. In both systems, there is also a limit to the expression of ideas and thoughts, although Yugoslavia is remarkably open by East European standards on this dimension. (The point is that Yugoslavia still is not West Germany, Scandinavia, or Austria on this score.)[2]

Under these circumstances, the relative structural and political similarities between Belgrade and Tirana, on the one hand, and Moscow, on the other, create a set of relationships that influence one another in important ways. Put briefly, the successes and failures of "real existing socialism" in the Soviet Union have an effect on all others who consider themselves "socialist."

This indirect influence of the Kremlin in Belgrade and Tirana is augmented by specific Soviet policies toward the two regimes and the reaction of these regimes to such policies. Albania, for example, has been highly critical of the Kremlin, for reasons that are peculiar to this bilateral relationship, castigating Moscow for its ideological laxity and its alleged abandonment of the principles of Marxism-Leninism. This Albanian fixation has remained a major feature of its domestic and foreign policy scene since the break with Moscow almost thirty years ago.[3] As a result of the self-imposed political and socioeconomic isolation of Albania from much of the rest of the world, the Soviets had little direct influence in Tirana. Thus the Albanians may be able to deal with their emerging problems of change outside the security considerations of the Kremlin or the other Balkan states. Only if the need for change *inside* Albania is ignored to the point of creating crisis conditions in the political order will security issues arise for others.

Soviet influence is much greater in the two other Balkan states under consideration here, because they are both members of the Warsaw Pact and the COMECON (Council for Mutual Economic Assistance), and thus directly involved in the Soviet security zone as well as in the economic network of socialist systems. There are, of course, considerable differences between Romania and Bulgaria on this dimension, mostly because of the concerted efforts by the Ceausescu clan to fashion and maintain an autonomist foreign policy. The Bulgarians, in contrast, have remained one of the closest allies of the Kremlin on all dimensions of foreign and security policy. But despite these differences, both these states are linked to the Soviet Union in ways that go beyond the experience of other Balkan systems.

This close relationship clearly affords the Kremlin a major opportunity to influence domestic politics in Sofia and Bucharest, both directly and indirectly. During the past few years (and continuing at the present time), the Soviet leadership has been remarkably reticent about direct intervention in the domestic affairs of any East European state, even as these entities experience the full force of developments that demand political, cultural, and socioeconomic change. Moscow seems preoccupied with its own problems and with the need to establish and manage détente with the United States. In Eastern Europe, the Kremlin's main focus is on Poland and its recurring crises and on the fast-moving developments in Hungary. In this context, the Communist states of Southeastern Europe seem less exposed and less prone to serious instability.

Whereas *direct* Soviet influence in Bulgaria and Romania has been limited in the Gorbachev era, the *indirect* impact of *glasnost* (political reform and openness), *perestroika* (economic restructuring), and the widening political debate in the Soviet Union has been considerable and will continue to grow in the future. The well-publicized process now under way in the USSR questions a number of political, socioeconomic, and cultural "givens" in the Communist-ruled systems and promises considerable change in the political process and the structures that control them. Such far-ranging debate is bound to affect the domestic political order in the Balkan states, even if the regimes in charge of these states reject developments in the regional hegemon or try to ignore them. Most important, the Soviet debate has sanctified the notion that one *can* question certain aspects of the established order and still be considered legitimate, a part of the system, rather than a traitor to it. This factor alone will open up the range and scope of political discussion and will have a considerable effect on the political systems of Southeastern Europe, regardless of regime efforts.[4]

Specifically, Soviet developments have encouraged elements of the technical and managerial elites in the Balkan states to criticize the performance of the *apparatchiki* still in charge of the party structures throughout much of the region. Furthermore, some members of the cultural intelligentsia have begun to write about matters hitherto considered out of bounds by the literary establishment, and plays and movies now discuss themes that could not be examined a few years ago. (This is true even in Romania, despite the efforts of the Ceausescu clan to stamp out such discussion.) Historians have been encouraged by Soviet developments to examine their own past in a more systematic manner, and other academics also are in the process of reassessing their fields of inquiry in terms of new developments. All this has clear implications for the regimes of the region. The winds of change are blowing in the Balkans, and this time they are driven largely by developments in the East. Such a phenomenon is bound to be destabilizing, in that it forces the issue of regime adaptation or resistance to change.[5]

Shared Misfortune: The Crisis of "Real Existing Socialism"

The Communist-ruled states of Southeastern Europe are part of the community of "socialism," whether or not they accept the notion of Soviet influence and the Soviet sphere of interest. This means that they have shared experiences and therefore a set of shared problems and expectations. At present, the Soviet Union, Romania, Bulgaria, Yugoslavia, and Albania are experiencing major upheavals and challenges that some scholars have characterized as a "systemic crisis." This crisis is both internal and external, because it deals with those characteristics that all Communist-ruled states possess, as well as national peculiarities that exist in each case. This, then, is the *international* crisis of communism. It behooves us to examine it in some detail.

All the regimes in this region share in the crisis of legitimacy. *Legitimacy* is commonly defined as the acceptance by the populace of the elites' right to rule.[6] Under present conditions in Southeastern Europe (and in the Soviet Union) legitimacy as defined is sorely lacking. This is so whatever the sources of legitimacy that are examined—instrumental, charismatic, symbolic, procedural, or performance based. In all cases, the regimes of all Eastern Europe are notoriously malfunctioning, thus endangering the very ability of each regime to rule, and certainly to prosper. To be specific:

To consider these sources in reverse order, there is little legitimacy derived from performance, because performance as commonly seen is faulty and woefully inadequate. Throughout the entire region, the economy is in dire straits, with severe problems of low productivity, lack of incentives, waste, corruption, inadequate technological sophistication, and the perennial problem of agricultural underproduction. No regime in Eastern Europe (and certainly none in Southeastern Europe) can expect public support on this dimension.[7]

The political order also is performing poorly. There is inadequate opportunity for representation of social strata and societal elites. The youth are clearly "turned off" from political sloganeering and the constant haranguing of regimes that demand much but deliver little. Limited forms of representation cannot solve the real need for an opening up of the political system to people with new ideas and the ability to solve the problems of modernity (which the old and tired leaders of the region have failed to solve in the past, even as they must be made responsible for the policies that created such conditions in the first place).[8]

There is also little procedural legitimacy (if we define it in standard fashion as the legitimacy that stems from the proper and predictable functioning of political procedures, processes, and institutions). The fact is that, procedurally, all Communist systems are "irregular"; much decision making is based on personal power, nepotism, graft, and other considerations, and ordinary citizens cannot expect to be treated fairly or equitably by the "authorities." The experiences of forty years have shown the man and woman in the street that communism is a system of rule that favors the privileged and provides little opportunity for others to redress grievances. The regime's attitude of arrogance and disregard for the rights and needs of the masses has produced widespread cynicism and a virtual lack of procedural legitimacy.[9]

Symbolic legitimacy under "real existing socialism" is of little consequence. This is a paradoxical fact in political systems that pride themselves on an internationalist ideology that originally provided the main impetus for the revolution and the establishment of the political power of the Communists. By now, few believe in the ideology of "Marxism-Leninism" (whatever that may be at any one time and in a specific country or situation), and the few believers there are feel that the practical policies of the regimes belie the faith in many ways. Thus the Communist regimes of Southeastern Europe are caught between the cynicism of the masses and the idealism of the few remaining true believers. Either way, symbolic legitimacy may no longer be derived from the ideology itself.[10]

The problems of performance and lack of faith in the official ideology are compounded by the emergence of counterideologies. The most important of these is nationalism, and nationalistic nostalgia for a glorious past that often exhibited animosity toward the Russians and one's neighbors in the volatile region of Southeastern Europe. The old faith in traditional symbolism has acquired some new features during the past two to three decades, but basically it represents traditional nationalism (coupled with religion) that vastly overshadows any support for other symbolism. In addition, there has emerged a symbolic counterculture in the region whose members uncritically admire the West and equally uncritically reject all (or most) manifestations of "real existing socialism."

Another source of legitimacy, charisma, is virtually nonexistent in Eastern Europe, even though Mikhail Gorbachev provides such a source in the Soviet Union. For Eastern Europe, the unfortunate fact is that the leaders of the region tend to be old *apparatchiki* whose days as leaders clearly are numbered (e.g., Zhivkov in Bulgaria, Honecker in East Germany) or technocrats lacking in personal charisma (e.g. Grosz in Hungary, and Jakes Czechoslovakia) who fail to inspire the masses and the societal elites at a time when the political and societal orders desperately need such a fillip. Other leaders, such as Jaruzelski in Poland, have battled the monumental crises of a society that is characterized by stalemate and exhaustion; they must now share power with others in an unprecendented fashion. Still others, especially Nicolae Ceausescu and his clan, exist in a terrible vacuum of unreality, producing policies that slowly but surely sap the lifeblood of the nation and threaten to make the system prostrate for years after the inevitable demise of the clan.

In Yugoslavia, the faceless collective leadership previously failed to inspire anyone, except in a negative direction. During 1988, however, a colorful and forceful spokesman for Serbian nationalism, Slobodan Milosevic, has emerged as the most popular leader in Serbia. Milosevic has taken a strongly nationalistic stance against Albanian nationalism in the Kosovo region and thus has gained widespread public support in Serbia. In Albania, Hoxha's successors struggle to retain both the image and the policies of the "grand old man" in the face of accelerating societal change. This, in short, is not the stuff of charismatic leadership.[11]

The crisis of legitimacy is compounded by the crisis of nation building, as briefly discussed earlier. The Communist regimes of the region have failed to produce values, attitudes, goals, and objectives that are germane to the system they attempted to build. Instead, these regimes must now deal with the unpleasant fact that the pre-Communist "nation" has shown enormous staying power, whereas the development of a "socialist" nation and a "socialist" political culture have failed to materialize. Because this failure now has become manifest in the entire region, there is no reason for the current political systems there to endure on *this* dimension; they must prove their capabilities and value on the basis of other criteria. Failing that (and the regimes of the region are, in fact, failing that), the main reason for regime survival is the use or threat of the use of force, plus the external dimension of Soviet power and the possibility that the Kremlin, even in a situation of great domestic fluidity, will still use that force to maintain the basic elements of the socialist order in Southeastern Europe.

In some systems, the reemergence of the nation as the primary focus of political affection and activity has produced destabilizing tendencies in the extreme. This is primarily so in multiethnic societies, and most of these are found in Communist Southeastern Europe, in Yugoslavia and Romania, but also in Bulgaria, where the policy of "Bulgarizing" the Turkish minority has been carried out with great determination, even brutality. Thus much of the region is embroiled in the failure of Communist nation building and the "unbuilding" of the system on which the notion of the socialist nation is established. Instead, there emerges the traditional Balkan state of ethnic animosities and discrimination. This situation clearly has security implications, as is discussed later.[12]

The Communist regimes of Southeastern Europe must also contend with the fact that their social systems have ossified, creating class societies that provide little opportunity for upward social mobility and, indeed, increasing downward mobility for a number of individuals and groups. Thus one of the few sources of political and socioeconomic legitimacy available to the regimes of the region (as well as to the rest of Eastern Europe) has disappeared or has become much less important. There is little reason to support regimes that increasingly maintain the status quo and enhance only the offspring of those who are already in privileged positions.[13]

Among the disenchanted social strata that can no longer be satisfied through rapid upward mobility is the artistic, cultural, and academic intelligentsia. Members of this social stratum increasingly question the very nature of the regimes in which they function, not merely the specific performance of institutions and other political structures. This searching examination of the system itself provides one of the most important sources of instability now besetting the Communist regimes of the region.[14]

The international crisis of communism just discussed has different specific manifestations in various countries, depending on the level of development, political culture, and ability of the regime to engage in political activity designed to defuse the crisis. This is clearly the case in the three systems examined here. The main point is that they all experience *some* of these problems, and that they will suffer their consequences increasingly in the future. Only country studies can sufficiently examine the mix of ingredients in each case.

The Influence of the West

While the Communist regimes of Southeastern Europe struggle to deal with the crisis of communism just discussed, and attempt to relate to the confusing developments in the regional hegemon, the Soviet Union, they must also contend with the influence of the West, which appears to be growing in strength as these societies mature and modernize. This Western influence comes in two forms; namely, specific Western policies toward the region and, more generally, the model and image represented by the seemingly dynamic societies on the other side of the European divide.

The general influence of the West is of great importance in the current configuration of East European societies, including those in Southeastern Europe. In sharp contrast to the stagnating and declining socialist economies, the West appears dynamic and successful. The stifling atmosphere of controlled societies stands in sharp contrast to the academic and intellectual free-for-all of more open societies. Politically, the ability to voice one's opinion and to organize for the purpose of making that opinion prevail in the marketplace of ideas is a marvel. Mass culture from the West sweeps the region, especially youth, and sets the standard by which the "pride and joy" of the socialist order think and behave. The West has always been important in the history of Eastern Europe. Never has this been more true than it is today.

COUNTRY STUDIES: SECURITY RISKS AND STABLE ALLIES

Romania: The Quiet of Despair

Among the Communist systems of Southeastern Europe, Romania represents a paradox: There is virtually universal agreement that the policies of the Ceausescu regime have driven the economy to the brink of complete malfunctioning, with severe food shortages, malnutrition, and the gradual erosion of ability to generate change and

development. The cynicism, political withdrawal, and fear that now grip this unfortunate country are potentially destabilizing in the extreme. At the same time, the Ceausescu clan maintains its iron grip on the country through a variety of mechanisms, chief of which is continued control over the armed forces and the security police. The outward calm of Romania stands in sharp contrast to the turmoil of neighboring Yugoslavia, and this means that, for the time being, the former represents little in the way of security risks for anyone. Romanian foreign and military policies will most likely remain in their present form until Nicolae Ceausescu dies, is replaced, or becomes incapacitated. It therefore is important to examine the main features of Romanian foreign policy during the Ceausescu era, and then to attempt to determine the extent to which these policies represent a security risk for the Soviet Union.

Much has been written about the autonomous policy of Ceausescu's Romania in foreign and security matters. In the "socialist commonwealth," Bucharest has tended to take an autonomous position on matters such as ideology and the need for "national roads" to socialism and communism. In economic integration, the Romanian position has emphasized the need for a national industrial base and sovereign decisionmaking up to the point of autarky. In security matters, Bucharest has refused anything but a minimal amount of integration in the Warsaw Pact, and has preferred to develop its own relations, especially with neutral Yugoslavia. Specific Romanian policy toward the West, the Middle East, and much of the Third World is often seen as representing a counterpoint to Soviet interests.[15]

Much of the literature discussing this Romanian autonomism refers to policies conducted by the Ceausescu regime during the 1970s and the first few years of the 1980s. The amount and importance of Romanian autonomism were probably overstated, but there was nevertheless a certain amount of reality in these analyses. During the past five to seven years, however, Ceausescu's foreign-policy successes have been few and far between, largely because of the desperate economic situation in the country, which drains resources needed for the effective conduct of foreign policy, and the increasing paranoia of the general secretary, which has removed his credibility as a serious leader in the minds of most external elites. Romania has also been forced to reintegrate itself with the COMECON in economic matters, because it has no capability to develop and sustain economic contacts elsewhere. Finally, the increasingly virulent anti-Westernism of the general secretary and his entourage has isolated Bucharest from the once sympathetic circle of foreign-policy makers in the West. Ceausescu is now perceived as nothing but an oriental potentate who attempts to emulate the sultans of the decaying Ottoman Empire; he is also perceived in Moscow as an embarrassment to "real existing socialism" in which the emphasis is on reform, rationality, procedural legitimacy, and technocratic leadership.[16]

Under these circumstances, Romania represents both stability and instability in Southeastern Europe. The clan rule of Ceausescu ensures the continuation of political, economic, and cultural Stalinism. There is little likelihood that the fundamentals of communism as a system of rule will be threatened so long as the present regime maintains itself in power. As much as Gorbachev and the reformers in the Soviet Union would like to see changes in the political order in Romania that would bring Bucharest into line with other systems in the region, there is indeed much to be said for the stability and orthodoxy of a country on the southwestern border. Moscow has enough trouble on its own, in handling its domestic affairs and in dealing with the problems of Poland and, indirectly, Yugoslavia. Romania's seeming stability is therefore a welcome security feature, even if the domestic manifestations of Ceausescu's clan rule are unpalatable.

The calm that characterizes contemporary Romania is based on the keystone of public despair and apathy, on the one hand, and the tight grip on the reins of power still maintained by the dictator and his clan, on the other. Throughout much of the region, Ceausescu is now known as the "Genghis Khan of socialism," widely perceived as a relic of the past, an embarrassment, and an impediment to the processes that can (and must) transform communism as a system of rule. To some extent, criticism of Romania also incorporates fear that, at some time in the near or intermediate future, the slowly burning fuse of societal crisis will reach a hidden powderkeg, with unforeseen possibilities for chaos inside Romania and possible security implications for others. At the same time, all the East European states, fully cognizant of the dangers of spillover from such a conflagration, keep Romania at arm's length as they grapple with their own problems. Ceausescu remains isolated and despised.[17]

Whereas the short-term advantages of the current Romanian system are clear to the Soviet leadership, the underlying problems of this society must be disquieting to observers in Moscow. The political and socioeconomic dislocations of Ceausescu's Romania are such that no one can discount the possibility of systemic breakdown at some point in the future, manifesting itself as the outbreak of widespread civil disorder, disintegration of basic societal patterns of interaction, or a desperate attempt by disgruntled elites outside the Ceausescu clan to grasp power to stave off the more fundamental dislocations that may loom on the horizon. At that point, Romania would become a security risk. It would also become an economic liability of considerable magnitude, assuming that the Soviet Union and its allies would need to help in the rebuilding of a destroyed economy.[18]

Bulgaria: Trusted Ally in Trouble?

Compared with Yugoslavia and Romania with their deep-seated systemic crises (one overt, the other covert), Bulgaria appears to be a virtual paragon of stability, and its foreign policy remains closely attuned to that of the Soviet Union. Thus Bulgaria clearly represents less of a security problem for the Soviets than the other two states of the region. At the same time, it is necessary to point out that even Sofia has problems that are potentially destabilizing internally and, by extension, externally.

For example, Bulgaria is experiencing the same kinds of economic problems as all the other nations in Eastern Europe. The ossification of the social pyramid is quite familiar to those who study upward mobility. Cynicism and withdrawal from politics are familiar symptoms for analysts of Communist political systems after the *Sturm und Drang* of the revolutionary and early postrevolutionary periods. Ethnic strife exists in Bulgaria, primarily in the form of forced assimilation of the Turkish minority by the dominant Bulgarians. There is a looming leadership void as Todor Zhivkov approaches retirement age. All these problems exist, albeit in a muted form compared with Bulgaria's northern and western neighbors. Intelligent management and a traditionally quiescent political culture have helped mute the expression of the crisis phenomena. But the phenomena are merely muted, not solved; a solution still requires fundamental systemic overhaul.[19]

The main internal problems confronting Bulgaria are twofold. First, there is an element of gerontocracy in the leadership, even as Zhivkov attempts to manage the winds of change that sweep his country as well as the rest of Communist Europe. Second, the Bulgarian leadership appears unwilling to come to grips with the depth of the problems facing it and the likelihood that these are, indeed, potentially system-transforming problems that cannot be solved through mere computerizing, tinkering with the mechanism of planning and rule, and managing the economy more intelligently. Unless the Bulgarian leadership can come to grips with these problems, the crisis of communism, now relatively muted in that country, is merely postponed, not solved.

Bulgaria appears to represent only a minor security problem for the Kremlin at the moment. There may be considerable instability (as defined earlier) in the system as a result of the general maladies of "real existing socialism," which may lead to changes of some magnitude. But the elites or persons now poised for possible succession are very much in the mold of the Zhivkov era and cannot be expected to change fundamentally the direction of Bulgarian foreign and security policy. Hence Soviet concerns are primarily directed at possible fallout from serious socioeconomic and political trouble, and the economic costs that are likely to be associated with such an event. A second concern is the possibility of conflict (political or even military) between a Yugoslavia in turmoil and a Bulgaria in the throes of nationalism and Bulgarian chauvinism over the issue of Macedonia (discussed later). This possibility clearly has the contingency planners in the Kremlin worried.[20]

Albania: Stalinism in Transition

Albania is usually pictured in Western scholarship as a system locked into the tradition of Enver Hoxha, characterized by ideological rigidity, extreme centralization in economic planning and execution, repressive measures against all dissenters and nonconformists, and a policy of isolationism in relations with the rest of the world. Furthermore, Tirana's relations with other Communist-ruled systems tend to be strained, reflecting the emphasis by the Albanian leadership on its own ideological rectitude and the corresponding malfeasance of all others on this score.[21]

The most recent scholarship has pointed out that post-Hoxha Albania is in a state of "limited flux," characterized by expanding relations with other states (many of them "capitalist") and a general loosening up of the ideological order and economic mechanisms. The fact that these processes are still in their infancy has prevented the development of crisis conditions, at least so far as they are known in the West. Albanian society is still at a relatively low level of development and therefore lacks the social and economic differentiation that has emerged in the rest of Eastern Europe. Furthermore, the relative backwardness of this system makes Stalinist methods of planning and management more appropriate. Extensive industrialization is still beneficial under these conditions, and the technological revolution associated with computerization, advanced information systems, and more open political discourse is still in the future. Thus the malaise of the more advanced Communist systems in Eastern Europe generally and Southeastern Europe specifically is still to come in Albania.[22]

These conditions also make Albania less of a security risk for the Soviet Union. Albanian society, barely emerging from Stalinism, is not likely to be endangered in the near future by the systemic crisis discussed previously. On the other hand, Albania has established ties with a number of Western countries, notably Italy, West Germany, and the Scandinavian countries, and such ties imply at least the possibility of greater Western influence. This tendency is countered by the elite's firm and continued commitment to ideoligical and political orthodoxy. But, Albania is too small and isolated to represent any significant threat to Moscow's interests in the Adriatic and the Mediterranean. Indeed, Tirana's emergence from self-imposed isolationism may provide the Kremlin with opportunities rather than liabilities.

SCENARIOS OF INSTABILITY AND CONFLICT

The four Communist-ruled states of Southeastern Europe represent different cases of systemic instability and performance. They also differ widely on the dimension of security risks. A systematic assessment of the Communist states of Southeastern Europe must take into account these national variations. Those persons and institutions in the Kremlin charged with the task of examining foreign-policy scenarios for Southeastern Europe must contend with a number of possibilities, none of which seems to be particularly palatable, even though they all vary in terms of risks, potential costs, and political trouble for the Soviet Union. The most important of these are (1) systemic breakdown in one or more of the states of the region; (2) the societal crisis of communism as a system of rule becomes aggravated, and conditions in Yugoslavia and Romania are replicated in Bulgaria and, to a lesser extent, Albania; (3) the push for reform in the Soviet Union becomes a destabilizing element of influence in Southeastern Europe; (4) the region settles into a period of deceptive calm, in which the regimes of the area engage in crisis management and "muddling through"; and (5) the policies of other actors set in motion events that produce instability and potential security risks.

Systemic Breakdown

As already discussed, both Yugoslavia and Romania are in a state of actual or impending societal crisis. In Romania, the iron hand of the

Ceausescu clan holds the country in its deadly grip; failed (even irrational) economic policy has pauperized the people; arbitrary, capricious, and rapacious behavior on the part of the Ceausescu clan has created a debilitating atmosphere of cynicism and fear in the population. There is little overt manifestation of resentment, thanks to the continued ability of the security police, the armed forces, and the vigilante squads of the regime to intimidate and to separate groups and individuals who oppose specific policies or the system in general. Perhaps a submissive political culture also assists in the maintenance operation. Despite this calm, there are pent-up frustrations that can be ignited, locally or nationally, by further deterioration of the abysmal economic conditions, or by specific events, such as the death or disability of Nicolae Ceausescu. This is, indeed, the most likely scenario for change in Romania. And it is also likely that the successive struggle will be vicious, producing chaotic conditions and instability for a time.[23]

Domestic problems in one of the systems in the region may also spill over into others. This is particularly so in the case of ethnic strife and national chauvinism. Any real success in the quest for greater autonomy by the various nationalities of Yugoslavia may feed on the resentment of Hungarians in Romania, thus increasing the level of tension in that troubled country. National chauvinism among the Albanians of Kosovo will undoubtedly impair relations between Belgrade and Tirana, and the conflict between Bucharest and Budapest over the treatment of Hungarians in Transylvania may heat up further. The feedback effect of ethnic separatism on the largest ethnic groups also must be considered; thus Serbian nationalism is a potent factor in the troubled situation facing Yugoslavia. Romanian chauvinism, already a considerable factor in contemporary political life in that country, is likely to become more aggressive in response to manifestations of Hungarian national feeling. Finally, the long-standing conflict between Yugoslavia and Bulgaria over Macedonia may erupt under crisis conditions in the former, perhaps as a desperate attempt by Belgrade to produce an issue that may help with the fractious confederacy. Such a conflict will inevitably heighten Bulgarian nationalism, with predictable results in official policy and public attitudes toward the Turkish minority. A complicated chain reaction of interstate relations may occur, and the combined effects of it may amount to a major security problem for the Soviet Union.

Regional conflict could take many forms. The states in the region are unlikely to engage in military conflict with one another. Still, protracted political controversy between Bucharest and Budapest,

Belgrade and Tirana, Sofia and Belgrade, or Belgrade and the capitals of the constituent republics in Yugoslavia will inevitably produce instability and a preoccupation with foreign policy at a time when the leaders of the region would be much better advised to focus on the serious domestic problems confronting them.

Against the scenario of significant instability in the region, followed by a number of bilateral conflicts of considerable proportions, the analyst should juxtapose the concerted efforts by Communist leaders to contain such conflicts and to work out various mechanisms of diffusion. For example, the conflict over Macedonia, once a very vocal and volatile issue, now seems rather muted, perhaps because Belgrade and Sofia both face important internal challenges that must take priority. Albanian rhetoric against its neighbors, which once was verbal war in the extreme, has been toned down. The Bulgarians and the Romanians exchange barbs over pollution and economic policy detrimental to each other, but the two leaderships have made a consistent effort to maintain good and cordial relations. Only Romania's relations with Hungary are distinctly poor and deteriorating to the point at which the whole region must be concerned. But that is more a regional problem than one specific to Southeastern Europe.[24]

Should widespread conflicts occur, they would also enhance the opportunities for other parties (notably, the major West European powers and the United States) to become involved in ways that would further reduce Soviet influence in the region. This scenario is even more plausible because Western influence is already on the rise in the region, as the faltering economies there crave "high tech" and management skills. Political trouble among the states of the region would provide an opportunity for further enhancement of this influence. Insofar as the Soviet leadership continues to view any expansion of Western authority on the periphery of the Soviet Union as a threat to the Kremlin's interests, developments such as these are indeed detrimental.

By the same token, the ability of the Communist regimes of Southeastern Europe to keep conflicts at a relatively low level would introduce an element of stability and security in a region left adrift by the possible partial withdrawal of significant Soviet influence from this region.

Aggravated Societal Crisis in Bulgaria and Albania

The possibility of aggravated societal crisis of communism as a system of rule, resulting in a replication of the conditions in Yugoslavia and

Romania in Bulgaria and Albania, is realistic and should be one of the main areas of concern in the Kremlin. Mikhail Gorbachev has been very vocal in his assessment of the shortcomings of the Soviet political and socioeconomic systems; there is no reason to believe that he is ignorant of the nature of the problems besetting other Communist-ruled states in the region. Therefore the deepening of the societal crisis is a significant security threat, even if it does not result in open political conflict among the states of the region. Weak systems tend to be unstable, and instability is costly, in terms of both money and political involvement. Protracted and worsening crises affecting the Communist states of Southeastern Europe would represent a major drain on Soviet resources. This Gorbachev can ill afford at a time when *perestroika* is attempting to deal with the many ills of the domestic system.[25]

At the same time, it is clear that the current Soviet leadership welcomes change in this region and is prepared to live with a variety of political and socioeconomic forms and processes that may result from such developments. Basically, the Kremlin has realized that dynamic development in the political and socioeconomic order represents a form of instability, namely, *creative* instability, which is endemic to all functioning societal systems. *This* instability is necessary to ward off stagnation, crisis, and much more debilitating instability— the instability of chaos and systemic breakdown. The latter scenario must be avoided at all costs, and the former must be equally emphatically promoted. Mikhail Gorbachev understands the need for therapeutic instability precisely because he wants to avoid security implications in the future.[26]

Soviet Reform Destabilizes Southeastern Europe

The crises already discussed have produced a variety of proposals and plans for reform in Eastern Europe, but, in considerable measure, it is the *Soviet* reform that has driven the leaders of these systems to consider *perestroika* and *glasnost*. Thus, conservative Communist elites are faced with the unfamiliar spectacle of Soviet leaders upbraiding them for lack of attention to reform and democratization. This is clearly the case in East Germany and Czechoslovakia (with differing responses); in Southeastern Europe, this scenario pertains primarily to Bulgaria. In cases such as these, Soviet policies themselves become destabilizing, thus potentially setting in motion events in one state that may trigger events elsewhere, thus expanding the circles of the problem. Furthermore, the disquieting fact is that many of the reforms proposed by the current leadership in the Kremlin resemble policies of long standing in Yugoslavia, where they clearly have not worked. The result is a reduction in the credibility of Gorbachev's program—and possibly a heightened belief that nothing short of fundamental reform will cure the ills of the Communist order anywhere.

In other cases, such as Romania, Soviet pressure for changes in policy has been counterproductive in that is has resulted in further centralization, more control from the top, and more power grabbing by the Ceausescu clan. Such a process, in turn, inevitably deepens the Romanian societal crisis, making a future breakdown a distinct possibility.

For a number of East European leaders, the destabilizing tendencies that come with Soviet reform are coupled with clear signals from the Kremlin that massive Soviet efforts cannot be expected to help solve local problems in the former satellites. Gorbachev and his colleagues want change in Eastern Europe so that crisis conditions can be staved off and stability can be maintained, but they want all this to be accomplished with minimal cost to themselves, because their energies are concentrated in the massive problems of the regional hegemon itself. The states under examination here are left to their own devices. Although this situation promotes autonomy, it may also enhance the likelihood of real instability *before* the regimes of the area get their house in order. Again, the security implications of such a scenario are complicated and potentially dangerous.[27]

Area Regimes "Muddle Through"

The scenario in which the region settles into a period of deceptive calm and the regimes of the area engage in crisis management and "muddling through" is preferable from the Soviet point of view, because it buys time and allows the Kremlin to concentrate on its own reform. The security risks are reduced, and the opportunities for Western meddling are limited. But this scenario only buys time, and produces no solutions. It is akin to tinkering with the system, not fixing it.

Other Actors' Policies Produce Instability

The Soviets know that the states of the region are particularly vulnerable to the actions of others. Only two of the states in the area are in the Warsaw Pact (and one of them is a recalcitrant maverick). Two others are outside that control organization even while ruled by Communists. Two more states, Greece and Turkey, are members of a competing alliance. Furthermore, the United States and the major West European powers have security interests in this area and are producing policies in pursuit of these interests. All these factors may interact to the detriment of Soviet security interests. A few illustrations should suffice:

• The desperate socioeconomic needs of Yugoslavia may lead to a closer alignment of Belgrade with the West. Such a scenario would unravel part of the Soviet strategy in this area, which is predicated on Yugoslav neutrality with a tilt toward other "progressive" powers.[28]

• Efforts by Greece or Turkey to foster closer relationships between the states of Southeastern Europe may lead to cross-alliance ties that weaken Soviet control. This is particularly the case with Bulgaria and Romania (especially the latter), because Nicolae Ceausescu has been a forceful spokesman for just such a scenario for many years.

• The United States (and some of its Western allies) could decide to pursue a more aggressive policy of "bridge building" with the states of the region at a time of Soviet preoccupation with domestic issues. Such a development would be bolstered by the desperate need for technology, money, and management capability in all the Communist-ruled states of Southeastern Europe.

• The perennial instability of the Middle East may affect politics on the Balkan Peninsula because of geographic proximity. This kind of development, in turn, may have direct or indirect effects on the security interests of the Soviet Union.[29]

As the Soviet Union allows greater leeway in the formulation and execution of both domestic and foreign policy, opportunities for more intense political and socioeconomic relations with non-Communist countries are created. Two such countries, Greece and Turkey, have exhibited significant economic growth in recent years and therefore may represent attractive partners, at least in a limited sense, for the stagnant economies of Communist systems as the latter try to revitalize themselves. As briefly discussed already, there have been periods of relatively active political relations across ideological borders before, and these traditions may be expanded as a result of the trend toward greater foreign-policy autonomy for the East European Communist systems. Should Europe indeed become dominated by the Common Market after 1992, the Communist states of Southeastern Europe may find themselves a backwater outside the mainstream of economic development; stronger ties with other, more dynamic regional actors may therefore be preferable, indeed necessary.

SOVIET OPTIONS: MINIMIZING THE PROBLEMS

Confronted by a plethora of problems and scenarios in Southeastern Europe, the Soviet leadership has a number of options, most of them unpalatable. If we assume that prevailing patterns of Soviet foreign policy, characterized by prudence and a keen concern for possible U.S. reactions, will prevail, three choices are available, depending on the severity of the crises confronting the Kremlin in the region: (1) military intervention, (2) political intervention and influence, and (3) economic intervention.

Military Intervention

This option will be used only in extreme conditions, best characterized as a fundamental threat to the survival of the "socialist order" of the states of the region. And if such a threat exists, military measures are likely only in the case of Bulgaria and Romania as members of the Warsaw Pact. Intervention in Yugoslavia or Albania would represent direct Soviet aggression against states outside the vital Soviet defense perimeter and would carry the possibility of a massive confrontation with the United States and its allies, especially in the case of Yugoslavia.

Soviet military intervention anywhere in Eastern Europe is unlikely at present, and it appears that the Balkans are perceived as less a security threat to the Soviet Union than the Northern Tier of the erstwhile Eastern bloc (East Germany, Poland, Czechoslovakia, Hungary), thus further reducing the possibility of such action in the southern area. The leaders in the Kremlin are counting on the ability of local leaders to produce real reform that can stave off upheavals and chaos. They are, furthermore, assuming that the emerging political pluralism of the East European systems will retain a significant amount of power and influence for the local Communist parties and their organizations, thus ensuring rather friendly regimes on the Soviet border. Furthermore, there is an assumption that significant elements of the societal elites and the general population see their interests best served in a system of Communist influence and a special security relationship with the Soviet Union. Thus even if a process of "Finlandization" eventually results, the threat to the Soviet Union itself is minimized.

For the Kremlin, the policy options in Romanian relations are rather limited at the moment. On the one hand, it is clear in Moscow that Ceausescu's policies represent a considerable risk in the long or intermediate run, but any form of heavy pressure or direct political intervention (not to speak of military measures) is likely to rekindle Romanian nationalism—and chauvinism in favor of Ceausescu, thus prolonging his political life beyond any likely boundaries now present. It is, indeed, a catch–22 for the Kremlin.

Soviet military intervention in Southeastern Europe (or elsewhere in Eastern Europe) is likely only if other actors, (especially the main powers of Western Europe or the United States) attempt to take advantage of current or future problems of this region to expand Western control (as opposed to influence) into part of the former bloc. Under such circumstances, the Kremlin's preoccupation with friendly regimes on its borders may no longer be satisfied (whereas Finlandization *will* satisfy it), and drastic measures may be undertaken. This, then, is a factor that must be taken into account as the West examines options available (discussed later).[30]

Political Intervention and Influence

The Kremlin is likely to produce considerable political pressure on all the states of Southeastern Europe in the case of an important crisis, as already mentioned. This is likely to happen after a crisis has developed, in order to move toward a speedy and favorable resolution, or perhaps before a real crisis has occurred, in order to prevent the rush to such manifestations. Political intervention would be applied in varying degrees, depending on the location of each state on the chart of Soviet concerns and the position of each unit inside or outside the Warsaw Pact. But political pressure is much less dangerous than military intervention and can be applied to all parties in the region, even those in NATO.

Economic Intervention

The economic crises of the Communist states of Southeastern Europe will demand considerable infusion of monetary resources, either as a preventive measure or as a remedial effort after the crisis has erupted. The Soviet Union will almost certainly be required to provide such funds for Bulgaria and might be asked in the case of Romania (in the latter case, after appropriate concessions on the part of Bucharest). In the case of Yugoslavia such economic assistance from Moscow may be less appropriate and less likely to be either requested or allocated, at least on a major scale. The Albanians may not yet be at a crisis level, and they are likely to avoid serious entanglements with the Kremlin even if it is needed. Still, both Tirana and Moscow would be willing to bury their ideological and policy differences if it were necessary in order to safeguard the basic aspects of the socioeconomic and political systems of this recalcitrant state.[31]

CONCLUSION: THE NEW EUROPEAN ORDER AND THE BALKANS

During much of the period of socialism in Eastern Europe, a *pax Sovietica* descended on the region, including the erstwhile unstable Balkan area. The overwhelming power and influence of the Soviet Union, the similarities of the political and socioeconomic systems of the area, and the dependence of the local political leaders on the support of the Kremlin for their survival all combined to produce conditions favorable for the maintenance of Soviet control and the removal of overt conflict between the states and parties of the region. But after a relatively short period of time, a number of events eroded this control and produced political instability. Yugoslavia and Albania left the fold, Poland and Hungary experienced severe problems in the 1950s, and similar afflictions befell Czechoslovakia in the 1960s and Poland in the 1970s and 1980s. During the latter decade, even Hungary and East Germany exhibited autonomist tendencies. Romania remained a maverick throughout.[32]

Concomitantly, the process of modernization in each of the states of the region produced political and socioeconomic dynamics that resulted in instability, eventually showing the extent to which the political order was outmoded and incapable of dealing with modern and stratified societies. In the 1980s, these problems became crises in several states. And these crises helped resurrect old animosities between states and internally between socioeconomic strata and ethnic groups.

As this dynamic unfolded, Southeastern Europe once again became an area of actual and imminent instability and thereby a regional and country-specific security risk for the Soviet Union. This is the problem that the Kremlin must struggle with now. And as the process of decay in "real existing socialism" unfolds, so does the security problem for the Soviet Union. The 1990s will demand more sophisticated and varied solutions to this problem.

The rapid developments in the polity and in the socioeconomic orders of the Soviet Union and Eastern Europe have brought about a new set of security issues, concerns, and opportunities for all participants in East-West relations. The division of Europe into two political camps was established at Yalta and Potsdam and became a fixture of postwar politics, both in terms of Realpolitik and in a psychological sense. In the West, it became de rigueur to consider Eastern Europe as part of the Soviet sphere of interest. Among the populations of Eastern Europe itself (as well as the local elites) it was a given that certain kinds of political and socioeconomic change were precluded, because the Kremlin had the will and the ability to prevent such change or destroy its results. This is no longer a given in the West or in the minds of many in Eastern Europe; even in the Soviet Union itself, prevailing policies foresee a much looser relationship with the states and parties of the former satellite countries. The postwar order of Europe is changing, and this change may produce security relationships that leave Eastern Europe in an anomalous position between the Soviet Union, on the one hand, and a resurgent Western Europe, on the other. Such a development, in turn, is likely to have profound effects on the Communist states of Southeastern Europe. Let us consider the possibilities.

First, the current process of diversification in Eastern Europe will further enhance the differences between the Northern and Southern Tiers of the erstwhile bloc. The northern countries are more important to the Soviet Union strategically than their southern counterparts, but they are also more important to the major powers of Western Europe, culturally, economically, and politically. This may mean that the primary focus of expanded East-West relations across crumbling ideological walls in Central Europe will be on Poland, East Germany, Czechoslovakia, and Hungary, while the Communist states of Southeastern Europe are once again relegated to the position of relative "backwater states." The political and socioeconomic rejuvenation that may be triggered by pluralization of society in the north may lag behind in the south.

Such a circumstance has two consequences that are seemingly contradictory. In the early stages of the rejuvenation process, Bulgaria, Romania, and Albania will lag behind other states in political development, but they will also exhibit less of a tendency toward instability than their northern neighbors. But assuming that the current ferment in several of the northern countries is a necessary ingredient of a crucial rejuvenation process (if controlled and channeled), the relative calm in the south is deceptive and counterproductive. As political development presumably helps economic development, the northern countries can be expected to move ahead in the production of goods and services, whereas the three countries in the south under examination here will stagnate and, in fact, fall even further behind their more developed northern counterparts. Ultimately, such a development is likely to give rise to profound resentment and possible outburst of political unrest that cannot be channeled into the structures and processes of expanded pluralism. The challenge to the existing order in the three Balkan states may be more profound and debilitating, with concomitant risks of spillover into neighboring areas.

For the Soviet Union, this kind of development is a most undesirable prospect, which must be avoided. This is clearly one of the main reasons for the Kremlin's continued (if muted) insistence on the need for change in these areas. And this quest will continue as the process of change unfolds elsewhere in the region.

For the West, developments in Eastern Europe generally and in Southeastern Europe specifically produce a number of opportunities, but also considerable dangers. Policy must be fashioned carefully, taking into account certain fundamental facts about this region.

First, there is no longer any reason to treat Eastern Europe as a subdivision of the Soviet Union. The entire region is in flux, and much greater autonomy in foreign policy terms is being granted by the Kremlin, partly out of necessity, but also out of conviction. From this it follows that a *regional* policy is not feasible (except for general concerns such as greater political freedom and expanded civil rights for everyone). Instead, the West must produce *bilateral* policies with each of the Communist states of the area, taking into account country-specific conditions, leaders, and developmental trends.

Second, the West should realize that there is a need to focus more specifically on the three countries of Southeastern Europe discussed here, lest our attention is riveted on the exhilarating developments in Poland and Hungary, the potential for change in East Germany or Czechoslovakia, or the chaos of contemporary Yugoslavia. Increased concern with the three Balkan states of Bulgaria, Romania, or Albania will help fashion policies toward them that can foster change, reform, and *constructive* instability, which, in turn, will help reduce the likelihood of massive and destructive instability in the intermediate run. Such policies should focus on encouragement of those elements that work for greater political pluralism at home as well as expanded civil rights. Furthermore, it is in the interest of the West that economic liberalization be effected through mechanisms such as decentralization of planning and execution and a greater role for private agriculture. In the foreign-policy realm, the West should foster greater autonomy from the Soviet Union and further integration of the states of Southeastern Europe into the socioeconomic and cultural community that is Europe.

The challenge, therefore, is to pursue policies that encourage "constructive instability" in an *orderly* fashion. This objective is not easy to achieve, for it depends on events over which the United States has little control.

The alternative, to press for a "limited destabilization" of the states of the region, may therefore appear attractive. Such a policy would be easier to implement and can be defended on the ground that destabilization, within limits, places the Soviet Union on the defensive. This scenario, however, has obvious risks and requires a different set of policies, ones that go beyond the scenarios discussed here.

The obvious problem for U.S. policymakers in dealing with Southeastern Europe in the coming decade will therefore be that of discerning where orderly change becomes disorderly and invites systemic collapse. In at least one, Yugoslavia, the borderline between creative instability and disorderly change leading to systemic collapse may have already been crossed. In this case, challenges of a new order arise, some of which are dealt with in the chapters that follow.

NOTES

Appreciation is extended to Wolfgang Höpken for his valuable comments on this chapter.

1. For example, Robert C. Tucker, *Political Culture and Leadership in Soviet Russia* (New York: W. W. Norton, 1987), especially chapter 7, "To Change a Political Culture," 140–99. See also Richard Löwenthal, "Gorbatschow Und Die Zukunft Der Sowjetunion," *Osteuropa* (July-August 1988): 515–23.

2. I have summarized a great deal of literature here. The most important of these sources are Morris Bornstein et al., eds., *East-West Relations and the Future of Eastern Europe* (Winchester, Mass.: Allen & Unwin, 1981); Walter D. Connor, *Socialism, Politics and Equality: Hierarchy and Change in Eastern Europe* (New York, N.Y.: Columbia University Press, 1979); Stephen Fischer-Galati, ed., *The Communist Parties of Eastern Europe* (New York: Columbia University Press, 1979); A. Ross Johnson et al., *East European Military Establishments* (Santa Monica, Calif.: Rand Corporation, 1980); Christopher D. Jones, *Soviet Influence in Eastern Europe* (New York: Praeger, 1981); Daniel N. Nelson, *Economic Reforms in Eastern Europe for the 1980s* (Elmsford, N.Y.: Pergamon Press, 1980); George Schöpflin, *Eastern European Handbook* (London: St. Martin's, 1982); Stephen White et al., *Communist Political Systems* (London: Macmillan, 1982); J. F. Brown, *Eastern Europe and Communist Rule* (Durham, N.C.: Duke University Press, 1988); Hans-Joachim Veen, *From Brezhnev to Gorbachev* (New York: St. Martin's Press, 1987); Baruch Hazan, *From Brezhnev to Gorbachev* (Boulder, Colo.: Westview Press, 1987); Charles Gati, *Hungary and the Soviet Bloc* (Durham, N.C.: Duke University Press, 1986); Karen Dawisha, *Eastern Europe, Gorbachev and Reform* (New York: Cambridge University Press, 1988); Peter J. Potichnyj, ed., *Soviet Union: Party and Society* (New York: Cambridge University

Press, 1987); Robert C. Tucker, *Political Culture and Leadership in Soviet Russia* (New York: W. W. Norton, 1987).

3. The Albanians also reject the Soviet experiment with *perestroika*. See Louis Zanga, "Albania's Rejection of the Soviet Experiment," *Radio Free Europe Research*, RAD Background Report/145 (Albania), August 1, 1988.

4. For the official Romanian position on *perestroika*, see Ceausescu's remarks on the occasion of his recent visit to East Germany (*Scinteia*, June 1, 1988). In Bulgaria, open defiance of party rules among intellectuals was discussed at a recent central committee plenum. See *Rabotnichesko Delo*, April 26 and 27, 1988.

5. See ibid. on Bulgaria; on Romania, see Vladimir Socor, "Dissent and Social Protest," *Radio Free Europe Research*, Romanian SR/1, January 13, 1988.

6. For example, Karl W. Deutsch, *Politics and Government* (Boston, Mass.: Houghton Mifflin, 1974), 15–19.

7. See, for example, Ivan Volgyes, *Politics in Eastern Europe* (Chicago: Dorsey Press, 1986), especially chapter 9, 213–34.

8. The best recent study of these problems is Tucker, *Political Culture and Leadership*, especially chapter 7, 140–99.

9. See Volgyes, *Politics in Eastern Europe*, chapter 8.

10. A good discussion of the traditional importance of ideology is Nina Tumarkin, *Lenin Lives! The Lenin Cult in Soviet Russia* (Cambridge, Mass.: Harvard University Press, 1983).

11. This is a summary of a great deal of research and secondary literature. A useful overview is Brown, *Eastern Europe and Communist Rule*.

12. See, for example, ibid., especially chapter 10, 316–36. See also assorted issues of *Radio Free Europe Research* and major Western newspapers such as *Neue Zürcher Zeitung, Frankfurter Allgemeine Zeitung, Süddeutsche Zeitung, Le Monde*, and *Financial Times*.

13. One of the best analyses of this is Connor, *Socialism Politics, and Equality*.

14. Even in Romania such developments can be found. See, for example, Nicolae Ceausescu, discussing the role of literature in socialist society and criticizing recalcitrant writers, in *Scinteia*, April 3, 1988.

15. There are a number of good books on Romania's foreign policy, including Aurel Braun, *Romanian Foreign Policy Since 1965,* (New York: Praeger, 1978); and Ronald Linden, *Bears and Foxes: The International Relations of East European States* (New York: Columbia University Press, 1979).

16. Aspects of Romanian policies have been openly criticized by the Kremlin; see *Pravda*, July 1, 1988, on Romanian policies towards Hungary.

17. For a discussion of a policy that has alienated much of Europe, East or West, see Wolf Oschlies, "Tausenden Rumänischen Dörfer Droht Die Vernichtung," *Osteuropa* (November 1988): 1002–8.

18. The Soviet press hinted at these problems in veiled terms as the various papers reported on Andrei Gromyko's visit to Romania in May 1988; see, for example, *Pravda* and *Izvestia*, May 14, 1988.

19. Bulgarian *perestroika* was discussed in detail at a plenum of the central committee in July, 1987, and it was further fleshed out in November (see *Robotnichesko Delo*, November 20, 1987). Then, in December, the National Assembly ratified the decisions of the plenum (ibid., December 10, 1987).

20. This is indeed an old problem. See, for example, Stephen E. Palmer, Jr., and Robert R. King, *Yugoslav Communism and the Macedonian Question* (Hamden, Conn.: Shoe String Press, 1971).

21. The most thorough study of Albania is still Bernhard Tönnes, *Sonderfall Albanien* (Munich: R. Oldenbourg, 1980).

22. The post-Hoxha leadership is beginning to move in the direction of serious change; conservative elements, predictably, are trying to block such moves. For a scathing criticism of such elements, see *Zeri i Popullit*, January 13, 1988.

23. For an analysis of this and other scenarios, see my paper "The Ship of State in

Troubled Waters: Leadership Drift in Romania," presented to the annual convention of the American Association for the Advancement of Slavic Studies, Boston, Mass., November 1987.

24. See, for example, the sharpened rhetoric in the verbal dispute between Romania and Hungary by Matyas Szüros, a member of the Hungarian Central Committee Secretariat in *Frankfurter Allgemeine Zeitung*, November 8, 1988, and official Hungarian statements in *Nepszabadzag*, January 6, 1989.

25. For a good analysis of this and related problems, see Dawisha, *Eastern Europe, Gorbachev, and Reform.*

26. For Gorbachev's own analysis, see his *Perestroika i Novoe Myshlenie* (Moscow: Izdatel'stvo Politicheskoi, Literatury, 1988), especially chapter IV, 166–77.

27. See Charles Gati, "Eastern Europe on Its Own," *Foreign Affairs* (Winter 1989): 99–120.

28. See, for example, Brown, *Eastern Europe and Communist Rule*, chapter 2, pp. 30–62.

29. Gorbachev has attempted to fashion his own strategy for this troubled region; see, for example, Galia Golan, "Gorbachev's Middle East Strategy," *Foreign Affairs* (Fall 1987): 41–58.

30. Charles Gati, "Eastern Europe on Its Own," *Foreign Affairs* (Winter 1989): 99–120.

31. Economic aid is part of the Kremlin's strategy toward Eastern Europe. See Charles Gati, "Gorbachev and Eastern Europe," *Foreign Affairs* (Summer 1987): 958–76.

32. The Soviets must take these liabilities into account. See, for example, Karen Dawisha and Jonathan Valdez, "Socialist Internationalism in Eastern Europe," *Problems of Communism* (March-April 1987).

4

ECONOMIC CHALLENGES TO THE COMMUNIST STATES OF SOUTHEASTERN EUROPE

Roland Schönfeld

Throughout history, Southeastern Europe has been a favorite target of foreign hegemony. After the gradual breakup of the Ottoman and then the Habsburg empire, the countries of the region, one by one, became politically independent. But the powers only changed their methods: when direct foreign rule had to be abandoned, the powers still had a broad range of opportunities to make these states dependent and to meddle in their internal affairs.

As the region emerged from World War I, the states of Southeastern Europe remained dependent on one or more patrons for several reasons. First, they sought protection from foreign powers, perceiving the borders drawn in the peace treaties as arbitrary. These powers, in turn, guaranteed them their newly won possessions or promised to seek the revision of the peace treaties and the fulfillment of unsatisfied territorial claims. Second, most of them—made up of ethnic groups of different origin, language, religion, education, and customs—experienced serious conflicts among their nationalities. The ensuing internal conflicts prevented a balanced social development and national integration, as well as straining their external relations with their neighbors. Third, these internal and external tensions also became a prominent source of economic problems.

Throughout Southeastern Europe in the interwar period, economic progress was hindered by the inherited underdeveloped and antiquated economic and social structures; by small-state nationalism, which encouraged the creation of customs barriers cutting across prewar trade routes; and by the tremendous shock and devastation brought on by the Great Depression. There reigned "the vicious circle of population pressure, excessive reliance on under-productive agriculture, and low income."[1] Up to four-fifths of the populations of these countries subsisted on agriculture, whose yields stayed far below European standards. The few small consumer-goods industries, some scattered engineering factories around Budapest, in Slovenia and the Banat, were promoted and subsidized by the state governments. The region suffered from enormous shortages of domestic capital, skilled labor, and entrepreneurship.

Southeastern Europe had the potential for extensive industrialization, because it was rather well endowed with most of the necessary raw materials. Its rich, albeit unevenly distributed, deposits of nonferrous minerals included copper, chrome, lead, and zinc in Yugoslavia, Romania, Bulgaria, Albania, Greece, and Turkey; bauxite in Yugoslavia and Hungary; Europe's largest oil deposits in Romania; and lignite in most of the countries. All these countries lacked coal and superior iron ore. There was an abundance of timber, but the production of other agricultural raw materials was neglected. Still, in most areas all the natural resources remained seriously underused because of the lack of capital and only a rudimentary infrastructure. Transportation remained acutely underdeveloped throughout the region, and only Greece took advantage of coastal shipping routes. The favorable inland waterways could not be used because there were no canals. The network of roads was primitive, and the old railroad system hardly suited postwar economic needs.

In the interwar period, all the states of Southeastern Europe pursued national policies of industrialization and import substitution by setting up high customs barriers, which helped to complete the economic dismemberment of the Dual Monarchy. The creation of regional customs unions, discussed frequently, was never realized because of the ancient fear of economic and financial domination by Vienna and Budapest. Foreign capital was needed to fill the domestic savings gap. Foreign capital was obtained extensively for reconstructing, resettling refugees, stabilizing currencies and balancing state budgets, modernizing production and infrastructure, feeding the fast-growing populations, buying armaments, and maintaining an inflated public administration. At the outbreak of the worldwide depression of 1929, the countries of Southeastern Europe were over-indebted in terms of their long-term potential to service loans with exports of commodities. With the collapse of international credit markets, substantial short-term funds were withdrawn and the inflow of new capital ceased, making these countries insolvent.[2]

By 1932, all the countries of Southeastern Europe had introduced foreign exchange controls and, because a substantial part of their foreign debt was in default, moratoriums were arranged for Greece, Bulgaria, Yugoslavia, Turkey, and Romania. The effects of these huge cuts on international purchasing power and the rapid decline of the prices of agricultural exports on their domestic economies were devastating. Their main export markets—Germany, Austria, Italy, and France—resorted to extreme agricultural protectionism. The states of Southeastern Europe failed to secure preferential treatment for their exports from the industrialized European countries. Closer economic cooperation among the countries of Southeastern Europe either was not feasible or did not provide for the absorption of their agricultural surpluses. With the introduction of foreign exchange controls, their trade with partners such as Germany, Austria, Czechoslovakia, and Italy had to be regulated through bilateral clearing accounts, while their governments attempted to influence the flow of exports and imports through multiple exchange rates and other means.

Beginning in the mid–1930s, Germany, which had begun to recover from the economic crisis relatively early and developed a growing demand for agricultural produce and minerals, provided substantial relief to Southeastern Europe's export problems. German importers offered relatively high and stable prices, which, despite the complication of unbalanced bilateral clearing accounts gave great impetus to domestic demand and caused an upsurge in industry and mining throughout the region. Toward the end of the 1930s, higher revenues enabled most of the Southeast European governments to launch ambitious investment projects designed to expand arms production and to modernize infrastructures and utilities through public works. With the *Anschluss* in 1938, the breakup of Czechoslovakia in 1939, and, finally, the defeat of France in 1940, Germany became the predominant trade partner in the region.

In the course of the political upheavals following World War II, Southeastern Europe was divided into two distinct economic parts. The Soviet type of rigorous command economy was forced on Albania, Bulgaria, Hungary, Romania, and Yugoslavia just as on Czechoslovakia, East Germany, and Poland—but not on Greece and Turkey.[3] Mining, industry, banking, and trade were nationalized, and agriculture was forced into cooperatives. The state's intervention in the economy, which had increased considerably in the economic crisis of the 1930s, now reached extreme proportions. Industrialization was pushed forward, and economic and social development were accelerated—through the radical exploitation of natural resources, including manpower, forced savings at the expense of living conditions, state investment, and highly centralized planning—faster than anyone could have imagined in the interwar years. The growth rates of the socialist economies of Southeastern Europe exceeded those of Turkey and Greece, which were attempting to deregulate and liberalize their economies with financial and technical aid from their Western allies. The authoritarian policies of economic and social modernization appeared more efficient and successful in solving the problems of inherited underdevelopment than the mixed or free-market systems.

Yet the forced construction of heavy industry and the programmed neglect of agriculture, light industry, the crafts, and services caused serious dislocations in the production structure of the socialist economies. Miserable living conditions, political repression, and shortages of consumer goods promoted social unrest. Furthermore, the system of planning itself, with its fixed prices and state monopolies, was inefficient and wasted resources. As early as the late 1950s, the communist countries of Eastern and Southeastern Europe experienced their first economic crisis in the form of rapidly declining and even negative growth rates. Moscow gave the signal to fight stagnation with cautious reforms and increased trade and cooperation with the capitalist countries.

Whereas Greece and Turkey had resumed trade relations with the free world immediately following World War II and eventually benefited from preferential treatment as associate members of the European Economic Community (EEC) founded in 1957, the Communist countries were absorbed into the Soviet orbit not only politically but also economically. In the early postwar period their industrial production was adjusted according to Soviet needs, and their traditional close trade and capital relations with the countries of Central and Western Europe largely disappeared. The Soviet Union offered to serve as a supply base for a wide range of raw materials and energy to be exchanged for manufactured goods from their recently built industries. The Soviet Union gained control and influence of their trade and development through the Council for Mutual Economic Assistance (CMEA), established in 1949 to coordinate production in the socialist countries, including Albania, Bulgaria, Hungary, and Romania. At the same time, these countries' limited export potential and the low quality of their industrial goods hampered economic integration with the capitalist West. They had no choice but to cooperate closely with the Soviet Union.[4]

The large but undemanding Soviet market, in contrast, has not challenged these industrializing economies to improve the quality of their export goods and accelerate their technical progress. Until recently, selling to the USSR and the other CMEA countries was easy, compared with selling to the fastidious and chaotic world market. As a result, CMEA economists and governments have considered an increase in trade with the West indispensable to rapid and balanced growth. Yet, so far, the attempts to boost exports to the West have failed. The oil price boom since 1973—which affected the oil-importing Communist countries albeit less severely, though the USSR set a new price formula for CMEA in 1975—caused a worldwide recession and rising protectionism in the Western markets. Hardest hit have been exports from the Communist countries: foodstuffs, agricultural and other raw materials, semimanufactured products, and some industrial consumer goods, most of them regarded as "sensitive" imports in the West. The continued imports of Western machinery and other commodities have led to overindebtedness in convertible currency and heavy constraints in the balance of payments of the Communist countries.

Unfortunately, the rise in cost of imported energy and minerals and the curtailment of Western imports coincided with the exhaustion of natural resources that had supported the extensive phase of industrialization in Eastern and Southeastern Europe. When Poland became illiquid in 1981, the credit flow from West to East temporarily ceased. Several other Communist countries, including Yugoslavia, also found themselves in serious difficulties. Stagnating growth and the policy of austerity imposed on these economies in order to balance Western trade by cutting back imports caused severe problems of supply and sinking living standards. Attempts to strengthen trade among the CMEA partners, particularly with the USSR, failed.

YUGOSLAVIA'S ECONOMIC DISINTEGRATION

Since its expulsion from the Cominform in 1948, Yugoslavia has relied heavily on Western, particularly American, financial aid. Its liberation from Soviet dictates offered early opportunities for the development of new economic policies.[5] In the early 1950s, collectivization of agriculture was abandoned, and the peasantry overwhelmingly returned to private farming. Yugoslavia gradually departed from the Soviet type of central planning, and enterprises were given a certain degree of autonomy under the new system of workers' self-management. With the reform of 1965, Yugoslavia started on the road to "market socialism," later to be set aside in the constitution of 1974, which reaffirmed the party's direction of enterprises, increased planning, and abandoned competition as a principle of economic liberalization. From the beginning the Yugoslav reform process was accompanied by a consistent orientation toward foreign trade and economic cooperation with the industrialized West. Yugoslavia opened its frontiers to tourism; exported hundreds of thousands of "guest workers" to Austria, West Germany, and elsewhere; and was the first Communist-ruled state to allow joint capital ventures with Western firms on its territory. Yet the liberalization of imports revealed deficiencies in the Yugoslav economy. As trade deficits soared, foreign indebtedness rose to extremely high levels and, by the early 1980s, a domestic economic crisis had come about.

The disastrous condition of the economy—with its soaring inflation, high unemployment, and enormous foreign debt—deepened divisions between nationalities and further encouraged the drifting apart of the republics and autonomous regions. This situation not only has discredited Yugoslavia economically in the eyes of Western governments, banks, and business, but also has deprived it of much of its political authority and influence in the nonaligned camp. Once an alternative Communist model to the Soviet claim of ideological leadership, today Yugoslavia's system of workers' self-management confirms earlier Soviet warnings against experiments with the Communist economic order.

The early federal "Long-Term Stability Program" launched with enormous publicity in July 1983 has had virtually no effect. The attempts to halt the decline in the demand for exports and to quench the import-inducing overheating of the domestic market also failed. The government has not succeeded in fighting inflation in an economy with high, and rising, unemployment. The rapid devaluation of Yugoslavia's currency has been the most pernicious cause of its economic ruin, as consumers buy earlier and managers calculate less cautiously. It also affects the profitability of production and the export capacity of the economy. Since the federal government has failed to introduce a positive real interest rate—recommended by the International Monetary Fund (IMF)—it has encouraged enterprises to incur debts. Managers did not implement the repeated wage freezes announced by the federal government, lest they antagonize the already dissatisfied workers. The December 1986 law linking wage increases to productivity enhanced the confusion in the system which, through interference by state, party, and unions, prevents most enterprises from operating at a profit. The spread of small private enterprises, promoted by the stability program of 1983, is impeded by paralyzing taxes and bureaucratic chicanery. Returning guest workers who intended to start their own businesses at home have tended to leave most of their convertible savings in foreign bank accounts. Ideological intransigence also frustrates much needed new initiative. There are 1.2 million registered unemployed workers, 75 percent of them under age thirty.

The internal organization of enterprises provided for by the constitution of 1974 atomized the enterprise into the smallest possible "self-managing" units. A common policy for the entire enterprise was to be achieved by reaching a consensus among its basic units. This policy complicated, if not altogether paralyzed, the decision-making process in an enterprise. "Social agreements" between enterprises replaced competition, as well as the considerable advances already made toward creating a socialist market economy. The need to reform the political and economic system became evident. Already in 1982, the League of Communists of Yugoslavia (LCY) set out to publish a "Critical Analysis of the Political System of Social Self-Management," which was then published in January 1986. But the study did not question the system's underlying ideological principles. Instead, the study confirmed the system's success and restricted itself to appeals to eliminate "functional deficiencies." At the thirteenth Party Congress in June 1986, all demands for radical reforms were diluted in the congress's powerless working committees.[6]

So far, only a handful of suggestions made by the reform commission established in 1988 to prepare a radical economic reform have been half-heartedly realized. A new enterprise law adopted in December 1988 created opportunities to establish socialist, cooperative, private, and mixed firms and provided for the abolition of the old Basic Organizations of Associated Labor. The preamble to the constitution of 1974, which provides for the dominant role of socialist property, however, was not changed. In this situation, there is little hope for genuine competition, which would risk ruining most of the unproductive and overindebted Yugoslavia enterprises. Yugoslav experts doubt that the new bank law will be enough to make banks independent and to change their traditional status as service institutes for insolvent enterprises. Apart from an improved joint-venture law and some vague promotion of small private enterprises, anonymous socialist ownership will clearly prevail in the Yugoslav economy, because recent measures have reinforced the party's control of enterprises. More than thirty other reform bills cannot be adopted because of disagreements among the republics.[7]

Since the end of the 1970s, the pronounced orientation of Yugoslav trade toward the West has faltered as a result of shrinking sales on the world market. In the economic crisis of the 1980s, increased bilateral trade with the Soviet Union and other socialist countries has given Yugoslavia temporarily an easy way out. The Soviet Union has overtaken West Germany as Yugoslavia's most important trade partner, providing half its energy imports. Yugoslav industrial products, which cannot find a market elsewhere, are sought by Soviet importers because of their high content of Western technology. In recent years, Yugoslavia has accumulated considerable surpluses in bilateral trade with the Soviet Union as a result of the lack of usable Soviet commodities, amounting to a $2.1 billion Soviet debt, and has therefore been forced to reduce its exports to this clearing partner. With exports to the hard currency area stagnating, Yugoslav economy has proved unable to take good advantage of the rising import demand of Western industrial countries so far.[8]

Thus the causes of the Yugoslav economic crisis are largely home-made, having been initiated by the fundamental changes in the political structure implemented in Tito's last decade. Antiquated Marxist dogmas are as counterproductive as the power seeking of the regional party bosses and nationalistic animosities.

ROMANIA: CRISIS, AUTARKY, AND AUTONOMOUS POLICY

Romania's political reputation in the West as a mediator in conflicts and the maverick of the Soviet bloc has suffered considerably from its economic crisis, the most severe since World War II. This crisis was caused not only by deteriorating external economic conditions in the 1970s but above all by a flawed development strategy. Romania's rigorous policy of austerity, the result of more than just economic considerations, has imposed unbearable privations on the population and exacerbated the economic depression. The government has not chosen to increase supplies to the domestic market by slowing down the repayment of its foreign debt. For years, it has refused to engage in closer economic cooperation with the CMEA. This stance is determined by a foreign policy established in the 1960s. The regime has presented itself to the population as the advocate of national interests, repeatedly testing the limits to which it can go without risking Soviet intervention.

Recent attempts to liberate Romania's economy from its enormous dependence on foreign trade have failed.[9] Until the mid–1970s, Romania made a remarkable effort to reduce drastically the CMEA's, and particularly the Soviet Union's, share in its foreign trade, but the expected boost in sales on the world market failed to materialize. In its euphoric vision of the effects of world trade on its growth (a vision shared by other Communist countries), Romania had by 1981 amassed a foreign debt of nearly $10 billion in convertible currencies. Following the reduction of Western credits to Poland, Romania also began to experience difficulties. In 1982 and 1983, it was forced to ask its creditors for reschedulings. Export promotion failed to yield the desired results in the midst of worldwide recession, especially in view of the quality and technological standards of Romanian products. Romania chose not to increase its dependence on the Soviet Union again.

Since 1975, Romania has experienced a growing demand for imported crude oil, which has not been met by increased barter trade with the USSR but by choosing to pay a rapidly rising price in convertible currency for oil from the OPEC countries. Thus Romania lost most of the benefits of the intra-CMEA system of preferential prices. Instead, it opted for austerity to improve the balance of payments through rigorous savings. Foreign advice has been rejected, as has financial aid from the IMF, since 1984, because of the IMF's policy-related conditions. Thus the Romanian government succeeded in reducing its foreign debt from $9.9 billion in 1981 to $2.5 billion by 1987, and to less than $1 billion by early 1989. On April 14, 1989, President Ceausescu announced that Romania had paid off all its foreign debts.[10]

Yet the policy of austerity has had a devastating effect on supplies to the domestic market and the utilization of Romania's production capacity. The resulting restrictions on imports of machinery, spare parts, and raw materials from the West have impaired export production. The workers' harsh living conditions worsen their performance. The authorities have reacted to the problem of dwindling exports to the West with even more rigorous restrictions on imports. The competitiveness of Romanian products in the hard-currency area, particularly the Common Market, is clearly declining. According to official reports, Romania produces about 90 percent of its capital goods itself, proudly calling it the "national option"; but this practice has widened the technological gap between Romania and the industrialized West even further.

In 1986, Romania's economic relations with the Soviet Union changed. For the first time, Soviet oil deliveries increased considerably, from 3 to 6 million tons per year, but the price advantage vanished with dropping world-market prices. Soviet deliveries of energy have to be paid for with convertible currency and "hard" commodities such as foodstuffs and oil-drilling equipment.[11]

Various branches of Romania's industry will be modernized with the help of Soviet capital, Soviet technology, and probably Soviet specialists. The goal is to expand Romania's export production to include some industrial goods on the technological "world level" demanded by the USSR. The outdated and inefficient Romanian steel industry in particular may benefit from this policy. Complete plants producing oil and gas pipe will be delivered to Romania by the USSR.

This Soviet style of modernization is depriving Romania of the benefits of Western progress and will not increase the competitiveness of its industry on the world market. It will, however, create additional opportunities for barter trade with the Soviet Union in exchange for increased Soviet energy supplies.

Romania remains a difficult partner for the other members of the CMEA. Bucharest has continuously criticized the CMEA clearing system, the shortcomings of the financial and technical aid of its partners and banks to Romania, and unfavorable terms of trade with the Soviet Union. Romania is more willing to participate in joint investments in the Soviet raw-material and energy sectors; yet its share in these projects is limited by lack of capital. Soviet firms complain that their Romanian partners have not fulfilled deliveries and supplied labor for several joint projects.

The Romanian government has firmly resisted certain aspects of the CMEA integration process promoted by Gorbachev. In particular, it has rejected the Soviet proposal to establish direct links between manufacturers of member countries and to setup joint industrial enterprises.

In his recent speeches, Ceausescu has made it perfectly clear that Romania should have a highly centralized command economy, despite growing opposition among the intelligentsia and the young party cadres.[12] This attitude may represent resistance to Soviet interference in national Romanian affairs. It must be remembered that once before, in the 1960s, the Soviet Union forced the smaller states of the bloc into reforms that failed and had to be revoked a few years later. Romania's current refusal to decentralize planning and management has important political causes. The decentralization of economic decision making would weaken the influence and control of the party over the economy. Given the widespread popular unrest caused by the miserable living conditions, the government cannot afford even minor liberalization.

BULGARIA'S LAGGING GROWTH

Since the 1970s, Bulgaria has faced an economic crisis stemming from scarce energy supplies, wastefulness of raw materials, slow technical progress, lack of skilled labor, lack of growth of exports to the West, and worsening international conditions. The growth rate of the produced national income sank from a remarkable annual 8 percent in the early 1970s to an average of 3.7 percent during the 1981–5 plan. The nadir of 1.8 percent came in 1985. Western experts are skeptical about the announced official growth rate of 6.2 percent for 1988.[13]

In 1979, harsh official criticism of the system of planning was followed with the creation of the "New Economic Mechanism." This program was not so innovative as the Hungarian reforms: it was to be implemented gradually and did not question the party's central guidance and control in the economy. Therefore, from the beginning, it represented a conflict between decentralization and control.[14] It was intended to relieve enterprises from the numerous compulsory plan directives and focus on "economic regulators" such as prices, profits, and taxes. In April 1986 the Thirteenth Congress of the Bulgarian Communist Party demanded the "transition from direct to indirect planning"; at the same time, however, the party's daily re-jected the idea of "market socialism." The plan's directives were partly replaced by state orders, while central price setting, an indispensable instrument of imperative planning, was retained for most commodi-ties. A price reform has been postponed until the 1990s. State intervention into the economy remains enormous. It is difficult to judge whether the "rules for economic activity" which have been passed so far have been put into practice at all, and it is likely that most of the reform exists only on paper.

The reformers' caution points to massive resistance in the bureau-cracy, in the enterprises, and perhaps even among the party leader-ship. In July 1988, Chudomir Aleksandrov, the most prominent advocate of reforms in the politburo, was ousted. Todor Zhivkov, general secretary of the Bulgarian Communist party, called for a continuation of both economic and political reforms, including selling shares of industrial stocks to workers, in order to increase their interest in the enterprise's economic success.[15]

In view of this slow pace of reforms, the overdue modernization of industry and agriculture and an increase in labor productivity will be a lengthy process. Since the aggravation of external economic pro-gress in the 1980s, the Bulgarian leadership has reacted by relying increasingly on the CMEA.[16] Since 1986, the CMEA's share of Bulgarian exports has exceeded 80 percent. The Soviet Union has been by far Bulgaria's most important trade partner: for forty years now, it has regularly provided more than half of Bulgaria's imports, from which the Bulgarian economy has benefited greatly. For instance, Bulgaria was spared most of the consequences of the oil price increases of 1973–4 and 1979–80, because it bought oil from the USSR at prices considerably below world market prices. Until recently, Soviet imports could be easily repaid with Bulgarian exports, which could not be sold to non-Communist countries. Furthermore, since the mid–1970s, because Bulgaria could not produce enough goods to balance the value of Soviet energy supplies, the Soviets helped with generous credits. Thus, until 1985, Bulgaria accumulated deficits in bilateral clearing with the USSR of 3.6 billion valuta-leva.

Since 1986, Bulgaria has again had a trade surplus vis-à-vis the Soviet Union. We may assume that Bulgaria's policy to pay off Soviet credits was due to heavy pressure from the new Soviet leadership. In 1985, for the first time in public the Soviet media criticized the inefficiency of the Bulgarian economy and the low quality of Bulgaria's export goods. The camaraderie long cherished by the two countries has been strained since Gorbachev's accession to power. Gorbachev reacted promptly to the frequent complaints of Soviet companies about Bulgarian deliveries. In the Soviet-Bulgarian "Long-Term Agreement on the Development of the Economic and Scientific-Technical Cooperation Until the Year 2000," the Soviet Union promises to continue to supply energy and raw materials, but Bulgaria commits itself to improving its production structure in order to increase its capacity for delivering the "necessary products . . . of high quality and technological world level."[17] Bulgarian producers have been planning joint enterprises with Soviet partners. From them, Bulgaria can expect faster technology transfers from the USSR, and the Soviets will have even tighter control of Bulgaria's industrial production. The numbers of Soviet experts, technical staff, engineers, and other "advisers," many of whom already work in all the important branches of the Bulgarian economy, will increase.

To Bulgaria, the importance of economic relations with the USSR is enormous. First, Bulgaria owes its rapid industrialization to Soviet technical and financial aid. The USSR has continuously supplied it with energy and raw materials, so that Soviet resources meet two-thirds of Bulgaria's energy demand. More than 90 percent of Bulgaria's oil imports come from the USSR, and dependence on Soviet iron ore, pig iron, and cellulose is analogous. The machinery in the

Bulgarian industrial sector is chiefly of Soviet origin, because the Soviet Union has delivered hundreds of complete plants in all branches of industry. The Kremikovitsi (near Sofia) and Lenin steelworks are excellent examples of this practice, as are the petrochemical plant near Burgas and the Kosloduj nuclear power plant.

Still, the arbitrary adaptation of much of Bulgaria's production capacity to meet Soviet demands has been costly. Most Bulgarian industrial goods cannot be sold on the world market because production cannot keep up with the West's technological progress. The ease of selling to the USSR has spared Bulgarian producers from international competition. The rising Soviet demand for high-quality goods is unlikely to change, and more of the limited numbers of competitive Bulgarian goods will be withheld from export to the West. Close economic cooperation with the USSR will hardly help Bulgaria modernize its industry, agriculture, and services to world standards.

In December 1988, Minister of Trade Lukanov and Minister of Foreign Affairs Mladenov expressed their support for opening up the Bulgarian economy to the West, a change that would require far-reaching systemic changes. So far, reforms in various sectors of the economy have been incoherent, hastily implemented, and bewildering. The repeated restructuring and reorganization of the economy have contributed to restraining the growth of industrial output, which in 1987 was stagnating at 0.7 percent, and in 1988 may have reached a little over 1 percent in real value. These disappointing results, compounded by the disastrous harvests of 1985, 1987, and 1988, have been the main cause of the $0.4–1.1 billion annual deficits in the hard-currency trade balance, which, between 1985 and the end of 1988, created an increase in net foreign debt from $1.5 billion to $6.4 billion.[18] More than 40 percent of Bulgaria's hard-currency earnings are directed for debt service, which is a significant burden, considering the limited potential of the Bulgarian export industry to increase its sales to Western markets. Until recently, convertible currency earnings benefited greatly from exports of oil derivatives produced from crude oil of Soviet origin, but Bulgaria has recently suffered from reductions of Soviet oil exports. Economic reforms providing greater incentives for innovation and efficiency are likely to proceed slowly for fear of releasing social tensions and political demands.

ALBANIA: IDEOLOGY AND PRAGMATISM

Since its break with China in 1976, Albania, the smallest of the Balkan countries, has adopted a new commercial policy. Following a period of extreme dependence on one powerful trade partner—first the Soviet Union, then China—which interfered in its development strategy, Tirana chose political independence and economic self-sufficiency. With the need to import machinery and raw materials, a regional diversification of trade was established toward the end of the Hoxha era.[19] Albania increased its trade with several West European countries, notably Italy. It also strengthened economic contacts with some members of the CMEA, especially Czechoslovakia, East Germany, and Romania. As before, commercial relations with the USSR and with the United States were rejected for ideological reasons. With a share of 15 percent of total Albanian trade, Yugoslavia remained Albania's most important partner, despite their strained political relations until recently. Since 1988, Czechoslovakia has been Albania's biggest supplier.

In the 1980s, a domestic economic crisis has impaired Albania's projected trade increase. Agriculture has stagnated, the export industry has fallen short of targets, and oil and chromium outputs have declined, creating shortages and restricting the country's capacity to increase foreign trade. In a country with a fast-growing population (2.2 percent, the highest rate in Europe), economic stagnation inevitably leads to social tensions. This consideration may have led Hoxha's successor, Ramiz Alia, to launch violent attacks on plant managers and bureaucrats on several occasions since the ninth Party Congress in November 1986.[20] For the first time in the history of Communist Albania, the shortcomings of Enver Hoxha's highly centralized planning system were acknowledged, indirectly, as one of the causes of the economic crisis.

Alia has further blamed deficiencies in organization and management as well as bureaucratic behavior for the poor performance of the economy, technological backwardness, "amateurism" in machine building, and low productivity in agriculture. He also denounced "excessive centralization" for the lack of initiative in Albanian enterprises. Alia demanded more competence on the lower levels of the economy and announced the steps to increase economic efficiency. For instance, income incentives are to improve the workers' performance, and—in a departure from previous agricultural policy— private enterprise by cooperative farmers is to be encouraged.

Alia's speeches could be taken as evidence of a more pragmatic new course, but it still represents much less than a reform of the system of planning. Increased economic efficiency is feasible only if the Albanian leaders resolve to eliminate some of the ideological principles of the Hoxha era. These include the constitutional ban on seeking foreign credits and foreign investment, because this ban cuts off Albanian industry from foreign technology. Because Albania has categorically refused to have official relations with both "imperialist" superpowers, however, Albania can have no economic contacts with the Soviet Union. The new Albanian leaders have brusquely rebuffed Moscow's attempts to resume contacts after Hoxha's death. The Albanians even discern in Gorbachev's new thinking, a "deepening of the revisionist social-imperialistic course."[21] Here, the Albanians intentionally eliminate a potential source of supplies and, presumably, financial and technical aid.

CRISIS MANAGEMENT IN GREECE AND TURKEY

Following World War II, Greece and Turkey shared the fate of many developing countries of the free world. Their frequently changing governments—which oscillated between democracy and dictatorship, containing social unrest, corruption, and lethargy with difficulty— were less successful than most of the Communist countries at overcoming their antiquated production structures. Despite large-scale state intervention, modernization of their economies was hampered by the pressure of large populations, inadequate domestic savings, and mismanagement. Without the help of the World Bank, the IMF, the EEC with its "Consortium of the Aid for Turkey," and a variety of development funds, the situation in both countries would have been much worse. Industry developed slowly and in largely inefficient state-owned enterprises. Agricultural productivity remained far below Western standards. The governments invested heavily in the neglected infrastructure, which remains inadequate to support a self-sustaining economic takeoff.

Both Greece and Turkey suffered from the world-market recession that began in the 1970s. Even in these unfavorable circumstances, however, the two countries have so far performed better than most other countries in the region. In Greece, the ruling Socialist Party has compounded the problems with its lengthy discussions of "nationalization" and "socialist achievements," which caused a drop in private productive investments, frightened off foreign equity capital, and strengthened the role of the state in the domestic economy. Trade unions were encouraged to call strikes, wages were linked automatically to fast-rising prices, and the cost of labor grew at the expense of the international competitiveness of Greek industry. An increasing demand for imports exacerbated the balance-of-payments constraint, and foreign indebtedness became an ever heavier burden for the economy.

In October 1985, the government launched a program of stabilization and so far has adhered to its policy of restricting incomes. Since then, real income has dropped by 15 percent, and inflation was down to 14 percent in 1988. Nevertheless, the fight against inflation is hampered by a tremendous budget deficit.[22] The success of the stabilization program is an important condition for the IMF's continued financial support. Since Greece joined the EEC as a full member, on January 1, 1981, it not only has succeeded in taking advantage of all the financial and commercial preferences available to it, but also has adjusted better to the demands of the EEC market.

Turgut Özal's plan published in January 1980 for reconstructing and stabilizing the Turkish economy was the first radical reform of the "etatism" established by Atatürk in the 1930s.[23] In the late 1970s Turkey was riddled with political riots and terrorism, wildcat strikes, and corruption, and it faced financial ruin. Özal put an end to the extreme protectionist policy and exposed state enterprises to international competition by releasing the exchange rate and liberalizing imports. His policies combined with export promotions yielded immediate results. Exports again grew and the enormous deficits in the balance of payments were reduced, although they are far from eliminated. Foreign indebtedness has increased to more than $37 billion, swallowing up over 40 percent of Turkey's foreign currency receipts.

Half of Turkey's imports consist of crude oil bought mostly in the Middle East; this situation illustrates the country's heavy dependence on foreign trade. As before, inefficient, loss-producing state industry represents a tremendous burden and is the main reason for Turkey's $3 billion budget deficit in 1988. Attempts to sell some illiquid plants to domestic as well as foreign firms have not been successful. Despite a rigid high-interest policy, the rate of inflation again climbed to more than 80 percent in 1989 (it had been 120 percent in the early 1980s). In the last five years private incomes lost 50 percent of their purchasing power. Discontent among the population is spreading, all the more so since a new austerity program was launched in October 1988. Özal's policies are still successful, however. In 1988, Turkey had its first surplus in the balance of trade, services, and transfers in its history. Its 7 percent growth rate surpassed the rates of all the other southeast European countries in 1988.[24]

ECONOMIC DILEMMAS AND POLICY OPTIONS

The Soviet Union is facing a dilemma regarding its southeast European allies: the conflict between its interests in the economic viability of these countries and the political cohesion of the bloc. Economic viability demands the abandonment of central planning, a source of inefficiency and stagnation, and the freedom to choose one's own way to good economic performance without regard for ideology. But cohesion requires uniformity and discipline, and these aims are difficult to reconcile. For the time being, it seems, the Soviet leadership prefers viability that can be significantly improved only by implementing fundamental economic and political reforms. It is willing to risk cohesion by tolerating unprecedented diversification.

The reason for the apparent change in the Soviet attitude toward its allies lies in the devastating economic crisis endangering the stability of the Communist regimes. To legitimate their political power, the ruling parties need economic success—which entails an adequate supply of consumer goods, a rising living standard, and social security for the population. But to reach these objectives, Moscow's partners must be left on their own more than ever before. In the 1970s, the bloc's energy- and raw-material-importing economies benefited from the slower rise of CMEA prices than world market prices, as well as from cheap Soviet clearing credits, which balanced their bilateral trade deficits. They were able to maintain inefficient central planning, mismanagement, an absurd system of distribution, and excessive waste because the USSR bore part of these costs by accepting second-rate industrial products which the bloc countries were unable to sell on the world market. Even if the Soviet economy gained from its trade with the CMEA partners, the burdens were unevenly distributed.

Since the mid–1980s, however, under pressure of its domestic crisis, the Soviet Union has been less willing to subsidize its partners, insisting on better quality of trade and the repayment of clearing credits. Soviet deliveries of energy and other raw materials have stopped increasing in response to the needs of the CMEA customers, and are more dependent than before on CMEA members' earlier investments in Soviet oil and gas fields, mines, and generating plants. Thus, for most CMEA states as well as Yugoslavia, the previous deficits in bilateral trade with the USSR have changed to surpluses, and parts of them at least serve to pay off clearing debts. By reducing these countries' dependence on Soviet supplies, the Soviets have apparently decided to forgo an important political lever. The policy of increasing the efficiency of these countries' economies will strengthen their autonomy in choosing trade partners.

But greater autonomy for the satellites will not mean avoiding Soviet control altogether. It also will not mean unlimited choice to abandon the fundamental precepts of socialism, as long as these countries are economically dependent on the Soviet Union. Yet the gradual implementation of economic reforms combined with political and social restructuring, including a certain amount of *glasnost*, will foster an open evaluation of the costs and benefits of close economic cooperation with the USSR, a sensitive topic that cannot be discussed without stirring up deep emotions, even a deeply rooted anti-Sovietism. To increase the efficiency of CMEA cooperation and enhance lagging economic integration of the member countries, thereby invigorating this instrument of Soviet control, it will be necessary to equip it with supranationality (which has so far been rejected by the smaller member states) or to introduce a definite market orientation to be implemented equally in all these countries.

Soviet leaders may have hoped to gain influence in Yugoslavia with economic concessions and political détente. With its continuing domestic crisis, the USSR's ability to increase trade and cooperation with Yugoslavia is limited. In spite of a growing "clearing lobby" among Yugoslav politicians pleading for an even closer economic cooperation with other Communist countries, the Yugoslav government is apparently determined to promote a renewed westward shift in foreign trade and is trying to increase hard-currency receipts and Western equity investment in the Yugoslav economy. Should this crisis-ridden state fall apart, the wealthier northern republics may join the West, and the Soviet Union will attempt to find allies among the other republics.

Western Europe, with its high standard of living and wide range of political liberties, will remain attractive to the southeast European countries with their traditional cultural and economic European links. Increased economic integration will strengthen the European Economic Community (EEC) after 1992, and thus increase opportunities for trade. Competition within the EEC will, however, grow. The export structure of the Communist states of Southeastern Europe is very similar to that of Greece, Spain, Portugal, and Turkey, an associate member. Trade and cooperation agreements with the EEC, like those signed by Yugoslavia and Romania in 1980 and Hungary in 1988, offer exemption from duty for imported industrial products, but with restrictions for "sensitive" goods such as textiles, and limited quotas for agricultural produce. Thus, the only way to strengthen their commercial relations with the EEC permanently is to modernize their export structure and focus on the production of modern high-tech consumer and investment goods, which so far has guaranteed the success of several industrializing countries of Southeast Asia in their trade with the EEC.

The West is well advised to counteract Moscow's attempts to maintain its influence in southeastern Europe. Serious attempts at reform and increased opportunities for economic cooperation ought to be appreciated and honored, even with financial concessions. The transition from planned to market economies will be long and painful, and it will impose considerable hardships on the population. Since successful reforms require the reintegration of these economies in the European and world economy, Western involvement in the process of transition through financial and technical aid is indispensable. The continued recognition of Soviet hegemony in the region for the sake of a false and hollow "stability" would be contrary to the vital interests of these countries and to their traditional political and economic orientation. And it would be the wrong policy for safe-guarding peace in the region.

NOTES

I am grateful to György Enyedi for his comments on an earlier draft of this chapter, as well as to the participants of the conference on "Geopolitics, Peace, and Balkan Security" that took place in Tutzing on January 9–12, 1989, where this paper was presented.

1. E. A. Radice, "General Characteristics of the Region between the Wars," in M. C. Kaser and E. A. Radice, eds., *The Economic History of Eastern Europe 1919–1975*, vol. I (Oxford: Clarendon Press, 1985), 31.
2. See Radice, "General Characteristics," 50–62; Michael Kaser and Rudolf Nötel, "The East European Economies in Two World Crises," in Ivan T. Berend and Knut Borchardt, eds., *The Impact of the Depression of the 1930's and Its Relevance for the Contemporary World*, A/5 Session, 9th International Economic History Congress (Karl-Marx University of Economics, Budapest, 1986), 215–47. Roland Schönfeld, "Die Balkanländer in der Weltwirtschaftskrise," *Vierteljahrschrift für Sozial- und Wirtschaftsgeschichte* 62 (1975), 179–213.
3. See Nicholas Spulber, *The Economics of Communist Eastern Europe* (London: Chapman and Hall, 1957).
4. For a discussion of Soviet-CMEA relations, see Paul Marer, "The Political Economy of Soviet Relations with Eastern Europe," in Sarah Meiklejohn Terry, ed., *Soviet Policy in Eastern Europe* (New Haven, Conn., and London: Yale University Press, 1984), 155–88; and the contributions to Roland Schönfeld, ed., *RGW-Integration und Südosteuropa* (Munich: R. Oldenbourg, 1984).
5. Dennison Rusinow, *The Yugoslav Experiment 1948–1974* (Berkeley: University of California Press, 1978).
6. Thomas Brey, "Jugoslawien nach dem III. (*sic*) Parteitag: Zwischen Aufbruch und Stagnation," *Osteuropa* 37 (1987): 451f.
7. Jens Reuter, "Konfligierende politische Ordnungs-Vorstellungen als Hintergrund

der Krise in Jugoslawien," *Südosteuropa* 38 (1989): 1–8; and Oskar Kovac, "Wege zur Überwindung aussenwirtschaftlicher Schwierigkeiten Jugoslawiens," *Südosteuropa Mitteilungen* 28 (1988): 154–69.

8. David Dyker, "Yugoslavia," in *CPE Outlook for Foreign Trade and Finance* (London: The WEFA Group, July 1989), 10.5.

9. Marvin R. Jackson, "Romania's Debt Crisis: Its Causes and Consequences," in *East European Economies: Slow Growth in the 1980's*, vol. 3 (Washington, D.C.: Joint Economic Committee, U.S. Congress, 1986), 489–502; Roland Schönfeld, "Rumänien: Hoher Preis der Autonomiepolitik," *Aus Politik und Zeitgeschichte*, Beilage zur Wochenzeitung Das Parlament, B 36–37 (1987), 26–37.

10. Estimates by Bank für Internationalen Zahlungsausgleich (BIZ), *Neue Zürcher Zeitung*, April 5, 1989; Radio Bucharest, April 14, 1989.

11. Anneli Ute Gabanyi, "Von Gorbacev zu Gromyko—Zum Stand der rumänischsowjetischen Beziehungen," *Südosteuropa* 37 (1988): 257–71.

12. Alan Smith, "Romania," in *Centrally Planned Economies Outlook*, The WEFA Group (Bala Cynwyd, Pa.: Wharton Econometric Forecasting Associates, October 1988), 8.1ff.

13. *Rabotnichesko Delo*, February 23, 1989.

14. Marvin R. Jackson, "Bulgaria's Attempt at 'Radical Reform,' " *Berichte des Bundesinstituts für ostwissenschaftliche und international Studien*, no. 2 (Cologne: Bunderinstitut, 1988). Roland Schönfeld, "Wirtschaftsentwicklung mit besonderer Berücksichtigung des Aussenhandels in Bulgarien," *Österreichisches Jahrbuch für Internationale Politik*, vol. 3 (Vienna: Boehlau Verlag, 1986), 182–98.

15. *Neue Zürcher Zeitung*, December 17, 1988.

16. Roland Schönfeld, "Aussenwirtschaft," in Klaus-D. Grothusen, ed., *Südosteuropa-Handbuch Bulgarien*, vol. VI (Göttingen: Vandenhoeck and Ruprecht, 1989).

17. "Dulgorocna programa za razvitie na ikonomiceskoto i naucno techniceskoto satrudnicestvo mezdu NR Bulgaria i SSSR za period do 2000 godina" [Long-Term Treaty on the Development of Economic and Scientific-Technical Cooperation between the People's Republic of Bulgaria and the USSR for the Period until the year 2000], *Ikonomika* 8 (1985).

18. John Sheehy, "Bulgaria," in *Centrally Planned Economies Outlook*, The WEFA Group (London, April 1989), 9.3, 9.4 (overall total gross debt was $7.3 billion).

19. Angelo Masotti-Cristofoli, "Albania's Economy Between the Blocs," in Roland Schönfeld, ed., *Reform und Wandel in Südosteuropa* (Munich: R. Oldenbourg, 1985), 285–305.

20. Elez Biberaj, "Albanien nach Enver Hoxha. Gratwanderung zwischen Kontinuität und Wandel," *Europa Archiv* 42 (1987): 559ff.

21. Louis Zanga, "Albania's Rejection of the Soviet Experiment," *Radio Free Europe Research*, RAD Background Report/145 (Munich: August 1, 1988).

22. *Neue Zürcher Zeitung*, January 20, 1989, February 3, 1989, September 7, 1989.

23. Zvi Yehuda Hershlag, "Economic Policies," in Klaus-D. Grothusen, ed., *Südosteuropa-Handbuch Türkei*, vol. IV (Göttingen: Vandenhoeck and Ruprecht, 1985), 346–69.

24. *Neue Zürcher Zeitung*, January 14, 1989, May 3, 1989.

5

THE BACKGROUND AND IMPLICATIONS OF THE DOMESTIC SCENE IN YUGOSLAVIA

Christopher Cviic

A decade ago Yugoslavia was a stable federation, respected by East and West alike for its independent foreign policy. Under President Tito's leadership, it had come to play an influential role on the world stage that was out of all proportion to its size and economic and military power. Would-be reformers in the Communist world studied and sought to emulate its distinctive system of workers' self-management, evolved since Tito's break with Stalin in 1948. Yugoslavia was a source of inspiration for all those searching for a "third way" between state socialism and free-market capitalism.

Today Yugoslavia is but a shadow of its former bouncy, boundlessly confident self. Beset by grave economic problems (rampant inflation, large hard-currency debt, high unemployment), it is facing serious social unrest, perhaps even a social revolution. Its noisy internal conflicts—notably, the increasingly bitter strife among its nations—are making its neighbors anxious and causing concern further afield.

Yugoslavia's erstwhile admirers now regard that country rather like one of those Victorian paintings showing a bankrupt confronted with the bailiffs and surrounded by grief-stricken wife and children under the title "An Awful Warning"—in other words, an object lesson in economic recklessness and political irresponsibility. Yugoslavia's many friends in the West simply cannot comprehend why it has made so little of the material aid and political support extended to it over so many years. They watch with dismay as Yugoslavia's leaders are locked in passionate squabbles that leave them with little time or energy for dealing with the desperate economic situation. Ironically, Yugoslavia, which the West helped so much in the (never quite spelled-out but always discreetly entertained) hope that it would eventually evolve into a pluralistic polity with a market economy, is lagging behind the reform-minded Warsaw Pact members like Hungary and Poland, which have always had to operate in much more constrained circumstances.

Exasperating as those "Yugorows" are to all those wishing to see the country behave sensibly, there is a certain logic behind them. There are reasons why Yugoslavia seems to prefer to follow its own complex and often mutually contradictory sets of priorities rather than the agenda set for it by well-meaning outsiders. This chapter explores some of those internal Yugoslav agendas and assesses their effects on the country's internal and external positions.

THE NATIONAL QUESTION

To make sense of Yugoslavia's present turmoil, it is essential never to lose sight of the crucial importance in a multinational state of the "national factor." This is a self-evident proposition, but also one that is easily lost sight of when pursuing other themes such as self-management, nonalignment, North-South conflict, economic reform, the crisis of communism, and so on. Of course, living standards, jobs, pensions, health, education, and human rights matter to the citizens of multinational Yugoslavia as much as they do to the citizens of nationally homogeneous Hungary and Poland. But in Yugoslavia there is always something else besides: the fact that every person is a member of a community within the state, the nation, in which the person's identity is anchored and to which the first loyalty is owed. The fact that a few people (1.2 million out of the total population of 22.4 million in 1981) rebel against this by declaring themselves as "Yugoslavs" serves only to emphasize the rule that in Yugoslavia, everything is seen through the prism of "national" calculations.

One of the reasons why this should be so in Yugoslavia to a greater extent than, for example, in the Soviet Union is the continuing volatility of national identity. The process of ethnic differentiation has continued throughout the Tito era and may not be over yet. It was only two decades or so ago, in the 1960s, that the Bosnian Moslems received official recognition as a nation. At about the same time, in 1967, the process of the establishment of the Macedonian nation within Yugoslavia was completed with the setting up of an autocephalous Macedonian Orthodox church. There are still those, within Yugoslavia and abroad, who challenge the legitimacy of this process of ethnic development by denying the ethnic authenticity of the Bosnian Moslems and the Macedonians, and lately also, the nationhood of the Montenegrins has come to be challenged once again. The fact that it is possible, for whatever reason (for example, intermarriage, or political opportunism in strongly "Yugoslav" institutions like the army) to "flee" into being a "Yugoslav" illustrates this continuing national volatility perhaps most vividly of all—and helps to explain why anything pertaining to national identity plays such a role in Yugoslavia; why, for example, both party and government may find themselves obliged to discuss language questions amid a severe economic crisis. At times of external danger, as during the threat of a Soviet invasion after 1948 and again in 1968, the broader Yugoslav framework may loom larger for a while than the narrower national one. But these temporary exceptions simply serve to confirm the rule that in Yugoslavia it is nation, rather than class or race, that represents the most significant political category.

Yugoslav Communists have been grappling with the national problem right from the start. They were not very successful in the 1920s and 1930s. In 1937, in order to plug themselves more effectively into national politics, they created separate Croatian and Slovene parties within the Yugoslav party. The process was completed after 1945 with the formation of separate parties for each of the six federal republics. But these republican parties did not exercise any real power, despite the fact that each had its own central committee and politburo. Tight central control continued to be held by the party politburo in Belgrade under Tito.[1] However, the existence of these separate party organizations within the country's federal system had a certain political importance because it represented an acknowledgment of the national aspirations of those peoples of Yugoslavia such as the Croats and the Macedonians, but also the Bosnian Moslems, who considered themselves hard done by in the pre-1941 royalist and centralist Yugoslavia.

As Yugoslavia began to decentralize in the 1950s, local party leaders in individual republics and provinces began to find it politically advantageous to "speak up" for "their" republic or autonomous province. In most cases, they did this over the allocation of investment capital from central funds in Belgrade, but the fiction of the primacy of the class interest continued to be maintained. Any local nationalistic tendencies were to be dealt with by the republican or provincial leaders. These leaders were expected to keep such tendencies under control, "sweeping before their own door first," as the colorful Yugoslav saying goes—Serbs fighting Serbian nationalists, Croats fighting the Croat, and so on.

Tito presided over the process and managed it with considerable aplomb. From time to time, if a particular leadership looked as if it were likely to fall into the trap of "opportunism," of going too far in espousing local interests as a way of boosting its own popularity, Tito rapped its knuckles and ensured immediate compliance. The harshest of his interventions was in Croatia in 1971–2. Even after the party itself had become "federalized" in the late 1960s and early 1970s, Tito's unquestioned authority and charisma ensured the relatively smooth functioning of the system.

Because all senior party leaders, in effect, derived their legitimacy from Tito, his death in 1980 was deeply unsettling for the whole hierarchy, despite the elaborate rules he had left behind involving regular rotation of offices and rigorous observance of the so-called nationality "key" to prevent any single group from falling under the domination of any other. Many frustrations had accumulated over the years, but for a long time none of the leaders dared to challenge Tito's rules—especially the inviolability of federalism.

All this changed with the appointment of Slobodan Milosevic as Serbia's party president in 1986. To the great surprise of many, including those in his own republic, Milosevic boldly swept aside the Titoist "feudal" principle that had firmly tied each leadership to a particular territory and began to speak for the Serbs, first those in Serbia proper, then those in its provinces of Kosovo and Vojvodina, and finally all the Serbs of Yugoslavia, whose largest nation they are, making up 36 percent of the total population. By openly articulating the Serbs' frustrations, Milosevic has reaped huge political advantages, but at some cost to the state as a whole. In many ways, however, he should be seen as a catalyst of a change that was already happening, notably in the way each national group was reassessing Yugoslavia and its position in it.

The way in which Yugoslavia's nations have been reassessing their stake in Yugoslavia was vividly illustrated in the different attitudes they adopted toward the seventieth anniversary of the formation of the first, royalist Yugoslavia under the Serbian Karadjordjevic dynasty. That anniversary, which fell on December 1, 1988, was celebrated enthusiastically in Serbia. In contrast, most non-Serbs either ignored it altogether or used it as an opportunity to bring home to today's generation just what a bad place that old Yugoslav kingdom had been.

The noncelebrators of the 1918 *ujedinjenje* (union) went out of their way to make an even greater fuss than usual of the forty-fifth anniversary, on November 29, 1988, of the wartime meeting in Jajce in Bosnia of the so-called Anti-Fascist Council of National Liberation of Yugoslavia (AVNOJ), which laid the foundations, under the party's guidance, for a postwar federal Yugoslavia. That anniversary, which has been national day in Yugoslavia ever since the Communists came to power in 1945, provided an opportunity for Serbia for the airing of more doubts about the occasion's legitimacy—not least because of the absence from Jajce of a proper delegation from Serbia. Inevitably, this lack of a Serbian delegation was read by Yugoslavia's non-Serbs as a further proof of the Serbs' second thoughts about the federal system, particularly as it had developed in the latter period of Tito's rule, reaching its final form in the 1974 constitution.

THE SERBS

The Serbs' case against Titoist federalism is most clearly set out in the draft memorandum prepared by a working group of the Serbian Academy of Arts and Sciences in Belgrade under the chairmanship of Antonije Isakovic, its vice-president and one of Serbia's most prominent writers.[2]

The draft memorandum deals with a number of issues affecting the whole of Yugoslavia, but its most telling parts are those that concentrate on the position of Serbia and the Serbs within Yugoslavia. The document states three main objections to today's Yugoslavia from the Serbian point of view:

1. The alleged discriminatory policy toward Serbia in the economic field, reflecting the alleged anti-Serbian bias in the pre-1941 Communist Party of Yugoslavia and the Communist International in Moscow, and the predominance of Yugoslavia's western republics, Croatia and Slovenia, in economic decision making after 1945

2. The partition of Serbia under the leadership of Tito, a Croat, and Edvard Kardelj, his second-in-command and a Slovene, into three parts in the 1974 constitution: Serbia proper and the autonomous provinces of Vojvodina and Kosovo, with both Kosovo and Vojvodina allowed direct participation in decision making at the federal level, bypassing Serbia

3. The systematic anti-Serbian policy in Kosovo pursued by Albanian "separatists" and "irredentists" with support from other republics and resulting in the steady exodus of Serbs from Kosovo, the center of Serbia's medieval state, where the Albanians now represent the majority

The memorandum also deals with the allegedly unequal position of the Serbian minority in Croatia and claims that the Serbs in Yugoslavia are subjected to a policy of "genocide."

The authors of the draft memorandum saw the rationale behind this policy in the slogan "strong Yugoslavia, weak Serbia," and called for its reversal, especially the abolition of the 1974 constitution under which the autonomous provinces of Kosovo and Vojvodina were allowed to evolve into de facto republics. The draft memorandum was strongly criticized in the non-Serb parts of Yugoslavia, partly because of its antimarket, dirigiste economic assumptions, but above all as a manifestation of revived "Great Serbian hegemonism." Within Serbia, however, and among Serbs in other parts of Yugoslavia, the document's main thesis—that the Serbs have had a raw deal under the "anti-Serb Tito-Kardelj" coalition in charge of Yugoslavia since 1945—has found widespread acceptance. There is no question here—and never was in the past—of a Serbian rejection of Yugoslavia as such, but of a certain kind of Yugoslavia seen as harmful to Serbian interests and denying them, the traditional *Staatsvolk*, their proper share of power and a recognition of their sacrifices in both world wars.

In contrast, prewar Yugoslavia was a place Serbs could call their own and identify with. It was not perfect by any means—there was resentment in the 1920s and early 1930s that the war reparations and Western loans proved far below Serbian expectations and that the western parts, Slovenia and Croatia, preserved too much autonomy from the central government—but there were many compensations. Even though the state was not called Serbia, it had a Serbian dynasty; a special position for the Serbian Orthodox church; and Serbian dominance in the army, the police, the gendarmerie, the senior ranks of the civil service, and diplomacy. And, most important, all ethnic Serbs, barring small minorities in neighboring Hungary, Romania, and Albania, were inside Yugoslavia's borders. Within Yugoslavia, areas such as Kosovo, from which many Serbs had departed during the five centuries of Turkish rule, were being recolonized by Serbian settlers with the aid of special programs administered from Belgrade. No wonder that the breakup of Yugoslavia in 1941 was seen as a great tragedy by all Serbs. But even though today's Yugoslavia compares so unfavorably, from the national Serbian point of view, with the prewar royalist one, it still has one advantage: the bulk of all Serbs are within its borders.

This situation would change, however, if Yugoslavia were to continue to evolve from loose federation that it is now into a confederation and perhaps eventually into a number of smaller, independent states. Then the Serbs would become permanently divided and exposed to the danger of assimilation in the parts remaining outside Serbia. Today only 40 percent of Serbs live in Serbia proper. Even when Serbia is taken together with its provinces, Kosovo and Vojvodina, 24 percent of Serbs remain outside—mainly in Bosnia (32 percent of that republic's total population) and in Croatia (11.6 percent of the total). (There are only 3.3 percent declared Serbs in Montenegro, but the majority of Serbs regard the Montenegrins as Serbs anyway).[3] And so the preservation of Yugoslavia, preferably as a centralized (although, of course, not necessarily, in terms of individual civil rights, illiberal) state remains a high national priority for any Serbian policy.

THE SLOVENES

For the Slovenes, these calculations of national interest look different. Back in 1918, in the wake of the Habsburg Empire's breakup, when the Slovenes felt threatened by panGerman and Italian imperialism, they were eager to join the new Yugoslav state as a powerful shield against the enemy from the west and the north. A well-defined entity with a language different from the other peoples of Yugoslavia, Slovenia had little to fear from the rest. World War II and Yugoslavia's breakup brought the danger of national annihilation to the Slovenes as a nation targeted by Hitler for extinction. So rejoining Yugoslavia, albeit a Communist one, seemed natural for the Slovenes.

Now, after nearly four and a half decades of life in new Yugoslavia, the Slovenes are showing signs of restlessness—rather like tenants in a large apartment house who feel that the rent is too high and that they do not care for most of the neighbors and so they want out. It certainly helps that, instead of facing raging imperialists in the west and north, Slovenia now faces two peaceful and highly prosperous neighbors, Austria and Italy, whose virtues as democratic states all Slovenes are aware of through personal travel and watching Austrian and Italian television.

Since 1978, Slovenia (together with Croatia) has been participating in the work of an informal, low-profile body called Alpen-Adria in German and Alpe-Jadran in Croat and Slovene, whose purpose is cooperation in the fields of culture, energy, environment, sport, transport, and others. Other members are the two western regions of Hungary, five Austrian *Länder*, four northern regions of Italy, and, in West Germany, Bavaria. Through this cooperation as well as in other ways, the Slovenes (and the Croats) have discovered how much they still have in common with these former regions of the Austro-Hungarian Empire. By the same token, the new westward orientation emphasizes the distance from Yugoslavia's east, which to many Slovenes seems to be only bringing problems like trouble in the Kosovo province, resistance to fast economic reforms, and so on.

It is hard these days to find anybody in Slovenia who would say that "even the worst Yugoslavia is better than none," as Slovenia's foremost pre-1941 politician, Father Anton Korosec, who died in 1940, used to say. On the contrary, many intellectuals are arguing that, both in 1918 and in 1945, Slovenia took the wrong historic turn.[4] The political and business establishments did not share this view, but fears of a neo-centralist regime's coming to power in Belgrade and proceeding to curtail Slovenia's autonomy are real. Talk of secession if the situation in Yugoslavia becomes unbearable for Slovenia is becoming quite common, not just in private conversation but also in Slovenia's remarkably free press. On September 27, 1989, Slovenia's parliament in Ljubljana adopted a series of amendments to the republic's constitution, including the right to secede from Yugoslavia.

THE CROATS

The feeling that life in the same apartment house is becoming rather unpleasant is shared by Croatia. For the Croats, too, Yugoslavia represented in 1918 a shield against Italian aspirations to the Croatian Adriatic coast, agreed to by the Entente powers in the 1915 Treaty of London as an inducement to Italy to join the war on the Entente side.

For the Croats, pre-1941 Yugoslavia was a disappointment. Ironically, it was the Croats who invented the idea of a "South Slav" state and were its most fervent advocates within the Austro-Hungarian Empire. In Yugoslavia, however, they lost even the limited autonomy they had enjoyed as one of the empire's historic nations under the 1868 "*Nagodba*" (compromise) with the Hungarians, signed a year after the *Ausgleich* between the Austrian and Hungarian halves of the monarchy. Precisely because of their geographical and, even more, linguistic closeness to the Serbs, the Croats felt vulnerable to denationalization under the official policy of "three tribes—one nation" (Serbs, Croats, Slovenes = Yugoslavs). Indeed, in 1929, King Alexander officially forbade the use of national flags and other symbols on the ground that he recognized only "Yugoslavs."

There were also economic factors. Croatia's business community felt itself manipulated and exploited by the rapacious Belgrade *carsija* (establishment and Mafia rolled into one).[5] Many Croats welcomed the agreement on limited autonomy for Croatia in August 1939 as the first step toward a federal reorganization of Yugoslavia, but it was bitterly opposed by Serbian political parties.

When Germany and Italy attacked and dismembered Yugoslavia, Croats (like most other non-Serbs in Yugoslavia) were not sorry. This was in strong contrast to the Serbs, who experienced the dismemberment as a traumatic event and, perhaps in self-defense, produced a special variant of the "stab-in-the-back" story. This variant blames the defeat not on the overwhelming strength of the Nazi and Fascist invaders and the poor organization and leadership of the Serbian-led royal army, but on the "treason" of the Croats and other non-Serbs. Any joy felt initially by the Croats at the breakup of Yugoslavia in 1941 was soon dispelled when it was stripped of most of its coast, divided into two occupation zones (one German and one Italian), and placed under the rule of the notorious Ante Pavelic, whose regime organized systematic persecution and extermination of the Serbs and the Jews as well as Croats who opposed Pavelic. Large numbers of Croats began to join the Tito partisans. The persecution of the Serbs, particularly harsh in the mixed-population areas of Lika, Kordun, and Herzegovina, forced thousands of Serbs to flee to the forests to save their lives. Some joined the royalist *cetniks*, but the bulk opted for the Tito Partisans. The 1941–5 persecution left the Serbs, and not just those in Croatia, with feelings of bitterness and mistrust towards the Croats, a legacy that is still alive today.

The post-1945 territorial settlement brought back to Croatia the Adriatic coastal regions and islands Italy had taken after 1918 and 1941, including the Istrian Peninsula. Croatia also obtained something it had not had in the royalist Yugoslavia until 1939—recognition as a federal republic. But the Croats continued to feel ill at ease for a long time after 1945. Tito's crushing of the 1971 "Croatian Spring," followed by a largescale purge and many imprisonments, ushered in a political depression, not unlike that in Czechoslovakia after the suppression of the "Prague Spring" in 1968. Its effects are still being felt today. (Tito's purges of "liberals" and "technocrats" in Slovenia and Serbia were less harsh than in Croatia but led to the loss of many able, modern-minded party leaders.)

As in Slovenia, there is in Croatia, particularly in business circles, a strong feeling of disenchantment with Yugoslavia. In contrast to the situation in Slovenia, however, there is no talk of secession in Croatia, but instead, in the party establishment, an active search for a "Yugoslav synthesis." This search partly reflects the difficulties that a cutting of the umbilical cord with Yugoslavia's eastern part would involve for Croatia. In Slovenia, 82 percent of all Party members are Slovenes, 6.5 percent are Serbs, and 5 percent are Croats. In Croatia only 59.6 percent of Party membership is made up of Croats and 19.4 percent of Serbs.[6] It must also be assumed that at least a proportion of the 17.9 percent Party members in Croatia who consider themselves "Yugoslavs" are Serbs. The Serbs of Croatia would fiercely resist measures likely to separate them from the rest of Yugoslavia's Serbs, and that resistance could be expected to be effective, given the Serbs' disproportionate strength in the party (as well as in the army and the police) compared with their share in the total population of Croatia, which is 11.6 percent.

THE MOSLEMS

In terms of their specific national interests, all the other major national groups—the Moslems of Bosnia and Herzegovina; the Macedonians; the Montenegrins; and the two biggest national minorities, the Albanians and the Hungarians—have benefited under the post–1945 federal system. The Moslems were recognized as an ethnic group on a par with the Serbs, the Croats, and the others in Yugoslavia in the 1960s. They had been an object of historic rivalry in Yugoslavia between the Serbs and the Croats. Under the Turks, who had occupied the Bosnian kingdom in 1463, the province's territory had been enlarged as a result of Turkish conquests in the west. It enjoyed a considerable and fiercely cherished autonomy.[7] Under Austro-Hungarian rule, from 1878 to 1918, the Moslems were treated with respect and the province prospered. After 1918, the majority of the Moslem deputies in the Belgrade parliament declared themselves as Croats, but their leaders pursued a policy of accommodation with the various regimes in Belgrade. The Moslems' initial support for Ante Pavelic's Croat state in 1941 cost them dearly after 1945— although some Serbs still argue that the Moslems, in fact, got away too easily under the Titoist "symmetrical" view of the supposedly equal participation of the various peoples of Yugoslavia on the side of the Partisans.

Things changed for the better both for the Moslems and for the Croats in Bosnia after the fall of Aleksandar Rankovic, the powerful police chief and party cadre secretary, a Serb by nationality, in 1966. The fact that Yugoslavia cooperated within the Nonaligned Movement with many Moslem countries made the Bosnian Moslems a useful element in the country's foreign policy. The authorities allowed

financial help for the Islamic community from abroad. By 1981, the most recent census, the Moslems reached the figure of 39.5 percent of the population, compared with 32 percent for the Serbs and 18.4 percent for the Croats.

For the Bosnian Moslems, there is every merit in preserving Yugoslavia as a federation or confederation. Yugoslavia's breakup would revive the Moslems' nightmare: the dreaded prospect of division. But a return to centralism would be equally unwelcome, because it would bring with it the possibility of a return to Serbian dominance like that between the two wars. But if the division of Yugoslavia were to become a reality, the Bosnian Moslems would most likely throw their weight behind the idea of a linkup with Croatia and Slovenia. (Bosnia and Herzegovina is contemplating taking part in the work of Alpen-Adria at the urging of its business community).

THE MACEDONIANS

Under the Tito regime, Macedonia obtained the status of a federal republic and full support for the development of its national institutions and language.[8] In 1967 it obtained its own autocephalous Macedonian Orthodox church—with the full support of the authorities and in the teeth of bitter opposition from the Serbian Orthodox church, which has, however, until now managed to block the Macedonian church's recognition by other Orthodox churches. Abroad, the Yugoslav government has promoted the recognition of the Macedonian nation and regularly engages in disputes with Greece and Bulgaria over their refusal to extend such a recognition. All this is, from the Macedonian point of view, an immense improvement over the pre–1941 period, when Macedonia was simply a part of southern Serbia exposed to a policy of systematic Serbianization. Not surprisingly, like most other non-Serbs, the Macedonians welcomed the breakup of Yugoslavia in 1941, but what the Bulgarians offered proved disappointing, especially compared with the full nationhood offered by Yugoslavia later.

Today, Macedonia is in a parlous economic state, chiefly brought about by the mistaken investment policy that followed the large injection of capital after the Skopje earthquake in 1963. This experience makes Macedonia deeply mistrustful toward ideas of a free-market reform and supportive of a redistributive economic policy. Macedonia's alliance with, and support for, Serbia is a reflection of its sense of shared danger from the Albanians, who make up more than 20 percent of the total population of Macedonia and have a majority in its western parts. The possibility that one day an Albanian federal unit may be created within Yugoslavia—especially the strong possibility that such a unit would not simply be confined to Kosovo but might well include the Albanian-inhabited western districts of Macedonia—fills the Macedonians with alarm. And so the Macedonians, once bitter opponents of the Serbs, now consider them as allies in the struggle to contain the Albanian "tide." In this struggle, the Macedonian authorities operate an extremely repressive policy against their Albanians. In the long run, however, replacement of the current arrangements by another Great Serbia (in whatever guise) would not be a welcome prospect for the Macedonians.

THE MONTENEGRINS

The setting up of a separate federal republic of Montenegro after 1945 as the state of the Montenegrin nation represented victory for Montenegrin *zelenasi* (Greens), who had advocated the view that, for all their close connection with the Serbs, the Montenegrins are a separate people.[9] But union with Serbia has always enjoyed strong support among the so-called *bjelasi* (Whites). This group won in 1918 when Montenegro, in the teeth of strong opposition from the then King Nikola (living in exile) and his faction in the country, joined Serbia, and thus Yugoslavia. Currently, Montenegro is in the throes of an upheaval, one element of which is the strong showing of the *bjelasi*, warmly supported from Belgrade. The *zelenasi* group has been on the defensive since the overthrow of the entire Montenegrin leadership after mass demonstrations in January 1989, jubilantly welcomed in Belgrade. Milosevic's description of Serbia and Montenegro as "two eyes in one head" neatly sums up the Serbian view of the situation and explains the current sense of satisfaction in Serbia over Montenegro.

THE ALBANIANS AND THE HUNGARIANS

The Albanians, the worst-treated national group in old Yugoslavia, where they even faced the possibility of expulsion to Turkey and Albania in the 1930s, welcomed the defeat and collapse of the old regime in 1941. The Italians incorporated the largely Albanian areas in Kosovo and western Macedonia into a Greater Albania under their protectorate, and provided food and arms and a measure of local autonomy. Not surprisingly, few Albanians joined the Tito forces in the early days of the Partisan guerrilla struggle. In the later stages, the prospect that Kosovo and other Albanian-inhabited areas might be incorporated into Albania proper under the Yugoslav-supported Albanian Communist leadership of Enver Hoxha helped to raise the level of support for the Partisans. But when, at the end of the war, Kosovo returned to Yugoslavia together with western Macedonia, there was strong Albanian armed resistance, which continued for several years. For two decades, Kosovo remained under a special police regime. One of the justifications was the need to guard against infiltration from Albania, which in 1948 joined Stalin against Tito. But the government in Belgrade did not allow the return of Serbian colonists, settled in Kosovo under the royalist Yugoslav regime and chased away from there under the Italian occupation.[10]

After the fall of Aleksandar Rankovic, in 1966, the police regime in Kosovo was eased. Large-scale demonstrations in November 1968 led to measures aimed at appeasing the Albanians. These included increased material aid as well as the setting up of a university in Pristina, Kosovo's capital. Eventually, in the 1974 federal constitution, Kosovo was granted the status of an autonomous province of Serbia but with direct participation in the federal organs, including the collective Presidency of Yugoslavia and the party presidium. In the spring of 1981, after Tito's death in 1980, public demonstrations in favor of formally upgrading Kosovo to the status of a republic of the Yugoslav federation were crushed. A period of strong repression followed. The federal leadership rejected the demand on the ground that such an arrangement would pave the way for Kosovo's secession and annexation by Albania, with subsequent problems in areas of Macedonia and Montenegro, which are inhabited by the Albanians and perhaps also want to leave and join Albania proper.

The real reason for the rejection of the "Kosovo republic" idea was the Serbs' bitter opposition. Now, with the victory of Serbia in the battle for the revision of the 1974 constitution, Kosovo is back under full Belgrade control. Although formal autonomy remains in force, the Serbian government in Belgrade controls the police, the courts, and defense. Under the newly amended constitution adopted in March 1989, Kosovo no longer needs to be consulted about further constitutional changes affecting its status. These can, under one of the new amendments, be introduced by the Serbian assembly alone. Kosovo is represented there, but has no power of veto.

It had been clear for a long time that Kosovo's Albanians would resist the proposed changes tooth and nail. Evidence for that came first from the general strike in the province in February 1989, which included a hunger strike by the Albanian miners. In addition to demanding the retention of the "Tito" 1974 constitution, the Albanians also insisted on the reinstatement of Kosovo's former party leader, Azem Vllasi, and others (including the anti-Milosevic Serbs) who had been replaced by the province's openly pro-Belgrade police chief, Rahman Morina, an ethnic Albanian, and strongly pro-Milosevic local Serbs. The adoption of constitutional changes, first by a Kosovo assembly surrounded by tanks, on March 23, and then by Serbia's on March 28, led to provincewide unrest, which lasted six days and resulted in twenty-four deaths, including those of two policemen. Unofficial reports suggest a much higher casualty toll.

The bulk of Yugoslavia's Hungarians live in Vojvodina, the country's ethnically most complex region, with twenty-two registered national groups. Of these, the Hungarians, who account for 18.9 percent of the total population, are the second biggest—after the Serbs, who make up 54.4 percent. Under Yugoslavia's federal system as it evolved after 1945, the Hungarians of Vojvodina have enjoyed cultural autonomy as well as representation in the province's power structure commensurate with their numbers. In comparison with the position of the Hungarians in Czechoslovakia, Romania, and the Soviet Union, the Hungarians of Yugoslavia have been well treated by any standards.

It should be mentioned that, until 1944–5, Vojvodina had another large national group, the Germans, who had been settled there in the wake of the Turkish retreat from territories occupied at the height of the Ottoman expansion in Europe. At the last census before World War II, in 1931, the Germans numbered 350,000 (the figures include the Germans of eastern Srijem, which had historically been part of Croatia but has since 1945 belonged to Vojvodina).[11] Most of the Vojvodina Germans retreated with the German army in the autumn of 1944; those left behind were forcibly expelled afterwards. Today, only some 4,000 remain. The Germans' place in Vojvodina was taken by colonists from other parts of Yugoslavia, mostly Serbs and Montenegrins.

For Vojvodina's inhabitants, the post-1945 federal autonomy represented in some ways a continuation of the autonomous status it had enjoyed under Austro-Hungary until 1918, when it joined Serbia and thus Yugoslavia. The increased role within the federation after 1974, which represented de facto republican status, had an added attraction for the local political establishment in that it ensured, under a special federal "key," jobs at the level of the federation. Not surprisingly, therefore, the ruling group—the Serbian majority as well as the Hungarians and others—did not react favorably to the idea, which first surfaced openly after Tito's death in 1980, that the province, along with Kosovo, should be brought under the closer control of the Serbian government in Belgrade. They strongly resisted it, but the conflict that ensued between the Vojvodina "autonomists" and the Belgrade "centralists," which has now ended with the former's defeat, never had the emotional intensity of the conflict between the Serbs and the Albanians for the control over Kosovo.

THE KOSOVO TRIGGER

It was the problem of Kosovo that triggered Yugoslavia's nationality crisis after Tito's death in 1980. The nationality crisis coincided with two others: the onset of the financial crisis arising out of Yugoslavia's large hard-currency debt and the growing challenge to the party's monopoly of power. The financial collapse ended years of optimism about Yugoslavia's future, which had been an important glue of the federation's unity, and raised the painful and divisive question of how the burdens of austerity and economic restructuring would be distributed among the country's republics and provinces. In the emerging debate about the future of the political system after Tito, a different type of division appeared: between non-Serbs, who, even when favoring political changes, wanted to retain the federal system, and Serbs, for most of whom the chief—though by no means the only—purpose of de-Titoization was precisely the scrapping of what they saw as the iniquitous 1974 constitution.

The most frequently voiced Serbian grievance was that the Serbian government in Belgrade had no jurisdiction over the courts, the police, and defense in the autonomous provinces of Kosovo and Vojvodina while they, through their representation in the assembly for the whole of Serbia, had a say in the affairs of Serbia proper (*uza Srbija* or, as a Belgrade wit called it, *uzas*, meaning "horror"). The fact that no such arrangement existed in the other republics (Croatia, for example, whose province of Dalmatia had in the past enjoyed a certain historic distinctiveness) was in the eyes of many Serbs yet more proof that Serbia was being kept weak and divided as a matter of deliberate policy pursued by what the Serbs saw as an anti-Serb Croat-Slovene coalition. But to many non-Serbs, this lament was the voice of the Great Serbian "hegemonism" bewailing its lost dominance. These differences toward the federal system and, in particular, the Serbs' demand for a stronger Serbia and their evident preference for a more centralized Yugoslavia, which non-Serbs viewed with the greatest suspicion, have so far been the main barriers to the formation of a common opposition front in Yugoslavia.

Within Yugoslavia's political establishment, Serbia found little support for its demand for a thorough revision of Yugoslavia's federal system. In that sense, things had not changed all that much since Tito's days when, back in 1977, the then Serbian party leader, Draza Markovic, raised the issue of Kosovo and was brushed aside by Tito. After the 1981 riots in Kosovo, the non-Serbs seemed to think that they had done enough by rejecting the Kosovo Albanians' demand for Kosovo to be upgraded to a full republic and by acquiescing in the harsh repression of the (mainly young) local Albanian activists. From the Serb's point of view, however, the issue of the constitution's revision—and, in particular, the situation in Kosovo—was urgent and yet was allowed to drag on without any change for the better.

Under pressure from the local Albanian majority, migration of Serbs from Kosovo continued for economic reasons, according to the Albanians, who pointed to large sums in cash paid to the departing Serbs for their houses and farms by their land-hungry Albanian neighbors. This view of the Serbs' emigration continued to prevail in Yugoslavia's non-Serbian parts—to the dismay of the Serbs, who saw what was happening in Kosovo as part of a deliberate policy designed to force the local Serb population to leave and thus ensure an "ethnically pure" Kosovo for the remaining Albanian majority. But why so much fuss over Kosovo?

For the Serbs, Kosovo has enormous emotional significance as the centerpiece of the main national "Kosovo myth" in Serbian history. The province was the heart of the medieval Serbian state and still contains numerous historic Serbian Orthodox churches and monasteries. It was in Kosovo on June 28, 1389, that the Serbian army, led by Prince Lazar, was defeated by the Turks, a defeat that led to five centuries of life under Ottoman rule for the Serbs. The recovery of Kosovo was a constant hope and aim during the centuries. But by the time Serbia had regained it from the Turks in 1912, the bulk of the Serbs had left—some of them, in fact, settling in what is today Vojvodina—while the number of the local Albanians had increased. Principally because of their very high birthrate, the local Albanians now make up nearly 90 percent of the local population, whereas the Serbs' share has dropped to below 10 percent in the past ten years, according to the latest official estimates.

The political conflict between the two communities feeds on historic animosities: the Serbs see in the mainly Moslem Albanians the modern version of their Turkish oppressors. The feeling is reciprocated by the Albanians, who see the Serbs as the historic enemy. For many Serbs it is intolerable that the formerly despised Albanians should now be getting the better of them, indeed humiliating them. The event in Kosovo that has particularly influenced Serbian opinion is that of Djordje Martinovic, an elderly Serbian farmer who claims that in May 1985 he was sexually assaulted by hooded Albanian assailants. The local Kosovo authorities' conclusion was that Martinovic had injured himself while engaged in an act of self-gratification and had later invented the story of the attack to cover his embarrassment. The case is still before the courts. Martinovic is asking huge damages from the Kosovo government.

Despite the Serbs' growing frustration and unhappiness, the stalemate over Kosovo might have dragged on had it not been for the appearance on the Yugoslav political scene of a remarkable new leader, Slobodan Milosevic. His election as party president in Serbia in 1986 marked a decisive turning point not only for Kosovo but for the whole of Yugoslavia, though few expected anything exceptional from this relatively quiet party *apparatchik*. Soon after he took the top position in Serbia, Milosevic captured the control of the Belgrade press in a series of swift moves that astonished his party rivals and friends alike and left them breathless. In April 1987 he visited Kosovo to address a mass meeting of local Serbs which lasted all night. Having heard their grievances, he promised them that "nobody would ever beat them again." There were raised eyebrows among many of his party colleagues. One of them, Dragisa Pavlovic, the party boss in Belgrade, made a crack about "speed too lightly promised" at a briefing for editors. Milosevic had his revenge. At a central committee meeting in the autumn, not only Pavlovic but also many other supporters of the "softly, softly" approach lost their party posts in a major reshuffle, which Belgrade wits immediately compared to a famous "massacre of princes" carried out by Milos Obrenovic, Serbia's toughest nineteenth-century ruler in a period just before full independence. Shortly after, even Ivan Stambolic, Serbia's president and Milosevic's former mentor, also was out of a job.

Having consolidated his position within the Serbian party, Milosevic gave, through the press controlled by him, considerable public support to the unofficial Serbian movement in Kosovo led by men like the retired police colonel, Mica Sparavalo; Kosta Bulatovic, an engineer; and Miroslav Solevic, head of the local Kosovo office of a Belgrade electronics firm.[12] The "Kosovo committee," which had previously been cold-shouldered by the authorities in Belgrade and actively blocked by the local Albanian-controlled authorities in Kosovo, suddenly became the focus of a new populist movement holding public "solidarity" meetings throughout Serbia. At those, the plight of the Serbs in Kosovo was the constant theme, coupled with ever more strident calls for action against "unprincipled individuals" within the Serbian republic and outside it, obstructing the just cause of Kosovo's Serbs.

In October 1988 the new populist movement, operating with clear but still not fully open support of the Milosevic team, scored its first important triumph: after a mass demonstration and an all-night siege of the main party and government headquarters in Novi Sad, the capital of Vojvodina, its entire "autonomist" leadership resigned and was replaced by supporters of Milosevic. One such supporter, Brana Scepanovic, managing director of Jugoalat, one of Vojvodina's biggest factories, who had laid on the logistical support for the Novi Sad meeting, was rewarded with a post in the new leadership. A similar attempt by the Kosovo committee to hijack the mounting social protest in Montenegro in November 1988 nearly succeeded, but a police charge dispersed the demonstrators and the republic's deeply divided leadership, partly composed of Milosevic's supporters and partly of Montenegrin "own-roaders" (a continuation of the old *zelenasi* who had in the past supported an independent Montenegro) stayed in power. Not for long: in January 1989 another determined onslaught led to the leadership's fall and its replacement by a new, broadly pro-Milosevic team of populist, strongly Serbianminded radicals.

The Kosovo committee's threats to stage "solidarity" meetings in Bosnia and Herzegovina and Croatia at the end of 1988 to publicize their cause, but also to mobilize the support of the local Serbs (32 percent of the total population in Bosnia and 11.6 percent in Croatia), did not materialize because of threats from the authorities of the two republics that such incursions would be resisted. But the leadership of Croatia was shocked in February 1989 when local Croatian Serbs responded to the Kosovo committee's call and held meetings in Knin and some other places where the Serbian minority lives. At those, local speakers echoed slogans previously launched from Serbia about the "unequal position" of the Serbs in Croatia. In June 1989, the celebrations in Serbia of the six-hundredth anniversary of the battle of Kosovo were the signal for Serbian militants in Croatia and Bosnia to stage incidents designed to destabilize the situation in these two republics. These incidents continued throughout the summer.

The authorities in Bosnia and Herzegovina, which had been standing on the sidelines of Yugoslav politics since the 1987 Agrokomerc scandal involving nearly $1 billion worth of uncovered promissory notes, reacted robustly in November and December 1988 against the proposed incursions from across the Drina River, the border with Serbia, and succeeded in penetrating them. But the "Milosevic factor" opened up serious divisions among the new and inexperienced leaders who had replaced the old establishment toppled in the wake of the Agrokomerc scandal. These divisions appeared in the open at the Bosnian Central Committee meetings in March and April and ran very much along national lines: the Serbs on one side and the Croats and the Moslems on the other.

Among the Moslems, fears of a Serbian takeover in the republic under a future centralized regime in Belgrade fed on reports that, far from being a product of spontaneous journalistic investigation, the Agrokomerc affair had been deliberately stage-managed from Belgrade, starting with a leak in the main Belgrade evening paper. The aim, according to this version, was the removal of Hamdija Pozderac, the senior Moslem political figure in Bosnia and vice-president of Yugoslavia's state collective residency, who had been put in charge of masterminding the revision of the 1974 constitution and was a firm opponent of recentralization. After disclosures of the involvement of his brother in the affair, Pozderac resigned from all his posts; he died in 1988.

Slovenia, under the leadership of Milan Kucan, party president since 1986, consistently took a conciliatory line over Kosovo, agreeing with the need for more law and order in the province both for the local Serbian minority and the Albanian majority. The increasing stridency of the Serbian Kosovo campaign, however, eventually pushed the Slovene leadership in February 1989 into condemning the repression of the local Albanian protesters against the curbs of the province's autonomy imposed by Serbia. A public meeting was held in Ljubljana on February 26 in support of the Kosovo Albanian miners on hunger strike, who had been demanding the retention of the 1974 constitution and the reinstatement of Albanian leaders removed from their positions and replaced by pro-Milosevic supporters. At the meeting, Kucan spoke alongside Slovene opposition figures.

Television reports of that Slovene meeting so enraged public opinion in Belgrade that a mass rally was held in Belgrade in protest the following day. At the rally, the arrest of sacked Kosovo Albanian leaders was demanded—there were even calls for their death—and Milosevic promised that "there would be arrests." The following day, the arrests were announced of a number of prominent Kosovo Albanians, including Azem Vllasi, former party leader and one of those dismissed from the Kosovo Provincial Party Committee, though still a member of the Central Committee of the federal party. This arrest of a party figure still a member of top bodies, the first of its kind anywhere in the Communist world since Stalin's time, caused a shock in non-Serb parts of Yugoslavia, especially in Slovenia, not least because—as the Slovene press pointed out—Milosevic had no authority to promise arrests of any kind.

The conflict over Kosovo has highlighted the division that had existed for some time within the Yugoslav party between a more liberal, pluralistic concept espoused by the party in Slovenia and the more authoritarian one with strong pluralistic admixtures that had emerged in Serbia. Intriguingly, both concepts originated as means for the party to broaden its base of support within the republic. But later these paths diverged. In Slovenia, since Kucan took office, there has been a steady growth of tolerated "alternative movements," with causes such as environment (important in Slovenia, which has Yugoslavia's only nuclear power station in Krsko on the Sava River), peace and antimilitarism, feminism, and so on. The movements were allowed to operate within the official Slovene youth movement and to publicize their views in *Mladina*, the increasingly outspoken organ of the youth movement.

Behind the new political permissiveness lay a calculation. The top priority of Slovenia's leadership, ever since the shock of the 1982–3 financial crisis, has been to push Yugoslavia as a whole toward a market economy as fast as possible. It could only do so, however, from a secure position of political support from a wide constituency. That support could be obtained only by mobilizing the intelligentsia behind popular causes. In a republic such as Slovenia, bordering on Austria and Italy, pluralism was an obvious demand for the educated elites to voice. Another was the defense of Slovenia's national interests, not just in the economic field but also in matters such as culture.

The Yugoslavia-wide discussion in the early 1980s about the introduction of a so-called core curriculum for schools throughout the country in all subjects including history, literature, and language caused Slovenia to fear a cultural "Yugoslavization." Such a process would rob Slovenia of its cultural identity by reducing the amount of Slovene history, language, and literature taught in schools in order that those of the other peoples of Yugoslavia could become better known in Slovenia. The Slovene party leadership grasped that this issue was a popular one and consequently took a stand against the core curriculum proposal. This stand was sharply criticized, even ridiculed, in the Belgrade press as "little Slovenism," which, in turn, provoked a growing Serbian backlash in Slovenia's cultural circles.

This issue, as well as another that had been irritating the Slovenes for a long time—the use of the Serbian variant of Serbo-Croat as a language of command and general communication—was taken up in the press, notably the magazine *Mladina*. That magazine later widened its coverage of military matters by reporting various abuses, the most famous of which was the report in 1987 of how a retirement villa was being built in Opatija on Croatia's Adriatic coast for Admiral Branko Mamula, the defense minister, by soldiers doing national service. Admiral Mamula resigned before the expiration of his mandate in May 1988. Before he did so, the Supreme Military Council in Belgrade discussed the situation in Slovenia in March and sought, through the local military commander, to take preliminary soundings of what sort of measures could be carried out against the opposition in an emergency.

Mladina published the story, causing a political row between the Slovene leadership and the army command in Belgrade. Four people, three *Mladina* journalists and a Slovene noncommissioned officer who had supplied them with the information, were put on trial and sentenced in July 1988 to terms ranging from six months for the journalists to four years for the noncommissioned officer. The *Mladina* affair continues; only one of the four has so far started serving his sentence. The small but not insignificant concessions in an army context—such as the permission to take the military oath in one's native tongue, the use of Slovene on army buildings and barracks in Slovenia, and, last but not least, the permission for conscientious objectors (granted in April 1989) to do their national service in a civilian form—have not made much impact. In Slovene minds, the army, because of the vast preponderance of Serbs in the officer corps, continues to be identified with Serbia. Despite efforts by the authorities, few Slovenes want to serve in the army or the police.

Those conflicts have led to even greater national cohesion in Slovenia and, consequently, greater tolerance of opposition movements. In May 1988 the Slovene Farmers' Alliance with its own youth wing was launched, in the presence of an official observer from the Communist Party. In January 1989 the Slovene Democratic Alliance was launched, followed a month later by the Slovene Social-Democratic Alliance, both led by well-known public figures: the former by Dimitrij Rupel, a sociologist and one of the founders of the influential *Nova Revija*, where much of the material reviewing Slovenia's recent history and politics in an independent, critical way has been published; and the latter by France Tomsic, an engineer who in 1987 led a major strike in a big factory in Slovenia and, more important, had worked a long time in West Germany and has close connections with the West German Social Democrats. All those movements operate within the Socialist Alliance, which, however, is under pressure to change its statutes and drop the "leading role of the party" and even socialism from its statutes.

The "Milosevic factor" has strengthened the forces of national consensus in Slovenia, but its leadership is conscious of its weakness within the Yugoslav context. Slovenes account for only 8 percent of the total population and, perhaps more important, Slovenia as a whole has fewer members in the party than Belgrade. In fact, the party has been losing members steadily. The Slovene leaders as well as the opposition are particularly concerned about the army leadership's continued hostility and suspicion toward them, arising not only out of Slovenia's pluralistic experiments, but also from the fact that Slovenia has taken a leading part in debates about the armed forces' expenditures and demands that they be cut like the rest of state-sector spending. The Slovene demand for a civilian minister of defense has greatly upset the army. One of the constitutional amendments adopted by Slovenia in September 1989 gives the Slovene parliament the sole right to decide whether a state of emergency, proclaimed by the collective Presidency in Belgrade, should also cover Slovenia.

In Serbia, the build-up of the national consensus has been on a different basis. The Kosovo issue has, under Milosevic's leadership, strengthened the party, relegitimating it in the eyes of the population. As a result Serbian human-rights groups have been pushed into the background, not least because the national "Serbia" part of the opposition platform has been appropriated by Milosevic, on one side, and by the Kosovo committee on the other. The fact that Milosevic has gained back Kosovo (and Vojvodina, although this is less important and has never been much of a public issue) has given the Serbian party a new lease of life and legitimacy. Milosevic's assurance, at the Serbian party's Central Committee meeting in April 1989, that the Serbs would not sit on their laurels but would go on to make Yugoslavia as a whole and the party in it stronger also has proved popular among the Serbs: it means that the unity of all Serbs will be assured. From a position of strength that he now enjoys, Milosevic looks set to try to gain control of the whole of the Yugoslav party, either at the next extraordinary party congress due to be held early in 1990 or afterwards.

At the congress, the Milosevic forces will not be able to dictate the agenda entirely; the Central Committee of the federal party will do so, rather than the party organization in the now Milosevic-controlled Vojvodina, which initiated the process for the holding of the congress. But the position has improved from Milosevic's point of view since the changes in the provinces and in Montenegro. Serbia (with the provinces) will have 629 of the 1,668 delegates at the congress. Because most of Montenegro's 123 and Macedonia's 166 can be expected to follow the Milosevic line, he will not even need the 86 votes of the party organization in the army. There, Milosevic's advocacy of a strong, united Yugoslavia must be assumed to enjoy considerable support. But the army's "unitarism" is not necessarily synonymous with Great Serbian nationalism, even though an estimated 70 percent of the army's officers and noncommissioned officers are Serbs. It is reasonable to assume that senior commanders are well aware of problems that a more strongly Serbian-flavored army, let alone Yugoslavia, would create for them, especially when the ever higher proportion of Albanian and Moslem recruits is taken into account. In the autumn of 1989, following the adoption of the Slovene constitutional amendments, the army leadership rebuffed the Milosevic camp's attempts to mobilize the army politically against the Slovenes.

CONCLUSION

Among scenarios suggested for Yugoslavia, the one that is frequently mentioned is the Chinese—of "one state with two systems"—a rough division into a "populist" Serbia, with its reannexed provinces of Vojvodina and Kosovo and with Macedonia and Montenegro within its sphere of influence, on one side, and, on the other, a "pluralist" Slovenia, a Croatia that is becoming increasingly so, and a Bosnia and Herzegovina leaning toward them. The idea has been widely discussed in Croatia and Slovenia, although it was first launched by Aleksandar Tijanic, a well-known Serbian columnist from Belgrade now writing for Slovene and Croat papers. It was he who first publicly mentioned an "internal Yalta" in Yugoslavia.[13] *Mladina* later followed this up with a map showing what it called "the United States of Western Yugoslavia," consisting of Slovenia, Croatia, and Bosnia and Herzegovina under the caption: "Would you like to live in such a state?" Although the paper's own answer, tucked away on an inside page, was no, the map's publication caused an uproar in Belgrade.

How much reality is there in this division? In practical terms, a good deal. Evidence for it comes from many sources: the widespread Slovene goods boycott in Serbia; the bitter media war between Belgrade on one side and Zagreb and Ljubljana on the other, which reflects the deep rift within the party leadership; the decision of the Serbian writers' association to break off relations with the Slovene association in the wake of the famous "solidarity meeting" in Ljubljana on February 27, attended by both opposition and party figures, at which support was expressed for the striking Kosovo Albanian miners; the withdrawal of an invitation to Janez Stanovnik, Slovenia's president and a former UN official, to speak in Titograd after the uproar in Serbia over his criticisms of Milosevic while on a visit to the United States in November 1988; and many others.

The intriguing question is whether the existence of the two "models" could eventually be formalized, following the example of the Austro-Hungarian *Ausgleich* (compromise) of 1867 and the subsequent *Nagodba* (compromise) between Hungary and Croatia in 1868. In present-day Yugoslavia, such a compromise would imply a deal, first between Belgrade on one side and Zagreb and Ljubljana on the other (with Sarajevo included in this group), to be followed by another deal among Belgrade, Pristina, and Novi Sad as well as among Belgrade and Skopje and Titograd. It has even been suggested in Yugoslavia that such a deal could simplify the work of a reforming federal government in Belgrade and make the solution of broader conflicts easier.[14]

Attractive though the idea may sound in some respects at least, it is not a realistic proposition for the near future. For a political carve-up to be successful, both sides must see it as advantageous, or, at the very least, as a lesser evil. Austria saw the *Ausgleich* in that light after its defeat by Prussia in 1866. It (or rather the Habsburgs) saved the empire by agreeing to the idea of a dual monarchy. The Hungarians got their Greater Hungary—under the hated Habsburgs, true, but what mattered was the backing of the whole empire for the Magyars in their dealings with the non-Magyars in their sphere.

It is easy to see what such a deal could offer to Slovenia and Croatia, perhaps even Bosnia—in the economic sense, but also politically: economically, the greater freedom to pursue the introduction of a market economy and to establish closer relations with neighbors and other partners in Western Europe and the West as a whole; politically, a guarantee of autonomy and of the freedom to pursue national consensus policies within a pluralistic context.

It is less easy to see what such a dualist arrangement would offer Serbia and current allies, Macedonia and Montenegro. Economically, it would mean the prospect of tough bargaining over the terms of economic life together. In such negotiations, the eastern side (Serbia, with Macedonia and Montenegro) would have certain cards—its raw materials and its continuing role as a market for Slovene and Croat goods—but its current economic collapse would mean that it would be arguing from a position of extreme weakness. Politically, of course, the eastern republics' strongest card would be its ability to veto the western republics' economic and political reforms. So a trade-off should, in principle, be possible, but would be less good than an outright victory. In any case, it would be hard to visualize it under the leadership of Milosevic.

The very nature of populist movements makes it difficult for them to compromise, to make binding deals limiting their freedom to strike at new enemies, to win new victories. Milosevic is no exception. Besides, even if he himself and his colleagues were tempted to consolidate their victories for a while, the current situation in Serbia would not allow it. The republic has been spared the worst unrest because the heady victories of Milosevic in Novi Sad and Titograd as well as the continuing drama in Kosovo itself have distracted the attention of the population from serious economic problems—from the money-losing giant steel complex in Smederevo to the heavy unemployment, especially among the young. In Belgrade, Milosevic managed to calm the striking Belgrade workers last autumn, when they invaded the Federal Assembly of Yugoslavia by promising them that their just claims would be met. What helped even more was the payment of higher-than-average wage increases in Serbia. But any formalization of the current political situation that would have the effect of forcing Milosevic and the Serbian party to look inward could be dangerous for him. It would therefore be logical for him and his colleagues to extend the fight to embrace the whole of Yugoslavia. That he is thinking along these lines was confirmed by his statement at the Serbian Central Committee meeting in April that Serbia "would not sit on its laurels but that, stronger now, it would continue to fight for a stronger Yugoslavia."

But could the western republics simply split off rather than submit to the masterful Milosevic? In principle they could. Under the Yugoslav constitution, republics have a right to secede, a right emphasized by the Slovenes in their amended republican constitution of September 1989. The existence of such a right was used as an argument against granting the status of a republic to Kosovo in 1981 on the grounds that, once a republic of the Yugoslav federation, Kosovo could use its right to secede to join Albania. Now it is once again being argued among Yugoslav (mainly Serbian) theorists—with an obvious sense of relevance to the present situation—that secession is not a current right and that, on the contrary, each nation of Yugoslavia "consumed" it upon entering the federation in 1944–5.

But whatever the conditional theory, the secession of one or more republics is difficult to envisage in practice. This is not because, as has often been argued in the past, Slovenia and Croatia, either together or singly, could not survive on their own. On the contrary, there is every likelihood that they could, although the going would be very hard at first and much would depend on the external situation. The real reason why such an exercise is difficult to imagine is that various forces would combine to prevent it or, if it did take place, would ensure that the would-be defectors were brought back into the Yugoslav fold.

It is true, to use a relatively close parallel, that Austria-Hungary split into its "successor states" relatively easily. But that was at the end of a long war in which the central authority had lost its main enforcement arm—the imperial and royal army. There was nothing left to compel the Croats, the Czechs, the Hungarians, the Poles, and the others to stay together within the same state. This is not so in Yugoslavia. President Tito is no longer there, but the Yugoslav army is. It would do its utmost to stop a secession that would also undermine its own role. It could do so relatively easily, because no republic nowadays has at its disposal significant territorial military forces of its own.

This is even more true since the reorganization of the Yugoslav army command system, announced in 1988 and in force since January 1, 1989, under which the army headquarters are no longer in republican centers but in Belgrade, Split, Skopje, and Zagreb. It has been argued in Yugoslavia that the reorganization makes sense in purely military operations terms, but there is little doubt that it also makes the army less vulnerable to local pressures. This is why the reorganization was opposed in Slovenia. If no political leader ordered the army to act in an emergency to "keep Yugoslavia together," which it would obviously prefer, its own leaders would no doubt act to find such a politician or, at the very worst, take power themselves temporarily to carry out such an operation.

But if the secession scenario is not very likely, what of the possibility that is also much discussed in Yugoslavia because it would in many ways represent the worst possible outcome: fragmentation of the country into a number of armed cantons, a sort of Balkan Lebanon, in conflict with each other? The degree of tension among Yugoslavia's nationalities is so high at the moment, and it is aggravated by the economic crisis, that such a conflict cannot be ruled out, especially in and around Kosovo. But there are, happily, deterrents.

One is the country's still relatively fresh memory of the dreadful civil war in the 1941–5 period—perhaps no longer as much of a deterrent against communal violence as it was in the first decades after 1945, but still operating. The other reason why it may not happen is the general realization that no forces opposing the central authority of the state backed by the army and the security forces would be strong enough to carry on their activity for any length of time without help from outside, such as the warring factions in Lebanon are getting. No state in the current climate of East-West relations is likely to want to commit itself to an active role in the hornet's nest that is Yugoslavia. Albania is no Syria, as has been shown by its extremely circumspect behavior—often under great provocation, in view of what is happening to the Albanians in Yugoslavia. Nor is Bulgaria an Iran; even if somebody in Bulgaria wanted to stir things up in Yugoslavia, it is unlikely that the Soviet Union would be prepared to sanction this now. A campaign by Hungary to liberate its countrymen in Vojvodina from Milosevic is equally a nonstarter, especially when one remembers the far worse provocation the Hungarians have tolerated in Transylvania.

Unlike the situation that faced the pre-1941 Yugoslavia, when it had to cope with three revisionist states on its borders—Italy, Hungary, and Bulgaria—all having designs on its territory and actively supporting groups opposed to the regime, no Western state is now giving overt or covert support to forces trying to break up Yugoslavia. These days, Western governments would not dream of tolerating, let alone actively supporting, any anti-Yugoslav activity that could, however remotely, be construed as terrorism. And so, occasional references in Yugoslavia to a "special war" being waged against the country from the West is wide of the mark, indeed quite absurd.

Given all this and the 1975 Helsinki Final Act, which has fixed the present frontiers in Europe for good, there is little to challenge the Yugoslav state from the outside, and so it is likely to survive. Ironically, the same cannot be said of the Yugoslav Communist Party, the force that has always prided itself on being the glue that is keeping the country together. It is quite conceivable that it could split—perhaps after the extraordinary party congress called for early 1989. The Slovene party might walk out if the Milosevic camp tries to put the clock back by, as the Slovenes see it, reimposing centralization on the whole Yugoslav party. That action, however, could accelerate the very situation that the western republics fear most: the de facto dismantling of the federal system, not only in the state but also in the party. Such a change would have to be preceded by a wholesale change of party cadres in Croatia and Slovenia to bring into leading positions new, inexperienced men and women more open to the pressure from the center.

Significantly, one of the slogans of the Milosevic camp is precisely such a change, called, in party jargon, the "anti-bureaucratic revolution." The strength of the Milosevic challenge is that any call for a purge of the party *nomenklatura* (ruling group) that has been running Yugoslavia so long could be attractive to a lot of ordinary people, regardless of their national allegiance. Factors playing a part here would undoubtedly include Milosevic's personal honesty; his modest life-style; and the fact that, unlike so many in the Yugoslav party, he "has no butter on his head," to use a colorful Yugoslav expression.

His opponents' trouble is that, in defending themselves from his challenge, they would be handicapped by having to justify some parts of the old system—notably its federal character—while disowning many others. In Ljubljana such a defense would be relatively easy: few scandals are waiting to be uncovered, and few local Serbs support Milosevic. Even trainloads of Kosovo "solidarity" protesters imported there could not do a lot. The "Serbian factor" in Croatia could play an important part in weakening the Croatian leadership's ability to withstand Milosevic. In Bosnia this vulnerability is even greater, although mistrust of the Serbs among the Moslems has revived and would strengthen opposition to Milosevic.

It is difficult to say what Milosevic would do if he were to win supreme power in Yugoslavia. Could he turn out to be a reformer and modernizer? His supporters argue that he is one but cannot show his true liberal reforming force too soon for fear of upsetting his party conservatives. Unfortunately, little or nothing so far suggests that he is crypto-marketeer and pluralist. On the contrary, much points to the possibility that he would use his supreme power to pursue his own agenda rather than that of the IMF or any Western body—for example, more redistribution from Yugoslavia's developed north to the poor south. On his home ground, his economic credentials are viewed with skepticism by, among others, the respected *Ekonomska politika* in Belgrade, Yugoslavia's most consistent advocate of the free market over the years, which owes its freedom to publish material critical of Milosevic to the fact that it is part of the Borba publishing house—in other words, a federal rather than a Serbian publication. (No criticisms of the Serbian leader appear in his own domestic press.)

In previous times there would have been little doubt that the West would have wanted to support a strong leader "trying to keep the country together." Tito was supported on that basis, and this support paid off. Not necessarily in every respect, but at the very least it helped to deny Yugoslavia, a strategically important country, to the Soviet Union at a critical time during the cold war. Now there is more room for maneuver, for holding back, and for having second and even third thoughts about who exactly is doing what in Yugoslavia. Just as it would be wrong, I believe, to adopt any plan for a framework deal with the Soviet Union over Eastern Europe, so it would be wrong for the West to limit the Yugoslav peoples' choices now as they begin to exercise their preferences in a serious way by plumping for a wayward, populist politician whose authoritarian style raises serious doubts about his ability to rule a complex country like Yugoslavia in any way except by force.

As it happens, Western policy can afford to be a bit more laidback about Yugoslavia than it used to be in the extremely competitive atmosphere of the cold war. What this might mean in practice would be a policy of keeping an open mind, listening to all ideas, ruling out none, and, above all, applying to Yugoslavia the same criteria being applied to the rest of Eastern Europe: favors and help where free-marketry and liberalism advance; a cool detachment where there is no such advance; and active disapproval coupled with appropriate sanctions where human-rights offenses are being committed, either against individual citizens or against national groups, as in Kosovo against its Albanian majority, for example. This appears to have been understood both by the European Parliament and by the United States Congress: both have taken up the issue of the current repression in Kosovo very seriously. It is just possible that letting the peoples of Yugoslavia work things out among themselves within very clear rules such as these might be the right policy for the West to pursue. But there should be no illusions that solutions will be, or indeed can be, easy: as the foregoing analysis may have shown, Yugoslavia is a flawed country that many of its own citizens would not reinvent if they had a chance. It may one day dissolve, as the union between Sweden and Norway did in 1905. So, rather than talk of ideal solutions, it is more sensible to talk of limiting damage and of easing conflicts and tensions inevitable in a country of this kind.

NOTES

1. See Paul S. Shoup, *Communism and the Yugoslav National Question*, (New York: Columbia University Press, 1968), 119. For a summary of the main features of

political development during the Tito era and immediately afterward, see the essay by Christopher Cviic "The Nature of Government and Politics in Yugoslavia," in George Schöpflin, ed., *The Soviet Union and Eastern Europe*, 2d ed. (London: Muller, Blond & White, 1986). For an economic treatment in the context of the self-management system, see Harold Lydall, *Yugoslav Socialism: Theory and Practice* (Oxford: Clarendon Press, 1984), and the same author's *Yugoslavia in Crisis* (Oxford: Clarendon Press, 1989). For a more political treatment, see Dennison Rusinow, *The Yugoslav Experiment, 1948–1974* (London: C. Hurst & Company for the Royal Institute of International Affairs, 1977).

In Yugoslavia, one of the best general summaries is to be found in Dusan Bilandzic's *Historija Socijalisticke Federativne Republike Jugoslavije* (Zagreb: Skolska knjiga, 1978), and the same author's update, *Jugoslavija poslije Tita* (Zagreb: Globus, 1986). The most serious economic treatment is in Marijan Korosic, *Jugoslavenska kriza* (Zagreb: Naprijed, 1988), and in Aleksander Bajt, *Alternativna ekonomska politika* (Zagreb: Globus, 1986).

For a helpful overview of the current controversy over federalism, see Dennison Rusinow, ed., *Yugoslavia: A Fractured Federalism* (Washington, D.C.,: The Wilson Center Press, 1988).

2. The Belgrade mass-circulation paper *Vecernje novosti* published, on September 24–5, 1986, a long report on the draft memorandum, which sparked many other reports and commentaries. The 74–page document was not published but continued to circulate privately. It was eventually published in the Zagreb monthly *Nase teme*, Nos. 1–2/1989. For understanding the Serbian view of Yugoslavia, a book by the Serbian novelist Danko Popovic, *Knjiga o Milutinu* (Belgrade: Knjizevne novine, 1985), is essential. When I obtained it in the summer of 1986, it had already run into thirteen editions.

   Another book that perceptively analyzes the Serbs' psychology in Yugoslavia is Milovan Danojlic's *Dragi moj Petrovicu* (Zagreb: Znanje, 1987).

   For a rare (among any of the nations of Yugoslavia) self-critical analysis, see the article by Desimir Tosic, "Gresi i greske u srpskom politickom drustvu," in *Nasa rec* (London), April 1989. For a scholarly and remarkably objective treatment of the extremely controversial subject of the number of victims in World War II see Bogoljub Kocovic, *Zrtve drugog svetskog rata u Jugoslavije* (London: Nasa rec Publications, 1985). Also, Vladimir Zerjavic, *Gubici stanovnistva Jugoslavije u drugom svjetskom ratu* (Zagreb: Jugoslavensko viktimolosko drustvo, 1989), is close to Kocovic's findings.

3. These figures and those on the same subject quoted elsewhere in this paper are, unless stated otherwise, taken from *Statisticki godisnjak Jugoslavije 1988* (Beograde: Savezni zavod za statistiku, 1988).

4. For a selection of contemporary Slovene views on the nationality question, see *Nova Revija* (Ljubljana), No 57/1987 and Nos. 67–8/1987. Also, Ciril Zlobec, *Slovenska samobitnost in pisatelj* (Trst: Zaloznistvo Trzaskega Tiska, 1986); Matjaz Kmecl, *Slovenska postna premisljevanja* (Ljubljana: Cankarjeva zalozba, 1987); Ciril Zebot, *Neminljiva Slovenija* (Celovec: Druzba sv. Mohorja, 1988).

5. This view was documented in Rudolf Bicanic, *Ekonomska podloga hrvatskog pitanja* (Zagreb: Croatian Peasant Party, 1938).

6. These figures, for 1987, were given to the author by the party information departments in Ljubljana, Zagreb, and Belgrade in April 1989.

7. For a brief overview, see my "Yugoslavia's Moslem Problem," in *The World Today* (London), March 1980. Also Irna Hendrichs, "Die Muslime in Jugoslawien" in *Europäische Rundschau*, I/1989. For a broader treatment of Islam in Yugoslavia, see the same author's *Der Islam in Jugoslawien* (Eberhausen: Stiftung Eberhausen, 1988).

8. See Stephen E. Palmer, Jr., and Robert R. King, *Yugoslav Communism and the Macedonian Question* (Hamden, Conn: Archon Books, 1971), for a comprehensive treatment that takes in both the pre–1941 situation and the subsequent period.

Also, the chapter on the Macedonian question in Shoup, *Communism and the Yugoslav National Question.*

9. See the chapter on Montenegrin "Greens" in Ivo Banac, *The National Question in Yugoslavia. Origins, History and Politics* (Ithaca and London: Cornell University Press, 1984), 270–91. Banac's study is the most authoritative treatment to date of the national question in pre–1941 Yugoslavia. It was also published in Zagreb by Globus in 1988 under the title *Nacionalno pitanje u Jugoslaviji. Porijeklo, povijest, politika.*

10. Branko Horvat, a noted Yugoslav economist, published a study of the Kosovo problem under the title *Kosovsko pitanje* (Zagreb: Globus, 1988). The book provoked a fierce controversy. Many of the Serbian views of the book were collected in a special edition of *Duga*, a Belgrade magazine, and published in July 1988. For both the Albanian and the Serbian views, see the booklet by Stevan K. Pavlowitch and Elez Biberaj, *"The Albanian Problem in Yugoslavia: Two Views"* with an introduction by Hugh SetonWatson published by the Institute for the Study of Conflict in London, Nos. 137–8, 1982. See also for an up-to-date treatment, Jens Reuter, "Das Albanerproblem in Jugoslawien" in *Europäische Rundschau* (Wien), No. 1/1989.

11. For figures and other details about the Germans in Yugoslavia, see Johann Wuescht, *Jugoslawien und das Dritte Reich* (Stuttgart: Seewald Verlag, 1969), 256.

12. An interesting account of the work of the Kosovo Serbs' committee is to be found in Darko Hudelist, "Skica za portret Miroslava Solevica," *Start* (Zagreb), March 18, 1989. This issue of *Start* was temporarily banned because of the article about Solevic on the ground that it might cause public disquiet. Hudelist's book about Solevic was published in Zagreb by Centar za informacije i publicitet in May 1988.

13. *Nedjeljna Dalmacija,* January 29, 1989.

14. Slaven Letica, "Vodje, mase i modeli," *Danas* (Zagreb), March 3, 1989. Also by the same author, "Proizvodnja neprijatelja," *Danas,* April 4, 1989.

II

SECURITY PROBLEMS OF THE COUNTRIES OF SOUTHEASTERN EUROPE

6

THE WARSAW TREATY ORGANIZATION AND SOUTHEAST EUROPEAN POLITICAL-MILITARY SECURITY

Daniel N. Nelson

Observers of Southeastern Europe and its Balkan core understand well that principal conflicts of the region do not lie on the plane denoted by contemporary East-West alliances. Rivalries, disputes, and conflicts that remain embedded in Southeastern Europe predate by decades or centuries the two international treaty organizations, North Atlantic Treaty Organization (NATO) (1949) and the Warsaw Treaty Organization, also known as the Warsaw Pact (1955). The well-known enmity between Greece and Turkey, nominal allies within the context of NATO, is rooted in ancient territorial arguments, the Cyprus stalemate, and other issues. Within the Warsaw Pact, the resurgence of a Hungarian-Romanian dispute over Romanian treatment of ethnic Hungarians in Transylvania has overcome restraint urged by the USSR. Even those disputes between members of the opposing alliances have little or nothing to do with the East-West alliance confrontation. Bulgarian treatment of Turkish nationals has brought Ankara's protests, but the dispute is not one invoking NATO and the Warsaw Pact but rather a bilateral issue with roots in the Ottoman control of Bulgaria in past centuries.

The Warsaw Pact's inception, in May 1955, was a political act by the Soviet Union—a reaction to West German rearmament and integration into NATO and a rationale for the maintenance of troops in Hungary and Romania after the Austrian State Treaty was signed (also in May 1955). Beyond these immediate objectives, the Soviets no doubt saw the Warsaw Pact as a broader symbol of their determination to retain Eastern Europe in their grasp.[1] Yet, in 1955, no senior Soviet officer would have thought of East European armies as adjuncts to Soviet offensive capabilities against NATO; they were poorly equipped and lacked any training with Soviet forces, and Warsaw Pact structures were largely inactive until the early 1960s.[2] The inauguration of joint exercises in 1961 began to change the character of the Warsaw Pact, but did not result in a rapid transformation of East European armies into instruments for offensive operations against NATO.

Simply put, the Soviet intention has always been to use the Warsaw Pact to impose a superpower perspective on Eastern Europe's security. Ideally, Moscow sought a tightly knit, compliant, impermeable alliance characterized by high levels of intraalliance foreign-policy agreement; high responsiveness to Soviet signals and examples; and resistance to Western, Chinese, or other overtures. Had the USSR been entirely successful in that goal, the three original southeast European Warsaw Pact members—Bulgaria, Romania, and (until 1968) Albania—would have adopted security policies highly consistent with one another and with Moscow, and nationalistic issues would have faded in importance.

But the Soviets failed. East European members of the Warsaw Pact, particularly those of Southeastern Europe, have not understood their security in ways consistent with the USSR or each other. They have not responded uniformly to Soviet signals or examples, and all have flirted with powers that, at various times, Moscow has seen as threatening.

Important questions arise from such general observations. If the Soviets have not succeeded in imbuing East European Communist Party regimes or peoples with a collective view (that is, a Soviet view) of security, how is that failure evident in multilateral or bilateral relations and the alliance behavior of non-Soviet Warsaw Pact (NSWP) members in Southeastern Europe—that is, Romania and Bulgaria? Conversely, in what sense has the Warsaw Pact been instrumental in enforcing behavior among those Soviet allies that is consistent with collective security, notwithstanding perceptions of indigenous elites or masses?

For the two Balkan states outside the Warsaw Pact but with governing Communist parties, Yugoslavia and Albania, issues also arise about the effects of the Warsaw Pact. For Yugoslavia, the political-military implications of a hostile international treaty organization were ominous. For the first decade of the Warsaw Pact, the military contribution of NSWP states in Southeastern Europe to any threat Moscow wished to mount against Tito was small, and the pact therefore changed little from the standpoint of Yugoslav military planning. Yet when NSWP forces participated in the invasion of Czechoslovakia of August 1968, the military implications of the Warsaw Pact were heightened. For Albania, despite the ideological break of 1961, Tirana did not withdraw from the Warsaw Pact until 1968, and Hoxha's involvement with China reflected the political and military dangers implicit in a departure from the collective fold of the Warsaw Pact.

In the comments that follow, the focus is on the Communist states of Southeastern Europe: Romania, Bulgaria, Yugoslavia, and Albania. Both Greece and Turkey will be noted in terms of their relations with one or more of the Communist states in the region. The discussion is divided into two parts: first, the effects of the Warsaw Pact on the domestic politics and international policies of states in the region and, second, the military doctrine of, and principal security issues confronting, each country.

EFFECTS OF THE WARSAW PACT ON BALKAN DOMESTIC POLITICS AND FOREIGN POLICIES

Romania

Nicolae Ceausescu, in the first decade of his quarter-century in power, used the Warsaw Pact and the USSR artfully as threats against which to rally domestic support. These threats were, of course, not entirely figments of Ceausescu's political imagination. Indeed, in late 1968 and again in the early 1970s, there was cause for Romanian concern that a Soviet-led Warsaw Pact intervention would be mounted.[3]

The high-water mark of Ceausescu's domestic mass legitimacy came at an August 1968 rally in Bucharest, when he called for the defense of the homeland against those who posed an imminent threat. Romania's condemnation of the invasion of Czechoslovakia, close relations with Mao's China, and other behavior had incurred Brezhnev's wrath, and there were signs of preparations for an invasion.[4] Anti-Russian sentiment, historically strong in the old Romanian provinces of Wallachia and Moldavia, was heightened by Soviet occupation after World War II and the stationing of the Red Army in Romania until 1958. To these long-standing suspicions of Russian intentions was added, with vivid clarity because of the Czechoslovak invasion, antipathy toward the Warsaw Pact's role as an enforcer of Soviet hegemony and the role that might be played by two NSWP neighbors, Hungary and Bulgaria, in aiding the USSR in "multilateral" action against Romania.

The short-term effect of military action to enforce the Brezhnev Doctrine—the notion of limited sovereignty within the European "socialist commonwealth"—was to bolster the popular appeal of the regime of a then-young Balkan ruler. Ceausescu was able to accelerate the replacement of party elites who, as elements of a Gheorghiu-Dej cohort, had dubious loyalty to Ceausescu.[5] He was also able, for a few years at least, to pose as the benefactor of ethnic tolerance and cooperation, government reform, and intellectual and artistic liberalization.

In fact, of course, Ceausescu in 1968 was merely tapping a Romanian-Russian enmity that had, only two-and-a-half decades earlier, led to willing Romanian participation in the German invasion of the USSR.[6] Beginning in 1971, the legitimacy Ceausescu had been able to garner in 1968 began to dissipate. Ceausescu's true intentions became evident as an ideological crackdown was imposed in 1971 and intellectual freedom was rolled back over the next few years. And, as has been told elsewhere, the excesses of a cult of personality—first for Nicolae Ceausescu, and later for his wife, Elena, and extended family—began to consume the Romanian political landscape.[7]

Ceausescu has never given up his efforts to use the Warsaw Pact as a cause célèbre. A decade after the Warsaw Pact invasion of Czechoslovakia, Ceausescu abruptly returned from meetings of Communist Party leaders from all seven pact members in the Soviet Union to announce that Romania would not accede to Soviet insistence that all Warsaw Pact members raise military spending levels and pursue similar policies in out-of-area issues (such as the Middle East). In this instance, Ceausescu's lieutenants organized mass rallies in Bucharest to replicate in size, if not spirit, the 1968 event.[8]

By the late 1980s, however, Ceausescu's appeals, although still audible, have been overtaken by events. The advent of Mikhail Gorbachev has placed Ceausescu in the awkward position of trying to defend an "independent course" vis-à-vis Moscow that rejects reform, moderation, and pragmatism, while causing untold suffering for the Romanian population.

Ironically, even before Gorbachev, the path of a sometimes noncompliant member of the Warsaw Pact did not have uniformly positive political consequences. The domestic requirements of playing a disjunctive role in the Warsaw Pact included devoting a substantial social and economic effort to the foolhardy goal of near-autarky in the economy. Through his maintenance of very high levels of investment

(30 to 35 percent of national income) over long periods of time, Ceausescu's notion of *dezvoltare multilateral* never connoted much in the way of higher living standards for Romanians.[9] Instead, less and less efficient industry was created in the Stalinist mode of extensive growth, yielding huge enterprises that produced large quantities of unmarketable materials. When these policies yielded the inevitable economic disaster, Ceausescu could not turn to the Soviets or to the West for assistance, and so he imposed a policy of austerity that continues until today. It is small wonder that Ceausescu's regime has suffered a massive turnaround in levels of public support and now rules what may be the most disaffected population in Communist Europe.[10]

At the same time, a military doctrine that reduced the role of the professional army in national defense led to strained civil-military relations. This strain has become a political issue because of the interdependence of the army and party. Neither can keep its authority without the aid of the other, and each distrusts the other's intentions.

Signs of this disenchantment are imprecise, but suggestive nonetheless. There was, for example, the case of General Ion Serb who was arrested, in early 1972, for passing details of China's ties with Romania to the USSR's military attaché in Bucharest. Because this arrest was followed by a number of high-ranking personnel changes in the army high command and in the Ministry of Internal Affairs, some analysts have speculated about ties to a coup attempt.[11] Although other analysts have doubted these tenuous linkages,[12] Ceausescu certainly was not confident about his relationship with the army's officer corps during the early 1970s.

A decade later, Ceausescu could no longer be assured of the military's support. Because of Romania's desperate economic straits in 1982, the Romanian leader announced at a December 1982 party conference that military expenditures would be frozen at the 1982 level until 1985.[13] Although the announcement was couched in rhetoric about arms reductions, the officer corps was certainly not deceived. Once again, rumors of a military coup reached the West in early 1983—rumors that were made more credible by their coincidence with Ceausescu's attempt to squeeze the military budget further and by the evident failure of that attempt. In both those years, expenditure and manpower increases were apparent.[14]

By the end of 1985, Ceausescu was forced to admit that the army was plagued with dissatisfaction. His reassignment of Colonel General Constantin Olteanu from defense minister to head of the Bucharest party organization in early 1986 was a careful move, consistent with his long-standing policy to rotate cadres among posts. While avoiding any clear demotion of Olteanu (who has since also lost that position), Ceausescu sought to constrain the political voice of the army. For lower-ranking officers other tools were used in the effort to limit political challenges—intensive ideological training and the overlapping sources of authority available to Ceausescu through the Romanian Communist Party, the state, and the Defense Council (of which he is the chairman).

Out of necessity, Ceausescu has tried to placate the Romanian army as he has encountered more and more mass hostility. This effort to repair fences with the military is implied by the inverse trends of public support and defense expenditures in Romania.[15] Isolated from Soviet support, particularly in the Gorbachev period, and politically distant from the West because of a sordid human-rights record and undependable economic ventures, Ceausescu falls back on the military and secret police as his defense from the people he rules.

The elevation of Mikhail Gorbachev to the post of general secretary of the Communist Party of the Soviet Union (CPSU) propelled Ceausescu much further away from the Soviets than ever before.[16] Ceausescu has repeatedly denied that socialism and economic decentralization or political pluralism are compatible. Indeed, only hours before the former Soviet president Andrei Gromyko arrived in Bucharest in May 1988, Ceausescu went so far as to warn against "rightist deviation" as the "principal danger" to socialism.[17] From the perspective of other Warsaw Pact members, Romania's exacerbation of tension with Hungary over ethnic Hungarians in Transylvania has been perhaps the most dangerous aspect of Ceausescu's relations within the pact. The exodus of ethnic Hungarians from Romania during 1988 alone exceeded 12,000. The presence of *refugees* escaping from one Warsaw Pact member into another has created "an explosive political problem" within the Soviet-led alliance, which may become worse if Ceausescu goes ahead with his plan to raze thousands of villages throughout the country (thereby doing grievous harm to minority languages and cultures that survive only in the countryside), with populations moved into new "agroindustrial centers."[18]

Whereas once criticism of the Soviet Union and the Warsaw Pact served to raise Ceausescu's stature, the utility of attacking the pact for this purpose has faded long ago. Now, continued emphasis on going it alone means staying aloof from processes of change and reform, not the assertion of national independence from the USSR. Pact members now view Ceausescu not merely as a deviant of nationalist bent, but as a palpable danger to the region's peace and stability. Political costs from Ceausescu's adamant rejection of socioeconomic moderation can no longer be avoided by referring to implicit Warsaw Pact threats and limitations on Romanian sovereignty. Not only has the Romanian public abandoned its *Conducatorul*; even the Romanian army has set its sights on a post-Ceausescu era.[19]

Bulgaria

For Todor Zhivkov's Bulgaria, membership in the Warsaw Pact appears to have been a politically comfortable, albeit socioeconomically burdensome, association. Zhivkov has led the Bulgarian Communist Party (BCP) for the entire three-and-a-half decades of Warsaw Pact history. Fealty to the USSR—demonstrated through thorough political, economic, and military integration via both the pact and the Council for Mutual Economic Assistance (CMEA)—has been the hallmark of Zhivkov's foreign and security policies.

Unlike Ceausescu, Zhivkov's regime has never sought to maintain, or even to discuss, a war-fighting capability distinct from Bulgaria's role in the Combined Armed Forces of the Warsaw Pact. The idea of a territorial defense as undertaken by Yugoslavia and Romania is an anathema to Sofia. The BCP leaders have consistently directed a higher proportion of the country's gross national product (GNP) to military spending than has any other NSWP state, and have maintained the highest military manpower levels as a proportion of population among all Warsaw Pact members except the USSR.[20]

The country's militarization within the Warsaw Pact has meant that, notwithstanding Bulgaria's rising living standards relative to the USSR (Bulgaria has Eastern Europe's most quickly rising net material product—NMP—per capita from 1965 through 1981), very little of Bulgaria's economic growth has been controlled by Bulgarians.[21]

Bulgaria depends on the USSR and other East European Warsaw Pact members for more than three-fourths of all imports and exports, 57 percent of which are to and from the Soviet Union. As the least energy self-sufficient of all NSWP states, Bulgaria imports 70 percent of its oil and natural gas from the USSR.[22] The net effect of this profound economic dependency is to limit drastically Bulgaria's freedom to make decisions that might damage Soviet security interests. Indeed, Bulgarian discussions of this matter acknowledge that "full coordination [and] intensified . . . economic and military-economic integration [with the] entire socialist community and, above all [with] the Soviet Union" are vital.[23] It is quite clear that Bulgaria's defense expenditures, and entire defense industry, are adjuncts of Soviet security interests in the guise of coalitional Warsaw Pact efforts.

Political effects of Warsaw Pact membership on the status of Zhivkov's regime are less clear. Zhivkov and his defense minister, Dobri Dzhurov, must continue to justify the heavy commitments to the Bulgarian armed forces on the basis of ties to the Soviet Union and to the defense of socialism. But there seems to be little in those justifications that can rationalize the level of effort, which falls in the highest decile of all nation-states regarding military force levels per 1,000 population, and between the 80th and 90th percentile for military expenditures as a proportion of GNP.[24]

It is difficult to specify *socioeconomic* costs of Bulgarian military effort on behalf of the Soviets and the Warsaw Pact. Yet it is important to note the weaknesses in critical elements of the Bulgarian economic infrastructure. In transport, for example, Bulgaria has far less rail capacity than either Romania or Hungary, and its civilian airline is merely symbolic.[25] Moreover, the failure to develop alternatives to the Soviet Union in foreign trade leaves Bulgaria extraordinarily isolated from the world economy, notwithstanding the country's relatively high level of industrialization.

Bulgarian subservience to the Soviet Union has also led to tensions within the military. Although the history of party-army relations in Bulgaria has received more detailed comments elsewhere,[26] we should recount here that the Red Army never took the Bulgarian Army's obeisance to Soviet dominance for granted. Even as the Bulgarian army changed sides in the closing months of World War II, Bulgarian-born political commissars who had served in the Red Army and Soviet "training officers" began infiltrating the army's ranks.[27] At the same time, Red Army divisions bracketed the Bulgarian units.[28] Once the war had ended, the Soviets used this control over the Bulgarian army to reshape it into a "Bulgarian People's Army" (BPA), with Georgi Damianov, a Bulgarian national who had lived in the USSR for twenty-three years and held the rank of general in the Red Army, as the minister of defense. Hundreds of other Bulgarian Communist exiles formed a large contingent within the BPA officer corps.

Soviet control over the BPA apparently was not strong enough to overcome resentment in the army toward Bulgaria's subservient status. A number of coup attempts have been reported in Bulgaria, recalling the involvement of the army in politics prior to World War II. In 1961 rumors of a plot against Zhivkov spread to the West, but the coup attempt could never be corroborated.[29]

More solid evidence exists of a planned coup attempt in 1965. Early in that year, apparently prompted by the ouster of Nikita Khrushchev in October 1964, the commander of the Sofia garrison, General Tsviatko Anev, along with Todorov-Gorunia (a Bulgarian Central Committee member) and several others, planned to seize key party and state offices, as well as major transportation and communication centers, and to topple the Zhivkov regime. Although further details are sketchy, we know that the conspirators were discovered, arrested, and imprisoned before they had the opportunity to take any military action. Several years later, various BCP investigations indicated that the conspiracy had penetrated deeply into district party committees and into other military commands.[30]

We do not know precisely what led to the coup attempt, but there are grounds for informed speculation. First, the 1961 plot was rumored to have involved a core of top BPA officers who had served together as anti-Nazi Partisans in World War II. The Partisans, unlike the Communist Bulgarians who served with the Red Army, had fought to oust the Germans before a Soviet invasion. After the war the Partisan officers no doubt retained their allegiance to the Bulgarian nation and people. Several of the 1965 conspirators had also been Partisans, and the timing of the plot following Khrushchev's removal in the Soviet Union suggests a desire for greater autonomy on the part of Bulgaria in its relationship with the USSR at a time that leadership difficulties in Moscow provided an opportunity for distancing Sofia from the Soviet Union. Finally, there were indications in 1960 that BPA commanders were worried about their uncertain political control of the army and concerned about failures to abide by "the Party line in the army."[31]

More than two decades later, the Bulgarian leadership remains nervous about the army's loyalty. Party leadership within the military is continually emphasized in the army's principal organ, *Narodna Armiya*, and commentaries on the same theme also appear often in the BCP daily, *Rabotnichesko Delo*. Ideological knowledge is tested frequently, and criticism of party leadership in the BPA for insufficient political training of troops is direct.[32]

To these ongoing concerns about the army must be added the issue of ethnic mistrust and national conflict, which escalated in the 1980s into open hostility and violence. Ethnic Turks and Bulgarian Moslems (Pomaks) together constituted as of early 1989, 12–15 percent of Bulgaria's population, depending on whose estimate is used. Their birthrate is substantially higher than the rate for the Bulgarian majority, and the gradual enlargement of these minorities would have been expected had the expulsion and large-scale emigration of April-

September, 1989, not taken place. During those few months, perhaps 300,000 Turks fled to Turkey, many expelled and others fearing reprisals after ethnic protests.

In 1983–85, ethnic violence flared in many towns and border *okrugs* (districts) where one part of the Turkish population is concentrated. The protests were directed against Zhivkov's policies to end Turkish-language publications and educational programs, and to require Bulgarian surnames of all Bulgarian citizens.[33] Turkish sources reported more than 1,000 deaths.[34] In 1989, the situation once again exploded, as Turkish protests led to police and army crackdowns, followed by mass expulsions. It is apparent, in this connection, that the Turkish population in Bulgaria would be a great liability to Bulgaria in time of war, especially if the BPA's role in a Warsaw Pact offensive scenario would be to engage the Turkish army in an attack to secure the Bosporus. More immediately, the ethnic unrest raises problems concerning the conscription of ethnic Turks into the BPA, and the possibility that the BPA will be permanently involved in ensuring domestic order in regions of the country inhabited by the Turkish minority.

Before 1985, Sofia's international involvement consisted almost entirely of economic, political, and military associations with other Warsaw Pact members *or* of economic and military aid to Soviet clients in the Third World. Indeed, as late as 1986 less than one-twentieth of all Bulgarian trade was with Turkey, Greece, Yugoslavia, Albania, and Romania.[35]

Held in check by Soviet interests and Warsaw Pact integration, Bulgaria has, in the 1970s through mid-1980s, been a reluctant and cautious participant in Balkan diplomatic interaction. In the January 1976 Balkan Conference, Sofia's involvement was tentative and suspicious. Zhivkov began to explore avenues of bridge building with Western Europe in the early 1980s, but a planned a visit to Bonn in 1984 was canceled in response to Soviet pressures.

The latitude for Bulgarian foreign policy widened somewhat after 1985. The severe strains on Bulgarian-Turkish relations brought on by the nationalities policies described earlier, which became even worse in spring and summer 1989, no doubt contributed to the Zhivkov regime's improving relations with Greece. In September 1986, Bulgaria signed a protocol of friendship with the Papandreou government. The protocol committed Greece and Bulgaria to help each other combat "agitation"—that is, ethnic unrest among Turks in Bulgaria or among Macedonian nationalists in both Bulgaria and Greece. Furthermore, the Bulgarian regime tolerated, and perhaps encouraged, environmental protests in Ruse against pollutants emitted from heavy industry in the Romanian city of Giurgiu, suggesting that Sofia was reassessing its relations with Romania. In February 1988, after some initial caution, Bulgaria participated in the Balkan foreign ministers' conference. At the meeting, Bulgarian positions evinced further movement away from strict isolation within the Warsaw Pact, without signaling any basic changes in Bulgarian foreign policy.[36]

There are, then, signs that Bulgaria's foreign policy has become somewhat more flexible in recent years, with interests germane to Bulgaria and neighboring states beginning to reassert themselves. As long as Zhivkov is alive, Bulgarian foreign policy will nevertheless be guided by support of Warsaw Pact integration and close collaboration with the Soviet Union.

Yugoslavia

When the Warsaw Pact was created by the Soviet Union in May 1955, it meant little for the military situation confronting Tito and Yugoslav communism. Although non-Soviet armies in the new pact were not imposing at that time, Tito well understood the evident willingness of Moscow to use tanks to crush uprisings (as in East Germany in 1953).

Politically, however, the good news of 1955—the Soviet agreement to withdraw from Austria and the overtures by Khrushchev for rapprochement with Tito—was diminished greatly by the advent of the Warsaw Pact. Belgrade was suddenly confronted by an eight-member international treaty organization with implications for the diplomatic and economic isolation of Yugoslavia, and a convenient rationale for Soviet troop presence on Yugoslav borders. The avowed hostility of Warsaw Pact members toward Titoism became more threatening when the pact began to improve its military preparedness after 1961.

Although the rupture of Soviet-Yugoslav relations has been recounted many times, we should recall that Tito's behavior from 1945 through 1947 was not, in rhetoric or in policy, anti-Soviet. Indeed, Stalin's inauguration of a new international—Cominform—in September 1947 had been suggested by Tito himself a couple years earlier. For Stalin, however, Tito's ideological conformity and rhetorical support of the USSR were insufficient. Stalin wanted, via Cominform, to stamp out any diversity in his newly acquired cordon sanitaire—a diversity personified by Tito. Brzezinski is certainly correct when he notes that Stalin was responsible for Titoism, by forcing the

Yugoslav leader, who was convinced until the last that some accommodation for national autonomy could be found for a loyal party and ally, to find an ideological basis for differences.[37] Stalin's 1948 expulsion of Yugoslavia from the Cominform, because Tito refused to submit to a "far greater degree of Soviet involvement," launched Yugoslavia into a confrontation with the USSR that outlasted Tito and several Soviet leaders.[38]

Although Nikita Khrushchev tried—first in the 1955 Belgrade Declaration and again after the Twenty-first CPSU Congress in 1961— to reestablish cordial ties with Tito, the political effects of the Soviet— Warsaw Pact threat were clear. Yugoslavia had three sources of cohesion: Tito himself, the Yugoslav army, and the threat from the USSR and Moscow's East European allies. The "threat" has not necessarily been that of a Soviet invasion but has always included "progressive internal disintegration being manipulated by skillful Soviet diplomacy, tactics and covert interference."[39] Of course, as we witnessed the socioeconomic and political deterioration of Yugoslavia in 1980s, such internal disintegration became more and more plausible.

Notwithstanding the waxing and waning of Belgrade-Moscow ties over the past forty years, Tito and subsequent League of Communists of Yugoslavia (LCY) leaders have regarded their relationship with the USSR as one fraught with many risks. As a consequence, Yugoslavia has been made an assiduous political and military effort to reinforce its security.

Politically and diplomatically Tito pressed for greater stability in the contiguous region while he carried his search for Yugoslav security worldwide. In the contiguous region, Tito and later LCY administrations sought to reduce potential conflicts with all neighbors. This regional political and diplomatic effort is not new. Yugoslav statesmen have always seen it to be in their interest to encourage regional ties to counter the designs of outside interests. In the interwar period, the Yugoslavs were at the forefront of endeavors to create a "Balkan Union," in part because of their quite genuine fears of war with Fascist Italy. At the four Balkan Conferences in the early 1930s, and in the Balkan Pact signed by Yugoslavia, Turkey, Greece, and Romania on February 9, 1934, the Yugoslavs were particularly effusive about the possibilities for a Balkan Union.[40]

Two decades later, in the mid-1950s, in the aftermath of their expulsion from Cominform, the Yugoslavs again sought ways to limit the reach of powerful states—this time, of course, Soviet hegemony. Tito was cognizant of the limited nature of American (and, in general, Western) assistance, but also saw the need to initiate political cooperation with other anti-Soviet states in the Balkans. At Yugoslavia's initiative, the Turkish, Greek, and Yugoslav foreign ministers met in Ankara in early 1953, and the Ankara Treaty was signed in February.[41] This treaty laid the basis for a subsequent accord, another "Balkan Pact" signed in August 1954, which pledged each of the three signatories to "come to the defense of each other in the event of an outside attack."[42]

The Balkan Pact began to disintegrate soon after it was signed. Understandably, Greece and Turkey's preoccupation with NATO commitments (and increasingly concern about Cyprus and other bilateral disputes) were fundamentally incompatible with Tito's foreign and domestic policies. The USSR represented a threat to all three, but not the same kind of threat. Tito still hoped for party-to-party discussions, and for reconciliation with a post-Stalin Soviet leadership.

Apart from these ideologically induced doubts about where a Balkan Pact might lead, Tito also had begun in the mid–1950s to seek a broader framework in which to anchor Yugoslav security. It was Tito's "peripatetic summitry"[43] that launched what later became known as the Nonaligned Movement. With Gamal Abdul Nasser and Jawaharal Nehru, Tito brought twenty-five "third-world" leaders to Belgrade in 1961 for the initial meeting of nonaligned states. This worldwide movement, until it was split with dissension in the 1970s, was of substantial benefit to Yugoslavia. Not only did the Nonaligned Movement enhance greatly Tito's and Yugoslavia's visibility, but the notion of nonalignment as distinct from neutrality brought substantial diplomatic attention and some degree of additional economic assistance. Tito, it is safe to presume, *did* see his worldwide endeavors on behalf of nonalignment as a contribution to his country's security vis-à-vis the USSR and the newly created Warsaw Pact.[44]

It can be argued, however, that the first Nonaligned Movement conference, held in Belgrade in 1961, represented the highpoint in Tito's effort to fashion a truly worldwide association of states opposed to military alliances. Particularly as many more newly independent, poor nation-states joined the movement, its focus began to shift from the issue that concerned Tito most—the dangers of military alliances led by superpowers—to the economic demands of the world's under-developed "South" versus the developed "North." In the 1970s, the involvement of a bloc of radical governments, led by Cuba, in the Nonaligned Movement pulled the organization further yet from issues that concerned Yugoslav security. It was evident at the Algiers meeting of the Nonaligned Movement in 1973 that what had begun, in part, as a Yugoslav counterweight to the superpower alliances around it (and to threats against Yugoslav security that could not be limited from within the Balkans) would not in the future serve that purpose.[45]

This diminishing relevance of nonalignment, per se, for Yugoslav security was also becoming clearer as Tito's death became increasingly expected and the implications of his passing for Yugoslav unity were brought into sharper focus. The Croatian crisis in 1971, indications of mounting ethnic tension in the south where Serbs confronted a population explosion of Albanians in Kosovo, and ominous signs that the economic boom of the 1960s was not going to continue, made Yugoslav domestic conditions seem far more vital than the distant issues of nonalignment. East-West "détente" of the early to mid-1970s also appeared to reduce the security need for a worldwide Yugoslav commitment. In his final years, Tito continued to seek a Nonaligned Movement true to its original purposes, and under his guidance Yugoslavia remained firmly committed to such a movement.[46] For the LCY and the army, however, it had become clear that the real challenges for Yugoslavia's future were within and nearby. In December 1979, moreover, it was demonstrated brutally in Afghanistan that nonalignment, in any case, was no guarantee against Soviet intervention and occupation.

There was, as well, the irredentist issue of Macedonia raised by Bulgaria, which had been omnipresent throughout the postwar period. Although this has been a less active issue than, for example, the Romanian-Hungarian diatribe concerning Transylvania, or Greek-Turkish confrontations, the Yugoslavs see the Bulgarian claims in terms of possible scenarios for a larger conflict with the Soviets.[47] The Macedonian issue has recurred recently in the Greek-Bulgarian treaty of September 1986. From Belgrade's perspective, clauses in the treaty that promise Greek-Bulgarian cooperation against externally sponsored "agitation or action that might imperil" Greek or Bulgarian stability are clearly directed against the Macedonian nationalism that is politically visible in Skopje.[48]

Yugoslav participation in the 1976 all-Balkan (except Albania) conference in Athens was a move toward refocusing Yugoslav diplomatic efforts on Southeastern Europe and the eastern Mediterranean, perhaps to use regional cooperation as a deterrent against Soviet designs whenever Tito died.[49] The Yugoslav role in the Conference for Security and Cooperation in Europe (CSCE) reflected a desire to maintain the Helsinki momentum for similar reasons—to strengthen relations with Western Europe and to reinforce European recognition of Yugoslavia's importance. Belgrade hosted the 1977–8 CSCE Review Conference and was active as well at the CSCE Review Conference in Madrid (1980–1) and the meeting in Stockholm in 1985–6, which resulted in significant expansion of confidence- and security-building measures first included in the Helsinki Accord.[50] Throughout 1986 and 1987 the Yugoslav foreign ministry devoted considerable effort to bring together all Balkan foreign ministers (including Albania's) in a session that reflected former prime minister Branko Mikulic's conviction that these efforts at regional political rapprochement and diplomatic contacts have priority.[51]

These new priorities for Yugoslav foreign policy, and the notion that the country's security against Soviet-Warsaw Pact intervention may best be obtained through links with Western Europe and diplomatic initiatives in the Balkans, were not the products of farsightedness among LCY politicians. Rather, "party officials, intellectuals and the press" had increasingly criticized Belgrade after Tito's death "for its persistent policy of supporting third-world interests at the expense of strengthening economic relations with the highly developed nations of Western Europe [and for] not improving relations with the country's Balkan neighbors."[52] Moreover, as the Yugoslav army observed mounting ethnic unrest and worker discontent, one can well imagine a defense minister (as did Branko Mamula) warning civilian LCY politicians of the immediate internal dangers to state security and the army's impatience with the party's capacity to address problems at home.[53]

The Soviet threat to Yugoslavia, and the possible implementation of intervention through the multilateral facade of the Warsaw Pact (with Hungarian and Bulgarian participation), *appears* far less today because of Mikhail Gorbachev. Gorbachev's visit to Yugoslavia in March 1988 was, like his visits elsewhere, impressive. From the standpoint of Yugoslav security, he took care to say all the right things— especially by repeating his views about the inviolable right of people to "shape their own destiny."[54]

The changes in the USSR, planned reductions of Soviet military presence in Eastern Europe, and an improved climate of superpower relations—coming at a time when Yugoslavia is confronted by clear and present dangers to its survival from extremely high inflation, violent clashes between Albanians and Serbs, rampant corruption and a leadership vacuum—have created an environment for Yugoslavs to worry far less about external threats. This has not meant any talk about altering military doctrine or security planning. Nevertheless, the international political context at the end of the 1980s suggests little that is ominous, because for most residents of Yugoslavia every-thing that appears ominous lies within their own country.

Albania

Albania, which joined the Warsaw Pact when it was founded in 1955, officially withdrew in 1968. During this brief association with the pact, the alliance provided little utility for Enver Hoxha, and the multi-lateral facade of the Pact added nothing to Soviet influence over Albania. The Pact's effects on Albania were, however, felt in less direct ways.

Albania was the only country in Eastern Europe where the Com-munist Party came to power without assistance from the Soviet army. Yet the Communist regime in Albania could not have succeeded without substantial assistance from the Yugoslav Communists, who sent advisers to the Albanian Communist Party during the war, and troops and economic assistance to the Albanians when the war ended. Tito planned, it appeared, to include Albania in a Balkan union under his control.[55] When Stalin expelled Yugoslavia from the Com-inform in 1948, it was an opportunity for Hoxha to escape from one patron into the arms of another.

Implicit in this new dependence on Moscow was a heightened Soviet profile in Albania. From Moscow's standpoint, Albania provided dip-lomatic and military leverage against Tito, and served as an important base from which to operate in the eastern Mediterranean. Soviet submarines began to use the port at Valona,[56] and large Soviet-sponsored industrial projects were launched in Albania. After Albania joined in the Warsaw Pact, the treaty provided an expost facto, multilateral justification for Soviet presence in Albania, which, of course, was directed against Tito as much as against NATO.

The Soviet-Albanian dispute, which broke out several years later, had at its core Hoxha's dislike of Khrushchev's "revisionism" and the Soviet's extreme displeasure at close Albanian-Chinese relations.[57] By October, 1961, Khrushchev was calling for the removal of the Alba-nian leadership. Hoxha responded by throwing out Soviet advisers and closing the submarine base at Valona.[58]

The Albanians nevertheless delayed their departure from the War-saw Pact until after the Soviet invasion of Czechoslovakia in 1968. Several reasons for this delay seem plausible: (1) The Albanians may have believed that continued nominal membership in the Warsaw Pact was needed as a balance against the Yugoslavs. (2) The Albanian leadership may have anticipated the demise of Khrushchev, and hoped for a return to Soviet neo-Stalinism. And (3), as James Brown speculates, Tirana may have felt safer vis-à-vis the Soviets inside rather than outside the Warsaw Pact, *until* the Soviet-led Warsaw Pact action to end the "Prague Spring" in August 1968.[59]

From 1968 until the death of Mao Zedong in 1976, the Albanian leadership used the implicit threat of Soviet/Warsaw Pact intervention to extract very large amounts of economic and military assistance from the Chinese.[60] Chinese largess was based on Tirana's ideological support for Maoism, and the not inconsiderable Albanian reserves of a strategic metal such as chromium. At the same time, Albania provided an entrée to the USSR's "backyard" for the Chinese—a component of a larger strategic game between the two principal Communist Party states. For Albania, the alliance with China served as a deterrent against an extension of the Brezhnev Doctrine beyond states contiguous to the USSR, as well as a means to gain economic and military assistance without significant cost.

Mao's death in 1976, and the reemergence of Deng Xiaoping by 1978 to become the principal figure in Chinese politics, led to a cooling of relations. In July 1978 China cut off aid to Albania, the culmination of growing disagreements between the two countries over foreign policy and questions of revolutionary principles.

During the next seven years, Albania evinced antipathy toward everyone. Hoxha's regime scorned all major powers and most of Albania's neighbors (although there were tentative conciliatory steps with Greece and Italy). The safety of Albania was assured through its relative isolation and its insignificance to the great powers.

Hoxha's own death in April 1985, however, raised questions about the directions of Albanian domestic and foreign policy. Such a small and poor country, undergoing a rapid expansion of its population,[61] needs developmental assistance and markets for the products it can export. Although it is too early for definitive conclusions, the direction thus far taken by Ramiz Alia has been to resurrect ties with Western states, including those that are NATO members.[62] Prime Minister Carcani and Foreign Minister Malile have actively tried to remove obstacles to the normalization of relations with the rest of Europe. For example, after more than a year of discussion concerning territorial disputes and the large Greek minority in Albania, the official state of war between Greece and Albania (dating from World War II) was finally ended in 1987.[63] In October 1987, formal diplomatic relations with West Germany were instituted, and a September 1988 visit by Foreign Minister Malile to Bonn broke new ground with a wide-ranging cultural agreement between Albania and West Germany.

Substantial economic and cultural cooperation has also begun with Turkey, and contacts with other West European states have been initiated.[64] With ties to Turkey becoming warmer, principal frictions with Athens removed, and an evident willingness to participate in regional discussions such as the Balkan foreign ministers' conference early in 1988, it seems clear that Albanian policy is directed toward ensuring its own security rather than relying solely on finding a new patron. Significantly, Tirana hosted its first multilateral diplomatic conference since World War II in January 1989, when deputy foreign ministers from the six Balkan states convened for a follow-up session to the 1988 Belgrade meeting.

If the Albanian Communist regime has external security concerns today, they are unlikely to be focused on the Warsaw Pact or the USSR. Albanian diplomacy has begun to probe (since 1986) the possibilities of bilateral accords with NSWP states resisting reform. The first crack in decades of Albanian—Warsaw Pact hostility came in the summer of 1986, when a major trade accord was signed between Albania and East Germany, and a ministerial-level East German delegation came to Tirana for a meeting with Prime Minister Adil Carcani.[65] Albania's unremitting hostility toward Warsaw Pact states has waned. Tirana is not yet ready, however, to respond to the nudges from Moscow to normalize relations with Warsaw Pact states generally.[66]

Yugoslavia, particularly now that Serbian nationalism has begun a resurgence personified in the new Serbian party leader Slobodan Milosevic, represents a continued threat, and there is ample vitriol in Alia's rhetoric about Yugoslav treatment of Albanian nationals in Kosovo or elsewhere. Yet it is unlikely that Albanian leaders envisage a military confrontation with Yugoslavia. Recent events in Kosovo have nevertheless led to a deterioration in Yugoslav-Albanian relations. (This problem is dealt with in a subsequent chapter.)

For Albanian foreign policy, the Warsaw Pact has played a number of peripheral but nevertheless significant roles. The Warsaw Pact has been a signal of Soviet protection against Yugoslavia and a potential cover for Soviet intervention. At all times, the pact has been a thin veneer for Soviet strategic interests that affected Albania deeply. In the past decade, as Soviet attention has been drawn away from the Balkans, Albania has avoided a new patron. Since Hoxha's death, Albania has used an independent foreign policy as a means for security rather than seeking a return to the dependence that has characterized Albanian existence for decades.

THE SOVIET UNION AND SOUTHEASTERN EUROPE

Notwithstanding extraordinary effort over many years, the Soviets have failed to achieve their goals in Southeastern Europe. In Romania, Ceausescu has used the Soviet/Warsaw Pact presence to rally public support for his autocratic regime. The USSR has implored Warsaw Pact states to increase defense spending, maintain manpower levels, and undertake more performance effort (maneuvers, etc.), with only limited success. Bulgaria still confronts issues of political loyalty in the army and ethnic tension in the population. Yugoslavia under Tito was not intimidated by the Soviets and Warsaw Pact, and gained international stature by anchoring Yugoslav security in the Nonaligned Movement. Albania, emerging from self-imposed isolation, has spurned reintegration with the USSR and Warsaw Pact and focused on improving relations with Western Europe and non-Communist states in Southeastern Europe.

Why have the Soviets failed to achieve better results? What accounts for the inability of the USSR to use effectively instruments at its disposal—most notably the Warsaw Pact—to mold the Communist states of Southeastern Europe into a compliant and impermeable "Southern Tier" of a Soviet *cordon sanitaire*?

In Southeastern Europe the Soviet efforts to create a closely knit alliance have encountered a number of obstacles. In Yugoslavia and Albania, genuine leaders emerged from the war whose own legitimacy was only enhanced by Soviet attempts at intimidation. In the Yugoslav and Albanian cases, transit through other states was necessary before Soviet forces could be used against them. Romania, Yugoslavia, and Albania also adopted territorial defense strategies that eschewed prolonged conventional combat by their countries' standing armies if the Soviets or Warsaw Pact neighbors attacked. Such military doctrines added greatly to the uncertain consequences of intervention, and raised the possibility that very large occupation forces would be tied down by indigenous Partisan armies.

The USSR's inability to maintain tight control over most of the Communist states of Southeastern Europe also has had much to do with the kinds of centrifugal tendencies present in the region. After 1956, none of the political changes in the Balkans have challenged the leading role of the party. Events of such magnitude may yet occur in the region, but other constraints on Soviet/Warsaw Pact intervention have grown in the meantime.

It is often argued that the Southern Tier of the Warsaw Pact, and Southeastern Europe generally, lack the strategic importance for the Soviet Union of Central and Northern Europe. The argument is used to explain Moscow's decisions to allow Albania to walk away from the Warsaw Pact, to let Romania's deviance run its course, and to accept Hungary's failure to live up to the performance requirements of "core" Warsaw Pact members.[67] At the same time, the Southern Tier may have become less critical to the Soviets *because* of Tito, Albania's defection, and Romanian intransigence. Certainly, Russian historical interest in the Bosporus and Dardanelles is well understood, and the desire to protect Russian interests in the Balkans is a well-established historical fact.

Crediting nationalism for Moscow's inability to ensure its unquestioned dominance in Communist Southeastern Europe may likewise lead us astray. Certainly, the nationalism of Romanians is no stronger than that of the Hungarians in 1956 or Czechs in 1968. The nature of Romania's differences from Warsaw Pact norms and the creation of a territorial defense strategy, however, may have been stronger deterrents to Soviet action than any measure of popular devotion to the nation.

MILITARY DOCTRINE

Among the four Communist Party states in Southeastern Europe plus Hungary, there have been five distinct orientations for national military policy in the past two decades (roughly since the invasion of Czechoslovakia and the reorganization of the pact in early 1969). Although Romania and Bulgaria have been Warsaw Pact members throughout that period, their military policies have followed different directions. For want of better terms, I categorize these different policies, with Hungary as a third and intriguing comparison, as follows:

1. "Nominal Warsaw Pact"—Romania, which adopted a territorial defense strategy while refusing to participate in joint maneuvers, denying transit to Soviet troops, and withdrawing from officer education programs in the USSR

2. "Peripheral Warsaw Pact"—Hungary, which has adopted no doctrine that deviates from Warsaw Pact norms, but lowers its military

commitments to maintain those conventional capabilities at levels below any other integrated pact member

3. "Total Warsaw Pact"—Bulgaria, the military doctrine and defense economy of which are entirely absorbed into the coalitional warfare rubric of the Warsaw Pact

In addition, of course, the two non-Warsaw Pact Communist states have adopted military doctrines that distinguish them in other ways:

4. "Non-Warsaw Pact Autonomous Territorial Defense"—Yugoslavia (and Albania post 1978?), where a largely independent effort, based on historical experience, is made to prepare standing army, paramilitary, and irregular troops to engage in a war of the entire people against an invader

5. "Non-Warsaw Pact Externally Dependent Territorial Defense"— Albania, early 1960s through 1978, in which a major power provides the bulk of weapons and the ultimate guarantee of a territorial defense strategy's validity

Although all five military doctrines reflect different adaptations to opportunities, options, or the lack thereof, *all* are heavily influenced by the existence of the Warsaw Pact and its transparent roles within Eastern Europe. Were there no Warsaw Pact, Soviet bilateral ties alone could have provided justification for neither Bulgaria's burdensome military effort nor Soviet absorption of Bulgaria's defense economy. In Hungary, where the population long ago had decided that the Warsaw Pact was "expendable and a hindrance,"[68] even a modest military effort by East European standards would be difficult to extract were the Soviets present without any multilateral element. For Romania, Yugoslavia, and Albania, of course, the potential for Soviet or NSWP invasions has been behind the original development of territorial defense strategies—although Albania's preparations have been directed as well against Yugoslavia.

These five paths for military policies among Communist states in the region thus reflect varying points along a continuum largely defined by the degree of hostility between indigenous leaders or masses and the USSR and its core Warsaw Pact allies.

REGIONAL SECURITY ISSUES

As discussed in country-specific observations of the preceding section, few of the burning security issues of the Balkans are caused by, or can be solved by, the Warsaw Pact. Yet the Soviet presence, if only through a state's nominal Warsaw Pact membership, affects the disposition of these regional issues. Leaving aside Greek-Turkish conflicts, several significant issues may engender confrontations between states of the region. All involve Communist states, and most involve at least one Warsaw Pact member. These areas of real and potential conflict include the following:

• Hungary versus Romania regarding the Hungarian minority in Transylvania and Transylvania in general as a territorial issue, with debates raging about historical settlement of Transylvania and emotions high concerning Hungarian charges of Romanian human-rights violations
• Albania versus Yugoslavia concerning Albanians in Kosovo and Serbian treatment of them there and in other republics, with Yugoslavia viewing Albanian statements as provocative interference
• Bulgaria versus Yugoslavia over Macedonia, with Bulgarians suspicious of Macedonian nationalism and angered because Yugoslavia treats Macedonia as a separate nationality and language, while the Yugoslavs suspect Bulgarian territorial desires and Soviet intentions by manipulation of the Macedonian issue
• Bulgaria versus Romania regarding Dobrudja, a territory on the Black Sea coast divided between Romania and Bulgaria which Bulgaria claims entirely for itself while asserting that ethnic Bulgarians who reside in the Romanian part have been denied socioeconomic and political opportunities
• Albania versus Greece, with the issue being the Greek minority inside Albanian territory ("Northern Epirus," according to the Greeks)[69]

In the most notable current example, Hungarians have reacted bitterly not only to the continued political repression of the Hungarian minority in Romania, but to the renewed commitment by Ceausescu to destroy thousands of villages (many of them Hungarian) in order to modernize Romanian agriculture.[70] Hungarian interests, were the Warsaw Pact not present, would require that demands be made for the protection of its minorities, and punitive action if those demands were not met. In the Warsaw Pact environment, however, there are constraints on military or economic retaliation, and substantial disincentives to bringing the dispute to the UN. What Communist countries of Southeastern Europe can do to pursue matters of national interest and security are, in similar ways, always being affected by the Warsaw Pact's existence, reminding participants in disputes of Soviet interests. In the case of Hungary, for example, we can well appreciate the pithy observation by Peter Bender that "Hungary's security problem, so far as it is of a military kind, consists solely in its membership [in] the Warsaw Pact."[71]

CONCLUSION

As ideologically based blocs continue to decay in Europe, old bilateral, nationally rooted issues will gain in importance in Southeastern Europe. Little of the evidence presented here would suggest a large role for the USSR in Southeastern Europe in settling these disputes. There are few scenarios in which Moscow, with Gorbachev or any foreseeable leadership, would be inclined to intervene militarily in the region—and only in the most extreme case of an anti-Communist revolution in neighboring Romania or Bulgaria would the probability of armed intervention rise significantly during the 1990s.

The principal security orientation of Southeastern Europe—that is, where and how the states of the region seek to enhance their military, political, and economic capacities vis-à-vis adversaries—will be through ties with the European Community and the CSCE process. For almost four decades after World War II, the USSR loomed as the principal threat or overwhelming ally of Balkan states. Already in the 1980s and certainly in the 1990s, a resurgence of intraregional and national quarrels, the perceptible withdrawal of the USSR to tend to grievous domestic problems, and the advent in 1992 of European economic unity together imply strong currents pushing the security orientation of Southeastern Europe away from what we have known for decades. The relationship between the USSR and Balkan Communist states will increasingly be defined by these countries' own interests. The pact itself is unlikely to disband, but will be less useful to the USSR as a means of guaranteeing its security. At the conventional forces in Europe (CFE) talks in Vienna, of course, the Warsaw Pact will remain on the diplomatic stage, but both NATO and the pact will be susceptible to individual countries' priorities that would have been unthinkable in the past.

Bulgaria's fealty to Moscow is unlikely to change dramatically, but a genuine *Bulgarian* perspective on its own security focusing on a Turkish threat, rapprochement with Greece, and increased involvement in Balkan and European diplomacy, has now emerged. For Romania, the USSR appears now to pose an ideological rather than a military threat, and the Ceausescu regime may well see its greatest security danger emerging from Hungary and the Western indictments of Romanian human rights policies. A post-Ceausescu Romania will not simply reintegrate itself within Soviet/Warsaw Pact security planning, but will instead try to find ways to repair socioeconomic losses of the Ceausescu era via reconciliation with the European Community while placating Soviet concerns. For Yugoslavia, with its own dissolution at issue, external "threats" pale by comparison. Only the West can help economically; added Soviet involvement would solve nothing. For Albania, only Yugoslavia poses any "threat," and the Warsaw Pact or the USSR are largely irrelevant to the Kosovo dilemma. Certainly, the USSR has proved to be no model for resolving ethnic/national disputes.

In the years ahead, as the trauma of Yugoslavia unfolds, when Ceausescu and Zhivkov die, and Albania continues to emerge from decades of isolation, there will be little room for a Soviet reassertion of a multilateral or superpower security perspective in the Balkans. Obviously, the USSR will make every effort to have its interests and preferences known, using diplomatic visibility, military aid and credits, and energy and raw material exports as leverage. Aside from weapons and raw materials, however, Moscow's tools with which to impose its "will"—assuming, of course, that the Soviets had the wherewithal to make such an effort—are incomplete. Southeastern Europe needs capital investment to modernize, not just raw material imports to fuel existing industry. Southeastern Europe has little need for advanced weaponry that the USSR might export, and Yugoslavia and Romania have well-developed small-arms industries of their own. And Southeastern Europe is likely to view the USSR's capacity for sustained military intervention as less credible in the 1990s than in the 1960s or 1970s.

The historical cleavages of Southeastern Europe have, instead, penetrated and "overcome" the veneer of late-twentieth-century alliances. Superpower-led or -imposed treaty organizations affected, but did not determine, the course of post-World War II political-military affairs in the region bounded by the Black Sea, Aegean, and Adriatic. That diverse forms of one-party authoritarianism and an array of defense and international policies all developed within the geographic confines of four Communist Party states in Southeastern Europe suggests the limits of power for superpowers and their military alliances.

NOTES

Ali I. Karaosmanglu's comments on this chapter have been much appreciated.

1. Helene Carrere d'Encausse, in her book *Big Brother: The Soviet Union and Eastern Europe* (London: Holmes and Meier, 1987), 269, states that "the Pact had as its primary function to demonstrate that the socialist camp existed and that it could not be changed."

2. Viktor Kulikov, ed., *Varshavskii dogovor: Soiuz vo imia mira i sotsializma* (Moscow: Voenizdat, 1980), contains discussion of these early stages of the pact and, implicitly, its inactivity.

3. Particularly in the spring and summer of 1971, numerous Soviet and Soviet-Bulgarian-Hungarian exercises were clearly meant to signal to Ceausescu the limits to his behavior. Ceausescu's close contacts with China may have been the "final straw" that led Brezhnev to such demonstrative warnings. In any case, it is certain that Ceausescu was worried and anticipated the worst. See, for instance, the speeches in mid-August 1971 contained in the collection of Ceausescu's pronouncements, *Romania on the Way of Building Up the Multilaterally Developed Socialist Society* (Bucharest: Meridian Publishing House, 1972), 271–302.

4. For example, Jeffrey Simon counts "no less than seven exercises around [Romania's] borders" in the two years from the summer of 1969 through the early fall of 1971. See his account of these maneuvers and the threatening posture toward Romania (and Yugoslavia) in Jeffrey Simon, *Warsaw Pact Forces* (Boulder, Colo.: Westview Press, 1985), 83–7.

5. One must, of course, give credit to Ceausescu's political acumen, as Michael Shafir does, when accounting for his success in moving aside holdovers from the Gheorghiu-Dej years. See Michael Shafir, *Romania* (London: Frances Pinter, 1985). Yet the Standing Presidium (i.e., politburo) and the larger Political Executive Committee had remained unchanged from the Ninth Congress (July 1965) through the end of 1967, and 1969 saw departures of the Gheorghiu-Dej cohort from these bodies, with further changes at the Tenth Congress in August 1969. Certainly, the coincidence of Ceausescu's popularity and tie to nationalism in the face of Soviet/Warsaw Pact threat helped to make his position unassailable.

6. The "initial decisions [to fight alongside the Germans in their 1941 invasion of the USSR] were not unpopular," writes Barbara Jelavich. The "general public acceptance," however, was focused on the need to regain Bukovina and Bessarabia, which the Soviets had annexed a year earlier, and on the need to gain German approval for a return of that part of Transylvania ceded to Hungary via German "arbitration" in 1940. Furthermore, Romanians' "animosity was directed against their Soviet neighbor and had its base in . . . historical conflicts" Jelavich, *History of The Balkans: Twentieth Century"* (Cambridge: Cambridge University Press, 1983), 250–1.

7. See, for example, Mary Ellen Fischer, "Idol or Leader? The Origins and Future of the Ceausescu Cult," in Daniel N. Nelson, ed., *Romania in the 1980s* (Boulder, Colo.: Westview Press, 1981).

8. "Cuvintare la intilnire cu representanti ai clasei muncitoare," November 25, 1978; "Cuvintare la intilnire cu representanti ai taranimii, intelectualitatii, si tineretului," November 25, 1978; "Cuvintare la intilnire cu representanti ai armata si ai ministeriul de interna," November 27, 1978 (Bucharest: Editura Politica, 1978). The first two of these speeches were also carried in *Scinteia* (November 26, 1978), 1 and 3.

9. I have discussed specific aspects of the deteriorating socioeconomic conditions of the late Ceausescu period in Daniel N. Nelson, "The Romanian Disaster," in T. Anthony Jones, ed., *Research on the Soviet Union and Eastern Europe* (Cambridge, Mass: JAI Press, forthcoming 1989).

10. These data are gathered by professional polling organizations on behalf of Radio Free Europe through continuous sampling, over three-year periods, of East European nationals traveling to Western Europe. Findings are reported in Radio Free Europe, East European Audience and Opinion Research, "Political Legitimacy in Eastern Europe: A Comparative Study" (March 1987), Table 6, p. 18. For Romania, specifically, negative evaluations of the performance of the current political system have increased drastically as a proportion of all responses since the late 1970s. Indeed, what I have termed a "negative shift" of public opinion has been larger in

Romania than anywhere in the Warsaw Pact. See Daniel N. Nelson, "Eastern Europe and the Public Political Arena", in *Europa Archiv* (December, 1988).

11. RFE Background Report, "Rumanian Difficulties in Military and Security Affairs" (March 6, 1972).

12. Aurel Braun, *Romanian Foreign Policy Since 1965* (New York: Praeger, 1978), 154–5.

13. BBC Summary of World Broadcasts (December 16, 1982).

14. I have discussed these data and their implications in "Military Policies and Military Politics" in Daniel N. Nelson, *Romanian Politics in the Ceausescu Era* (New York: Gordon and Breach, 1989).

15. As public approval began to plummet in the early to mid–1980s (see sources cited in note 10), Romanian military expenditures as a proportion of GNP, central government expenditures, and per capita spending, as well as force levels as a proportion of population, all rose. The most dramatic increases were in 1982 and 1983, with 1984 and 1985 data indicating that the military effort was maintained even as the economic crisis lessened slightly. For data on military expenditures consult U.S. Arms Control and Disarmament Agency (ACDA), *World Military Expenditures and Arms Transfers* (Washington, D.C.: ACDA, 1987) [Hereafter "ACDA"], 74.

16. Henry Kamm, "For Bucharest, A Great Leap Backward," *New York Times* (February 15, 1988).

17. Nicolae Ceausescu, as quoted in *Scinteia* (May 4, 1988).

18. See, for example, William Echikson, "Hungarian Refugees Spark Rare East-bloc Row", *Christian Science Monitor* (June 13, 1988); and Echikson, "Hungarians Protest Romanian Plan to Destroy Villages," *Christian Science Monitor* (June 27, 1988).

19. See my discussion of the officer corps' likely attitudes in "Military Politics and Military Policies in Ceausescu's Romania" in Daniel N. Nelson, *Romanian Politics in the Ceausescu Era.*

20. Rankings of Bulgarian expenditures and manpower levels relative to all nation-states reveal this surprisingly high and consistent commitment. See, for example, ACDA, p. 51, for raw data, and p. 38 for Bulgaria's rankings in 1985. For instance, Bulgaria ranked twelfth in the world in military expenditures per capita and sixtenth in armed forces as a proportion of population, that is, above the 90th percentile of all nation-states on both indicators. One should note, moreover, that those rankings are *after* a modest decline in Bulgarian military effort generally from the late 1970s into the 1980s.

21. Regarding Bulgaria's economic performance, see George R. Feiwel, "Industrialization" in Stephen Fischer-Galati, ed., *Eastern Europe in the 1980s (Boulder, Colo.: Westview, 1982)*, 55–82; NMP data are from Thad P. Alton, "East European GNPs: Origins of Product, Final Uses, Rates of Growth and International Comparisons." In Joint Economic Committee, *East European Economies: Slow Growth in the 1980s* (Washington, D.C.: U.S. Government Printing Office, 1985), 115–16.

22. Central Intelligence Agency, Directorate of Intelligence, *Handbook of Economic Statistics* (Washington, D.C.: CIA, 1986) [Hereafter, "CIA"], 101–2 and 130.

23. *Narodna Armiya* (December 12, 1984), as translated in FBIS *Daily Report, Eastern Europe* (December 17, 1984).

24. ACDA, 1984, 1985, 1986, 1987.

25. CIA, 1987, 212, 222.

26. John D. Bell, *The Bulgarian Communist Party from Blagoev to Zhivkov* (Stanford: Hoover Institution Press, 1986); see also, John Jaworsky, "Bulgaria" in Teresa Rakowska-Harmstone et al., *Warsaw Pact: The Question of Cohesion*, Phase II, vol. 3 (Ottawa: Ministry of Defense, ORAE, 1985).

27. G. F. Vorontsov, *Voennye Koalitsii i Koalitsionnye Voiny* (Moscow: Voenizdat, 1976).

28. Bell, 86; see also Nissan Oren, *Revolution Administered* (Baltimore: Johns Hopkins University Press, 1972), 86.

29. James F. Brown, *Bulgaria Under Communist Rule* (New York: Praeger, 1970), 179.

30. Michael Costello, "Bulgaria," in Adam Bromke and Teresa Rakowska-Harmstone,

eds., *The Communist States in Disarray* (Minneapolis: University of Minnesota Press, 1972), 149; see also Brown, *Bulgaria Under Communist Rule*, 173–87, for the most complete account of the conspiracy and its aftermath.

31. General Velichko Georgiev as quoted in *Narodna Armiya* (June 12, 1960)
32. See, for example, an editorial in *Narodna Armiya* (December 12, 1984).
33. Radio Free Europe, Situation Reports-Bulgaria no. 14 (October 23, 1984), 1–4; see also Radio Free Europe, Background Report No. 150 (December 27, 1985), 12.
34. See reports on the ethnic unrest and Turkish claims in the *New York Times* (May 19, 1985 and August 5, 1985).
35. Stephen Ashley, "Bulgaria and the Balkan Foreign Ministers' Conference," Radio Free Europe Research, vol. 13, no. 10 (March 11, 1988), *Bulgarian Situation Report*, no. 3 (March 8, 1988), 6.
36. Ashley, "Bulgaria and the Balkan Foreign Ministers' Conference," 5–8.
37. Zbigniew Brzezinski, *The Soviet Bloc* (Cambridge, Mass.: Harvard University Press, 1967), 62–4.
38. Ibid., 64.
39. James F. Brown, *Eastern Europe and Communist Rule* (Durham, N.C.: Duke University Press, 1988), 363.
40. T. I. Geshkoff, *Balkan Union* (New York: Columbia University Press, 1940); see also a brief discussion of the Balkan conferences and ancillary cooperation during the 1930s in Ioan Mircea Pascu, "The Balkans: A Romanian Perspective," in David Carlton and Carlo Schaerf, eds., *South-Eastern Europe After Tito* (New York: St. Martin's, 1983), 137–40.
41. Aurel Braun, *Small State Security in the Balkans* (Totawa, N.J.: Barnes and Noble, 1983), 44.
42. Hans Gunter Brauch, "Confidence-Building Measures in the Balkans and the Eastern Mediterranean," in Carlton and Schaerf, eds., *South-Eastern Europe After Tito*, 85.
43. Ronald Linden, *Communist States and International Change* (New York: Allen and Unwin, 1986), 12.
44. Braun, *Small State Security in the Balkans*, 46.
45. Changes within the Nonaligned Movement toward North-South issues and the attempt by radical states to view the USSR and Warsaw Pact states as the "natural partners" of nonalignment are discussed by Richard L. Jackson, *The Non-Aligned, the U.N., and the Superpowers* (New York: Praeger, 1983), 24–36. Generally, as well, see Ernest Corea, *Non-Alignment: Dynamics of a Movement* (Toronto: Canadian Institute of International Affairs, 1977).
46. Works devoted specifically to Tito and Yugoslavia's role are Alvin Z. Rubinstein, *Yugoslavia and the Nonaligned World* (Princeton, N.J.: Princeton University Press, 1970); and *Tito and the Non-Aligned Movement* (Belgrade: Socialist Thought and Practice), especially pp. 75–92 with Tito's speech to the Algiers conference in 1973.
47. Paul Shoup, *Communism and the Yugoslav National Question* (New York: Columbia University Press, 1968), 144–83.
48. Stephen Ashley, "Greek-Bulgaria Friendship Treaty," in Vojtech Mastny, ed., *Soviet-East European Survey, 1986–1987* (Boulder, Colo.: Westview Press, 1987), 318–25.
49. Braun, *Small-State Security in the Balkans*, 52.
50. Regarding Yugoslav involvement in the CSCE process, and the specific issue of confidence-building measures, see Hans Gunter Brauch, *Vertrauensbildende Massnahmen und Europaische Abrüstungskonferenz* (Gerlingen: Bliecher, 1986).
51. The Balkan foreign ministers' conference of February 24–6, 1988, was arranged and hosted by the Yugoslavs. Yugoslav Foreign Minister (now vice president in the State Presidency) Raif Dizdarevic issued formal invitations on April 6, 1987, in a letter to his four counterparts. Tanjug dispatch, April 22, 1987.
52. Milan Andrejevich, "The Balkan Foreign Ministers' Conference from the Yugoslav

Angle," Radio Free Europe Research, *Yugoslav Situation Report*, no. 2 (March 10, 1988), 6.

53. Defense Minister Branko Mamula, interview in *Narodna Armija* (September 23, 1987).

54. In a speech to Yugoslav Federal Assembly, in Belgrade on March 16, 1988, Gorbachev noted that "democratization requires an unconditional recognition by the international community of the right of each people to shape its destiny, its right to dispose of its own resources. This is a universal, general right. It cannot belong to some 'chosen' peoples, and the more so be measured by the economic or military potential of states . . . each people has its interests that are not subordinated to the interests of other states." See Tass dispatch, March 16, 1988, as cited in *News and Views From the USSR*, distributed by the Soviet embassy, Washington, D.C. This statement, in direct contrast to the so-called Brezhnev Doctrine, was well received.

55. Jelavich, *History of the Balkans*, 274.

56. Michael MccGuire, *Soviet Naval Developments* (New York: Praeger, 1975), 345.

57. One standard source that describes events from the late 1950s through the early 1960s is William E. Griffith, *Albania and the Sino-Soviet Rift* (Cambridge, Mass.: MIT Press, 1963). Other useful sources, with details about the long Chinese-Albanian relationship, are Peter R. Prifti, *Socialist Albania Since 1944: Domestic and Foreign Developments* (Cambridge, Mass.: MIT Press, 1978), and Berhard Tonnes, *Sonderfall Albanien* (Munchen: F. Oldenburg, 1980).

58. Braun, *Small-State Security in the Balkans*, 38.

59. Brown, *Eastern Europe and Communist Rule*, 373.

60. Michael Kaser, "Trade and Aid in the Albanian Economy," in U.S. Congress, Joint Economic Committee, *East European Economies Post-Helsinki* (Washington, D.C.: U.S. Government Printing Office, 1977).

61. For a general analysis of Albania's socioeconomic and political conditions, including issues of food production and population growth, consult Michael Kaser, *Albania Under and After Enver Hoxha* (Washington, D.C.: U.S. Congress, Joint Economic Committee, 1986).

62. For a discussion of these foreign-policy options shortly after Hoxha's death, see Elez Biberaj, "Albania After Hoxha: Dilemmas of Change", *Problems of Communism*, vol. XXXIV (November-December 1985), especially pp. 41–6.

63. Brown, *Eastern Europe and Communist Rule*, 380.

64. For example, discussions between Albania and Britain, in part over the Corfu incident more than four decades ago, were resumed in secret after Hoxha's death—although noted in the press. See J. Cooley, "Albania Expected to Resume Secret Talks with Britain", *Christian Science Monitor* (August 26, 1985).

65. Louis Zanga, "Reform Albanian Style," in Vojtech Mastny, ed., *Soviet-East European Survey, 1986–1987*, 297; Zanga cites the Albanian news agency, ATA, dispatch of June 23, 1986.

66. Within months after Hoxha's death, the USSR began a concerted effort, through signals in Soviet media coverage of Albania and in broadcasts to Albania, to demonstrate that there were advantages to be found in renewed ties with the "socialist commonwealth." For example, see various Soviet broadcasts and articles in principal Soviet newspapers cited in FBIS, *Daily Report, Soviet Union* (May 17, 1985, pp. F13–14 and May 30, 1985, pp. F1–2).

67. Nelson, *Alliance Behavior in the Warsaw Pact*, especially pp. 71–107.

68. Peter Bender, *East Europe in Search of Security* (Baltimore, Md.: The Johns Hopkins University Press, 1972), 104.

69. Author's adaptation from Anthanassios G. Platias and R. J. Rydell, "International Security Regimes: The Case of a Balkan Nuclear Free Zone," in Carlton and Schaerf, eds., *South-Eastern Europe After Tito*, 118.

70. Daniel N. Nelson, "The Romanian Disaster," in T. Anthony Jones, ed., *Research on the Soviet Union and Eastern Europe* (Cambridge, Mass: JAI Press, forthcoming 1990).

71. Bender, *East Europe in Search of Security*, 102.

7

YUGOSLAVIA'S FOREIGN POLICY AND SOUTHEASTERN EUROPE

Zachary T. Irwin

In recent years, Yugoslav foreign policy has acquired a disjunctive character. Traditionally, the strengthening of Yugoslav security, regional cooperation, and nonalignment policies contributed to stability of the regime. During the 1980s, it became doubtful whether pursuit of these policies was able to promote the country's stability. The armed forces increased their involvement in domestic affairs, and some Yugoslavs and foreign observers believed that the armed forces threatened civilian political control. Active republican involvement in the implementation of foreign policy suggested an alternative to nonaligned identification, or even a prelude to disintegration. Regional cooperation was jeopardized by events in Kosovo. Disagreement over Yugoslav economic reform and commercial policy raised questions about whether closer association with the European Community was compatible with principles of nonalignment. Thus Yugoslavia faces severe foreign-policy challenges in the decade ahead, most of which can be traced to the country's domestic situation.

This essay analyzes several elements of Yugoslavia's foreign policy, past and present: the country's efforts to provide for its security, the development of nonalignment, Yugoslavia's role as a regional power in the Mediterranean and the Balkans, and republican foreign policy. A concluding section examines Yugoslavia's relations with the United States and the effect of the deteriorating economic situation on Yugoslavia's foreign policy.

THE SECURITY DIMENSION

At the time of Yugoslavia's expulsion from the Cominform in 1948, Yugoslav armed forces included some 350,000 men under arms.

Approximately the same number were available for mobilization.[1] Although Yugoslavia's army then was the second largest in Europe (after that of the Soviet Union), it confronted a tangible Soviet threat. In his memoirs Khrushchev said that he was "absolutely sure" that Stalin would have invaded Yugoslavia if the countries had shared a common boundary.[2] In late 1949, the United States lifted restrictions on the purchase of arms by Yugoslavia, but military cooperation between the two nations developed slowly. Talks between Yugoslav authorities and Anglo-American-French officials proceeded in 1952 and 1953, yet Beatrice Heuser notes that "full scale talks on defense coordination" proved to be impossible because of the hostility between Yugoslavia and Italy and Western opposition to sharing NATO secrets.[3] The British chiefs of staff opposed creating a separate Balkan Command for Yugoslavia, Greece, and Turkey. However, a Greek-Yugoslav rapprochement created conditions for a treaty of friendship among these three powers in February 1953 and a military alliance, the Balkan Pact, the following year.

In October 1954, President Tito's remarks on the Balkan Pact indicated that Yugoslavia was no longer interested in cooperation with NATO. In an address to the Yugoslav Federal Assembly, Tito stated that compared with previous years "the danger of aggression is less" and that "in the present situation the treaty may serve primarily for the further development of economic and political cooperation."[4] Although the Balkan Pact formally remains in force, Yugoslavia's loss of interest in maintaining its consultative institutions was probably linked to the 1955 Soviet-Yugoslav accommodation. Yet the treaty still lingers as a source of Soviet concern.[5]

The prospects for regional military cooperation between Yugoslavia and its neighbors have been revived periodically. Presidents Tito and Ceausescu conferred just after the 1968 Soviet invasion of Czechoslovakia and after Soviet accusations that Yugoslavia and Romania had been "actively helping Czechoslovak antisocialist forces."[6] Since 1968, military contacts between the two states have become routine.[7]

In 1979, the Soviet invasion of Afghanistan provoked Albania to offer assistance if Yugoslavia were threatened. The Albanian Communist Newspaper *Zeri i popullit* condemned the invasion, warning that, "Soviet social-imperialists and their Bulgarian tools have not failed at blackmailing and threatening Yugoslavia," adding that if Yugoslavia were attacked, Albania would "do the same thing as we have done in the past and fight the common enemy."[8] Unfortunately, the prospects for cooperation were dashed the following year by the Albanian insurgency in Kosovo. Albanian endorsement of republican statehood for Kosovo brought Belgrade to denounce Albania's "crude interference" in Yugoslav affairs and to accuse Tirana of entertaining "territorial claims."[9] Cooperation with other regional states remains an emergency option for Yugoslavia, but Tito and his successors have considered reliance on Yugoslav forces to be more consistent with nonalignment and with the developing role of the Yugoslav People's Army (YPA) and the country's self-defense forces.

Initially, the Yugoslav All-People's Army evolved as a response to the Soviet invasion of Czechoslovakia.[10] The Yugoslav All-People's Defense is a decentralized system consisting of the YPA and the Territorial Defense Forces. The army component consists of approximately 200,000 men, the navy of 12,000, and the air force of 36,700.[11] According to an interview with President Tito in 1978, the total number of reserve units permits Yugoslavia to enlist more than a million men under arms. This number has probably increased in the past decade.[12] Yugoslav doctrine does not identify either the YPA or the Territorial Defense Forces with exclusively conventional frontal defense or with guerrilla warfare in occupied areas.

According to Adam Roberts, the YPA is to be prepared for "descending transformations" so that it could continue to offer resistance even after frontal setbacks, whereas the Territorial Defense Forces are prepared for "ascending transformations" by which small guerrilla units would coalesce into larger units against an invading army. The system enables Yugoslavia to maintain the largest number of active troops in the region and to devote the smallest share of its gross national product (GNP) to defense. National defense laws, adopted in 1969, 1974, and 1982, have consistently upgraded the YPA relative to the territorial units. These changes have been reflected in the federal constitution and in the YPA command structure.[13]

Yugoslav defense policy includes several novel elements. The constitution provides that "no one shall have the right to acknowledge or sign an act of capitulation, nor to accept or recognize an act of capitulation" (article 238). Similar provisions in the national defense law outlaw the invitation of foreign forces on Yugoslav soil. Also, Yugoslavia possesses a developed defense industry. Approximately 80 percent of Yugoslavia's defense needs are met by domestic producers, excluding the mainstay of the air force, the MIG-21. In 1988, the Soviets agreed to transfer the MIG-29 to Yugoslavia; sixteen aircraft are scheduled for delivery, and by 1995, Yugoslavia will reportedly produce the *Novi Avion Orao*, a supersonic fighter. Recent military talks with the United States apparently did not involve the transfer of any major weapons systems. During the mid-1970s, the sale of advanced American antitank technology was postponed indefinitely when premature news of the sale's approval embarrassed both sides.[14]

Yugoslav attitudes toward nuclear weapons are somewhat ambiguous. Although the country ratified the Nonproliferation of Nuclear Weapons Treaty, in 1975 General Dimitrije Seserinac Gedza warned that this position would be "reconsidered" should an enemy contemplate "the use of mass terror or other weapons of mass destruction be used." He went on, "Because today the possibility exists—both in the East and the West—of manufacturing nuclear weapons costing a few hundred dollars . . . cheap and easily manufactured mini-nuclear weapons, capable of destroying entire units or headquarters of the aggressor, would have a sobering effect on anyone contemplating invasion of our country.[15] It is reasonable to describe Yugoslavia as a "near-nuclear country," although the extent of its capability is uncertain.[16]

In the event of conventional war, the areas most vulnerable to invasion lie along the Pannonian plain bordering Hungary and Romania. The 623-kilometer Hungarian boundary is "virtually a classical invasion route for tank formations,"[17] and an invader could penetrate the area between the boundary and Belgrade, a distance of 160 kilometers. The 557-kilometer Romanian boundary is vulnerable but less threatened because of the absence of Soviet divisions in Romania. The 536-kilometer boundary with Bulgaria is relatively secure owing to geographical barriers, but Yugoslavs are sensitive to any Albanian rapprochement with Bulgaria because of the proximity of the two countries.

In May 1987, Soviet Marshal Viktor Kulikov, the former supreme commander of the Warsaw Pact, granted an interview to the Yugoslav periodical *Danas* in which he was asked about the "very interesting" fact that the only military assistance treaty Albania had not renounced was that with Bulgaria. Kulikov denied that the treaty was more than a "formality." In his words, "There is now no military cooperation between these two countries."[18] From Belgrade's perspective, an Albanian-Bulgarian accommodation conjures up images of encirclement. At the height of the Cominform blockade in 1950, Moscow maintained five airfields in Albania, and more than fifty daily flights were scheduled between those airfields and Bulgaria.[19]

At present Soviet intentions appear to preclude military intervention in Yugoslavia, but the Brezhnev Doctrine has not been formally renounced. Soviet accounts of recent events in Yugoslavia have implied dangers to socialism. A recent article in the Soviet armed forces newspaper *Krasnaya Zvezda* observed that "excessive decentralization has divided Yugoslavia into a series of independent isolated islands."[20] The article pointed to Albanian separatism and verbal attacks on the YPA as evidence of "antisocialist forces trying to climb onto the political stage." In November 1988, General Dmitri Yazov, the Soviet defense minister, visited Yugoslavia—the first such visit by a Soviet defense minister since 1980—and reaffirmed long-standing military ties. The Soviets appear to be acting on the assumption that the Yugoslav armed forces represent the most effective source of Soviet influence and a likely bulwark against Western-inspired liberalization.

The Yugoslavs have long perceived worsening relations with Albania and Bulgaria as a security threat. In the past, the Yugoslavs considered Bulgarian interest in Macedonia as Soviet inspired and an indication of Soviet attitudes toward Yugoslavia.[21] Recently, Yugoslav statements have identified a threat originating in the Balkans. In an address to the Federal Assembly on December 17, 1987, Admiral Branko Mamula, the minister of national defense, warned, "Under the pretext that some parts of our territory are of strategic interest for the security of some neighboring countries, the possibility of military intervention has been discussed."[22] According to Mamula, some "neighboring countries both last year and this formed significant military forces for rapid intervention."

It is unclear which forces were the object of Mamula's remarks, but the concern illustrates a general characteristic of Yugoslav threat perception. As domestic conditions in Yugoslavia have deteriorated, the perceived danger of intervention has increased. This perception extended to the West and the Reagan administration's interest in a military doctrine envisaging the proliferation of "low-intensity conflicts" as a new form of East-West struggle. In this connection, in a December 1986 address, Mamula branded the "doctrine of low intensity" as a "real threat to our security and independence. We are studying it . . . as a possible form of use of military force against our country . . . particularly in the case of serious internal difficulties."[23] Mamula's speech coincided with the increasing involvement of the armed forces in domestic affairs.

Several factors have accelerated the influence of the armed forces in Yugoslav politics; these include the appointment of a former chief of military counterintelligence to head the state security apparatus in 1966; the decade-long tenure of YPA Colonel General Franjo Herljevic as federal secretary for internal affairs; and the reliance on the armed forces to restore order, indirectly, during the Croatian Crisis in 1971, and, directly, in Kosovo since 1981.[24] Marko Milivojevic maintains that the federal secretary for national defense functions as a *de facto* commander-in-chief of the armed forces, owing to the rotating chairmanship of the State Presidency.[25] Yugoslav military doctrine traditionally defines a circumstance in which foreign military and subversive internal elements combine in a "special war" as a "coordinated political economic, psychological propaganda and socially-subversive [form of warfare] which may include military action."[26] The examples of "special war" are drawn principally from instances of U.S. involvement in Latin America, yet in Yugoslavia's current crisis, it is reasonable to conclude that the YPA could use the techniques to confront a hostile or apathetic Yugoslav population.

Intervention by the YPA in domestic politics appeared possible in 1988 for two reasons: the inability of the central government to stop the increasing disorder and specific army objections to developments in Slovenia.[27] Slovenian student activists arrested in the spring of 1988 had in their possession a plan for YPA intervention in Slovenia. Although the contents of the document are not available, they undoubtedly provided for direct action. By affirming the authenticity of a "military document" and disputing its constitutionality, the Slovenian State Presidency implied the innocence of those on trial.[28]

Intervention by the armed forces in Yugoslavia could occur through the replacement of officials or their arrest, perhaps coinciding with an intensification of the struggle against "enemies" by the "committees of nationwide defense and social self-protection."[29] Milivojevic concludes that "in all *probability* the YPA High Command is now involved in some sort of contingency planning [for a military takeover], but that the associated '*problems*' of such an attempt have made it extremely *cautious*"[30] [emphasis in the original]. The multinational character of the YPA is certainly one reason for this caution. Nor is it certain a military regime could be more effective than a civilian government under Yugoslav conditions. The case of Poland's Jaruzelski may be less relevant in Yugoslavia's case than that of the Greek colonels.

NONALIGNMENT

The origins of Yugoslav nonalignment lie in the diplomatic and political conditions of the 1950s. Newly independent countries sought to avoid provoking the Soviet Union or the United States by remaining uncommitted to either side in the cold war. In Yugoslavia, the ideology of self-management provided a basis for Communist rule distinct from Soviet socialism, yet implied no distinct foreign policy. At a meeting of Asian socialists in 1953, Milovan Djilas discovered a "common ground" with the participants in the "wish to resist exploitation by the West and hegemony by the USSR."[31] Contacts among Yugoslavia, Burma, and India indicated possible political cooperation. Initially the Bandung Conference of Asian and Middle East States excluded Yugoslavia, but the opportunity for Yugoslav involvement soon followed. The failure of the Bandung conference to create a durable identity for "positive neutralism" provided Tito the opportunity to pursue a separate agreement with Nehru and Egypt's Nasser. In 1955 Nasser and Tito met on Tito's yacht at Suez after the latter's trip to India, and the following year Nasser, Tito, and Nehru met on Brioni to support "positive neutralism" and appeal for a system of "collective security on a world scale."[32]

Zimmerman notes that nonalignment allowed the leadership "to hold a diverse coalition together" and "to distinguish Yugoslavia from the Soviet Union without giving proof to Cominform charges that Yugoslavia had become a lackey of Anglo-American imperialism."[33] By avoiding identification with the West and finding an authentic platform for anti-imperialism, Tito strengthened his position with the rank and file of the LCY. The global character of the movement permitted a legitimating, if shallow, universalism.

Nonalignment has often brought Yugoslavia into conflict with the United States. Specifically, Tito furnished mediation and critical transport facilities for the Soviets during the 1955 Czechoslovak arms transfer to Egypt. Yugoslavia has also vigorously criticized American involvement in Vietnam and unhesitatingly supported powers hostile to the United States in the Third World, including Cuba and North Korea as fellow nonaligned states. In addition to helping the Soviet Union resupply Arab states after wars with Israel in 1967 and 1973, Yugoslavia has fully backed the Palestine Liberation Organization. In 1985, U.S. Secretary of State George Shultz angrily and publicly criticized his Yugoslav counterpart in Belgrade for his refusal to extradite Mahmoud Abdul Abbas, wanted in connection with the hijacking of the *Achille Lauro*.[34] During the 1988 session of the UN General Assembly, a commentary in the newspaper *Borba* sharply criticized the American ambassador to the United Nations, Vernon Walters, for stating that the nonaligned "are not nonaligned. They are united against the United States."[35]

Yugoslavia's commitment to nonalignment has been the subject of debate within the country. The late Croatian Communist leader Vladimir Bakaric expressed skepticism about the claims of some states to be authentically nonaligned. He scoffed at the "socialist" claims of such states and suggested that Yugoslavia's contribution to nonalignment would be best realized by adapting to "world market conditions" instead of supporting nonaligned economic initiatives.[36] In a 1986 interview, the chairman of the Federal Executive Committee, Ante Markovic, called for Yugoslavia's deeper involvement in the "Alps-Adriatic Work Community" as a means of "our internal strengthening" and the "socialization of our unified foreign policy."[37] This organization was created to promote functional cooperation among a regional group of states and federal units. Because of the group's commitment to Western-style integration, membership of Yugoslavia's western republics provoked controversy. For Markovic, the commercial, cultural, and scientific cooperation typified by the Alpen-Adriatic Community represented a form of "opening up to the rest of the world" that was retarded by the "fears" of unnamed Yugoslav officials whose "rigid schemes" of foreign policy were inappropriate to accelerated development.

It is not surprising that these views were contested by Yugoslavs from the less developed republics. The dilemma is long-standing. In 1974, the Slovenian premier, Stane Kavcic, was ousted for allegedly attempting to make Slovenia "an economic appendage of Western Europe," among other political errors.[38] More recently, the Slovenian president, Janez Stanovnik, criticized the federal government's secretive preparations for the Ninth Summit of Nonaligned Nations scheduled for Belgrade in 1989 and for "errors and illusions" of the nonaligned regarding Europe.[39] In rebuttal, former foreign minister Milos Minic criticized the "dual track" foreign policy implied by Stanovnik.

The most controversial set of questions concerning nonalignment has arisen from Yugoslavia's relations with the European Community (EC). Despite Yugoslavia's renewed commitmentto economic cooperation with the nonaligned, the overall share of Yugoslavia's exports to developing countries fell from 20.8 percent in 1982 to 14.5 percent in 1987, and imports declined from 22 percent to only 13 percent.[40] Meanwhile, developing countries' debt to Yugoslavia reached $3.8 billion, nearly a fifth of Yugoslavia's total debt to industrial countries. Concurrently, Yugoslavia's exports to the EC increased 17 percent between 1987 and 1988, (to a total of 38 percent of all exports), while imports increased only 4 percent to $4.3 billion—for a balance-of-payments deficit of $183 million.[41]

EC-Yugoslav relations have been regulated by a series of five-year agreements that provide substantial commercial concessions for Yugoslav products, social and legal benefits for Yugoslav workers in Western Europe, and most-favored-nation status for EC imports to

Yugoslavia.[42] Many Yugoslav economists, particularly those in Slovenia and Croatia, have argued that only closer association with the EC can offer a means of resolving the economy's structural problems. The urgency of the situation has increased as a result of the economic crisis in Yugoslavia and the EC's scheduled integration in 1992.

Most recently the Nineteenth Plenum of the LCY Central Committee in December 1988 called for associate membership status in the EC. The meaning of "associate membership" is not entirely clear. Presumably, it would broaden the treaty arrangements Yugoslavia enjoys with the EC as well as indefinitely extend commercial preferences with the Common Market, which are now negotiated periodically. The policy of seeking closer ties with the EC remains controversial. Ranko Petkovic observes the existence of

> two voices today, a majority of which are from Slovenia although not all are from there, that claim Yugoslavia should turn more towards West Europe . . . [and it follows] as an automatic reflex almost always that this would mean a sacrifice of nonalignment and defacto *Anschluss* to the West. But also vice versa: that the increase of trade with the eastern countries [would intensify] . . . as omens of a possible rapprochement to the East and, yes, even a return to the long left ideological family circle.[43]

Adoption of the economic reforms in December 1988 coincided with the most far-ranging negotiations between Yugoslavia and the EC conducted to date. Talks on economic relations were held at the ministerial level in the Council for Cooperation between Yugoslavia and the EC, and political talks were held between Federal Secretary for Foreign Affairs Budimir Loncar and the Greek foreign minister, who spoke for the EC. The economic talks reaffirmed

> the unique treaty status Yugoslavia enjoys with EC as a non-aligned, European and Mediterranean developing country, which in practice means maintaining its present privileges at a time when the community is defining and redefining its relations with nonmembers [and] stresses the significance of economic reform which is in progress in Yugoslavia and whose fundamental preoccupation is a market economy and a wider inclusion in contemporary world and in particular the European economy.[44]

The talks included additional matters of finance and commerce involving Yugoslavia. The impact of the EC in shaping the economic reform in Yugoslavia is unmistakable. The head of the EC delegation in Belgrade, Marc Janssens, stressed the "essential" importance of reform legislation in making Yugoslavia attractive to European investors and its "application to all republics and provinces."[45] EC-Yugoslav economic talks coincided with political talks related to nonalignment—that is North-South economic relations, U.S.-Soviet relations, and the organization of a Middle East peace conference. Reportedly, the political exchange recognized "very similar views" on these questions.

Nonalignment continues to be important for maintaining Yugoslavia's political independence from the superpowers. Within Yugoslavia, the debate about the depth of commitment to the Nonaligned Movement is a result of growing diplomatic demands of the movement itself and the development of West European independence from the United States. By the late 1980s, the cost of Yugoslavia's involvement in the Nonaligned Movement and its distance from Western Europe became unacceptable to Yugoslavia's developed republics. This situation could be resolved if Yugoslavia relinquished its leadership role among the nonaligned countries or ceased to recognize any contradiction between nonalignment and closer participation with Europe.

REGIONAL ASPECTS

Yugoslav authorities consistently promote the idea that the countries of the Balkans have been the victims of extraregional involvement and that only nonalignment offers protection from foreign subordination. Condemnation of the "Yalta system" or "spheres of influence" in regard to the region has been a consistent theme in Yugoslav foreign policy. Evidence of this is seen in Western reports of Soviet intentions to invade Yugoslavia, suggestions for joint U.S.-Soviet accord over Eastern Europe, and the notorious "Sonnenfeldt Doctrine" recommending an "organic link" between the USSR and Eastern Europe.[46]

Yet if Yugoslavs are concerned about the consequences of a Yalta style agreement for their independence, they are no less fearful of superpower rivalry, especially under conditions in which the region would become a "grey zone" of intervention. The former Yugoslav foreign minister, Josip Vrhovec, referred to this image in an address to the Federal Assembly shortly after the Soviet-supported Vietnamese invasion of Cambodia: "The strengthening of security on the European continent is impossible if military interventions, organized foreign domination and hegemony spread . . . should these principles [sovereignty, independence, noninterference, territorial integrity and inviolability of frontiers] not be respected, the Balkan area could turn into a special 'grey zone' in which foreign countries would try to demonstrate their presence."[47] Vrhovec also mentioned the importance of the 1955 Soviet-Yugoslav Declaration, which committed the Soviet Union to respect Yugoslavia's "sovereignty, independence and territorial integrity."

Yugoslavia's perception of its position emphasizes both a Mediterranean and a Balkan dimension. Radovan Pavic offers an example of the Mediterranean aspect.[48] To the extent that Yugoslavia may be said to pursue a Mediterranean policy, it has involved several components. The first is a commitment to organizing a group of nonaligned Mediterranean states, including Cyprus, Malta, and those of North Africa and the Middle East, and an attempt to represent their views through the CSCE process.[49] In addition, Belgrade has organized conferences of Mediterranean foreign ministers and, in 1984, a conference of twenty-eight "Progressive Parties and Movements of the Mediterranean," a group that emphasized the "connection and interdependence of Mediterranean developments and general development of the world, especially in Europe with the Balkans, the Middle East and Africa." Yugoslav policy has also endeavored to promote certain functional areas within the Mediterranean, such as commercial exchange, investment, energy, and tourism.

Yugoslav proposals for Mediterranean disarmament fall into four areas.[50] Confidence-building measures seek to win acceptance of several propositions by all major powers. They include (1) the notification of littoral states twenty-one days prior to major naval exercises; (2) acceptance of on-board observers from littoral states or the joint participation in such exercises of vessels belonging to other nonaligned countries; and (3) the inclusion of all significant military forces under regulations of the Helsinki Final Act such as prior notification of military maneuvers and similar confidence-building measures. A second set of proposals seeks to freeze the military budgets of the superpowers and to reduce fleets to bring about a "balanced reduction of military forces." A third proposal aims to commit the superpowers not to create additional military forces in the region. Finally, Yugoslav spokesmen have considered a "non-nuclear" Mediterranean as an eventual goal.

NATO forces are not likely to show interest in these proposals. But in an address to the Yugoslav Federal Assembly on March 16, 1988, General Secretary Gorbachev proposed limiting the "naval potential" of Soviet and U.S. fleets in the Mediterranean, requiring advance notice of naval exercises and unspecified "principles and methods" to protect shipping lanes.[51] In June the previous year, Foreign Minister Shevardnadze had proposed a U.S.-Soviet ban on the transport of nuclear weapons. It is unclear whether Soviet support could make Yugoslavia's ideas of naval disarmament more acceptable. The Soviet initiative helps promote proposals among nonaligned Mediterranean states. It also draws attention to the fact that this and other Soviet initiatives are unacceptable without substantial troop reductions in central Europe as well as a reduction of tension in the Middle East.

In the past, Yugoslav perceptions of its Balkan identity had minimal impact on foreign policy. As recently as 1976, Yugoslav officials insisted that the government had "no special Balkan policy."[52] Thus, Yugoslav policy considers the region an aggregate of individual states with whom Yugoslavia carries on bilateral relations. This perception is gradually changing with the development of Balkan multilateralism.[53]

In 1988, Yugoslavia was host for the Balkan Foreign Ministers Conference. The conference discussed a number of common problems, including economic, cultural, scientific, environmental and transport policy. The contentious issue of a chemical- and nuclear-weapons-free zone was deferred. Bulgarian Foreign Minister Petar Mladenov proposed a "multilateral moratorium and subsequent cuts of military expenditures [and] the establishment of a hot-line between heads of state, ministers of defense and border troops to prevent undesired incidents."[54] The communique of the conference implicitly endorsed a traditional Yugoslav perception of security enunciated by Ljubisa Adamovic at a 1972 conference on European security in Varna: "The *basic dilemma* concerning the evolution of relations in Europe [is]: will there be a gradual *transformation* into a basically new system of relations *or* will there be a *de facto preservation* of the structure with some unavoidable adjustments which do not affect its essence [emphasis in original]."[55] To achieve such a "transformation," Adamovic had called for "functional integration" and warned against U.S.-USSR "bilateralism" and the "imposition of a 'condominium' on third countries."

The conference's communique approached the question of minorities obliquely, stating "that national minorities, in the Balkan countries on whose territories they exist, should be a factor of cohesion, stability, friendly relations, and cooperation."[56] Of course, the question is on "whose territories" do they exist? Albania's support for republican status of Kosovo would imply elevating this "nationality" to a constituent "nation" of Yugoslavia. Greece and Bulgaria deny that a distinct Macedonian national identity exists.

Before the conference, the chairman of the LCY Commission for International Cooperation, Dobrivoje Vidic, condemned Albania for fostering "Greater Albania designs on Kosovo." He asked pessimistically, "What is the extent to which unsettled questions in bilateral relations among Balkan countries influence the realization of multilateral objectives[?]"[57] The LCY Macedonian representative, Vasil Tupurkovski, answered the question elsewhere: "Relations [in the Balkans] will depend on how these minorities are treated with the context of *our revolutionary criteria* of settling the national question [emphasis added]."[58]

In view of the tense national situation in Macedonia, Tupurkovski's remark is understandable, but it does not bode well for interstate cooperation. It was, therefore, especially significant that Albanian Foreign Minister Reis Malile acknowledged that minority problems were "one of the problems that has made and continues to make it difficult for Balkan countries to establish open, sincere and truly friendly and promising relations among them. Certainly the stance towards minorities and their treatment is an internal question of each country, a field of its complete sovereignty."[59]

The promise of continued Balkan cooperation remains intact. Early in 1989, the deputy foreign ministers of the Balkan states met in Tirana to reaffirm the objectives of the 1988 conference, to confirm a second foreign ministers' summit for 1990 in Tirana, and to schedule a series of ministerial meetings in many areas of functional interest.

Finally, Yugoslavia's regional diplomacy includes its activity within the European Conference on Security and Cooperation (CSCE). From the outset, Yugoslavia has sought to advance CSCE proposals in disarmament, human rights, and economic cooperation through cooperation with neutral and nonaligned states.[60] An exhaustive content analysis of all CSCE speeches of delegates between 1974 and 1980 demonstrates an increasing coincidence of views among neutral, nonaligned, and Mediterranean states.[61] The 1988 CSCE follow-up meeting in Vienna accepted neutral and nonaligned proposals in ecology and human rights, as well as some disarmament recommendations. Yugoslav Ambassador Ignac Golob took particular satisfaction that "collective rights of national minorities have indirectly been recognized for the first time and the rights of national minorities have been entered into chapters of human contacts, information, culture and education."[62] The influence of Yugoslavia within the CSCE process is necessarily limited, but, unlike diplomatic activity, CSCE participation does not provoke domestic controversy.

THE REPUBLICS AND FOREIGN POLICY

Yugoslavia's role in Southeastern Europe also involves the activity of the republics in implementation of the country's foreign policy. Since the passage of a series of constitutional amendments in 1968, the republics and autonomous regions have taken an active role in broadening foreign economic relations and representing the interests of Yugoslav minorities in neighboring states.[63] Hungary, Italy, and Austria have received republican representatives acting on behalf of common conationals. By contrast, Romania's assimilationalist policies toward Serbs and other non-Rumanian groups have strained relations with Belgrade, and Greek and Bulgarian refusal to recognize the Macedonian nationality remains a source of conflict with the Macedonian People's Republic.

The case of Slovenia's relations with Austria's Carinthian Slovenians demonstrates the potential for republican activity in foreign policy. After years of intermittent polemics between Yugoslavia and Austria concerning the latter's observance of minority guarantees in the Austrian State Treaty, foreign ministers Vrhovec and Pahr marked a breakthrough in 1979.[64] Austria guaranteed "respect" for the rights of its Slovenian and Croatian minorities and recognized the "great significance of contacts . . . between Yugoslav socialist republics and autonomous provinces and Austrian federal lands."[65] Despite the promise, results did not meet Yugoslav expectations, and in 1984 Slovenian President Mitja Ribicic denounced Austria's minority policy as "a shame for modern Europe and a challenge to democracy."[66] Evidently the republic, not the federation, had become the principal spokesman on the question.

The potential for conflict between republican foreign policies is clear. Despite repeated denunciation of "Khomeini socialism" and Iran's charge of "persecution" of Muslims in Yugoslavia, the Iranian president, Ali Khamenei, met with leading officials of the Muslim republican organizations in Sarajevo and led prayers in its main mosque.[67] Meanwhile the Slovenian assembly "sharply condemned" Khomeini's death threat against Salman Rushdie for the book *Satanic Verses*. Also there is little doubt that Serbian and some federal officials considered cultural relations between Albania and Kosovo to have been disruptive. Cultural relations were suspended after the 1981 demonstrations in Kosovo and Macedonia, and they were only resumed recently. New amendments to the Serbian constitution specify that "the autonomous provinces realize international cooperation within the framework of the international cooperation of the SR

Serbia."[68] At the same time, Montenegro is free to export its manufactured goods to Albania and import relatively cheap power from
Albania for an alumina complex at Titograd.

Ties between Montenegro and Albania are strategically important;
in 1979, Tirana and Belgrade agreed to complete a 476-kilometer
rail link between Shkoder and Titograd, linking Albanian railroads
with the rest of Europe, which was inaugurated in 1986. Direct trade
between Albania and Montenegro reached a level of $125 million by
1980, about a third of Albania's total trade with Yugoslavia and double
the amount of trade with Kosovo.[69] At a session of the Montenegrin
Presidency, Veljko Milatovic praised the republic's "intensive" role in
relations with Albania.[70] There is little doubt that federal officials
encouraged Montenegro's involvement.

The extent of indebtedness to foreign banks and governments by
the less developed republics remains controversial, because such loans
must be repaid in convertible currency, which is disproportionately
earned by the developed republics. From the overall viewpoint of
Yugoslavia, the differences in trade orientation of the republics may
be more important than the distribution of foreign debt. For example, by the early 1980s, Montenegro's trade with the predominantly socialist clearing area stood at 72 percent, while the federation's percentage amounted to 49 percent.[71] Macedonia's trade with
the clearing area was 63.3 percent in 1981, although it fell to 54.9
percent in 1984.[72]

The level of Soviet contact with individual republics has increased
following Gorbachev's visit to Yugoslavia in 1988. Politburo member
Vitaliy Vorotnikov visited Montenegro and Serbia in April. In a
meeting with Slobodan Milosevic, Vorotnikov spoke of relations between Serbia and the Russian Soviet Federated Republic as "an important supplementary channel" to federal relations, expressed in Soviet
technological and economic assistance and "a jointly written document" for relations through 1990.[73] Serbian trade with the Soviet
Union currently amounts to about 41 percent of total Soviet-Yugoslav
trade.[74] Vorotnikov added that bilateral republican cooperation was
"reinforced" by "direct contacts" between Krasnodar territory and
Vojvodina, Dagestan and Kosovo, Moscow and Belgrade, and Kursk
and Titovo Uzice. Although Slovenia's share of trade with the Soviet
Union is relatively small compared with that of other republics, the
chairman of Slovenia's Executive Council visited Belorussia and Moscow in 1988, where he was received by Nikolai Ryzhkov, the Soviet
chairman of the Council of Ministers.[75]

These contacts at the regional level, which have great potential economic value for both sides, can be expected to grow more frequent in the future, but this development presents several distinct problems for Yugoslav foreign policy. One problem concerns the integrity of nonalignment. Greater republican autonomy in the conduct of foreign economic policy has been accompanied by a tendency for the less developed republics to trade with Communist countries and for the more developed to trade with Western Europe. Second, greater republican involvement in foreign trade and investment may undermine the fragile unity of the Yugoslav market and the implementation of common economic policies. Some foreign institutions, such as the International Monetary Fund, can deal only with the federal government. Finally, republican developments concerning minorities in neighboring states will increasingly affect the conduct of foreign policy and the prospects for Balkan cooperation.

RECENT DEVELOPMENTS AND U.S. POLICY

U.S. foreign policy has traditionally sought to maintain Yugoslavia's territorial integrity and political stability and to support Yugoslavia's independence from the Soviet Union. In an interview in the fall of 1988, the former U.S. deputy assistant secretary of state, Thomas Simons, Jr., recognized the country as "very important for the United States" and recalled the 1948 break with the Soviet Union: "This development was of great strategic signification [*sic*] and in the years since has proved to be an important factor in preserving the peace in Europe. The stability of this situation has been and remains the primary goal of the United States in its relations with Yugoslavia."[76]

For Simons, a corollary of this goal was to "encourage political pluralism and systemic market reform." Simons's statement followed a meeting between U.S. Secretary of State George Shultz and Federal Secretary of Foreign Affairs Loncar. Shultz first expressed concern about Yugoslav domestic events to Loncar, mentioning the situation in Kosovo. According to David Binder, "The message was that while Washington felt the problems were essentially an internal matter, Yugoslavia's credibility as an economic partner was being damaged."[77]

The United States soon became indirectly involved in Yugoslavia's domestic situation. Within a few days of the Shultz-Loncar meeting, Slovenian President Janez Stanovnik sharply criticized political developments in Serbia in an interview granted to the *New York Times*.[78] In a subsequent address to the National Press Club in Washington, Stanovnik spoke of the importance of the "full-fledged development of democracy," while fearing that demonstrations had left the country "truly on the edge of civil war."[79] The comments were condemned by Belgrade's *Politika* as an "anti-Serbian outburst [that was] slanderous, absurd, and full of malice."[80] Stanovnik was implicitly appealing to the West for support against Milosevic.

The Bush administration will apparently continue the Reagan administration policy. At his confirmation hearings, Under Secretary of State Lawrence Eagleburger was questioned about Kosovo. He admitted the "very dangerous" situation created by Serbian party leader Milosevic, adding, "There's no question in my mind that the Albanians are more sinned against than sinning." But he also spoke of the need for "caution": "If I know anything about Yugoslavia, it's when you come at them not to do something that is precisely the time they'll go ahead and do it. All I'm really saying here is this is an issue we ought to be talking to Belgrade about."[81] Eagleburger acknowledged the problem Yugoslavia represents for U.S. concerns about human-rights practices. In its 1988 *Country Reports on Human Rights Practices*, the State Department noted recent violations, including the trial of several journalists of the Slovene youth magazine *Mladina*. The report estimates the number of political prisoners to be between 500 and 1,000, and it states that authorities "have been more willing" recently to discuss particular cases. As Yugoslavia's economic crisis worsens, Western opportunities to influence the authorities may also increase, either through the International Monetary Fund or through the provisions of credits for imports of emergency provisions.

In late March shortly after Eagleburger's remarks, armed clashes in Kosovo between Albanians and security forces left twenty people dead.[82] The *Economist* noted that within Yugoslavia few non-Serb Yugoslavs believed the official explanation that the Kosovo events amounted to an organized revolt inspired in Tirana.[83] The event further exacerbated the mutual resentment between the Serbian political leadership and Yugoslavs who consider Serbian behavior at once brutal and demagogic. The Slovenian Communist Milan Kucan remarked that "the lives lost in Kosovo are on the conscience of Yugoslavia."[84]

The deterioration in nationality relations in Yugoslavia coincided with its prolonged economic crisis, which has given new urgency to the problems of foreign trade. With an inflation rate in excess of 200 percent in 1988, the value of the dinar fell from about 15 dinars to the U.S. dollar in 1980 to approximately 6,500 dinars in 1988 and drastically limited internal sources of investment capital.[85] External debt and the need to prevent economic collapse have made exports critical. According to the Yugoslav economist Davor Savin, "Exports have become an exorganic [exogenous] category, and they can no longer be manipulated so as to adjust other macroeconomic aggregates . . . . Maintenance of external liquidity requires the opposite approach, that is, adjustment of other aggregates to exports, which must increase literally at any cost."[86] But the prospects are poor, he adds, because of excessive demand on the internal market. "Fewer than a third [of Yugoslav firms] are able to export at prices higher than on the domestic market." To make exports more competitive requires structural changes, the elimination of unprofitable firms, and the import of new technology. New technology, in turn, requires more exports.

The economic crisis has thus become the central concern of Yugoslavia's foreign policy. Foreign Secretary Loncar has described Yugoslavia's "key shortcoming" in foreign policy as "insufficiently translating [global economic trends] into our internal situation." Thus, Loncar stressed the imperative of "insuring a greater [commercial] exchange with foreign partners and their greater preparedness for cooperation in ways which will have an impact on our economic reform." Yugoslavia's ability to carry out this objective requires close cooperation with Western market economies, and the confidence of their governments that Yugoslavia is committed to respect for human rights. Not only have the United States and Albania been concerned about the situation in Kosovo, but the European Parliament has condemned Yugoslavia's use of force against the protesters—a fact certain to affect Yugoslavia's suitability as an economic partner with Western Europe.[87]

The most challenging problem for U.S. foreign policy, however, may be the attitude of the Soviet Union. Soviet efforts to win influence in the armed forces and in Serbia have already been described. *Izvestia* has implicitly supported the Milosevic leadership by its description of a mass rally in November 1988 in Belgrade as "an earnest discussion."[88] *Izvestia* also supported Serbia's viewpoint by describing the Kosovo uprising as a "conspiracy," implying support for a policy of violent repression.[89] The extent and consequences of Soviet support for Milosevic are difficult to judge. Nevertheless, *Izvestia* and other Soviet accounts have not been reticent in describing Albanian "terrorism" as the source of the problem in Kosovo. In brief, there are indications that Moscow has taken an approach to the Kosovo situation opposite to that of the United States.

During the 1970s, scenarios for a post-Tito Yugoslavia focused on the danger of national disintegration followed by Soviet intervention. Although the possibility of direct Soviet intervention has diminished, the threat of national disintegration and political upheaval in Yugoslavia is now more relevant. Two sets of scenarios are suggested by Radovan Vukadinovic and Marijana Koroshica.[90] Vukadinovic considers external developments decisive. He envisages several possible outcomes:

1. A *"Yalta formula" model* in which Yugoslavia would become the object of a superpower "settlement" delineating U.S.-Soviet interests and reducing rivalry. Vukadinovic considers this scenario unlikely because the necessary superpower cohesion is lacking. Also the nature of such an agreement is difficult to imagine.

2. A *"regional" model* emphasizing the destabilizing economic developments in Eastern Europe generally and demanding radical economic reform. This scenario emphasizes the difficulty of all socialist states in overcoming economic and political stagnation. Closer commercial relations with Western Europe and domestic reform are thus appropriate for Yugoslavia.

3. A *"Balkan" model* in which Yugoslavia would divide into a "Greater Serbia" and "Greater Albania." Vukadinovic avoids explaining any details of the territorial concessions involved by the creation of successor states to Yugoslavia. Presumably they would require external support and perhaps a federative arrangement of the western republics.

Koroshica also suggests these scenarios for Yugoslavia:

1. A *"prolonged crisis"* of declining living standards and the strengthening of "nationalistic movements, bureaucratic centralism, and national confrontation."

2. A *"program of economic reform"* characterized by the "independence of economic subjects and a steady narrowing of the guardianship of politics over the economy."

3. A *"radical change" program* whose "essence is economic efficiency regardless of ideological coloration and the integrity of the system." Like Vukadinovic's second scenario, Koroshica's third scenario would mean closer affiliation of Yugoslavia (or certain republics) with the EC.

Yugoslavia's greatest challenge is to make sure that the promise of economic reform outweighs the appeals of national separatism. The greatest threat to Yugoslav integrity consists less in a prolonged "muddling through" than in a sudden outbreak of violence that could not be quickly suppressed. Surely if any national leadership were to detach itself from the federation, a civil war could become inevitable. The threat of military intervention, however, may have a prophylactic effect in limiting the claims of republican leaders. Now that Slovenian Janez Drnovsek has become chairman of the State Presidency, debate about EC and European Free Trade Association affiliation is likely to intensify, in view of his commitment to eventual membership.[91]

Supporting the goals of pluralism and stability in Yugoslavia represents a major challenge for the United States. More specifically, conditions for stability will require an improvement in Yugoslavia's economic situation, yet it is unclear how this can be achieved. Beyond bilateral talks with Belgrade, Washington would be wise to seek a common front with Western Europe, maintain lines of communication with all major actors in Yugoslavia, and counsel their patience. The success of such a policy will require continued U.S.-Soviet dialogue about European disarmament and security.

NOTES

Radovan Vukadinović 's valuable comments made an important contribution to my study. I am much indebted also to Paul S. Shoup for his numerous helpful comments and assistance in the various drafts of my paper.

1. John Berryman, "The Soviet Union and Yugoslavia's Defense and Foreign Policy," in Marko Milivojevic, John Allcock, and Pierre Maurer, eds., *Yugoslavia's Security Dilemmas* (Oxford: Berg, 1988), 194.
2. *Khrushchev Remembers: The Last Testament*, Strobe Talbott, ed. (Hammondsworth: Penguin, 1977), 224, cited in ibid., 195.
3. Beatrice Heuser, "Yugoslavia in Western Military Planning 1948–1953," cited in ibid., 150.
4. Address of President Tito to the Yugoslav National Assembly, October 25, 1954, cited in *Documents on International Affairs 1954*, Denise Folliot, ed. (London: Oxford University Press, 1957), 205. The pro-Soviet, neo-Cominform "Communist Party of Yugoslavia" called for renunciation of the pact at its clandestine 1975 congress in Bar.
5. Andrew Borowiec, *Yugoslavia After Tito* (New York: Praeger, 1977), 68.
6. *New York Times*, August 25, 1968.
7. Besides regularly exchanging military delegations, Yugoslavia and Romania have collaborated in the production of the *Orao*, a twin-jet fighter. Radio Bucharest, April 12, 1969, in FBIS (Foreign Broadcast Information Service), East European Series, April 14, 1969, cited in Alex Alexiev, *Romania and the Warsaw Pact: The Defense Policy of a Reluctant Ally* P-6270 (Santa Monica: Rand Corporation, 1979), 15.
8. ATA (Tirana) 900 Greenwich mean time (GMT), January 19, 1981, in FBIS East European Series, July 1, 1981.
9. TANJUG, Domestic Service 1957 GMT, November 24, 1981, in FBIS, East European Series, November 25, 1981.
10. A. Ross Johnson, "The Role of the Military in Yugoslavia: An Historical Sketch," in *Soldiers, Peasants and Bureaucrats: Civil-Military Relations in Communist and Modernizing Societies*, Roman Kolkowicz and Andrzej Korbonski, eds. (London: Allen and Unwin, 1982), 186.

11. *Brassy's Defense and Foreign Affairs Handbook 1987–88*, Gregory R. Copley, ed. (Washington, D.C.: Perth Corporation, 1988), 1139.

12. *International Herald Tribune*, March 6, 1978, cited in Adam Roberts, "The Yugoslav Experiment in All-People's Defense," *R.U.S.I and Brassy's Defense Yearbook 1978–79* (London: Brassy's Ltd., 1978) 112.

13. Robin Alison Remington, "Political Military Relations in Post-Tito Yugoslavia," in *Yugoslavia in the 1980's*, Pedro Ramet, ed. (Boulder, Colo.: Westview, 1985), 60-2.

14. *New York Times*, May 14, 1976, and Berryman, "The Soviet Union and Yugoslavia's Defense and Foreign Policy," 203.

15. *Borba*, December 7, 1975, in *Survival* 18, no. 3 (June 1976): 117.

16. Ted Greenwood, Harold Feiveson, and Theodore Taylor, *Nuclear Proliferation* (New York: McGraw-Hill, 1977), 129, 151.

17. Robert Bartos, "National Security," in *Yugoslavia: A Country Study*, Richard F. Nyrop, ed. (Washington, D.C.: U.S. Government Printing Office, 1981), 236.

18. Cited in "Marshal Kulikov's Exclusive Interview with *Danas*," *Radio Free Europe Research*, Yugoslavia SR/3 (May 4, 1987): 31.

19. Joseph S. Roucek, "Geopolitical Trends in Central-Eastern Europe," *Annals of the American Academy of Political and Social Science*, no. 271 (September 1950): 40.

20. *Krasnaya Zvezda*, October 29, 1988, cited in Milan Andrejevich, "The Latest Developments in Yugoslav-Soviet Relations," *Radio Free Europe Research*, Yugoslavia SR/11 (December 2, 1988): 26.

21. Pedro Ramet, "The Soviet Factor in the Macedonian Dispute," *Survey* 24, no. 3 (Summer 1979): 131-2.

22. Cited in "Yugoslav Defense Minister Warns Neighboring Countries," *Radio Free Europe Research*, Yugoslavia SR/1 (January 18, 1988): 20.

23. Branko Mamula, "The Irrevocable Yugoslav Course," *Socialist Thought and Practice* 27, no. 1-2 (January–February 1987): 35. According to Sam C. Sarkesian, the low-intensity conflict includes "the range of activities and operations on the low end of the conflict spectrum involving the use of military or a variety of semi-military forces (both combat and non-combat) on the part of the intervening power to influence and compel the adversary to accept a particular political-military condition," cited in Richard M. Swain, "Square Pegs from Round Holes: Low Intensity Conflict in Army Doctrine," *Military Review* 67, no. 12 (December 1987): 9.

24. Marko Milivojevic, "The Political Role of the Yugoslav People's Army in Contemporary Yugoslavia," in Milivojevic, Allcock, and Maurer, eds. *Yugoslavia's Security Dilemmas*, 16–27.

25. Ibid., 29.

26. "*Specijalni Rat*," *Vojna Enciklopedija* 9 (Belgrade: Vojna izdavacka zavod 1975), 7.

27. The trial of the Slovene students coincided with a number of objections to political developments in Slovenia which YPA spokesmen had criticized: Slobodan Stankovic, "The Role of the Army," *Radio Free Europe Research*, Yugoslavia SR/4 (June 4, 1987): 12 [Slovene disinterest in the YPA]; *Borba*, October 22–3, 1988, in FBIS-EEU–88–207 (October 26, 1987): 57 [proposal for "territorialization" of the YPA]; TANJUG, Domestic Service 1839 GMT (October 17, 1988), in FBIS-EEU–88–206 (October 25, 1988): 51. [objections to financing the YPA independently of the federal budget]; *Borba*, September 27–8, 1988, in FBIS-EEU–88–176 (September 12, 1988): 80 [trial of Slovenes].

28. *Politika*, September 2, 1988, in FBIS-EEU–88–176 (September 12, 1988): 81.

29. A 1986 article in *Danas* revealed certain instances in which the committees had "overstepped their authority" in confronting "hostile demonstrations" or had been activated in the face of labor unrest. *Danas*, December 9, 1986, in *JPRS*-EER–87–027 (Joint Publication Research Service, East European Report, Political, Sociological, and Military Affairs) (February 17, 1987): 96.

30. Marko Milivojevic, "The Yugoslav People's Army: Another Jaruzelski on the Way," *South Slav Journal* 11, no. 2–3 (Summer-Autumn 1988): 13.

31. Milovan Djilas, *Rise and Fall* (San Diego: Harcourt Brace Jovanovich, 1985), 311.

32. "The Brioni Document," July 19, 1956, cited in Leo Mates, *Nonalignment—Theory and Current Policy* (Dobbs Ferry: Oceana, 1972), 379.
33. William Zimmerman, *Open Borders, Nonalignment and the Political Evolution of Yugoslavia* (Princeton, N.J.: Princeton University Press, 1987), 27.
34. *Keesing's Contemporary Archives* 32(December 1985): 34632.
35. *Borba*, January 19, 1989 in FBIS-*EEU*–89–019 (January 31, 1989): 87.
36. According to Bakaric, adapting to world market conditions was essential for Yugoslavia's nonalignment; "if we fail to achieve that, all our crying for cooperation with the nonaligned and developing countries will have been in vain because then our system will not suit them." *Borba*, August 16, 1981.
37. *Vjesnik*, November 28–30, 1986, in JPRS-EER–87–019 (February 27, 1987): 53.
38. *Borba*, September 20, 1972, cited in Slobodan Stankovic, "After the Slovenian Central Committee Plenum," *Radio Free Europe Research* (November 8, 1972): 1. The disagreement between Stanovnik and Minic was not simply a matter of abstract principles. Despite the absence of diplomatic relations between Yugoslavia and South Korea, Seoul and Ljubjana had exchanged permanent commercial commissions, in apparent defiance of the nonaligned boycott of South Korea. *Danas*, February 14, 1989.
39. *Danas*, February 21, 1989.
40. Vuk Ognjanovic, "Yugoslavia and the Developing Countries," *Review of International Affairs* 29, no. 929 (December 20, 1988): 1. See also Marijan Svetlicic, "Economic Cooperation Among the Developing Countries as a Factor of their Security," *Review of International Affairs* 29, no. 919 (July 5–20, 1988): 23–25.
41. Milodrag Trajkovic, "Nova etapa u odnosima Jugoslavije i Evropske zajednice," *Medjunarodna politika* 30, no. 931 (January 15, 1989): 5.
42. For a comprehensive description of Yugoslav-EC agreements, see "Economic Relations between Yugoslavia and the European Economic Community (Institutional Frameworks)," *Yugoslav Survey* 28, no. 1 (1987): 75–101.
43. *Danas*, January 19, 1988, cited in Jens Reuter, "Jugoslawien und Europa," *Sudosteuropa* 37, no. 5 (1988): 23.
44. Trajkovic, "Nova etapa u odnosima Jugoslavij i Evropske zajednice," 6.
45. *Danas*, February 21, 1989.
46. On the origins and reaction of the "Sonnenfeldt Doctrine," see Joseph S. Nye, Jr., *The Making of America's Soviet Policy* (New Haven: Yale University Press, 1984), 192–3.
47. *Borba*, November 1, 1979. See also Stevan K. Pavlowitch, "The Grey Zone on NATO's Balkan Flank," *Survey* 26, no. 3 (Summer 1980): 40.
48. Radovan Pavic, "Osnove suvremenih geopolitickih odnosa u bazenu sredozemlja," *Nase teme* 21, no. 3 (1977): 603–5, 610. Pavic offered a detailed description of Mediterranean geopolitics from a Yugoslav viewpoint. He warned that Yugoslavia could become an "object of speculation or eventual Soviet military intervention" if the Soviet Union were transformed into a "direct Mediterranean power."
49. See "Belgrade CSCE Communique 9 March 1978," *Survival* 20, no. 3 (May-June 1978): 131–3; and Mihajlo Javorski, "Yugoslavia and the CSCE," *Review of International Affairs*, 21, no. 732 (October 5, 1980): 1–4.
50. Radovan Vukadinovic, "Tri nivoa aktivnost u pravcu mira i sigurnost; na Mediteranu," *Pomorski zbornik* 24 (1986): 78–80. Also, Ksenija Klaric, "Mediteran Na KESS-u," *Pomorski zbornik* 24 (1986): 53–62. This article offers a history of preparatory talks of Mediterranean states regarding CSCE.
51. Cited in Douglas Clarke, "Gorbachev's Mediterranean Proposals," *Radio Free Europe Research*, RAD Background Report/54 (March 25, 1988): 1.
52. Borowiec, *Yugoslavia After Tito*, 70. A Yugoslav professor, Branimir M. Jankovic, has written that the idea that geopolitical significance of the region was generally held by outsiders "who want to rule over these expanses, rather than that of the peoples who live there. . . . As applied to the Balkans, geopolitics has been far more interested in the history of the area than that of the indigenous peoples" (*The*

Balkans in International Relations, Margot and Bosko Milosavljevic, trans. [New York: St. Martin's, 1988], 2).

53. Ranko Petkovic, "Istorijski geostrateski polozaj i znacaj Balkana juce i danas," *Socijalizam* 31, no. 3 (1988): 74–5.
54. "Documentation," *Review of International Affairs*, 29, no. 910 (March 5, 1988): 22.
55. A. Acimovic and V. Glisic, "Intra-European Relations in the 1970s," in Lilita Dzirkals and A. Ross Johnson, eds., *Soviet and East European Forecasts of European Security: Papers for the 1972 Varna Conference*, R–1272–PR (Santa Monica: Rand Corporation, 1973), 43.
56. "Documentation," 16.
57. Dobrivoje Vidic, "What Are the Unsettled Questions in the Balkans?" *Review of International Affairs*, no. 906 (January 5, 1988): 8.
58. Vasil Tupurkovski, "We Want the Best Possible Relations with Our Neighbors," *Review of International Affairs*, no. 909 (February 20, 1988): 5.
59. "Documentation," 19.
60. Yugoslavia's policy toward the initial CSCE meetings is included in the speeches and documents collected in *Yugoslavia and European Security and Cooperation* (Belgrade: Medunarodna Politika, 1978).
61. Daniel Frei and Dieter Ruloff, *East-West Relations: A Systematic Survey*, vol. I (Cambridge: Oelgeschlager, Gunn & Hann, 1983), 16–21.
62. Ignac Golob, "On the Concluding Document of the Vienna CSCE Meeting," *Review of International Affairs* 40, no. 932 (February 5, 1989): 3.
63. The history and significance of the 1968 amendment and the transition to the 1974 document are discussed in Ivan Padjen and Bizidar Bakotic, *Vanski poslovi Jugoslavije* (Cakovec: Zrinski, 1972), 44–9, 65–9, and 81–9.
64. A background of the Slovene question from the Yugoslav viewpoint is provided in *Problem manjina u jugoslovensko-austrijskim odnosima* edited by Bogdan Osolnik, ed. (Belgrade, 1977); see also Thomas M. Barker, *The Slovene Minority of Carinthia* (Boulder, Colo.: East European Monographs, 1984).
65. TANJUG, Domestic Service, 1615 GMT, October 19, 1979, in FBIS-WEU (West European Series) (October 22, 1979): E–1.
66. *Delo*, August 27, 1984, in FBIS-EEU–84–170 (August 30, 1984): I–7.
67. *Borba*, February 22, 1989. See also Zdenko Antic, "Yugoslav Officials Concerned about Pan-Islamic Nationalism," *Radio Free Europe Research*, no. 64 (March 16, 1982); and Slobodan Stankovic, "Yugoslav Moslem Nationalists Condemned," *Radio Free Europe Research* no. 210 (September 2, 1983).
68. Amendment 29, *Nacrt amandmana na Ustav SFRJ*, *Borba*, Special Supplement, February 1, 1989.
69. *Rilindja*, February 22, 1981, in FBIS-EEU (February 26, 1981): I-5.
70. TANJUG (Domestic Service) 1401 GMT, (February 24, 1981), in FBIS-EEU (February 25, 1981): I–2.
71. "Robna razvenjena sa innostranstvom," *Mjesecni statisticki pregled*, Titograd 29, no. 9 (July 1981) (Supplement); and *Statisticki Godisnjak Jugoslavije* (Belgrade: Savezni zavod za statistiku, 1982), 310.
72. *Statisticheski godishnik SR Makedonija* (Skoplje: Republichki zavod za statistika, 1986), 267.
73. TASS (English) 1402 GMT (April 25, 1988), in FBIS-SOV–88–080 (April 26, 1988): 26.
74. TANJUG, 2001 GMT (January 27, 1989), in FBIS-EEU–89–018 (January 30, 1989): 57.
75. *Pravda*, October 5, 1988, in FBIS-SOV–88–193 (October 5, 1988): 33–4.
76. Thomas Simons, Jr., "The United States Supports Yugoslav Independence, Unity and Nonaligned Policy," *Review of International Affairs* 39, no. 927 (November 20, 1988): 2.
77. *New York Times*, October 12, 1988.
78. Ibid., October 15, 1988.

79. Cited in Milan Andrejevich, "Slovenia's State President Calls for Democracy," *Radio Free Europe Research*, Yugoslavia/10 (November 11, 1988): 27.
80. *Politika*, November 5, 1988, cited in ibid., 28.
81. "Confirmation Hearings of Lawrence Eagleburger, Deputy Secretary of State-Delegate," before the Senate Foreign Relations Committee, March 15, 1989 (processed).
82. *Washington Post*, April 3, 1989.
83. *Economist* (April 1, 1989): 41.
84. *Washington Post*, April 3, 1989.
85. James Seroka, "Socio-Political Deterioration and Economic Reform in Yugoslavia," unpublished paper read at International Studies Meeting, London, March 29–31, 1989, 6–7.
86. *Ekonomska Politika* (November 10, 1986), in JPRS-EER–87–005 (January 9, 1987): 25.
87. *Minutes of the Proceedings of the Plenary Session of the European Parliament*, April 13, 1989, 159.
88. *Izvestia*, November 22, 1988, in FBIS-SOV–88–225, (November 22, 1988): 30.
89. Ibid., March 7, 1989, in FBIS-SOV–89–053 (March 8, 1989): 27.
90. Radovan Vukadinovic, "Scenario of Yugoslavia's 'Disintegration,'" *Review of International Affairs* 39, no. 927 (November 20, 1988): 4–5. And Marijana Koroshica, "Tri scenarije moguce buducnosti," *NIN* (Nedeljne Informativne Novine), no. 1986 (January 22, 1989): 20–1.
91. Milan Andrejevic, "Slovenia Elects its State Presidency Member," *Radio Free Europe Research*, Yugoslavia/6 (April 15, 1989): 11.

8

THE SOUTHERN PERIPHERY: GREECE AND TURKEY

F. Stephen Larrabee

In the post-World War II period, the Balkans, especially the southern periphery, have been a source of instability and turmoil. Many American policymakers, in fact, initially questioned whether it was wise to accept Greece and Turkey into NATO, fearing that their inclusion would prove disruptive over the long run. In the first decade after their entry these doubts significantly diminished. Both Greece and Turkey went out of their way to prove their fidelity to the alliance, often subordinating their own national interests to the dictates of alliance cohesion and the need for collective action.

In the 1960s and the 1970s, however, the security consensus that had characterized the early postwar period began to erode, and many old problems and tensions reemerged, complicating relations with the United States and NATO. These first surfaced in a serious way during the 1963–4 Cyprus crisis, which led to a deterioration of U.S. relations with both allies. Over the next decade, relations with both allies were exacerbated by a number of other events: the April 1967 military coup in Greece, the growing political turmoil in Turkey that led to military intervention in 1971, and the eruption of the second Cyprus crisis in 1974.

The 1974 Cyprus crisis was a watershed. It not only led to the near outbreak of military conflict between Greece and Turkey, but resulted in a serious estrangement between the United States and both allies. As a consequence of the Turkish invasion, Greece withdrew from the military structure of NATO. The Caramanlis government also began to strengthen and diversify its ties, especially to Western Europe, and to reduce Greece's dependence on the United States. The strong push by Caramanlis for Greece's integration into the European Economic Community (EEC) was one manifestation of this effort. His opening to the Communist countries of the Balkans was another. At the same time, the 1975 arms embargo imposed by the U.S. Congress on Turkey in the aftermath of the Cyprus crisis led to a deterioration of U.S. relations with Ankara and created bitterness that lingers today. As in the Greek case, the crisis prompted an effort by Turkey to broaden and diversify its ties, particularly with the Arab countries of the Middle East and with the Soviet Union. Ankara also sought to improve its ties to the Balkans.

Perhaps equally important, the crisis exacerbated relations between Greece and Turkey and bred animosity that has important security implications for NATO and Western interests in the area. Today, fifteen years after the Cyprus crisis, relations remain strained over a host of issues in the Aegean ranging from the continental shelf to command and control arrangements for the Aegean. These disputes severely impair the political coherence of the alliance as well as hinder its ability to coordinate military activities in the area. Moreover, they carry with them the danger that at some point tensions may erupt into open confrontation, as almost happened in 1976 and again in March 1987.

In addition, the Cyprus conflict today remains little closer to resolution than it did in 1974. A number of diplomatic initiatives conducted by the United States, Britain, and the UN have all run aground on the questions of how political power and territory are to be distributed between the Greek Cypriot and Turkish Cypriot populations. In the meantime, the status quo has solidified, making any return to the status quo ante more difficult. The Turkish Cypriot side, supported by Ankara, is relatively content with the existing state of affairs, whereas the Greek Cypriot side wants to change it but is unwilling to make the compromises acceptable to the Turks. There thus remains a danger that at some point frustration and resentment may again erupt and embroil both communities—as well as their patrons—in a new conflict.

The problems on the southern periphery are made more acute, moreover, by a number of extraregional issues in contiguous areas, particularly the growing potential for instability in the Balkans. The deterioration of the Yugoslav economy and the rise of ethnic conflicts, especially in the Kosovo region, highlight this problem. Any major political instability or change in Yugoslavia's nonaligned status would have important implications for the security of Greece and Turkey. But the problem extends beyond Yugoslavia. Romania also seems headed for a period of prolonged instability once Ceausescu leaves the scene. This instability, too, could affect developments in Greece and Turkey, especially if it were to lead to a shift in Romanian policy toward closer ties with Moscow.

In addition, the fall of the shah and the war between Iran and Iraq have increased the importance of the Mediterranean for any "out of area" contingencies and given the area greater strategic significance. In the future the most serious threat to Turkey's security could come from an unexpected confrontation in the Persian Gulf rather than from an attack on Europe by the Soviet Union. This situation has inevitably affected Turkey's security perceptions and foreign policy. At the same time, Turkey's proximity to the gulf has increased the strategic importance of Turkey in the eyes of U.S. policymakers.

To these developments must be added the important changes in Soviet foreign policy under Gorbachev. Gorbachev's "new thinking" has added an important new element in East-West relations and given East-West détente and arms control new momentum. A continuation of this trend, especially a reduction of conventional arms, could affect not only central Europe but also the flanks, reducing the sense of threat felt by Turkey and Greece. This sense of reduced threat could, in turn, accentuate the centrifugal trends on the southern periphery, which have manifested themselves with increasing intensity over the past two decades and have made both countries even less willing to contribute to collective defense.

Finally, domestic changes in the United States could aggravate recent problems. President Bush is confronted by major budgetary pressures that will require hard choices, especially regarding foreign military assistance. In the face of these pressures, it is unlikely that either Greece or Turkey will receive the level of military assistance that they believe they need. Thus foreign assistance issues could lead to new acrimony, and to a more vigorous search for alternatives by both allies.

At the same time, domestic changes in both Greece and Turkey could add a new element of uncertainty to the current security outlook in both countries. Turkish Prime Minister Turgut Özal has done a commendable job in restoring democracy in Turkey, but he faces major domestic hurdles, above all in the economic area, which could significantly weaken Turkish defense policy. Moreover, his weak showing in the September 1988 referendum and the March 1989 local elections suggests that his popularity may be waning.

Similarly, Greece faces a period of uncertainty and potential change. As a result of the deterioration of the Greek economy as well as a series of personal and political scandals, support for former Prime Minister Andreas Papandreou and his Pan-Hellenic Socialist

Party (PASOK) has declined significantly since 1987. The party came in second in the June 1989 elections, gaining 39 percent of the popular vote and 125 out of 300 seats in Parliament. However, the New Democracy, a party which placed first with 44 percent of the popular vote, was unable to win the necessary 151 seats needed to achieve a majority in Parliament and agreed to form a temporary alliance with the Communist-dominated Alliance of the Left until the convocation of new elections in November 1989. If the New Democracy fails to win a majority in the November election, Greece could face a period of unstable coalition governments in which the Communist Party (KKE) becomes the critical swing factor and "kingmaker"—a development that would give the party unprecedented influence in Greek politics.

Taken together, these trends underscore the changing security environment on the southern periphery and the need to give the area more systematic attention. Over the next decade, trends there could intersect with trends elsewhere, particularly in the Balkans, to make the area an even more acute policy problem for the West. Against this background, it may be useful to look at some of these issues in closer detail.

GREECE

Greece plays an important role in U.S. and NATO policy in the southern periphery. Air and naval facilities in Greece, especially on Crete, provide the United States and NATO with important staging, logistic, communications, and intelligence support in the eastern Mediterranean.[1] The most important facility is the Souda Bay complex on Crete—the largest deep-water port in the eastern Mediterranean—which can accommodate nearly the whole U.S. Sixth Fleet. In addition, there is a large military communications center in Nea Makri, just outside Athens. The Hellenikon air base, also on the outskirts of Athens, performs important intelligence-gathering missions. There are also five NATO Air Defense Ground Environment (NADGE) centers dispersed throughout Greece. Loss of these installations would severely hinder U.S. intelligence-gathering capability and reduce the flexibility of the Sixth Fleet.

As noted at the outset, U.S.-Greek relations have witnessed periodic strain over the past two decades. During the late 1960s and early 1970s the United States was blamed for its support of the Greek dictatorship—or at least for not doing enough to get rid of it. The perception of U.S. support for the colonels, while not entirely accurate, is widespread in Greece and has discredited the United States in the eyes of many Greeks, especially younger Greeks, who are now beginning to assume positions of increasing power and influence.[2]

The United States was further hurt by its handling of the 1974 Cyprus crisis.[3] Greece perceived the failure of the United States to halt the Turkish invasion of Cyprus, as it had done a decade earlier, as a tacit "tilt" toward Turkey. The subsequent violent outbreak of anti-Americanism and anti-NATO feeling compelled the Caramanlis government to withdraw Greece from the military wing of NATO.

Although the most virulent forms of anti-Americanism and nationalism have subsided, both significantly contributed to the election of Andreas Papandreou as prime minister in 1981 and 1985, and they remain strong political forces in Greece today. Papandreou has both exploited and manipulated this latent nationalism to his political advantage, assailing the "colonial" nature of U.S. policy and calling for a restructuring of U.S.-Greek relations under the slogan "Greece for the Greeks." He repeatedly threatened to close the U.S. bases in Greece—which he portrayed as a major symbol of Greece's "colonial" status—and has insisted that the bases must serve "Greek national interests."[4]

On a number of issues, moreover, Papandreou broke ranks with NATO. He refused to impose sanctions against Poland after the introduction of martial law in December 1981. He also refused to condemn the Soviet shooting down of the KAL 007 airliner in September 1983, claiming that it was on a CIA spy mission, and he did not support the deployment of intermediate-range nuclear missiles in Europe. Finally, Papandreou's support for the creation of a nuclear-free zone in the Balkans also irked many of his NATO allies, as did Greece's rather lenient position on terrorism.

Papandreou's bark, however, was worse than his bite. Although he departed from the NATO consensus on a number of marginal issues—largely for domestic reasons—he showed a strong streak of pragmatism on the key security questions of concern to the West. He did not close the U.S. bases or withdraw from NATO. In September 1983 a new Defense and Economic Cooperation Agreement (DECA) was signed. Under the terms of the agreement, which was to run for five years, the United States was guaranteed use of the facilities until 1988, when the agreement expired.[5] In early 1987 Greece and the United States also signed an agreement for the purchase of forty F-16 fighters, another sign that Papandreou's periodic anti-Americanism has not inhibited military cooperation with the United States when cooperation is seen to serve Greek national interests.

The inconclusive outcome of the June 1989 elections has left U.S.-Greek relations somewhat in limbo. The base agreement expired in December 1988. However, negotiations have been put on hold until after the convocation of new elections in early November 1989. Papandreou has been hurt by charges of corruption—he was indicted on charges of bribery in September—and this may give the New Democracy, which came in first in the June elections, enough extra votes to be able to obtain an absolute majority. If the New Democracy fails to win an absolute majority, then Greece could be faced with a series of unstable coalitions, and agreement could be endangered.

Even if the New Democracy wins an absolute majority, however, it would be wrong to assume that all problems would be resolved should the New Democracy be returned to power. Although the rhetoric would certainly change, the substance of the New Democracy's policy on many issues would not vary all that much from PASOK's. Faced with a vociferous campaign against the bases by PASOK and the Communists, the New Democracy would be under strong pressure to make some visible reduction of the U.S. presence in order to show that it had not sold out Greek national interests. Thus, regardless of the outcome of the next elections, some facilities like the Hellenikon air base are likely to be closed, and others may have certain functions curtailed or transferred to other facilities.

But even if an accord is worked out allowing the bases to function relatively unimpaired for another five-year period, the long-term future of the bases remains clouded. There is a belief in some parts of the U.S. government, especially the Pentagon, that the military benefits of maintaining the bases in Greece are not worth the continued political aggravation and economic costs. Although this belief is not widely shared at the moment, the sentiment could grow if the base negotiations prove contentious and if pressures mount in the United States to cut the U.S. defense budget further.

Other contentious issues that have plagued U.S.-Greek relations in recent years, such as the level of military assistance, are not likely to disappear. Under the DECA signed in 1983, Greece receives roughly $500 million annually in foreign military sales credits on favorable terms. Greece considers the assistance critical for maintaining the modernization of its armed forces, particularly in light of the threat it perceives from Turkey. In the past several years, however, both Greece and Turkey have experienced severe cuts in their military assistance,[6] a fact that has periodically caused tension with both countries.

Greece has been particularly sensitive to any effort to abandon the

7-to-10 ratio informally set by Congress regarding aid to Greece and Turkey. Greece sees the preservation of the 7-to-10 ratio as vital for maintaining the balance of power in the region and has tended to regard any effort to eliminate it as a de facto tilt in favor of Turkey. Greece also complains that much of the military assistance received by Turkey is in grant aid rather than credits, whereas Greece gets foreign military sales credits, which have long grace periods but relatively high interest rates.[7] Finally, Greece has periodically sought a security guarantee against Turkey.[8]

Previous U.S. administrations, including the Reagan administration, have generally rejected the 7-to-10 ratio, arguing that aid should be provided to Greece and Turkey on the basis of their NATO-related needs, not according to some artificial and mechanical ratio. The Reagan administration also refused to provide a security guarantee to Greece on the ground that it could not give special security guarantees to one member of NATO against another. The Bush administration is likely to maintain both these positions. For political reasons, however, Congress will probably preserve the 7-to-10 ratio, as it has done in the past.[9]

Greek-Turkish differences also continue to complicate NATO planning. Under the Rogers Agreement, which permitted Greece's reentry into NATO, a new Allied air force command (7th ATAF) similar to the command in Izmir (6th ATAF) was supposed to be set up in Larissa in central Greece.[10] Greece, however, has refused to proceed with the establishment of the command until the operational responsibilities of the two headquarters have been agreed upon. Greece has also refused to participate in a number of NATO exercises because the exercises have excluded Lemnos, which Greece claims prejudices its legal position in the Aegean dispute with Turkey.

Greece, however, is unlikely to withdraw from NATO, even if PASOK returns to power. Whatever Greece's dissatisfaction with the alliance, the fact is that Greece is more secure inside NATO than outside. Greek membership in NATO acts as an important constraint on Turkey and on U.S. support for Turkey. Were Greece to withdraw from NATO, it would be even more vulnerable to Turkish pressure, and U.S. assistance to Turkey would increase. By remaining in NATO, moreover, Greece can better mobilize support for its position in the Aegean and prevent, due to the unanimity principle, the adoption of decisions by NATO that would prejudice command and control arrangements in the Aegean.

In January 1985 Greece announced a new defense "doctrine" that declared the threat from the east (i.e., Turkey, not the Soviet Union) the primary threat. The announcement, however, appears to have been designed largely for domestic consumption. In practical terms it has had little impact on Greece's defense posture. Whereas troop deployments in the north near the Turkish border have been strengthened, most of these moves had been made before Papandreou's assumption of power. Nor do arms purchases and modernization programs reflect a special concern with Turkey rather than with the Warsaw Pact. Many of the recent improvements—a more highly mechanized infantry, the purchase of new tanks to replace aging M-48s, and the improvements in the Greek navy—are as important for defense against attack by the Warsaw Pact as they are against Turkey.

Greece has also sought to play a more active role in other European organizations, especially the European Community (EC). Initially opposed to Greece's entry into the EC, Papandreou modified his opposition to membership once he assumed power, emphasizing instead the importance of improving the terms of Greece's entry. Today there is little chance that Greece would withdraw from the EC. Greek agriculture has benefited significantly from EC subsidies, a fact for which Papandreou ironically has received the political credit. The creation of a single European market, however, will require important adjustments on Greece's part, particularly on the part of small businesses, many of which are still largely family-owned and run.

Greece's application to join the West European Union (WEU) at the end of 1988 represents another example of the increased accent on integration with Western Europe lately. Although the main motivation for the application appears to be to gain greater West European support for Greece's position vis-à-vis Turkey, it signals an important shift in PASOK's antinuclear stance, because membership entails the explicit acceptance of nuclear deterrence as a means of ensuring Western security. Whereas at present the prospects for Greek entry into the WEU are dim (due largely to the WEU's fear of importing Greek-Turkish differences into its ranks), the general trend toward greater integration with Western Europe is likely to receive greater impetus if the New Democracy returns to power.

In short, regardless of the outcome of the elections scheduled for the fall of 1989, some restructuring of U.S.-Greek relations is likely. A large portion of the Greek population, especially the younger generation, sees Turkey, not the Soviet Union, as the main threat. At the same time, although anti-Americanism has receded from its highpoint in the mid-1970s, a gradual erosion of Greece's ties to the United States is likely to continue as Greece's integration into the EC proceeds. As a result, some reduction of the U.S. military presence is probably inevitable. The dimensions of this reduction will depend to a large extent on factors over which the United States has relatively little influence, above all, the course of Greek domestic politics (a subject to which we return at the end of this chapter).

TURKEY

Turkey plays a key role in NATO. The Turkish army is the second largest in NATO. Although in need of modernization, it would nonetheless tie down some twenty-one Warsaw Pact divisions, which otherwise might be committed to the central front. Turkey's control of the Turkish straits would also be critical in preventing entry of the Soviet Black Sea fleet into the Mediterranean. Turkish air bases, especially the air base at Incirlik, allow the forward deployment of U.S. tactical bombers and put these aircraft within striking distance of Transcaucasia. Furthermore, access to Turkish air bases would also be critical in any contingency in the Persian Gulf.

Turkish installations also play an important intelligence-gathering role and help in monitoring Soviet missile tests and other military activities. Facilities in Turkey provide an estimated 25 percent of NATO's hard intelligence, some of which is not available from other sources. The importance of Turkish facilities has increased, moreover, as a result of the loss of intelligence-gathering installations in Iran.[11] Turkey also provides important early-warning, regional, and sea surveillance capabilities that would help warn the Sixth Fleet of any attacks.

Turkey's relations with the United States and NATO, like Greece's, have undergone an evolution. Turkey joined NATO in 1952 largely as a reaction to Soviet pressure, and during the 1950s relations with the alliance were quite harmonious. But the security consensus began to break down in the 1960s. Like other West European countries, Turkey began to question whether the United States would actually come to its defense once the Soviet Union had acquired intercontinental ballistic missiles. These fears were reinforced in the aftermath of the Cuban missile crisis by the Kennedy administration's unilateral decision to withdraw the Jupiter missiles stationed in Turkey, the stationing of which Turkey had regarded as an important symbol of the U.S. commitment to Turkish security.[12]

The real catalyst for the deterioration of relations, however, was the 1963–4 Cyprus crisis. President Johnson's letter to Turkish President Inonu, warning that the United States might not come to Turkey's defense if a Turkish invasion of Cyprus provoked Soviet intervention, shocked many Turks and precipitated a search to broaden and diversify Turkey's relations, especially with the Soviet Union and the Arab countries of the Middle East. This effort was intensified in the wake of the second Cyprus crisis and the 1975 arms embargo. The embargo seriously impaired the modernization program of the Turkish army and led the Turkish government to suspend the operation of a number of the U.S. installations. The main effect of the embargo, however, was psychological. It significantly increased Turkey's doubts about the credibility of the United States as a reliable ally and left a feeling of bitterness and betrayal that continues to have a subliminal effect on relations between the two countries.

U.S.-Turkish relations have generally improved since the lifting of the embargo in 1978, but they have been marred in recent years by increasing differences over the issue of security assistance, which has directly impaired defense cooperation. Although Turkey is one of the largest recipients of U.S. military assistance, the Congress has reduced the level of aid since 1985 in order to maintain a rough 7-to-10 balance, in accordance with the Foreign Assistance Act. It has also linked the assistance to Turkey's position on Cyprus. In 1987, for instance, Congress cut the Reagan administration's request for aid to Turkey from $925 million to $569 million and tied the aid to prohibition of the use of U.S. arms by Turkish troops in Cyprus.

The Turkish government considers the level of U.S. military assistance to be below Turkish needs, which the Turks estimate to be at least $1 billion per year over the next decade. Moreover, Ankara deeply resents the attempt by the U.S. Congress to link the assistance with Greek needs, because it gives Greece direct leverage over Turkish security. This resentment was dramatized in May 1987 when Turkish President Kenan Evren canceled a scheduled visit to the United States to protest the congressional reduction of Turkish aid. The 1980 DECA, which was signed in March 1987 after eighteen months of difficult negotiations, entered into force in February 1988 and will remain in force until 1990.

The problems related to foreign assistance, moreover, are likely to get worse rather than better in the future. Strong pressures to reduce the U.S. budget deficit are likely to reinforce the general trend toward cutbacks in foreign assistance which has been gaining ground in Congress in recent years. Moreover, as long as Greece does not leave NATO, Congress seems likely to limit the amount of foreign assistance available to Turkey and to ensure that the issue remains an irritant in U.S.-Turkish relations.

At the same time, Turkey's relations with Western Europe remain problematic. The key issue concerns Turkey's ties to the European Community. From the outset Turkey has seen membership in the EC as a natural complement to its ties to NATO and as an indispensable element of the process of modernization initiated by Kemal Ataturk, the founder of modern Turkey. Indeed, the debate about ties to the EC has been part of a larger and more profound debate about Turkey's identity and place in the world—that is, whether Turkey should be oriented toward the secularized West or should stress its Islamic traditions and ties to the Arab world.[13] Most of the Turkish elite view the tie to the EC as a way of completing the Ataturk revolution and tying Turkey more tightly to Europe and the West.

West European interests in Turkey's association with the EC, however, are primarily political-security: to strengthen Turkey's ties to the West. The EC has no vital economic interest to extend the relationship beyond that embodied in the 1963 Association Agreement. On the contrary, Turkish membership in the EC would create a host of economic, political, and social problems that many members wish to avoid. Thus there is a basic asymmetry of interests between Turkish goals of full membership in the EC and the EC's desire for some association short of membership.

This asymmetry of basic interests could be patched over as long as the issue of membership could be put off to the distant future. A number of developments in the 1980s, however, increased Turkey's interest in expanding ties to Western Europe, and particularly in applying for full membership in the EC:

1. The cooling of relations with the United States since 1985, and especially the inability of Turkey to find a receptive market for an expansion of its exports in the United States, has increased Turkey's interest in developing stronger ties to Western Europe
2. Turkey's desire for Western credits has made ties to Western Europe more attractive
3. The fall in the price of oil has led to a reduction in Turkish exports to the Middle East and made it clear that the Middle East option is no alternative to Europe
4. The entry of Greece and Portugal into the EC has intensified Turkish fears that the EC's "southern expansion" would be stopped, leaving Turkey the only member of NATO not a member of the EC— an unacceptable position for the Western-oriented Turkish elite

These factors, together with continuing differences over the conditions for labor migration contained in the 1963 Association Agreement, prompted the Özal government to switch its policy and to apply directly for membership in the EC in April 1987 rather than seek an improvement in the Association Agreement. However, whereas many West European governments want to see closer ties with Turkey, they have reservations about a permanent and irreversible integration of Turkey into the EC in the near future. Many fear that membership could lead to an increase in Turkey's balance-of-payments deficit, as a result of the liberalized access of West European agricultural and industrial goods to Turkish markets, and could contribute to rising unemployment as less competitive enterprises are forced to fold.

The most powerful concerns, however, are political and relate to the effect of Turkey's entry on the EC itself. The entry of Turkey would strengthen the growing divergences between North and South within EC and push the center of gravity more to the south, thus contributing to the development of a two-tier EC and sharpening its political-cultural heterogeneity at a time when it is already finding the absorption of Greece, Spain, and Portugal problematic. Turkey's entry could also further weaken the decision-making process and diminish the ability to achieve consensus, already difficult, within the EC. Finally, many fear that Turkish entry will result in importing the Greek-Turkish conflict into the EC ranks, thereby transforming the Greek-Turkish conflict from a marginal problem into a significant internal issue.

The Turkish application has thus confronted the EC with a dilemma. None of the major European governments wants Turkish entry, but for political reasons, none wishes to say so openly. This continued ambivalence allows the EC to finesse the issue and avoid a clear answer. Yet this situation cannot go on indefinitely. Sooner or later the EC will have to decide what form of relationship it wants with Turkey. The problem is that if Turkey pushes for a clear answer in the near future, it is likely to be no. A negative response, however, could deepen Turkey's alienation from the West and weaken the hands of those forces in Turkish society that have been advocating stronger ties to Europe.

Unlike the situation in Greece, however, Turkish threat perceptions and defense policy remain oriented primarily toward the Soviet Union. Turkey shares a common border with the Soviet Union. Moveover, the USSR has twenty-one divisions stationed in the Transcaucasus Military District. The Soviet Mediterranean Fleet is stationed in the Black Sea and would have to pass through the Turkish Straits in order to enter the Mediterranean. All this gives Turkey a far greater reason to remain concerned about the Soviet Union than Greece has.

The difficulties with the United States and Western Europe, together with Turkey's growing economic problems, have prompted Turkey to broaden its ties to other areas, particularly the Middle East.[14] This process began in the mid-1960s as part of Ankara's general effort to diversify its policy in the aftermath of the 1964 Cyprus crisis. It was given new momentum in the 1970s, however, by economic considerations. Turkey is highly dependent on Middle East oil, and the proportion of imported oil has rapidly risen in recent years. As a result Turkey has a strong incentive to expand its ties to the leading oil producers in the Middle East and the Persian Gulf, especially Iran and Iraq, as well as Libya. Domestic factors, including Özal's strong religious convictions as a practicing Muslim, also appear to have played a role in Turkey's effort to expand ties with the Arab world. The fall in the price of oil, however, has reduced demand for Turkish goods throughout the region and led to a decline in Turkey's economic position in the Middle East. This decline has underscored the limits of Özal's Middle East opening and has contributed to Turkey's renewed interest in strengthening ties to Western Europe since 1985.

At the same time, Turkey's proximity to the Persian Gulf has increased its strategic significance in the eyes of Western policymakers, who have stressed its importance in any future Gulf contingency.[15] However, Turkey's geographic proximity to the Gulf as well as its economic interests in the region have made Ankara more cautious and reluctant to take actions that could endanger its ties to the Gulf states and other Arab states in the region. These ties, along with doubts about the utility of the rapid deployment force against low-level conflict, make it increasingly unlikely that Turkey will allow its facilities to be used for non-NATO contingencies in the Gulf. During the 1973 Arab-Israeli conflict Turkey refused to allow the United States refueling and reconnaissance facilities in order to aid Israel. Given its increased ties to the Arab states, Ankara is even less likely to provide such assistance today, unless it perceived a direct threat to its security.[16]

None of this means that Turkey is about to turn its back on the West or to withdraw from NATO. It does suggest, however, that NATO's relationship with Turkey, like that with Greece, is likely to remain uneasy. Over the long run Turkey seems likely to continue to diversify its contacts, particularly with the Middle East, while remaining a member of the Western alliance. Under these circumstances, unrestricted use of facilities and installations cannot be taken for granted. Moreover, Turkey seems increasingly likely to use access to these facilities as a bargaining chip to obtain greater security assistance and achieve other foreign-policy aims, a practice that could exacerbate current tensions.

CYPRUS AND THE AEGEAN

Since 1974, Greek-Turkish relations have been marred by two sets of issues: Cyprus and the Aegean. These issues are often lumped together, although politically they are quite separate. There is, however, an obvious *psychological* linkage between them in the sense that a resolution of one would have an important psychological impact on the resolution of the other.

Of the two, the dispute over the Aegean is the more important because it touches more directly on vital national interests: The Aegean issue, in fact, is actually a set of issues.[17] These include:

• *Air space.* Turkey claims that the eastern half of the Aegean air space should fall under Turkish control. Greece, however, argues that this would jeopardize the sovereignty and security of the Greek islands in the Aegean and the Dodecanese, because under such an arrangement, these islands would lie within Turkey's security zone.

• *Continental shelf.* There is no agreement on what constitutes the continental shelf. Turkey insists that only the continental land masses, not the islands, have continental shelves. Consequently it proposes that the proper line of delimitation is a median line between the two land masses. Greece, basing its claims on the Geneva Law of the Sea Convention (1958), defines the shelf along lines dictated by the Greek islands and wants exclusive control of the shelf and its resources. Acceptance of the Turkish position would, in effect, undermine the Greek claims to sovereignty of the Greek islands off the coast of Turkey.

• *Fortification of the eastern Aegean and Dodecanese islands.* After the 1974 Turkish invasion of Cyprus, Greece accelerated the fortification of the Aegean and Dodecanese islands (which began in the 1960s). Turkey claims that this action contradicts the provisions of the Lausanne Treaty (1923) and the Paris Peace Treaty (1947).

• *Limits of territorial waters.* Greece claims a six-mile limit around its mainland and islands, but reserves the right to extend this to twelve miles. Such a move would have a direct bearing on the issues of air control and continental-shelf delimitation. Turkey, however, has said that it would regard such a move as a casus belli, and so far Greece has refrained from implementing its twelve-mile claim.

These differences are felt particularly deeply because, unlike the Cyprus issue, they touch directly on questions of sovereignty and security for both Greece and Turkey. On several occasions, in fact, these differences have nearly led to armed conflict. In March 1987 a confrontation was only narrowly avoided when Turkey dispatched a research vessel into a disputed part of the Aegean claimed by Greece. The vessel was later recalled, but not before the two countries had gone to the brink of war. Had cooler heads not prevailed, the incident could have led to armed conflict.

The 1987 crisis, however, appears to have had a salutary effect on the attitudes and policy of both powers. Like the Cuban missile crisis in 1962, this one prompted a reassessment of ties and contributed to a thaw in relations between the two countries. This process of rapprochement was initiated at a bilateral meeting between Papandreou and Turkish Prime Minister Turgut Özal in Davos, Switzerland, in January 1988. The Davos meeting did not try to resolve the really tough political issues. Instead, it concentrated on expanding contacts and cooperation in nonsensitive areas, in the hope that expanded contacts might create a better climate for the later resolution of the larger issues. At the meeting the two leaders agreed to set up a hot line for instant personal contact. Two working groups were also established, one on economic cooperation, and a second on political issues.

In the wake of the meeting in Switzerland an effort was made to institutionalize the "Davos process." Contacts between the two countries increased, at the ministerial and popular levels. The two sides also took several small but encouraging political-military steps designed to build trust and to reduce tension; these included signing a memorandum on "rules of the road" for naval exercises similar to the U.S.-Soviet Incidents at Sea Agreement and agreeing to end their long-standing dispute over NATO infrastructure funds. The two prime ministers also met twice—once in Brussels, in March 1988 and again in Athens in June 1988. The Athens meeting had a strong symbolic significance: it was the first visit by a Turkish prime minister to Greece in thirty-six years. The atmosphere of the meeting was cordial, but little progress was made toward resolving the outstanding core issues between the two countries.[18]

Since the Athens meeting, moreover, the Davos process has lost considerable momentum. In August 1988 Papandreou canceled a scheduled visit to Ankara, ostensibly because of scheduling difficulties. The real reasons, however, seemed political: to avoid giving the impression that he put a dialogue with Turkey ahead of Greek national interests. Air incidents have also marred relations and eroded the spirit of cooperation. The promulgation in January 1989 of a new law that puts half the Aegean and the area of northern Cyprus under Turkish jurisdiction for search and rescue operations in the event of an accident also led to new polemics between the two countries, prompting a formal protest from Greece. Greek-Turkish differences also nearly derailed the final deliberations for the mandate for the talks on conventional forces in Europe in Vienna, when Greece protested the exclusion of a small portion of Turkish territory around the port of Mersin from the area for force reductions on the grounds that Turkey had mounted its 1974 invasion of Cyprus from the region and that Turkish forces on Cyprus were supplied from the area.

The most important factor contributing to the loss of momentum, however, has probably been the weakened domestic position of each leader. Since June 1988, the popularity of both leaders has waned considerably. Both face domestic challenges that seriously threaten their political power. Hence neither has felt confident enough to take the necessary political risks to infuse new life into the dialogue.

This situation, in fact, highlights one of the main weaknesses of the Davos process: it depends to a large extent on the commitment and involvement of the two leaders, both of whom are politically weakened and may not be in power much longer. Their political defeat could seriously undercut, or at least delay, the fragile process. For the process to succeed over the long run a broader constituency for increased cooperation over confrontation needs to be developed.

Cyprus also remains an important stumbling block to improved Greek-Turkish relations.[19] Although Cyprus was not a formal part of the Greek-Turkish agenda, during the Athens meeting Papandreou made clear that the course of Greek-Turkish rapprochement depended on a solution to the Cyprus dispute. A resolution of the Cyprus dispute, however, remains as elusive as ever. The election of George Vassiliou as president of Cyprus initially raised hopes that progress toward a settlement might at long last occur. However, despite some initial signs of movement in the summer of 1988, the intercommunal talks remain deadlocked, with little sign of a breakthrough. Moreover, Özal's domestic weakness, highlighted by his stinging defeat in the March 1989 local elections, has diminished his room for maneuver and makes it less likely that he will be willing to take the risks necessary to facilitate a withdrawal of Turkish troops from northern Cyprus. Under these conditions a major breakthrough in the near future seems unlikely.

THE BALKAN CONNECTION

Whereas the security situation on the southern perimeter will be most vitally affected by the course of bilateral relations between Greece and Turkey as well as their relations with the United States, developments elsewhere, especially in the Balkans, also are likely to play an important role. Consequently, both Greece and Turkey have sought to strengthen ties with their Balkan neighbors in recent years and have shown an interest in increased bilateral as well as multilateral regional cooperation. This is particularly true in the case of Greece. In the aftermath of the 1974 Cyprus crisis, Greek Prime Minister Constantine Caramanlis launched a major opening to the Communist states of the Balkans. His policy essentially followed two tracks: (1) a bilateral path emphasizing personal diplomacy, designed to strengthen bilateral ties to all the Balkan countries; and (2) a multilateral path aimed at creating indirect but increasingly institutionalized links among the countries of the region.[20]

Papandreou has sought to build on Caramanlis's efforts and has given them new momentum. Ties to Albania have been expanded as a result of a cross-border trade agreement signed in April 1988 and the official termination of the theoretical state of war that existed since the end of World War II. In August 1987 Greece also renounced claims to southern Albania (known in Greece as "Northern Epirus"). These developments have opened a "new era" in Greek-Albanian relations and put relations on the soundest footing they have been on in the postwar period.

Greece has also made a visible effort to improve relations with Bulgaria. In 1986 a Declaration on Good Neighborliness, Friendship, and Cooperation was signed between the two countries, which foresees an expansion of ties in a number of important areas. Perhaps most noteworthy in this regard has been the expansion of military ties, highlighted by the visit of the deputy defense minister and chief of the Bulgarian General Staff, Atanas Semerdzhiev, to Athens in April 1988. The visit by Semerdzhiev was the first visit to Greece by a high-ranking Bulgarian military official since the end of World War II and was in return for a visit to Sofia in July 1987 by chief of the Greek General Staff, General Nikos Kouris. The expansion of defense cooperation should not, however, be exaggerated. It seems primarily designed to ensure Bulgaria's neutrality in case of any conflict between Greece and Turkey and has not gone beyond the exchange of visits by the respective chiefs of staff of each country.

Greece's relations with Yugoslavia also have improved considerably over the last decade. As with Bulgaria, the improvement of relations has resulted in an expansion of military cooperation, which has included exchanges between the chiefs of staff of the two countries' armed forces. This military cooperation, however, has largely been symbolic and has not extended to other areas such as weapons procurement.

Political relations also have improved, but relations continue to be marred from time to time by the flare-ups over the Macedonian issue. Greece has reacted sharply to claims that the people living in the Macedonian part of Greece are Macedonians—a claim which Athens categorically rejects—and to the increased agitation on the issue recently by Macedonians living in Yugoslavia.[21] Athens views the resurgence of the Macedonian issue, however, largely as a by-product of the recent growth of ethnic nationalism in Yugoslavia and the loss of control from the center, rather than as a reflection of a concerted campaign directed by the central government in Belgrade.

Relations with Romania have been stagnant since mid 1987, in part because of poor personal chemistry between Ceausescu and Papandreou. Ceausescu appears to resent Papandreou's effort to seize the high ground on the issue of the creation of a nuclear-free zone in the Balkans, an issue with which Ceausescu has been closely identified in the past. At the same time the deterioration of the domestic situation in Romania, particularly the increased repression of human rights, has tarnished Ceausescu's image abroad and made him a less attractive partner. In addition, Greece has sought to keep its policy in tune with that of the EC, which has been increasingly critical of Ceausescu's domestic repression over the past several years.

Papandreou has been of the strongest supporters of the creation of a nuclear-free zone in the Balkans, at least rhetorically. His championship of the idea, however, has largely been tactical and motivated by domestic politics, particularly a desire to appease his left-wing. Support for the concept is a relatively cost-free exercise. It allows Papandreou to portray himself as a champion of regional détente and disarmament without really risking anything, because the creation of such a zone is highly unlikely in the near future.

At present there is no strong regional consensus within the Balkans in favor of the idea. Greece, Romania, and Bulgaria back the establishment of such a zone, but Turkey strongly opposes it and has made any withdrawal of nuclear weapons from the area contingent on a European solution to the problem. (Ankara refused, for instance, to attend the Balkan summit in Athens in February 1984 until the issue was given a less prominent place on the agenda.) Yugoslavia, while supporting the idea in principle, has made clear that it does not regard the issue as a top priority.

As a result, since the Athens conference the issue of the creation of a Balkan nuclear-free zone has been played down. The topic was given relatively little attention at the Balkan foreign ministers' conference held in Belgrade in February 1988, which focused primarily on practical ways to increase cooperation in areas like trade and tourism. At the conference, Greek Foreign Minister Karolaos Papoulias referred only fleetingly to the issue, and the communiqué issued at the end of the conference specifically noted the existence of "differences of view" on the subject.

All told, the Belgrade conference was a modest success. The meeting underscored the overall improvement of the climate in the Balkans in recent years and added impetus to the general trend toward increased regional cooperation among the Balkan states. The foreign ministers from the six Balkan countries attending the conference (Greece, Turkey, Yugoslavia, Romania, Bulgaria, and Albania) agreed in advance not to air grievances but to concentrate on establishing a framework for fostering greater multilateral cooperation in a number of well-defined and uncontroversial areas such as trade, tourism, industrial cooperation, and environmental protection. Controversial issues such as minorities were purposely treated bilaterally in order to avoid issues that could spoil the generally positive atmosphere at the conference.[22]

The most noteworthy aspect of the conference was the participation of Albania, which had previously refused to take part in such regional meetings. Albania's participation was a clear signal of Tirana's desire, since the death of Stalinist leader Enver Hoxha in 1985, to break out of its self-imposed isolation and to forge closer ties with its Balkan neighbors. The Belgrade conference was followed by a conference of Balkan deputy foreign ministers in Tirana in January 1989—the first time that such a meeting had taken place on Albanian soil since the end of World War II—and a follow-up meeting on confidence-building measures in Bucharest in May 1989, in which Albania also participated.

Turkey has also attempted to improve its ties to its Balkan neighbors. Although Ankara remains opposed to the creation of any nuclear-weapons-free zone in the Balkans, it has pursued an active policy in the Balkans in an effort to gain support for its policy objectives and to avoid being outflanked by Greece. Ankara's diplomatic effort has been complicated, however, by differences with Bulgaria over Sofia's treatment of the Turkish minority in Bulgaria. The Bulgarian campaign to "Bulgarize" the Turkish minority in 1984–5 and force all of them to adopt Bulgarian names caused a major outcry in Turkey and resulted in a serious deterioration of relations.[23]

Relations improved for a short while after the signing of a Protocol on the Promotion of Good Neighborliness, Friendship, and Cooperation on the eve of the Belgrade meeting of Balkan foreign ministers in February 1988. However, the decision by the Bulgarian government at the end of May 1989 to expel forcibly thousands of ethnic Turks created new tensions in relations and caused servere domestic problems for Turkey, which was forced to absorb hundreds of thousands of refugees on short notice (some 300,000 by October 1989). In August Turkey was forced to close its borders to the refugees, requiring would-be immigrants to obtain entry visas as tourists. The move was taken in part to regulate the chaotic border travel and gain time to overcome the difficulties posed by having to resettle so many refugees. At the same time the Turks hoped to put pressure on the Bulgarian government to negotiate an emigration agreement, which the Bulgarians have to date refused to do.[24]

In short, neither for Greece nor for Turkey does Balkan cooperation represent a realistic substitute for ties to the West. Despite the growing bilateral and, to a lesser extent, multilateral cooperation in recent years, the Balkans remain a highly diverse and politically fragmented region where common interests are still overshadowed by important political differences. None of the other Balkan countries want to involve themselves in an intra-NATO affair or to complicate their relations with the other NATO ally. Thus, at best, the Balkan opening can complement ties to the West, not replace them.

SOVIET POLICY

The Soviet Union has traditionally had a strong interest in the Balkans and Mediterranean. The Soviet Mediterranean fleet, the *Eskadra*, is based in the Black Sea, and its activities are subject to restrictions under the Montreux Convention of 1936, which regulates movement through the Turkish Straits. Despite its impressive expansion over the past two decades, the fleet is still made up of warships with limited ability to sustain distant operations,[25] which hampers the

fleet's flexibility. Hence Soviet policy in the region has been characterized by a continuous search for access to shore facilities and support.

During the past three decades the Soviet naval presence in the
Mediterranean has expanded dramatically. It reached its zenith between 1968 and 1973 when Moscow negotiated access to a number of
facilities in Egypt, which permitted the Soviet navy to expand the
number of days it spent at sea. Sadat's expulsion of the Soviet Union,
however, significantly circumscribed the *Eskadra*'s flexibility and the
sustainability of its deployment strength. Although Moscow has managed to obtain access to facilities in Syria and Libya, these are not as
good as those in Egypt. As a result, since 1978, Soviet operations have
stabilized at about 16,000 ship-days per year—down from a high of
21,000 in 1972.

These limitations give the Soviet Union a strong interest in finding
permanent shore support in the area. Yet the prime Soviet goal is
probably to restrict the flexibility of the U.S. Sixth Fleet in the area,
especially its ability to provide support and rapid reinforcement to
the countries of the southern perimeter in any conflict. As a result,
Moscow has a strong interest in seeing a weakening of Greece and
Turkey's ties to NATO and a withdrawal of the Sixth Fleet from the
Mediterranean.

In this sense, Moscow has reason to be encouraged by developments
over the past decade. NATO's difficulties on the southern flank,
however, have not led to a significant strengthening of Soviet ties with
either Greece or Turkey.[26] Moscow did sign a Document on Principles
of Good Neighborliness and Friendly Cooperation with the Ecevit
government in 1978, but this document fell far short of the non-
aggression pact that Moscow apparently desired. The Soviet invasion
of Afghanistan and the fall of the shah, moreover, revived Turkish
fears of Soviet expansionism and led to a cooling of relations with
Moscow. In short, despite the gradual improvement in relations since
the mid-1960s, Turkey still sees the Soviet Union as the main threat
to its security and remains wary of Moscow's long-term aims.

Moscow's efforts to woo Greece have been even less successful. The
deterioration of U.S. relations after the 1974 Cyprus crisis and
Papandreou's assumption of power initially gave Moscow some hope
that its political relations with Greece might take a turn for the better,
but these hopes have remained largely unfulfilled. Although Papandreou has been highly critical of the United States, he has not sought
to cultivate overly cordial ties to Moscow. He did visit the Soviet Union
in 1982 to attend Brezhnev's funeral, but the visit brought few

concrete results. All told, Soviet relations with PASOK have not been qualitatively better than those with the New Democracy.

Nor do they seem likely to witness any major warming. A Greek tilt toward Moscow would only drive the United States to support Turkey even more strongly. Moreover, on the issues that count for Greece—the Aegean and Cyprus—the Soviet Union lacks any real leverage. The really important external factor is the United States, not the Soviet Union. Only the United States has the power and influence to exert pressure on Turkey in ways conducive to Greek interests. Thus, although Papandreou may continue to make life difficult for the United States and NATO, he is unlikely to make a major overture to Moscow. This is even more true should the New Democracy return to power in the near future.

Yet, if Greece and Turkey are not about to leave NATO, there are few reasons for complacency. Gorbachev has proved to be a much more sophisticated and shrewd politician than his immediate predecessors. His increased emphasis on détente and arms control is likely to further erode Greece's and Turkey's perceptions of the Soviet threat, already significantly diminished in the past decade, and to spark new centrifugal tendencies in the area. A further diminution of the Soviet threat could make it even harder to maintain a sense of common purpose and alliance cohesion in the future.

Eventually, moreover, Moscow is likely to seek to obtain constraints on the activities of the Sixth Fleet, possibly pushing for its elimination from the Mediterranean entirely. Gorbachev's proposal during his trip to Yugoslavia in March 1988 for a freeze on Soviet and U.S. naval forces and an eventual withdrawal of these forces from the Mediterranean should be seen in this light. The proposal seems designed to reduce the nuclear threat posed to the Soviet homeland by the Sixth Fleet as well as constrain Washington's ability to resupply its Greek and Turkish allies in any conflict in the area.[27]

DOMESTIC CHANGE

Domestic changes in Greece and Turkey could also affect the security outlook in the area. Both countries seem headed for periods of political change and possibly even instability. This is particularly true in the case of Greece. The June 1989 elections resulted in a significant loss of support for PASOK, which came in second with 39 percent of the vote and 125 seats in Parliament. But the New Democracy, which came in first with 44 percent of the vote, fell short of the 151 seats needed to win a majority Parliament and agreed to form a coalition with the Alliance of the Left, an amalgam of six leftist parties dominated by the Communists, until the convocation of new elections in November 1989. As noted earlier, if New Democracy fails to win a majority in the next election, Greece could face a period of unstable coalition governments in which the Communist Party (KKE) would hold the balance of power or become the critical swing factor.

The dangers of another military coup like that which occurred in April 1967, however, seem remote. The military intervention in 1967 was a sobering experience, for the military and the civilian population alike, and there is little enthusiasm among the military to try its hand at running the country again. Moreover, under Papandreou the military was thoroughly purged of top-level officers associated with the military dictatorship.

In addition, since 1974 important structural changes have occurred in Greek politics which diminish the prospects of military intervention. The old "personalistic" parties that characterized Greek politics in the postwar period—and contributed to the political instability and military intervention in the late 1960s—have begun to be replaced by the new organizations more closely resembling modern mass parties.[28] One of the keys to PASOK's success, for instance, was its tightly knit organizational structure, with its extensive network of local chapters and regional communities. It also made extensive use of American-style campaign techniques. In part because of PASOK's example, the New Democracy after 1974 was forced to develop an organizational structure with its own system of local chapters that reached down into the villages. The New Democracy, in fact, is the first party in modern Greek history to change leaders through an organized process at a party congress.[29]

Papandreou's victory in 1981 can, in fact, be seen as a indication of the health and "maturity" of the Greek political system. It demonstrated that an orderly transfer of power was possible and that the ascent to power of the left need not lead to instability or political ferment, as was the case in the 1960s. In effect, the left has been reintegrated into the political system and today is considered a legitimate component of the system.[30] Thus, although Greek politics seems headed for a period of fluidity, the moderation of the deep polarization of Greek politics—so characteristic of the interwar and early postwar period—has enhanced the prospects for a stable political evolution over the long run.

Like Greece, Turkey also faces a number of critical challenges in the future that could significantly affect its political orientation and foreign policy. Since taking over as prime minister in 1983, Turgut

Özal has pursued pro-West, rapid-growth policies and done a credible job in returning Turkey to democratic rule. The economic situation has improved, and many of the most acute problems that led to the military intervention in 1980, particularly the growth of terrorism, have been significantly reduced.

At the same time, since 1983 a gradual process of "redemocratization" has occurred. A new constitution, with strengthened powers for the president has been introduced, and the military has gradually returned power to the politicians. Many of the political groupings that existed before the military intervention in 1980 have been revived, and representatives of the old political system such as former prime ministers Suleyman Demiral and Bulent Ecevit (both of whom had been banned by the military from taking part in politics) have formally reentered political life.

Despite these encouraging developments, Turkey faces a number of problems that could erode recent progress and pose a threat to domestic stability. The Turkish economy, which witnessed a strong recovery in the first years after Özal took over as prime minister, has recently begun to sputter. In 1989 inflation rose nearly 75 percent over 1988. Unemployment is about 20 percent. The fall in the price of oil, moreover, has hurt Turkish exports, especially to the Middle East, and has undercut Özal's economic strategy, which has been based on export growth. A failure to arrest these trends could endanger Özal's economic stabilization program and lead to renewed social discontent.

In addition, Özal's personal popularity and political support have shown marked signs of erosion. He won only 35 percent of the vote in the referendum held in September 1988, which was widely regarded as vote on his performance. In the local elections in March 1989 his Motherland Party did even worse, winning only 22 percent of the vote and placing third behind the left-of-center Social-Democratic Populist Party, led by Erdal Inonu, which drew 28 percent of the vote, and the conservative True Path Party, led by former prime minister Suleyman Demiral, which came in second with 26 percent. To add to the ignominy, the Motherland Party lost control of the city halls in Turkey's three largest cities: Istanbul, Ankara and Izmir.

Much of the erosion of support for Özal has been due to his handling of the economy—once considered his great strength—particularly his inability to control inflation. This has lost him the support of the Turkish business community, previously among his strongest backers. Against this background Özal may be tempted to run for the presidency when the current Turkish president, Kenan

Evren, steps down in November 1989. If Özal decided to run and won, he would become the first civilian president of Turkey since 1960.

However, Özal's departure (either by elevation to the presidency, or by erosion of his parliamentary majority) could foreshadow a period of weak coalition governments and political instability. Renewed instability would be particularly worrisome because it could exacerbate ethnic unrest, particularly among the Kurdish population, most of which is located in the southeastern part of Turkey, near the border with Iraq, Syria, and Iran. The breakdown in law and order in the 1970s resulted in increased unrest in the Kurdish areas and the imposition of martial law in the Kurdish provinces. The 1980 military takeover brought an improvement in security. Since 1984, however, there has been an upsurge of insurgency, led by the Marxist Kurdish Workers Party, forcing the Turkish government to maintain martial law in five of the wild and mountainous southeastern provinces where the guerrillas operate. The guerrillas do not have widespread support among the Kurdish population, but the Kurdish problem remains potentially explosive because of the possibility of outside support for the guerrillas from Turkey's neighbors, particularly Syria and Iran, both of which have large Kurdish populations. The problem has been complicated, moreover, by the recent influx of Kurdish refugees from Iraq, who remain confined to makeshift camps and represent an added source of potential discontent and unrest at a time when Turkey already faces problems with its own Kurdish population.

If serious political instability or unrest were to occur, the military, which has traditionally seen itself as the custodian of the Ataturk revolution and the ultimate guarantor of democratic order, might feel compelled to intervene again. Military rule, however, would solve little and could even exacerbate Turkey's problems, leading to greater polarization at home and increased isolation abroad. NATO would again be faced with dilemma, and Turkey's bid to enter the EC would be set back years, perhaps decades. Such an event, in turn, could intensify anti-Western feeling and lead to a weakening of Turkey's ties to the West.

Over the last decade there has been a visible increase in Islamic sentiment and traditions in Turkey. The political implications of this trend, however, should not be exaggerated. Although religion continues to play an important role in the countryside,[31] and has recently made some gains in the city, the Turkish elite, especially the military, are strongly committed to keeping Turkey a secular state. This sentiment is shared by the vast majority of the population. Opinion polls show that only about 10 percent of the population favor Turkey's becoming an Islamic state. Moreover, the forces that more or less openly favor such a development, such as the National Salvation Party, have actually lost popular support in recent years.[32] Thus whereas Turkey is likely to continue to expand its ties to the Muslim states of the Arab world, there is little real danger of Turkey's becoming a radical Muslim state or turning its back completely on the West.

WESTERN POLICY

The preceding discussion strongly suggests that regardless of who comes to power in Greece and Turkey in the coming decade, the West is likely to face continued difficulties on the southern periphery. The sense of common purpose, once so strong, has seriously eroded, and it is unlikely that it can be fully restored. Indeed, Gorbachev's détente policy could accentuate the centrifugal forces at work in the region in recent years and even unleash new destabilizing forces that have been relatively dormant to date. It thus behooves the United States and its West European allies to pay more attention to the southern periphery than they have in the past—particularly in light of the potential for instability elsewhere in the region (Yugoslavia).

What can and should the United States do? First, the United States (and its West European allies) should strongly support and encourage a reinvigoration of the Davos process, which offers the best hope for resolving many of the current differences between Greece and Turkey. If the effort collapses, antagonism between Greece and Turkey could intensify. A Greek-Turkish rapprochement could have important side benefits for the United States and NATO. It might create a better atmosphere for the resolution of U.S.-Greek bilateral problems, particularly the base issue. It might also make the resolution of certain NATO-related issues easier, particularly those related to the NATO command.[33]

Second, the United States should try to maintain a sense of even-handedness and avoid being drawn into bilateral disputes. In many instances, it may be better for Washington to use its influence behind the scenes and let other organizations such as the UN take the lead. In the long run such a strategy may be more productive than trying to mediate the disputes directly. This is particularly true in the case of Cyprus.

Third, the United States should encourage a strengthening of Greece's and Turkey's ties to Western Europe. Both should be made to feel a part of a larger European political community. As a result, their willingness to contribute to Western defense might increase, even if, as is likely, ties to the United States are gradually reduced. Stronger ties with Western Europe could have important domestic benefits as well, strengthening the somewhat fragile roots of democracy in each country.

Fourth, the United States needs to take a broader view of its security interests and not see them solely in narrow military terms (a key weakness of U.S. policy in the past). In particular, it needs to pay more attention to underlying political, social, and economic trends in the area. Over the long run these are likely to improve the security situation in the region more than marginal changes in the military balance.

Finally, the United States needs to view relations with both Greece and Turkey in the broader geostrategic context of developments within Southeastern Europe as a whole. As noted earlier, instability elsewhere in the region, especially in Yugoslavia, would directly weaken Greek and Turkish security. Hence the United States and its West European allies need to devise a more responsive and active policy toward the current Yugoslav crisis. Such a policy not only would help to dampen the current destabilizing trends within Yugoslavia itself but also would contribute to strengthening regional security as a whole and help to prevent any spillover of tensions into the eastern Mediterranean.

NOTES

The author would like to express his appreciation for the comments on an earlier draft of this chapter by Nikiforos Diamandouros.

1. For a detailed discussion of the bases and their functions see Foreign Affairs and National Defense Division, Congressional Research Service, "U.S. Military Installations in NATO's Southern Region," report prepared for the Committee on Foreign Affairs, U.S. House of Representatives, Washington, D.C., October 1986, pp. 4–5. Also John Chipman, ed., *NATO's Southern Allies: Internal and External Challenges* (London: Routledge, 1988), 60–1.

2. There is no clear evidence that the United States actually engineered the 1967 coup, but many of the main figures in the coup—particularly the head of the junta, George Papadopoulos—had close ties to the U.S. military and security forces. Moreover, during the Nixon administration the restrictions on arms sales imposed by President Johnson were eased and a number of high-level U.S. officials, including Vice-President Agnew, paid official visits to Greece, which gave the impression that the United States tacitly supported the colonels.

3. For a good discussion of the U.S. policy during the Cyprus crisis, see Lawrence Stern, "Bitter Lessons: How We Failed in Cyprus," *Foreign Policy* (Summer 1975): 34–78; see also Monteagle Stearns, *Updating the Truman Doctrine: The U.S. and NATO's Southeastern Flank*, International Security Studies Program, Working Paper no. 86 (Washington, D.C.: Wilson Center, 1989), especially pp. 3 and 19. For a conspiratorial view stressing the continuity in U.S. policy, see Van Coufoudakis, "American Foreign Policy and the Cyprus Problem, 1974–78: The 'Theory of

Continuity' Revisited," in Theodore A. Couloumbis and John O. Iatrides, *Greek-American Relations: A Critical Review* (New York: Pella Publishing Company, 1980), 107–29.

4. For a detailed discussion see F. Stephen Larrabee, "Dateline Athens: Greece for the Greeks," *Foreign Policy*, no. 45 (Winter 1981–82), 158–74. Also, F. Stephen Larrabee, "Papandreou: National Interests Are the Key," *Atlantic Monthly* (March 1983): 24–32.

5. The terms of the agreement contain an important ambiguity. The Greek text of the agreement states that the agreement terminates after five years, whereas the U.S. text says the agreement is "terminable" after five years. The United States regarded the language difference largely as a face-saving device to allow Papandreou to present the agreement as a step toward the eventual closure of the bases. In an accompanying letter the United States also agreed to secure $500 million worth of foreign military sales (FMS) credits on favorable terms. In contrast to the agreement with Turkey, however, the Greek DECA made no reference to any NATO-related functions for the bases.

6. In 1988, Greece received about $344 million in assistance, almost all of it in the form of FMS credits, whereas in 1984 and 1985 it received $501.4 million in FMS credits. The figure for 1989 is expected to be about the same as that for 1988. See Ellen B. Laipson, "Greece and Turkey: U.S. Foreign Assistance Facts," *Issue Brief IB86065*, Congressional Research Service (November 25, 1988): 3 and 7.

7. In 1988, for instance, Turkey received $526 million in military assistance, of which $156 million was in grant aid and the rest mostly in FMS credits. It also received $32.7 million in economic assistance. Greece received $344.1 million, almost all of it in FMS credits, and no economic aid. For comparative figures over the past five years, see Laipson, "Greece and Turkey: U.S. Foreign Assistance Facts," 3–4.

8. It is worth noting that the demand for a security guarantee did not originate with Papandreou. The previous conservative government under George Rallis also demanded such a guarantee and insisted on the maintenance of the 7-to-10 ratio.

9. The traditional pattern has been for the U.S. administration to submit a large request for military assistance to Turkey based on Turkish needs to modernize its armed forces. This usually exceeds the 7-to-10 ratio. The administration's request is usually cut back by Congress in order to preserve the 7-to-10 ratio, angering Turkey but not satisfying Greece, which usually claims that the amount allotted to it is still unsatisfactory. As a result, the whole assistance process becomes highly politicized, with both countries engaging in heavy lobbying of the administration and the Congress. For an insightful discussion of the assistance process by an experienced insider, see Stearns, "Updating the Truman Doctrine," 9–24.

10. For the text of the Rogers Agreement, see Robert McDonald, *Alliance Problems in the Mediterranean—Greece, Turkey, and Cyprus: Part II*, Adelphi Paper 229 (London: International Institute for Strategic Studies, Spring 1988), Appendix A, 7.

11. Congressional Research Service, "U.S. Military Installations," 49, and Chipman, *NATO's Southern Allies*, 60–1.

12. For a good discussion of the effect of the Cuban missile crisis on Turkish security perceptions, see George S. Harris, *Troubled Alliance* (Washington, D.C.: American Enterprise Institute, 1972).

13. See Heinz Kramer, *Die Europäische Gemeinschaft und die Türkei* (Baden-Baden: Nomos Verlag, 1988), 17. Kramer's study is by far the best and most comprehensive treatment of Turkey's relations with the EC.

14. For a detailed discussion see Ali L. Karaosmanoglu, "Turkey's Security and the Middle East," *Foreign Affairs* (Fall 1983): 157–75.

15. For a strong argument along these lines, see Albert Wohlstetter, "Die Türkei und die Sicherung der Interessen der NATO," *Europa Archiv*, Folge 16 (1985): 507–14.

16. In November 1982 the United States and Turkey signed a joint memorandum of understanding which provided for the construction and joint use of airfields mainly in eastern Turkey. Turkish officials have stressed, however, that these

airfields are limited to NATO uses in pursuit of agreed Allied missions. For a good discussion of Turkish perspectives on this point, see Karaosmanogolu, "Turkey's Security in the Middle East," especially pp. 167–75.

17. A detailed discussion of these issues is beyond the scope of this study. For a comprehensive treatment, see Andrew Wilson, *The Aegean Dispute*, Adelphi Paper 155 (London: International Institute for Strategic Studies, 1979/80).

18. Roberto Suro, "Few Gains Seen as Greek-Turkish Talks End," *New York Times*, June 16, 1988. Also, Loren Jenkins, "Greek-Turkish Premiers Conclude Athens Summit with Plea for Patience," *Washington Post*, June 16, 1988. For a more detailed assessment, see Ronald Meinardus, "Eine Neue Phase in den Griechisch-Türkischen Beziehungen," *Europa Archiv*, Folge 14 (1988): 403–12. Also, Ellen Laipson, "Greek-Turkish Relations: Beginning of a New Era?" Congressional Research Service, December 1, 1988.

19. A detailed discussion of the Cyprus issue is beyond the scope of this chapter. For a balanced, comprehensive study, see Robert McDonald, *The Problem of Cyprus*, *Adelphi Paper* 234 (London: International Institute for Strategic Studies, Winter 1988/89). For a discussion of recent developments in the intercommunal talks, see Gülistan Gürbey, "Zypern zwischen Moratorium und Stagnation—Neuere Entwicklungen um Zypern," *Suedosteuropa*, Heft 4 (1989): 213–23.

20. For a good discussion of Caramanlis's Balkan diplomacy, see Nikolaos A. Stavrou, "Greek-American Relations and Their Impact on Balkan Cooperation," in Couloumbis and Iatrides, eds., *Greek-American Relations*, 149–68.

21. Like Bulgaria, Greece has no territorial claims on Yugoslav Macedonia and recognizes the existence of a Macedonian republic, which is part of the Yugoslav federated state. But Greece does not accept the effort by the Macedonians in Yugoslavia to appropriate the Macedonian name to define a Slavic population in the Balkans. Greece views the name *Macedonian* as merely a geographic term that applies to any native of the wider Macedonian region, irrespective of national identity. Greece particularly resents efforts by the Macedonians in Yugoslavia to lay claim to historical events and personages such as Alexander the Great, who are regarded by the Greeks as an internal part of their history and cultural heritage. For a good discussion of the changing role of the Macedonian issue in recent Balkan politics, particularly the Greek point of view, see Evangelos Kofos, *The Macedonian Question: The Politics of Mutation* (Thessaloniki: Institute for Balkan Studies, 1987), 1–16.

22. For a detailed discussion see Dietrich Schlegel, "Are the Balkan Countries Closing Ranks," *Aussenpolitik*, no. 4 (1988): 391–405. Also Jens Reuter, "Die Aussenministerkonferenz der Balkanländer in Belgrad," *Südosteuropa*, Heft 4 (1988): 128–41.

23. The Bulgarian policy of "Bulgarizing" the Turkish minority has been part of a step-by-step process to limit minority rights which can be traced back to the late 1950s. Until the late 1970s, however, the Bulgarians still were willing to admit the existence of the Turkish minority. The name changing campaign marked an important shift in the Bulgarian position. For a good discussion of Bulgarian policy on this issue, see Wolfgang Höpken, "Im Schatten der nationalen Frage: Die bulgarisch-tuerkischen Beziehungen," *Südosteuropa*, Heft 2/3 (1987): 75–95; and by the same author, "Im Schatten der nationalen Frage: Die bulgarisch-tuerkischen Beziehungen (II)," *Südosteuropa*, Heft 4 (1987): 178–94.

24. The exodus has also caused hardships for Bulgaria. Many of the ethnic Turks were from important agricultural and industrial areas and their departure has caused a significant labor shortage in these regions. The tobacco industry has been particularly hard hit. However, a complete picture of the damage will not be available until 1990, when statistics for the past year's economic performance are published.

25. For an excellent discussion of these problems and the Soviet search to alleviate them, see Gordon McCormick, *Soviet Strategic Aims and Capabilities in the Mediterranean: Part II*, *Adelphi Papers* 229 (London: International Institute for Strategic Studies, 1988): 32–48.

26. For a good overview of Soviet policy toward both countries, see Robert S. Eaton, "Soviet Relations with Greece and Turkey," *Occasional Paper No. 2* (Athens: Hellenic Foundation for Defense and Foreign Policy, 1987).

27. For Gorbachev's proposal, see *Pravda*, March 17, 1988. See also Jackson Diehl and David Remnick, "Soviet Urges Naval Cuts in Mediterranean," *Washington Post*, March 17, 1988.

28. For a discussion of the old "personalistic" system that dominated the early postwar period, see Keith Legg, *Politics in Modern Greece* (Palo Alto: Stanford University Press, 1969); and David Holden, *Greece without Columns* (London: Faber and Faber, 1972), especially pp. 271–86. The Communist Party (KKE), which was always a mass party, was the exception during this period.

29. I am particularly indebted to Nikiforos Diamandouros for many of the insights here regarding the structural shifts that recently have taken place in the Greek party system.

30. Ironically, much of the credit for the reintegration of the left into Greek politics belongs to Constantine Caramanlis, Greece's prime minister from 1974 to 1978 and a staunch anti-Communist. It was Caramanlis who legalized the Greek Communist Party and formally ended all extraordinary legislation from the cold war period, thereby making it possible for the political refugees who fought in the civil war on the side of the rebels to return to Greece.

31. The Kemalist revolution was confined largely to the city and rested primarily in the military, the state bureaucracy, the large industrialists, and the urban intelligentsia. Hence the emphasis on secularization never penetrated deeply into the countryside. For a good discussion of the role of Islam in Turkish politics and society, see Serif Mardin, "Religion and Politics in Modern Turkey," in James P. Piscatori, ed., *Islam in the Political Process* (Cambridge: Cambridge University Press, 1973), 138–59. Also, Ilkay Sunar and Binnaz Toprak, "Islam in Politics: the Case of Turkey," *Government and Opposition* 18, no. 3 (1983): 421–41.

32. In the local elections in March 1989 the National Salvation Party received just over 9 percent of the popular vote.

33. Although there is no direct connection between the command issues and Greek-Turkish bilateral differences over civilian air traffic and other airspace matters, if the civilian airspace issues were resolved, both sides might feel less anxious about the command issues, and some sort of a compromise allowing the activization of the seventh ATAF in Larissa would probably be easier to achieve.

III

THE GREAT POWERS AND SOUTHEASTERN EUROPE

9

THE SOVIET MILITARY VIEW OF SOUTHEASTERN EUROPE

Phillip A. Petersen and Joshua B. Spero

The Balkan Peninsula, long the tinderbox of Europe, remains a highly unstable microcosm of world problems, tensions, and frustrations. The déjà vu quality of sociopolitical and economic events in the Balkans at the end of the decade masks the geopolitical importance of the region to stability in Europe. The Soviet General Staff, however, has long recognized that the composition, dimension, and strategic situation of the Balkan states make them especially susceptible to being drawn into a war.[1] Appreciating that the incipient instability of Southeastern Europe may once more make the region a focus of great-power politics, the Soviet General Staff has prepared operational plans to provide the basis for the application of military power in specific circumstances. It would be extremely negligent if such perspectives are not brought into the Western policy calculus. This chapter attempts to contribute to this process.

MILITARY POWER AS AN INSTRUMENT OF SOVIET SECURITY POLICY

The conventional wisdom among most Western social scientists holds that Soviet security policy can be understood in terms of civilian-military tension. A U.S. congressional policy panel concluded in September 1988 that the ongoing debate in the Soviet Union over military doctrine should be viewed as a political struggle over who determines "how much is enough" for Soviet security.[2] Some have even concluded that this "taming of the military" is largely complete and has set the stage for permanently altering the relationship between the use of military means and the use of political means to provide security.[3] The fundamental assumption is that Soviet military leaders as an interest group are committed to the exercise of force in meeting foreign-policy and security objectives. Although such a model of the Soviet security policy process is clearly a useful tool in assessing contemporary decision making, it just as clearly has fundamental weaknesses as an instrument of prediction. For example, despite the fact that professional soldiers opposed the use of military power in Afghanistan to solve what was understood to be a political problem, the Soviet military intervened in December 1979.[4]

It seems reasonably certain that the Soviet Defense Council today has no intention of employing military power as an instrument of policy in Southeastern Europe. Yet it must not be forgotten that whereas the Warsaw Pact military doctrine announced in May 1987 gave the armed forces the new mission of preventing war, the new doctrine did not absolve the armed forces of the responsibility for achieving victory if they failed in their new mission. Consistent with this latter responsibility, the Soviet General Staff continues to refine its military contingency planning. Although decisions about security policy in the Soviet Union are made by the Defense Council, security recommendations to the Defense Council are generally made by the Headquarters of the Supreme High Command on the basis of specific operational plans prepared by the appropriate geographic sector in the Operations Directorate of the General Staff (see Figure 1). These sectors in the Operations Directorate are responsible for preparing strategic-scale defensive and offensive plans for Theaters of Strategic Military Action or TSMAs (*Teatr voyennykh destviy* or *TVD*).[5]

THE SOUTHWESTERN TSMA

For purposes of strategic planning, the Soviet General Staff has divided Europe into three TSMAs: Northwestern, Western, and Southwestern (see Figure 2). According to lectures presented at the Voroshilov General Staff Academy in Moscow, the "Balkan countries constitute the center of the Southwestern TSMA."[6] The theater extends about 3,000 kilometers from east to west and 2,500 kilometers from north to south and includes the territories of Albania, eastern Algeria, Austria, Bulgaria, Cyprus, northern Egypt, Greece, Hungary, Italy, Libya, Malta, Monaco, Romania, San Marino, Tunisia, western Turkey, and Yugoslavia; the Odessa and Kiev Military Districts of the Soviet Union; the western part of the Azov and Black seas; the Marmara, Adriatic, and Aegean seas; and the eastern part of the Mediterranean Sea. Since the operational boundaries of TSMAs are scenario dependent, under some circumstances the Southwestern

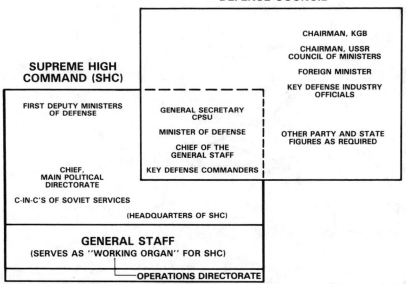

DEFENSE COUNCIL

CHAIRMAN, KGB

CHAIRMAN, USSR
COUNCIL OF MINISTERS

**SUPREME HIGH
COMMAND (SHC)**

FOREIGN MINISTER

KEY DEFENSE INDUSTRY
OFFICIALS

FIRST DEPUTY MINISTERS
OF DEFENSE

GENERAL SECRETARY
CPSU

MINISTER OF DEFENSE

OTHER PARTY AND STATE
FIGURES AS REQUIRED

CHIEF OF THE
GENERAL STAFF

CHIEF,
MAIN POLITICAL
DIRECTORATE

KEY DEFENSE COMMANDERS

C-IN-C'S OF SOVIET SERVICES

(HEADQUARTERS OF SHC)

GENERAL STAFF
(SERVES AS "WORKING ORGAN" FOR SHC)

OPERATIONS DIRECTORATE

Figure 1   Soviet Strategic Planning Organization

Source: Adapted from "NATO and the Changing Concept of Control for Theater War,"
LTC John G. Hines and Dr. Phillip A. Petersen, Signal, Vol. 41, No. 9, May 1987.

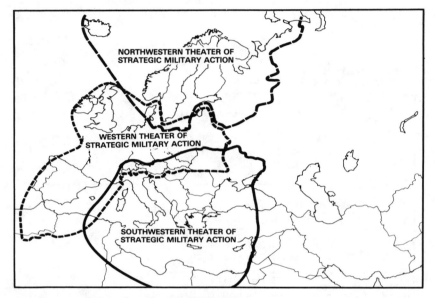

Figure 2   European Theaters of Strategic Military Action

Source: Signal (See Figure 1)

TSMA could also include the territories of southeastern France, Switzerland, Austria, southern Poland, and eastern Czechoslovakia.

In support of the large number of scenarios that could potentially require the conduct of combat actions in the Southwestern TSMA, the Operations Directorate has worked out detailed operational plans for five army-scale offensives. These operational assessments concerning the Southwestern TSMA should not be interpreted as indications of Soviet intentions, but rather as operational contingency planning requirements flowing from military-strategic concerns. Thus the five offensives could be executed in any of the possible variants to support the use of military power, ranging from general war to some lesser requirement for the employment of military force in Southeastern Europe. In anticipation of the complex requirements in the conduct of strategic operations in the Southwestern TSMA, the Headquarters of the Supreme High Command has also established an intermediate-level High Command Of Forces (HCOF) for the control of forces in this theater.

According to a Soviet military lecture presented in the mid-1980s, the command element of the Southwestern TSMA was "made known in 1984." At that time, Army General I. A. Gerasimov was appointed as commander-in-chief (CINC) of the HCOF in the Southwestern TSMA.[7] This same lecture from the mid–1980s also identified the following possible operational directions[8] for the Southwestern TSMA (Figure 3):

Alpine Direction—frontage, 180 to 240 kilometers; depth, 550 kilometers; operational density, six to eight divisions. The Alpine Operational Direction is intended to destroy or fix forces in the region of the Alps so that they cannot be committed to the decisive strategic operation in the Western TSMA. The southern boundary of this direction may overlap with that of the North Italian Direction.

North Italian Direction—frontage, 100 to 200 kilometers; depth, 600 to 750 kilometers; operational density, six to eight divisions. Since the Soviets are concerned that the infrastructure of northern Italy could be employed to support Western military efforts in Central Europe, Soviet strategic planners have designated an operational direction intended to eliminate that possibility. The terrain transited by forces moving on the North Italian Operational Direction could be limited to southern Austria or could include northern Yugoslavia depending on the scenario of the crisis and war.

Adriatic Direction—basically the territory of Yugoslavia. Frontage, 300 to 500 kilometers; depth, 500 to 700 kilometers. It allows control

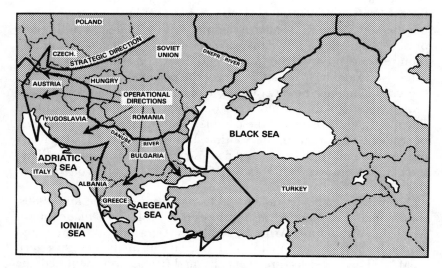

Figure 3   Southwestern Continental Theater of Strategic Military Action

Source: Adapted from <u>Signal</u> (See Figure 1)

of the Adriatic coastline, prevents a major assault landing by NATO, and thus creates favorable conditions for a grouping of forces operating on the North Italian Direction. Besides this, by operating on this axis, the forces of the Warsaw Pact can cover the primary economic regions and industrial centers of Yugoslavia, Hungary, and Romania and control the important lines of communication—Vienna-Belgrade-Athens. The most convenient places for crossing the Dinaric Alps are the valleys of the Bosna and Neretva rivers. The operational density of the axis is ten to fifteen divisions (toward the west from the Sava River, it is four to five divisions).

Ionian Operational Direction—frontage, 180 to 400 kilometers; depth, 400 to 500 kilometers. This direction provides a grouping of forces exit from the lower Danube plain to the coast of the Ionian Sea and the Strait of Otranto. The natural conditions of this direction are complicated; therefore, a wide use of combat equipment with high trafficability, airborne assaults, transport aviation and helicopters is advisable. The operational density is only five to six divisions.

Bosporus-Dardanelles Operational Direction—provides the creation of conditions for the breakout of a large grouping of Warsaw Pact forces in the straits. The terrain on this direction allows for the use of tank formations as part of combined-arms groupings and for the rapid exploitation of success with the aim of establishing control over the straits. The operational density of this direction is five to six divisions, including two tank divisions.

The Alpine, North Italian, and Adriatic Operational Directions probably would be grouped into a single strategic direction,[9] and the Ionian and Bosporus-Dardanelles Operational Directions probably would be grouped into another strategic direction aimed at establishing control of access to the Black Sea and control of the eastern Mediterranean. It is important to note that the Soviets do not consider the Turkish border with the Soviet Union to lie in the same TSMA as the Bosporus and Dardanelles, but to lie instead in the Southern TSMA. This arrangement apparently reflects at least two Soviet considerations: (1) a Soviet military conflict with Pakistan and Iran might involve the United States and Turkey, but not necessarily NATO as an alliance; and (2) in an operational sense (i.e., the establishment of unit boundaries), combat actions against the Bosporus and Dardanelles would not involve the coordination of *front* operations against eastern Turkey.

The Alpine Operational Direction

Traditionally, the main axis of a Warsaw Pact attack on Austria has been perceived as being directed from Hungary up the Danube Valley into southern Germany. If the main objective lies in Bavaria, however, there is no reason for the Soviets to take this long route when an axis directed from Czechoslovakia would quickly bring them to the key Danube city of Linz. The terrain between the border and Linz is relatively open and rolling country, not difficult if the tactical route does not stray too far north. This tactical axis also has a rail route, and a four-lane highway is being built from Linz toward the Czechoslovak border.

Fortifications have been constructed around the Linz area, and the speed of the Danube River itself makes it difficult to get into the water and out of it except at two points. Thus, only a quick air-land assault on Linz would offer the possibility of obtaining the tempo of operations necessary for success on the southern arm of encirclement against CENTAG (Central Army Group) in the Western TSMA (Figure 4). Even with forces at Linz, however, the advance against Munich would be difficult, because the initially open terrain subsequently becomes more restricted as the axis approaches Salzburg, and the rivers along the southwestern banks of the Danube repeatedly provide potential defensive lines.

To the south, because Vienna lies exposed to the east of the Alps, the Austrians would probably not even attempt to defend the city. To the north of the city, however, the mountains lie closer to the Danube, facilitating defense against a Warsaw Pact advance up the valley. Austrian defense plans have identified key areas such as this, which dominate transit routes through the country, and have taken actions to ensure their control. Beyond these key areas to be defended, the Austrians have also prepared a national redoubt into which their forces can withdraw to ensure protracted resistance.[10]

Soviet hopes for any early Austrian capitulation could evaporate rather quickly, because the Austrians have repeatedly demonstrated their courage in the face of threats from the East. All bridges constructed since the end of World War II have been prepared for deployment of a barrier system and for total destruction. Furthermore, an extensive fortification system has been constructed to cover the barrier system as well as points of access into the national redoubt. The national will was reflected in the fact that Austrian forces stood ready to defend the frontiers during the Soviet invasion of Hungary in 1956 and Czechoslovakia in 1968. More important, preparations undertaken by the government to remove itself to the national redoubt in 1968 suggest that the politicians are determined to avoid decapitation of the defense effort.

Since the Soviet General Staff intends the Alpine Operational

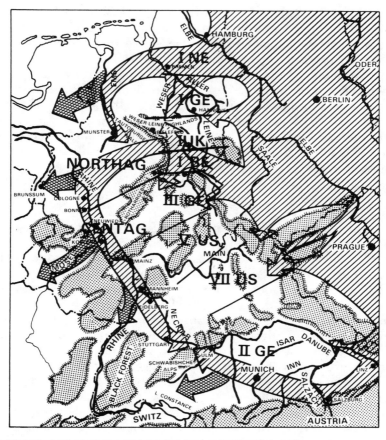

I NE = 1st Dutch Corps	I GE = 1st German Corps	I UK = 1st British Corps
I BE = 1st Belgian Corps	III GE = 3rd German Corps	V US = 5th U.S. Corps
VII US = 7th U.S. Corps	II GE = 2nd German Corps	

Abbreviations:
NORTHAG = Northern Army Group
CENTAG = Central Army Group

Figure 4   Textbook Application of Soviet Encirclement Principles in NATO Central Region

Source: "Soviet Offensive Operations in Central Europe," Dr. Phillip A. Petersen, <u>NATO's Sixteen Nations</u>. Vol. 32, No. 5, August 1987.

Direction to fix Western forces in Italy so they may not be redeployed to the Western TSMA, it is important to understand the Soviet assessment of the potential roles of the Swiss armed forces. From the Soviet perspective, the Swiss air force could play a decisive role in Austrian defense plans along the Linz-Salzburg axis by substituting for the weak Austrian air force. Even more important, however, is the potential role of the Swiss army in supporting the German II Corps in Bavaria. To reduce the possibility that Swiss forces might be committed to northwest Austria and southwest Bavaria, therefore, Soviet military planners have prepared a potential "threat" to southern Austria.[11]

The North Italian Operational Direction

The threat to Italy's role as operational rear of either the Southwestern TSMA or the Western TSMA comes from the air and missile threat to Italian ports and airfields, as well as from ground forces by way of Austria and the Yugoslav provinces of Croatia and Slovenia. If Soviet forces on the southern arm of encirclement into Bavaria were especially successful, a Soviet tactical axis directed from occupied Innsbruck against the Brenner Pass also becomes a possibility. The early capitulation of the Austrian government could be instrumental in this case. It would also be important to Soviet planners with respect to the North Italian Direction, because the Soviets plan for advances west up two wide river valleys (Lafnitz and Raab) toward Graz, then on to Klagenfurt and Italy.

The system of barriers and fortifications constructed by the Austrians in the passes south into Italy clearly suggests the potential for security cooperation between Italy and Austria. Furthermore, the Italians have positioned three corps in the north to defend the ground axis into northern Italy. "The IV Corps (HQ Bolzano) sees to the defense of the high mountains, and its five Alpini brigades are garrisoned on the flanks of the Dolomites."[12] The "V Corps (HQ Vittorio Veneto) is responsible for guarding the flatter ground towards the coast, and its formations and units are disposed in depth along the approaches to Venice."[13] Behind the IV and V Corps, the III Corps (HQ Milan) functions as a reserve in depth, having an armored brigade at Novara west of Milan; a motorized infantry brigade at Turin; and four more mechanized infantry brigades in Milan, Bologna, Brescia, and Bergamo.

Warsaw Pact forces operating on the North Italian Operational Direction would be limited to one principal point of entry: the

Tarvisio area. Secondary axes would likely be employed by trying the Pramollo and Plöcken passes and moving up the Drava (Drau) River Valley (see Figure 5).

The objective of the North Italian Operational Direction would be the north Italian plain near Verona. Just to reach the plain would involve the transit of some 170 kilometers of difficult terrain. Before Soviet forces could reach the Italian heartland, they would have to advance through the successive lines of the Piave, Brenta, and Adige rivers, and, finally, the Po and its left-bank tributaries.

From a Soviet perspective, unless they have total air supremacy, the ground offensive on the North Italian Operational Direction would constitute a most difficult assignment for the six to eight divisions allocated. Obviously, seasonal conditions could make the conduct of operations even more difficult. Furthermore, a spell of heavy rain in the mountains would cause rapid and unpredictable rises in the rivers. It is not surprising, therefore, that Soviet strategic planners consider the four to five divisions operating "west from the Sava River" on the Adriatic Operational Direction to be a key element for "the creation of favorable conditions" for those forces operating on the North Italian Operational Direction.

Socialist Yugoslavia has organized its defense in such a manner as to ensure that any invader would be met by a widespread and protracted struggle. The main force of the Yugoslav People's Army (YPA) and the territorial defense units are slated to defend the central part of the country, relying on the hilly and mountainous terrain. Under this concept, operational forces of the YPA must provide the time for mobilization (approximately forty-eight hours) of the territorial defense forces. Subsequently, the operational and territorial forces would attempt to defend both along fronts and in depth. As explained by Adam Roberts, "To achieve this object, part of the operational army would have to execute a 'descending transformation': that is, to transfer partially or completely from the frontal to the partisan form of warfare, and simultaneously, to transform a heavy organization depending on heavy weapons into light organizational forms appropriate to partisan-type operations."[14]

The operational implications of the Yugoslav strategy for NATO forces defending on the North Italian Operational Direction are that there could be little to prevent the Soviets and Hungarians from exploiting the axis of the Sava River for an offensive westward into Italy. The coastal plain, extending 20-odd kilometers from the northeastern corner of the Adriatic, provides the Soviets with an opportunity to outflank the Italian defenses in the mountains to the north.

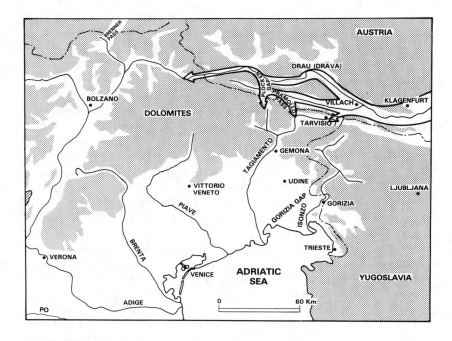

Figure 5   North Italian Operational Direction

Source: "Italy in Soviet Military Strategy," Phillip A. Petersen, <u>The International Spectator</u>,
         Vol. XXIII, No. 1, January - March 1988.

Near the Italian city of Gorizia the coastal plain extends into Yugoslavia. With the high ground on three sides of Gorizia in Yugoslav territory, there is every reason to believe that the Soviets would attempt to transit Yugoslav territory, with or without the cooperation of the Yugoslavs.

The multiple channels of the Taliamento River represent the first line of defense on the plain if the Gorizia Gap were lost. The Italian army has gun emplacements at a number of important points along the river from the coastal plain to the upper valley in the mountains. Although the riverbed is more like a flood plain and is both dangerous and unpredictable, it is just as often no barrier at all. Behind the Tagliamento position, the Piave River provides a more dependable barrier if the bridges (three highway and two autostrada) were taken down.

The Drava-Sava axis through Yugoslavia also would provide the Soviets with additional opportunities to stretch Italian defenses further north. As the Italian border retreats from the Isonzo River upstream from Gorizia, the Yugoslav road net allows for access to Italian territory in the direction of Udine, although with no immediate access to the coastal plain. Farther north, near the Austrian border, Yugoslav territory also would facilitate an attack on the Tarvisio area from multiple directions.

Given the Yugoslav strategy, which does not exclude the possibility of "some degree of military support from outside the country,"[15] and the fact that most of the high terrain to the east of the coastal plain lies on the Yugoslav side of the border, it is possible to suggest that in a crisis both governments could find their respective positions "improved immeasurably by pre-emptive advances across the border"[16] by Italian forces. By moving less than 100 kilometers into Yugoslavia, the Italians could completely neutralize the Soviet advance toward the Gorizia Gap at the nodal road junction of Ljubljana. "An even shorter move north across the Carnic Alps into Austria might just as effectively block the Soviet advance up the valley of the Drava by way of Klagenfurt and Villach."[17] Clearly, "the Italian strategy is to hold the ground well forward, so as to exploit the obstacle value of the mountainous terrain along the borders with Yugoslavia and Austria."[18] Just how far forward might well depend on whether the Italians could take up defensive positions before the Soviets could seize this key terrain by airborne/heliborne assault.

The Adriatic Operational Direction

The main tactical axis of Warsaw Pact forces operating against Yugoslavia would probably be directed from Hungary onto the Danubian

Plain (see Figure 6). The spearhead of any such operation would seek to capture Belgrade as quickly as possible. The defenders of the city could expect that the ground assault on the city would be assisted by airborne or heliborne forces in an attempt to keep the defenders off balance. The Soviet strategy would undoubtedly be linked to some political attempt to break up the People's Republic of Yugoslavia, unless the entire operation were tied to some sort of internal military coup.[19]

If the combat action against Yugoslavia were part of a larger strategic operation in the Southwestern TSMA or were directed at the complete occupation of the country, the axis south out of Hungary toward Belgrade would be joined by an axis directed up the Sava and Drava (Drau) river valleys to occupy the northwestern quarter of the country. Bulgaria could best support the offensive on this operational direction by launching a drive from the southeast against the Nisava Valley, which penetrates the mountainous terrain along the Yugoslav border with Bulgaria.

With the immediate Soviet operational objectives lying in the northern and eastern parts of the country, the Yugoslav coastal defense command would probably not find itself being significantly challenged during the initial stages of any Soviet invasion. It would therefore be in a position to assist units withdrawing into the mountainous terrain along the coastal side of the country, where the Yugoslavs managed to maintain as many as thirty divisions during World War II,[20] and to assist in the movement of and security for any supplies from the West that might land along the coast. At least another eight divisions could probably operate in the mountainous terrain in southeastern Yugoslavia.[21] Historical precedent, as well as geography, suggests that Yugoslavia would find the West willing to provide at least military goods, although the first assistance Yugoslavia could feel confident of receiving is the assurance that its military forces could be diverted from the Austrian, Italian, and Greek borders.[22]

The Ionian Operational Direction

From the perspective of the Soviet General Staff, the Ionian and the Bosporus-Dardanelles Operational Directions are inextricably locked into the same Strategic Direction, for two reasons: First, even if the Warsaw Pact should successfully seize control of the Turkish Straits, Soviet naval forces would still face the problem of making the 600-kilometer passage between the Dardanelles and the Mediterranean.

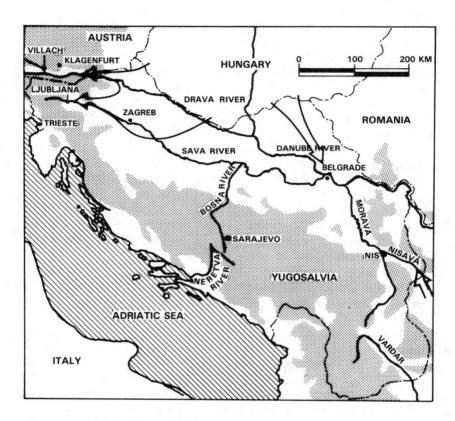

Figure 6 Adriatic Operational Direction

Second, the easiest access to the open rolling terrain of Turkish Thrace is on the Greek side of the Evros (Maritsa) River.

Regardless of the political overtures made by the Warsaw Pact toward Greece, the main attack on the Bosporus-Dardanelles Direction would probably swing south of Edirne across Greek territory to avoid Turkish defenses west of the city. One tactical axis would turn east toward Istanbul and another south toward the Dardanelles. Since the Bulgarians would be expected to provide as much as half the ground forces in the operation, they might also choose to assume the opportunity to continue south along the plain of the Evros (Maritsa) River toward Alexandroupolis to reacquire some Aegean coastline. If the Warsaw Pact were to engage the Greeks on this axis, the objective would probably be Kavala (see Figure 7).

As noted in the Soviet military lecture from the mid-1980s, the natural conditions of the Ionian Operational Direction would necessitate extensive combat actions by airmobile forces. For, in addition to the multitude of islands, 80 percent of the mainland is dominated by mountainous terrain. The principal axis of ground advance would undoubtedly be along the road and rail route from Sofia to Thessaloniki to Athens. To move along this axis, however, would require not only air mobility but also air superiority.

Although the terrain of northern Greece is generally mountainous or otherwise inhospitable, the geographical obstacles may have little more than a temporary canalizing effect, given the high mobility of Soviet forces. The least tenable ground on the frontier is the nearly 200-kilometer Aegean coastline of eastern Macedonia and Greek Thrace. This terrain poses the threat of encirclement for its defenders should the Warsaw Pact move down the Struma (Strymon) River against Thessaloniki. In this case the tactical axis from Bulgaria would likely split at Lake Kerkinitis once the difficult 10-kilometer stretch from the border had been breached. One axis would move south along the floor of the Struma (Strymon) River valley to Serre, where it would turn east to Drava, and then back south to Kavala to link up with the axis moving west from the Evros (Maritsa) River.

Since fortifications have been constructed on the right bank of the Struma (Strymon) River, and the routes through the Vertiskos Mountains provide very little room for maneuver off the roads, the main tactical axis from Bulgaria to Thessaloniki would probably follow the rail route north of Lake Kerkinitis toward Lake Doiranis, and then south over wide open plains leading directly to the Aegean. This route never narrows to less than 3 kilometers in width, and it could be supported by an axis cutting through the southeast corner of

Figure 7   Ionian Operational Direction

Yugoslavia. Such a supporting axis would attempt to move into Greece along the Vardar (Axios) River Valley. Even though such an attempt would probably result in a meeting engagement—a combat action in which the opposing sides engage while on the move, with units incompletely deployed in battle—with Greek forces in the vicinity of Strumica, it would clearly spread the defending forces.

Any attempt by the Warsaw Pact to seize Thessaloniki would probably reflect a Soviet decision to occupy the entire country. The route south from Thessaloniki is blocked by the edge of the western Macedonian plateau facing east over the Axios (Vardar) Plain. Referred to as the Aliakmon Line in 1941, the northern end of the portion is anchored on the Vevi Pass, Mount Kajmakcalan, and the northern end of Lake Vegoritis. The city of Veroia would anchor the center of the line and Mount Olympus the right flank. The only four passes through the position are Vevi, Edhessa, Veroia, and along the coast. Although the main axis would probably follow the coast, the route to Larisa and the Plain of Thessaly could become very difficult near Platamon and again in the narrow valley of the Pinios River between Olympus and Ossa.

A full-scale invasion of Greece would probably be structured as a *front* operation in the Aegean Strategic Direction. The immediate *front* objective in Greece would be the Corinth Canal, which would provide the most readily defensible line should the offensive have to be halted to support the diversion of reserves elsewhere. The subsequent *front* objective would involve heliborne operations against the Peloponnese and a joint assault landing operation against Crete.

The Bosporus-Dardanelles Operational Direction

Within the Southwestern TSMA, the most important strategic region is that of the Turkish Straits. In the ethnic rhetoric of the Soviet General Staff, it is the Balkans where "the Slav people, led by Russia, had been committed for a long time in wars with Turkey. The struggle for domination over the Black Sea, occupation of the Straits and freedom of the Balkan people from Turkish domination continued until the 20th century."[23] Thus the Soviet military makes no distinction between the twentieth-century Turkish Republic and the Ottoman Empire, and believes "the Straits" should be liberated from "occupation."

The Turkish Straits Strategic Region is centered on the 300-kilometer passage between the Black and Aegean seas. The strategic region comprises three parts: the Bosporus, which is 30 kilometers long but only about 2 kilometers wide; the Sea of Marmara, which measures 200 kilometers by 70 kilometers; and the Dardanelles, which are about 5 kilometers wide and lead for 70 winding kilometers to the Aegean Sea.[24] This entire Turkish Straits Strategic Region is defended by the First Turkish Army.

Although the Soviets would undoubtedly prefer to husband their resources for the main battle in central Europe, the temptation to fulfill the Slav dream of liberating Constantinople might be too strong to postpone until the struggle in the Western TSMA had been successfully resolved. Much would depend upon the attitude of the Greeks and the NATO resources available to support the Turks and Greeks.

The main axis of the Bosporus-Dardanelles Operational Direction would probably be directed from the west. A secondary axis would likely be directed at Kirklareli from the north. The low, wooded Yildiz daglari constitutes a defensive barrier to penetration from the north, but the terrain to the south is superb tank country. Furthermore, the east-west transportation net of Turkish Thrace supports a direct advance on Istanbul. The only natural defensive lines are the valleys of the streams that flow through rolling downland, at least some of which have been fortified.

The last defensive line west of Istanbul is that of the Catalca Position, which runs for a total of 24 kilometers as the isthmus narrows, and lakes and arms of the sea can be exploited. Unfortunately, the Black Sea coast to the east of the Catalca Position provides the Warsaw Pact with a well-recognized opportunity to outflank this defense line with an air-sea assault landing. The terrain in northwestern Anatolia is also conducive to the conduct of air and amphibious assault landings, but the route to the Bosporus is difficult and the defending garrisons are well positioned.

On a maritime axis, such as that directed against the Bosporus, an operational-strategic assault landing would probably involve amphibious and airborne forces supported by naval surface combatants as well as aircraft of the navy and the air forces. In addition, such an operation would be quickly reinforced by especially trained motorized rifle troops that would be landed by air or sea in the objective area.[25] Joint airborne/amphibious combat actions resembling such an assault landing operation were conducted in Exercise SHIELD-82, held between September 28 and October 1, 1982, in Bulgaria. The assault in SHIELD-82 was preceded by attacks on the "enemy" artillery and defensive positions by Warsaw Pact aircraft and naval vessels. Minesweepers and specially equipped mine-clearing helicopters led the assault, clearing paths for the trailing craft. Surface ships and submarines provided security for the naval task force conducting the landing and deployed to counter an "enemy" that was capable of surface, subsurface, and air counterattack. Acoustic devices were used to monitor the movements of the "enemy" submarines and antisubmarine operations were conducted.[26]

Naval infantry led the assault landing by ship and helicopter, which included the landing of tanks and armored personnel carriers. Soviet air cushion vehicles were used to land the heavy equipment. Once the initial beachhead was secured, helicopters cleared minefields along the shore and inland. Soviet naval aviation, employed in a ground support role, and attack helicopters supported the landing and subsequent attack. The attack following the landing concluded with an assault of the "enemy's" position from the flank, in conjunction with an attack by the forces landed by parachute.[27]

The parachute insertion was preceded by fire preparation of the landing zones by Soviet and Bulgarian bombers and fighter-bombers. Movement to the drop zones was by Soviet Il-76/CANDID heavy transport aircraft, carrying both paratroops and combat equipment. Security for the heavy transports was provided by Soviet and Bulgarian fighters; the air superiority missions and the paratroop drop continued despite rain and fog in the exercise area. The airborne force seized an airfield, subsequently using it to land more troops and equipment. Once the airfield was secured, the force captured a special weapons storage facility, conducted a "raid," and linked up with the amphibious force.[28] Exercise YUG in 1971, ten years earlier, had a similar scenario: "An airborne division was dropped or airlanded at a captured airfield 'within half an hour,' and almost certainly tasked to link up with naval infantry landed on the Black Sea coast that same day."[29]

As noted by Charles Pritchard, "The Soviets are well aware of both Turkish fixed defenses such as the fortified areas near the Bosporus and NATO plans for a mobile defense of the Thracian beaches."[30] The Soviets are also aware that success in the defense of Turkish Thrace depends on the timely arrival of NATO air and antitank reinforcement, given the rapid pace of Warsaw Pact deployment of reactive armor.[31] There can be little question that Turkish antitank capabilities are inadequate, given the open rolling terrain the First Army has been assigned to defend.

Possible Operations Against Romania[32]

Romania presents a relatively simple landform pattern consisting of a sharply curving line of mountains, with, along its outer edge, foothills and plains, and a series of mountains (including the Bihor massif) extending like a chord across its open side (Figure 8). This "chord" of mountains is much more open, and, in fact, consists of broken hills in a few places in the far north. The circuit formed by these mountain ranges contains the Transylvanian Basin, which measures about 145 kilometers from east to west and about 195 kilometers from north to south. The Transylvanian Basin itself is a high plateau that is frequently broken by wooded hills and rivers.

On the west side of the ring of mountains that encircle the Transylvanian Basin lies a flat plain running from the Soviet border in the north along the entire border with Hungary to about half the border with Yugoslavia. To the eastern and southern sides of the ring of mountains lie plains that run to within 72 kilometers of the Romanian Black Sea coast. The coastal area consists of a delta area in the north, where the Danube flows into the sea, and low plateau to the south. Thus, although the landforms of Romania leave its capital and largest city wide open to a quick armored thrust from the Odessa Military District, the Carpathian Mountains do provide a natural fortress to which the Romanian military forces could withdraw in the face of a Soviet onslaught.

A Soviet ground advance into Romania could be expected to be concentrated along the Prut River, which forms the eastern boundary between Romania and the Soviet Union. The spearhead of the operation would undoubtedly be directed out of southeasternmost Odessa Military District, across the plains to the south of the Carpathian Mountains and straight to the capital. The Romanian leadership could expect Soviet airborne or airmobile forces to assist ground units in the assault on Bucharest.

It is highly unlikely that the Soviets would attempt to use the Bulgarians as proxy for their own intervention, if only because of the inability of the Bulgarians to mount the type of lightning-quick military operation that would seem to be required in order to have any chance of crushing the Romanian will to resist. This does not preclude, of course, a Soviet attempt to reduce Romanian determination through the use of Bulgarian attacks along the Danube. Should the Soviets wish to take into account the full-scale protracted resistance that the Romanians threaten, Soviet thrusts from the Odessa Military District and Bulgarian attacks across the Danube might be joined by drives directed from the Carpathian Military District north of the Bihor massif and from Hungary to the south of the Bihor massif in an attempt to breach the chord of mountains surrounding the Transylvanian Basin. Such action would most certainly find Soviet

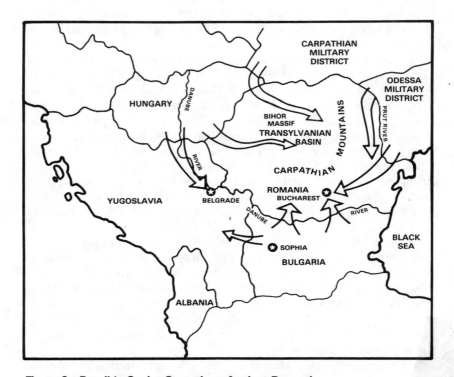

Figure 8   Possible Soviet Operations Against Romania

Source: Adapted from "Military Intervention as a Solution to Soviet Problems in the Balkans," Phillip A. Petersen, <u>Soviet Policy in the Post-Tito Balkans</u>, Edited by Phillip A. Petersen, Studies in Communist Affairs, Vol. 4, U.S. Government Printing Office, 1979.

airborne or airmobile forces being employed against the most critical terrain involved, as well as against the major cities of Transylvania.

The first task of the armed forces of Romania would be to delay enemy penetration long enough to allow for total mobilization. This task would involve employing frontal tactics (although taking care to ensure that large losses were avoided) across invasion routes and making quick and effective responses to the Soviet employment of airborne and airmobile forces. Once the Soviet "blitz" had been slowed, it might then be transformed into a protracted conflict in which a mixture of combined and partisan tactics could be employed to exact the maximum cost from the invaders. The defenders can only hope that the maximum cost would be too high for the Soviet military and Western political sensitivities.

The Romanian leaders would hope to use their landforms in the event their country was invaded. The army has, therefore, an area organization composed of two military regions and the Bucharest garrison.[33] Military units to the east and south of the Carpathian Mountains would have as their principal task the responsibility of opposing any land invasion from the Soviets' Odessa Military District, any naval landing along the Romanian Black Sea coast, and any operations launched from across the Danubian border with Bulgaria. A secondary, but critical, task would be the isolation and destruction of any Soviet airborne or airmobile forces that could be expected to be employed against Romanian cities and other crucial points. As these Romanian military forces withdrew in the face of the enemy, they would make their way to the eastern and southern Carpathians, where they could use the terrain in an attempt to keep the Soviets out of the Transylvanian Basin. Romanian military units in the north and west would also attempt to slow any Soviet advance in order to prepare defensive positions along the western Carpathians.

Success on the part of the Romanian military would allow for the existence of an independent Romania in the "heartland" of the country. The continued existence of this heartland fortress would depend on many factors, not the least of which is the ability of the Romanian military to keep Soviet armor out of the Transylvanian Basin and to deal effectively with Soviet airborne and airmobile force operations against the basin and its shielding ring of mountainous terrain. Should the potential Romanian fortress break down, the Romanians would attempt to resort to guerrilla operations based in the Carpathians, but operating throughout the entire country as well.

SOUTHEASTERN EUROPE IN A PERIOD OF TRANSITION

Clearly, any Soviet use of military power in Eastern Europe involves a risk of great-power confrontation. That risk, according to conventional wisdom, is now at its lowest point. The very change encouraging this optimism will nevertheless come at the price of the stability that inhibited great-power miscalculation. As a result, the last decade of the twentieth century may well constitute a dangerous period of transition to a new strategic environment. The institutionalization of pluralization in Eastern Europe, and indeed even in the Soviet Union, is as heady for the West to observe as it is for the East to experience. Enthusiasm being no substitute for analysis, the revolutionary processes taking place in Eastern Europe and the Soviet Union must be seen not simply in terms of the philosophical struggle between egalitarianism and freedom, but also as the release of potentially explosive social tensions and political frustrations.

In a manner not unlike that of the American officers in Vietnam who concluded that they had to destroy a village in order to save it, the revolutionaries now in control of the Soviet state have found they have to destabilize the system in order to change it. In the process of destabilizing the system, however, ethnic and religious tensions and frustrated economic and nationalist aspirations have resurfaced. Except perhaps for the Soviet Union itself, Southeastern Europe represents the most dangerous vortex of these explosive forces. The culturally destructive policies of Ceausescu's village reorganization plan in Romania have provoked nationalist tensions with Hungary.[34] Nationalist tensions have also erupted in violent riots between Albanians and Serbs in Yugoslavia.[35] In both cases, as Soviet power recedes from its pervasive role in the politics of Eastern Europe, forces that for the most part have been held in abeyance since the end of World War II are rushing to fill the political vacuum.

With the exception of Hungary in 1956, the Soviets have traditionally forgone the overt use of military power to maintain stability in Southeastern Europe. The potential cost of military intervention as a Soviet policy tool in the Balkans has simply been perceived as too great. Consistent with this traditional approach, since Soviet General Secretary Mikhail S. Gorbachev's accession in March 1985, Soviet policy toward the Balkans has remained cautious and conciliatory, even though the economic and political instability of the region continues to increase.[36] In fact, during 1988 Gorbachev visited both Yugoslavia and Romania to sign important joint communiques pledging Soviet nonintervention. In Yugoslavia, for example, he agreed to "attach special significance to the strict observance of the universally binding principles of . . . fundamental international legal documents prohibiting aggression, the violation of borders, the seizure of other country's territories, all forms of the threat or use of force, and interference in other countries' internal affairs on whatever pretext."[37] The agreement signed by the Soviets and Romanians constituted implicit approval for the Romanians to pursue their own security arrangements:

> We firmly come out for a Europe united within the diversity of social systems, for the deepening of political, economic, scientific and technical, and cultural collaboration between all states of the continent, for a Europe of peace and cooperation, a Europe of independent and free nations. We are also in favor of relations that would rule out any interference in internal affairs and would ensure all peoples independent socioeconomic development in accordance with their wishes, without any outside interference.[38]

In support of this noninterventionist policy, Soviet Foreign Minister Eduard Shevardnadze has argued that the Ministry of Foreign Affairs should play a larger role in the political-military decision-making process. The foreign ministry, he posits,

> must finally assert in the code of professional behavior such norms as a rejection of force and the threat of force as political instruments, respect for the positions and views of others, tolerance and the readiness to perceive what is different not necessarily as bad or hostile, and the ability of partners to live together peacefully even though they may be different and not agree with one another on everything.[39]

Thus Shevardnadze not only voiced concern over the use of force to resolve international conflict and asserted that the Ministry of Foreign Affairs should be just as integral to political-military decision making as the Ministry of Defense, but implicitly laid claim to a senior role within the Defense Council or some new body that would replace it.[40]

In the past, political instability in Eastern Europe was seen largely as a Soviet problem. Stability was purchased by fostering dependence through aid and differential prices. As the Soviet approach to security in Europe continues to change, however, the declining willingness and capability of the Soviet Union to accept sole responsibility for stability in Eastern Europe is likely to have the effect of transferring greater responsibility to the West. The West has long claimed that it wanted to see greater independence for the non-Soviet Warsaw Pact states. Now the West may be asked to pay for that independence. Having already determined that military power is not a practical policy tool in the Balkans, Gorbachev has apparently also concluded that the Soviet Union is no longer able to subsidize the region to the same extent as previously. The consequences of the West's rejection of any responsibility could ultimately produce circumstances not unlike those prevailing at the beginning of this century prior to World War I. Altered political and strategic circumstances could thereby return previously discussed "operational contingency planning requirements" to the foreground of Soviet policy considerations.

NOTES

The authors appreciate comments on an earlier draft by Raymond Hutchings.

1. "Preparation of the Territories of Theaters of Strategic Military Action," *The Voroshilov Lectures: Materials From the Soviet General Staff Academy, Issues of Soviet Military Strategy*, compiled by Ghulam Dastagir Wardak, edited by Graham Hall Turbiville, Jr. (Washington, D.C.: National Defense University Press, 1989), 114.
2. *General Secretary Mikhail Gorbachev and the Soviet Military: Assessing His Impact and the Potential for Future Changes*, Report of the Defense Policy Panel of the Committee on Armed Services, House of Representatives, 100th Cong., 2nd Sess. (Washington, D.C.: U.S. Government Printing Office, September 13, 1988), 6.
3. Jack Snyder, "The Gorbachev Revolution: A Waning of Soviet Expansion," *International Security* (Winter 1987/8): 115–16.
4. Artem Borovik, "Afghanistan: Podvodya Itogi" [Afghanistan: Final Results], *Ogonyek*, no. 12 (March, 1989): 6–8, 30–1; Also see Bob Keller, "General Recalls Soviet Rift in War: Says Military Staff Opposed 1979 Afghan Intervention," *New York Times*, March 19, 1989.
5. *Teatr voyennykh destviy (TVD)* has also been translated as "theater of military operations" (TMO) and "theater of military action" (TMA). See John G. Hines and Phillip A. Petersen, "Translating a Concept," *International Defense Review*, no. 3, 1986. A TVD is defined by the Soviets as "that part of the territory of a continent with the coastal waters of the oceans, internal seas and the air space above them (continental TVD); or the water areas of an ocean, including its islands, the contiguous coastlines of continents and the air space above them (oceanic TVD), within the boundaries of which are deployed strategic groupings of the armed forces and within which military operations are conducted." *Voyennyy entsiklopedicheskiy slovar'* [Military Encyclopedic Dictionary] (Moscow: Voyenizdat, 1983). A TVD, in turn, comprises strategic and operational directions.
6. *The Voroshilov Lectures*, 113.
7. There have been two CINCs of the HCOF in the Southwestern TSMA since 1984. The current CINC, Colonel-General V. V. Osipov, replaced Army General Gerasimov in February 1989.
8. An operational direction is a zone of terrain, including contiguous coastal waters and its airspace, within which an operational formation (army or corps) conducts its operation. Within the context of the continental TSMA in which they lie, operational directions may be internal or coastal.
9. A strategic direction consists of a wide strip of land, including contiguous coastal

waters and airspace, leading the armed forces of one warring party to the other's most important administrative-political and industrial-economic centers. Strategic directions involve operational-strategic scale operations, undertaken by combinations of *fronts*, fleets, independent armies, and flotillas.

10. *Background Information about Area Defense: Information on Military Defense* (Vienna: Bureau of Defense Policy, undated).

11. Two Soviet articles dealing with Soviet planners' concern about the Swiss armed forces, for example, are V. Kuznetsov, "Training and 'Interpretations,' " *Izvestiya*, January 1, 1985; and "In the Role of Potential Ally?" *Krasnaya zvezda* (Red Star), July 16, 1985. Both articles critically assess the Swiss armed forces' attitude toward NATO and attack the wisdom of decisions by Switzerland to modernize its forces with NATO-compatible equipment. The first article also questions the training of Swiss pilots on a NATO air base in Sardinia. It implies that the defense of a neutral country does not require such sophisticated air training and, therefore, makes the accusation that the Swiss air force is preparing to fight against Warsaw Pact aircraft. The article also attacks the Swiss decision to purchase the Leopard 2 main battle tank. The second article makes a special point of "the growing U.S.-Swiss military ties." (The authors wish to express appreciation to Stephen Kux for drawing their attention to these unclassified examples of Soviet perceptions.) Soviet perceptions with regard to the Swiss have been summarized most clearly as follows: "The Russians obviously regard armed neutrality as a charming paper phrase. They associate Switzerland with the North Atlantic Treaty Organization, even if Switzerland adamantly does not. The Russians appear to look upon Switzerland as a kind a capitalist Alamo—a likely position of ultimate defense for a falling Western Europe." John McPhee, *La Place del la Concorde Swisse* (New York: Farrar/Straus/Giroux, 1984), 24. In fact, the former chief of staff to the minister of defense in Czechoslovakia and assistant secretary to the Czech Defense Council has noted that since 1963 the Soviets have assumed they would have to occupy Switzerland to ensure it did not become a bastion for Western forces. Jan Sejna, *We Will Bury You* (London: Sidgwich and Jackson, 1982), 121.

12. Hugh Faringdon, *Confrontation: The Strategic Geography of NATO and the Warsaw Pact* (London: Routledge and Kegan Paul, 1986), 185–8.

13. Ibid., 188.

14. Adam Roberts, *Nations in Arms: The Theory and Practice of Territorial Defense* (New York: Praeger, 1976), 174–5.

15. Ibid., 175.

16. Faringdon, *Confrontation*, 190.

17. Ibid.

18. Ibid., 188.

19. During a "protest meeting in Niksic" in the fall of 1988, the slogans "We want arms" and "We want the Russians" were heard. The Belgrade Domestic Service asked, "Who is inviting the Russians and why?" The broadcast concluded that "there are also those whose apparent aim is to break up and destroy socialist Yugoslavia," thus suggesting the continuing existence of pro-Soviet sympathies in the country. Belgrade, TANJUG, Domestic Service, September 19, 1988.

20. See map facing page 61 in U.S. Department of the Army Pamphlet Number 20–243, *German Antiguerrilla Operations in the Balkans (1941–1944)*, August 1954.

21. Ibid.

22. In 1968 the Italians informed the Yugoslav government that they would guarantee the security of Yugoslavia's border with Italy so that Yugoslavia could redeploy troops stationed along this border to the east. See Dennison I. Rusinow, *Yugoslavia and Stalin's Successors, 1968–1969*, American Universities Fieldstaff Report, Southeastern Europe Series XVI, no. 7, (August 1969): 7, footnote 1. Furthermore, the United States has supplied Yugoslavia with military equipment such as antitank mines and, during the crisis of August 1968, the United States president warned the Soviets against military intervention in Yugoslavia. See Robin Alison Reming-

ton, "Czechoslovakia and the Warsaw Pact," *East European Quarterly* III, no. 3 (September 1969): 329.

23. "General Concepts on Theaters of Strategic Military Action and Methods of Studying Their Strategic Characteristics," *Voroshilov Lectures*, vol. 1, p. 113.

24. Faringdon, *Confrontation*, 163.

25. See Phillip A. Petersen, "Turkey in Soviet Military Strategy," *Dis Politika* (Turkish Foreign Policy), XIII, nos. 1–2 (1986).

26. John L. Jensen, *SHIELD–82*, DDB–2680–185–83 (Unclassified) (Washington: Defense Intelligence Agency, 1983), 7.

27. Ibid.

28. Ibid., 10.

29. Graham H. Turbiville, Jr., "Soviet Airborne Operations in Theater War," *Dis Politika* (Turkish Foreign Policy) XIII, nos. 1–2 (1986): 176.

30. Charles Pritchard, "Warsaw Pact Amphibious Forces and the Turkish Straits," *Dis Politika* (Turkish Foreign Policy) XIII, nos. 1–2 (1986): 158.

31. See Benjamin F. Schemmer, "Interview with Phillip A. Karber," *Armed Forces Journal International* (May 1987): 42–59.

32. This section is adapted from Phillip A. Petersen, "Military Intervention as a Solution to Soviet Problems in the Balkans," in Phillip A. Petersen, ed., *Soviet Policy in the Post-Tito Balkans*, Studies in Communist Affairs Series 4 (Washington, D.C.: U.S. Government Office, 1978), 93–117.

33. Eugene K. Keefe, Donald W. Bernier, Lyle E. Brenneman, William Giloanne, Neda Al Walpole, and James M. Moore, Jr., *Area Handbook for Romania*, DA PAM550–160 (Washington, D.C.: U.S. Government Printing Office, 1972), 213.

34. Gheorghe Deaconu, "Romanian Rural Civilization," *Contemporanul* (in Romanian) (January 1, 1989): 4; Doina Cornea, "An Open Letter to President Nicolae Ceausescu: The People are Fed Up With This Socialism," *Sueddeutsche Zeitung* (in German) (April 17, 1989): 7; reports appearing in the Romanian newspaper *Scinteia* for May 4, 1989, and June 29, 1988; and Henry Kamm, "Rumania Makes Threats, Hungary Says," *New York Times*, July 11, 1989, p. 3.

35. "Obstanovka v Kosovo obostryayetsya" [The Conditions in Kosovo Become Exacerbated], *Krasnaya zvezda*, March 27, 1989; "Obstanovka ostayetsya slozhnoy" [The Situation is Deteriorating], *Krasnaya zvezda*, March 31, 1989; John Tagliabue, "In a Yugoslav Province, Aflame for Six Days, the Resentments Still Smolder," *New York Times*, April 4, 1989; "Methods of Spontaneous Organization," a speech by Stipe Suvar, president of the Presidium of the Central Committee of the League of Communists of Yugoslavia at the Session of the Central Committee of the Croatian League of Communists on April 12, 1989, *Borba*, April 13, 1989, p. 4.

36. An example is the resignation of the entire Yugoslav cabinet under the leadership of Branko Mikulic on December 30, 1988, as a result of the faltering economy. See TASS, "Otsenivaya minuvshiy, Prognoziryua nastupirskiy—Belgrad" ["Past Value, The Coming Prognosis—Belgrade"], *Pravda*, January 1, 1989, p. 4; see also Barry Newman, "Yugoslav Cabinet's Resignation Shows Communist Fragility in Fractious Land," *Wall Street Journal*, January 3, 1989, p. 12.

37. "Soviet-Yugoslav Declaration," *Pravda*, March 19, 1988, p. 2.

38. "Soviet-Romanian Joint Communique," *Pravda*, October 6, 1988, p. 3.

39. E. A. Shevardnadze, "On Practical Tasks of the Ministry of Foreign Affairs for Implementing the Ideas and Points Contained in the Speech by M. S. Gorbachev in the UN on 7 December 1988," *Vestnik Ministerstva Inostrannykh Del SSSR* [Bulletin of the USSR Ministry of Foreign Affairs], December 15, 1988, p. iii.

40. Another prominent political-military body contributing to the policy debate resides in the Congress of People's Deputies' Committee on Defense and State Security.

10

PREMISES AND PRACTICES OF SOVIET POLICY IN SOUTHEASTERN EUROPE

Ronald H. Linden

PREMISES OF SOVIET POLICY IN EASTERN EUROPE

Since World War II Soviet policy in Eastern Europe has been based on the pursuit of three kinds of security: physical, political, and economic. These goals apply to Southeastern Europe as part of the East European region, but, as this chapter shows, the variety of problems posed by the states of Southeastern Europe creates special nuances in Soviet policy for that region. This chapter briefly addresses each of these goals before dealing with Soviet practices in the region. The chapter concludes with consideration of several scenarios for Eastern Europe.

Physical Security

The USSR has invested immense political, economic, and military resources to keep its western border free from potential attack by hostile conventional and, to a lesser extent, nuclear forces. This goal has little to do with the Communist nature of the Soviet government or with the existence of any actual current threat. The Soviet Union absorbed the brutal lessons of the past and, given the scope of the country's destruction and suffering in World War II, the maintenance of an adequate buffer in the west took on a life of its own as a foreign-policy given.

The threat emanating from Southeastern Europe, however, has clearly been perceived to be much less than the threat from Central Europe, a view that accurately reflects at least twentieth-century

European history. Soviet troop-stationing patterns show a much greater emphasis on the central and northern regions of Eastern Europe than on the southern region. No Warsaw Pact troops have been stationed in Bulgaria, and such troops were withdrawn from Romania in 1958. Outside the Warsaw Pact, neither Albania nor Yugoslavia has accepted Soviet troops.

Political Security

Political security has been a goal dating from the time of the Bolshevik Revolution and the period between the world wars during which the USSR was the only socialist state. The operative premise is that the Soviet Union must have in this region friendly states which in their domestic and international policies will be cognizant of and responsive to Soviet interests. This was certainly not the case during the interwar period, when large and small powers alike either ignored Soviet desires or were hostile to them. Political security since the late 1940s until very recently has been guaranteed in Eastern Europe by the dominance of Soviet-supported Communist parties in these states.

At a maximum, such as during Stalin's time, the Communist Party of the Soviet Union (CPSU) sought the duplication of its own forms and policies in each of the East European states. Such an approach both provoked and was reinforced by the split with Yugoslavia of 1948. After Stalin's death the policy of the Soviet leadership was to press for general adherence to, if not exact mimicking of, Soviet domestic and international initiatives. At a minimum, political security in this region has meant resisting the influence of countries seen to be the key Soviet adversaries, primarily the United States but also, during the 1960s and early 1970s, China. Chinese diplomacy was very active in Southeastern Europe during the 1970s; Beijing succeeded in attracting a vocal if small ally in Albania and in maintaining full and supportive ties with Romania.

Since 1948 the Soviet Union has seen greater threats to its political security in Central Europe. But the challenge in Southeastern Europe has also been complicated, because of the varied environment, including Yugoslav independence, Albanian hostility, and Romanian pursuit of a distinctive foreign policy.

Economic Security

The Soviet Union has clearly viewed Eastern Europe as a region whose resources are available to be used to satisfy Soviet needs. As a result, for the first fifteen or so years after World War II, the Soviets extracted by various measures (reparations, joint stock companies, unequal trade relations) immense material resources to build and rebuild the Soviet economy.[1] During the next twenty years, however, the relationship shifted to one in which the Soviet Union provided the raw materials and fuel and received in exchange more complex manufactured goods. Owing to declining terms of trade and increased involvement of several East European countries with the West, this relationship turned increasingly unfavorable for the USSR. The USSR, as Michael Marrese and Jan Vanous have shown, subsidized the East European economies, including those of Southeastern Europe,[2] in order to keep the alliance politically cohesive and, to the extent possible, to support the ability of some of the regimes to buy peace at home with better economic performance.

More recently, the Soviets have called attention to the need to "restructure" the trade relationship more to their advantage and in a way that serves their greatest need: better-quality machines, equipment, technology, and technological know-how to help the Soviet economy perform better.[3]

Historically, the Soviet search for economic security in particular has provoked greater conflict in Southeastern Europe than in other regions. Postwar attempts to force Yugoslavia to develop its economy along lines dictated in Moscow contributed to the 1948 break. Later, Khrushchev's move to "perfect" the Council for Mutual Economic Assistance (CMEA)—in a way that would have increased the specialization, and thus the advantage, of the more industrially developed Northern-Tier countries—drove Romania to search for other economic partners and to accompany this search with a foreign-policy reassessment. Bulgaria, in contrast, has consistently demonstrated its willingness to accommodate itself to the dominant premise of Soviet–East European economic relations and has generally prospered through its extremely close ties with the USSR.

PRACTICES OF SOVIET POLICY

Since Stalin's death the Soviet Union has attempted to keep the domestic and international behavior of the East European states within certain behavioral parameters. These boundaries have not been rigidly applied over time, nor have they been applied uniformly throughout the region. Nor, of course, are they explicitly delineated, although some indicators are derived from authoritative pronouncements such as that of September 1968 defining what became known in the West as the Brezhnev Doctrine.[4] In general, however, by forceful intervention of all types Moscow had, until recently, regularly indicated the following three boundaries of acceptable behavior: Communist Party dominance of the political and economic system, at least minimum participation in the Warsaw Pact, and maintenance of civil peace.

Communist Party dominance of the political and economic system meant, in part, Soviet, and usually local regime, hostility to and suppression of challenges to the political structure, which ensured that the Communist Party maintained a monopoly on political power. Whether threats to this monopoly came from outside the political elite, as in the case of Solidarity in Poland, or from within the party itself, as in Czechoslovakia during 1968, the Soviet reaction had been, sooner or later, to brand such movements as "anti-Soviet" or "anti-socialist" and to link them to "counterrevolutionary" support from the West. All challenges were seen as threats to the goal of political and, in some instances, physical security, and were either directly or indirectly suppressed.

Minimum participation in the Warsaw Pact has been enforced differentially, as might be expected, given the greater Soviet emphasis on northern and central Europe. For example, Soviet fears about breaching of the alliance by Czechoslovakia or Poland have been more pronounced, even exaggerated, than those over Romania's deviance, despite the fact that Bucharest's participation in the Warsaw Pact has been the least supportive over the past two decades. The USSR has tolerated a low and sometimes declining level of defense expenditure by Romania and Bulgaria, consistent Romanian nonparticipation in maneuvers, and often some distance from Warsaw Pact foreign-policy pronouncements and initiatives. However, Romania has remained a member of the pact, has renewed its bilateral and multinational treaties, and proclaimed its loyalty to the alliance and the necessity of keeping it in force. Indeed, after the ascendance to power of a Solidarity government in Poland in August 1989, Bucharest even reversed its long and loudly trumpeted position on self-determination and called for the pact to act against this new government.[5]

Critical to the Soviet view of events in Hungary in 1956 and Poland during 1980-1 was the perception that the party was losing not just its "leading role" but the political initiative and the ability to maintain the order on which the postwar system—and their regimes—were built. The party was losing control of events in the streets.[6] Especially because the original "revolutions" occurred in times of chaos and upheaval, the increasingly conservative Soviet leadership has been sensitive to the appearance of situations that might allow popular disaffection and disruption to threaten either of the other two parameters.

In this regard the pace of change has been an important factor, because a more moderate pace allows the local regime to appear to be in charge, to avoid the uncontrolled growth of "antisocialist" forces (and to execute tactical crackdowns against certain opposition groups), and to demonstrate the continued leading role of the party (and to try to reassure those who might be nervous in Moscow).

In establishing and enforcing these behavioral boundaries, the Soviets have not insisted on uniform practices throughout the region. Even before the sensational changes in Poland and Hungary, the Soviet Union since Stalin had tolerated a range of diverse social and economic phenomena both of a more capitalist nature (such as private agriculture in Poland) and a more retrograde character (such as Stalinism in Romania). Externally, states such as Poland and Romania pursued extensive contacts with Western countries before Moscow and other members of the alliance did, while Romania maintained good relations with China as well as a number of countries with whom the USSR had either few or hostile ties. For Warsaw Pact members, as long as the basic three boundaries were respected, the Soviets did not insist on duplication of the Soviet system and tolerated considerable diversity in domestic economic and social structure and on international issues.

The two non-Warsaw Pact members in Southeastern Europe— Albania and Yugoslavia—have been the furthest, literally and figuratively, from Soviet pressure and, despite Soviet intervention within the pact, not subject to threats of intervention, at least since 1948. Moscow has not seen domestic developments in these two countries as directly affecting Soviet physical or political security, but reacted with hostility to the increased presence or influence of its adversaries in these states, in particular of China in Albania, and the United States and the West in Yugoslavia.

Old Threats

For the Soviet Union in Eastern Europe as a whole, the greatest threats have been those posed to the dominance of the political system by the Communist Party. Such threats have been present in Hungary, Czechoslovakia, and Poland and have carried dangerous implications for other Soviet goals in the region. The possibility of full-scale overthrow or even radical reform of the political system was seen by the pre-Gorbachev leadership as potentially allowing a more fluid, less predictable domestic political situation, or even the possibility that antisocialist and anti-Soviet forces would take power. In addition, in Hungary and Poland during previous episodes the threats of civil disorder were real and growing. Foreign-policy adjustments or even major changes that might have eroded the Soviet power base in the region were not inconceivable.

As is evident, these threats have occurred most often in the Northern Tier. Indeed, in Bulgaria and Romania, except for a coup attempt in the former in 1965, Communist Party dominance and domestic tranquility have never really been in question. In ideological terms, Ceausescu's rule in Romania has undermined the role of the party, in that the party has been replaced by an individual, a return to the days of the cult of personality. And various aspects of behavior by Romania (e.g., its relations with China) clearly provoked displeasure in Moscow. But neither its domestic deformations nor its various acts breaking ranks internationally, such as unilaterally and loudly announcing a cut in defense expenditures, have been perceived as actionable threats against the three main Soviet goals. For its part, Romania has been careful not to directly challenge Soviet security interests either in the region or globally.[7]

Yugoslavia's creation and continual reforming of its system of self-management has represented a threat to Soviet-style socialism only in the abstract, as a possible model for others in the region to duplicate. The Yugoslavs themselves have eschewed any such role, and, because since 1956 no alliance member has appeared to move in a "Yugoslav" direction, this potential "threat" has not materialized. Internationally, Yugoslavia has endeavored to follow a form of nonalignment that has been highly considerate of Soviet foreign-policy concerns and has often aligned itself with Soviet views. On the Middle East, for example, Yugoslavia's policy has been closer to Moscow's than Romania's has. There has been no suggestion of joining the opposing alliance or allowing a larger U.S. military presence in the country, nor has there been any express desire to redraw Balkan boundaries at the expense of Soviet ally Bulgaria. Albania's close alliance with China during the 1960s and early 1970s did raise the possibility of further defections, but after 1968—and owing to Romanian prudence—this possibility also faded.

Soviet "New Thinking" and the Region

Soviet "new thinking" on Eastern and Southeastern Europe has to be viewed in the context of overall Soviet foreign-policy changes. The

Gorbachev era has seen demonstrable and significant revisions in Soviet foreign-policy conceptions about the world and, more important, about actions toward that world. Clearly, the Gorbachev leadership team has been striving to reduce Soviet exposure abroad, in order to cut the costs and consequences of an overextended foreign policy. This effort has involved several overtures toward China, which appear to be bearing fruit, and less successful moves toward Japan. The Soviets' own withdrawal from Afghanistan and pressure on Vietnam to do the same from Cambodia have served both the immediate Soviet goal of reducing the costs of those involvements and of warming the environment for improving relations with China and the United States. Toward the latter, the continuous concessions on medium-range missiles followed by the intermediate-range nuclear forces (INF) treaty have been both preceded and followed by pressure for renewed and more vigorous strategic arms-control measures— both marked switches from the late Brezhnev-Andropov-Chernenko period. Soviet feelers for improved relations with Israel, as well as with a number of Arab states with whom the Soviets did not previously have relations, and support for an agreement in southwestern Africa have been complemented by a rapid growth of interest and opportunity for expanding economic relations with the West. This policy has been directed at private capital (e.g., through joint ventures), increasing bilateral trade, and capitalist global institutions, such as the International Monetary Fund and the General Agreement on Tariffs and Trade.

These moves and numerous others should not be interpreted as some kind of Soviet desire to "behave" according to standards determined in the West or, as some analysts have crudely put it, "to join the civilized world." Nor should they be seen as coming primarily in response to aggressive Western pressure. These policies stem from the Soviet leadership's perception of the needs of the country itself, its economy, its society, and its socialist system. The Gorbachev team explicitly recognizes that the Soviet economy is in desperate straits. Far from competing internationally with the advanced West, it is falling behind even the newly developing countries of the Pacific rim and cannot even effectively provide what the country itself needs to function properly in manufactured goods, communication and information technology or computers; in food production, processing or distribution; in housing, health care or most areas of social welfare. In their discussions of these problems the Soviets acknowledge that the question may not be one of production; sometimes it is a problem of the application, distribution, and utilization of technology, goods, and resources. These problems are seen to be related to questions of investment; prices; and the social/cultural issues of initiative, incentive, and labor productivity. Finally, Gorbachev himself, more than any other of the current leaders, insists that without reform of the political system, very little of what is needed will be accomplished.

On the international plane, Gorbachev has also made clear the link between domestic *perestroika* and new thinking in foreign policy. He and his supporters recognize the need to ease the pressure on the Soviet economy—and in some cases on the political system—stemming from global involvement and conflicts. Doing this would allow both attention and resources to be devoted to the compelling domestic tasks.

With respect to Eastern and Southeastern Europe, the new thinking is directly related to the international role of the Soviet Union and to its domestic needs. First, there is the question of whether the Soviet Union should and will seek to maintain this increasingly costly sphere of influence, by following the policies outlined earlier. In their public statements, Gorbachev and other Soviet leaders have gone out of their way to cast out "old thinking" on this score, rejecting the notion that they arrogate to themselves a monopoly on truth or that they want to duplicate Soviet systems in the region. Such statements have been cast as rejections of the "Brezhnev Doctrine," though they are not combined with acknowledgments of its existence. Long-time heretics such as Yugoslavia have been assured that the Soviet Union accepts the idea of many and independent paths of socialist development. But nothing spoke as loudly on this score as the Soviet toleration of—and even reportedly granting of permission for—the installation of a non-Communist government in Poland.[8] The significance of this forbearance cannot be overstated. After more than forty years of insisting that only a Communist-dominated political system could provide the necessary reassurance, Moscow belatedly recognized the need to see if its goals could be secured through another arrangement.

Through their actions in Eastern Europe, as elsewhere in the world, the Soviets have indeed indicated a desire for reducing their political and economic exposure. The troop cuts and withdrawals announced by Gorbachev in 1988 included significant reductions in forces in Central Europe; several of the states themselves also have cut their troops. Furthermore, while making it clear that *perestroika* is the wave of the future, Moscow has not been exerting any real pressure on the more recalcitrant of its allies (East Germany, Czechoslovakia, Romania) to get in line. The Soviets are following a policy of "differentiation" toward their allies—a warmer relationship exists ironically with

Poland and Hungary, for example, than with Romania and East Germany—but there is little evidence of, for example, an economic squeezing of Romania to force it to apply the principles of *perestroika*.

Soviet new thinking toward the region also involves a rethinking of the role and function of CMEA. It is clear from Soviet writings that the Soviets are displeased over what is seen as an unfavorable economic relationship, in which the Soviets supply raw materials and fuel at great opportunity costs and sometimes lower than world prices in return for more expensive but often poor-quality manufactured goods. Aside from the price and cost factors, the benefits of such trade—including the ability to improve and diversify the national economy and trade profile—are seen as disproportionately accruing to the East European countries, especially the more advanced ones.[9]

Second, Moscow wants the organization itself to function better, to begin to act more as a genuine economic union, with more effective mechanisms for price formation, currency exchange, and specialization of production. The Soviets are demonstrating increasing impatience with CMEA, particularly compared, in recent years, with the looming counterexample of the European Community. Finally, Soviet pressure to change CMEA has been driven by the Soviet commitment to *perestroika*, which has taken the form of pressure for the member states to restructure their own economies in a way that will allow more direct production ties between Soviet and East European enterprises, thus facilitating the spread of advanced science and technology throughout the region.

What does all this add up to? First, the whole—that is, Soviet policy toward the region—does not equal the sum of its parts. There is clearly a tension between the Soviets' pronouncements and actions that indicate a willingness to let each state go its own way and the clear desire to get the region to improve its economic performance and change its relationship with the USSR. If in fact all the states pursue what they see as their own best economic interest, they are likely to want to continue to rely on cheap Soviet raw materials and fuel, payable with goods, not hard currency. The CMEA junior partners' incentives to accommodate the USSR on the issue of restructuring the trade relationship, although not absent, will be overcome by the evident advantage of continuing the current system, by their desire not to aggravate an already difficult domestic economic situation, and by their desire to trade their more complex goods to the West.

For the Soviet Union, the problem will be how to get the CMEA states to satisfy Soviet economic needs without relying on "old thinking" (i.e., hegemonic interference from Moscow) and without pressing these states economically so much that their domestic situation becomes even more difficult and the regimes more vulnerable to political challenge.

More broadly, there is the question of whether "new thinking" and "new acting" are reversible with regard to Eastern Europe. While Soviet declarations and actions seem to reject the notion of intervention, a change in leadership in the USSR or in the perceived "security" situation in the region could put this option back on the table. Before the emergence of the Solidarity government in Poland, statements by Soviet leaders made *in* Eastern Europe were always hedged by admonitions that the leaders of these parties had responsibility not only to their own nations but to the "common interests of socialism."[10] In the last two years of the Gorbachev regime such views have evidently lost in battle with more universalistic values, such as those expressed by Gorbachev in his speech to the United Nations. Presumably those harboring such sentiments—and Gorbachev himself has broadened the notion of socialism but by no means abandoned its pursuit as a national goal—are not yet far from power. Soviet writings have not explicitly rejected the basic premise of the Soviet invasion of Czechoslovakia in 1968. Instead, Moscow has essentially accepted the assessment of that period made by the regime in Prague, acknowledging mistakes but continuing to point to "antisocialist forces" and extensive Western influence.[11]

It would be foolish to assume that the Soviet Union, new thinking or not, will rapidly, or ever, abandon the desire for physical and political security in a region it sees as vital. The means of achieving these ends, however, clearly has changed and includes a substantial broadening of the Soviet notion of what kind of regimes and what kind of region serves these interests. Even if the Soviet Union were to become a non-Communist country, its great-power imperatives would continue to operate in this region. A new leadership in Moscow would still work to protect its national security, very broadly defined. Moscow would still fret about and work against any military presence or threat in the area, and could be expected to react negatively against any political developments in the region that made this threat more likely.

New Threats

The major new development in Eastern Europe as a whole, although not in Southeastern Europe, is the erosion of the political monopoly of the Communist Party. This erosion has already been formalized in

Hungary and Poland and can be seen in the Soviet Union itself. Thus one of the key Soviet goals in Eastern Europe, maintenance of party control, is lost—and in states that are central to Soviet thinking about the region. Although in Poland and Hungary such changes are accompanied by assurances that international alliances are not subject to radical change, new political forces, especially should they become ruling parties, can change this equation. Indirectly, then, the possibility arises that a second value, that of minimum participation in the Warsaw Pact, could come under threat. Indeed, in the case of Hungary, the idea of eventual neutrality has already been publicly broached.

In Southeastern Europe, neither of these developments seems likely, but more dramatic and potentially more dangerous developments are threatened in Yugoslavia. The increasingly desperate economic situation there, coupled with the renewed force of nationalist hostility exemplified by the events in Kosovo, raises the possibility of internal military action in that country (martial law, coup d'état, civil war). Although such an event in itself is not likely to be seen as threatening the USSR, a military struggle in the Balkans with the inherent possibility of external involvement cannot be welcomed by Moscow. Indeed, Soviet statements on Kosovo have been fully supportive of the Belgrade government.[12]

Moscow has been more circumspect with regard to the other national conflict in the region, between Hungary and Romania. The Soviets have not officially intervened in the ongoing dispute over the national roots and rights in Transylvania, nor has the Soviet leadership been assertive on Hungarian claims of Romanian mistreatment of their conationals inside Romania. On the former question, it is very unlikely that the USSR would support a redrawing of national boundaries in this region. It has already opposed such action within the Soviet Union, with regard to Nagorno-Karabakh, and would be loath to see such a precedent established in Southeastern Europe.[13] But on Budapest television Soviet historian Roy Medvedev did indirectly criticize Ceausescu's destruction of small villages, a policy that, among other things, will wipe out many Hungarian communities. Moreover, in November 1988 in Moscow, an unofficial group, *Democratic Perestroika*, protested Romanian policies.[14]

How then might Soviet policy toward Eastern and Southeastern Europe evolve? Under what conditions would Soviet concern or even intervention be more or less likely? In the next section we consider some scenarios and factors that may affect Soviet actions in the region.

SCENARIOS IN EASTERN EUROPE: FACTORS AND ACTORS

Scenario 1: "Don't Call the Question"

In this scenario, we can envisage continued change in the region, even significant change, including an increasing role for opposition political forces and erosion of the system of state socialism. The Soviet Union would accommodate itself to the loss of the party's monopoly of power, if as in Poland and Hungary the situation evolves rather gradually, if civil peace and order hold, and if opposition political forces are willing and able to effect an agreement to share power and responsibility in running the country.[15] This scenario also demands that, in the absence of an all-European transformation, the new governments assure Moscow that the system of international alliances will be maintained. The regimes, whether Communist, social-democratic, or some kind of coalition, will have to be careful to restrain overtly anti-Soviet groups and give obeisance to Soviet security needs, broadly conceived.

If all this were to happen, and especially if economic performance in the region were to improve, allowing for the development of domestic regime support and improved supply of Soviet needs, the question of what are the limits of new thinking for the region might never have to be faced. In this scenario the pace of change, if not its ultimate effects, would be moderate; the political and social environment would remain relatively secure.

In addition, given Soviet sensitivity to Western involvement, the United States, as an adversary involved in and committed to changing the existing situation in the region, would have to remain in the background. Public U.S. support for change could and should be forthcoming, but provocative actions that might stimulate a severe Soviet reaction would have to be avoided.

Scenario 2: Heightened Soviet Concern

In scenario 2, the significant economic and political developments noted in scenario 1 are accompanied by overt and provocative Western involvement, especially by the United States. In this instance, the Soviets' concern over the rapid destruction of virtually everything the USSR had sought to achieve in Eastern Europe since World War II would be greatly heightened. In this scenario, the Soviets would be alarmed by statements or actions, particularly by the United States, which seek somehow to demonstrate our "right" and "stake" in determining the future of this region. Such actions would very likely produce a strong Soviet counterreaction and results directly opposite from those that Washington, and certainly the people of the region, would want, but which the United States would in the event be unable to block.

Scenario 3: Soviet Intervention

In scenario 3, the changes in Eastern Europe begin to multiply and conform to the worst Soviet fears of a disappearing buffer. This scenario might include a rapid dissolution of the Communist Party or its marginalization and replacement by forces less inclined to appease Soviet sensitivities about its security. Given the history of this region, anti-Soviet or, less likely, antisocialist forces might gain legality or act forcefully even without official sanction. Moscow is unlikely to view the appearance of such groups or their approaches to real power with equanimity.

Especially if such changes were accompanied by civil disorder, anti-Soviet demonstrations, prosecution of ousted Communist leaders by non-Communists, or declarations hostile to Soviet foreign-policy goals in the region, Soviet pressure would increase and intervention could not be ruled out. A similar reaction can be expected should the issues between Hungary and Romania cause relations to deteriorate to the point at which the existence of the alliance is threatened or the possibility of military action becomes heightened.

There should be no illusion that Soviet desire for a peaceful and controllable "neighborhood" has been abandoned, or of Gorbachev's "willingness" to act forcefully when he sees vital Soviet political or national interests in danger. The "coup" of October 1988, the use of new laws against demonstrators during 1988 and 1989, and especially the response to "the national question" in the Soviet Union are illustrations of the forcefulness of this regime *in extremis*. A region like Eastern and Southeastern Europe, long seen as vital to Soviet international security, will not be let go if Mikhail Gorbachev or any other Soviet regime perceives developments there as dangerous.

Scenario 4: Difficulties in Yugoslavia and Albania

As noted, the Soviet government strongly supports the central Yugo-slav government and in particular the Serbian government's approach to the difficulties in Kosovo, an approach not unlike its own in

Armenia, Azerbaijan, and Georgia. It can be expected that Moscow will continue to see no gain for itself in a civil war or breakup of Yugoslavia, especially one in which its own hand or that of its ally Bulgaria would be discerned or alleged. At the very least, Moscow will not favor the disappearance of good economic relations through which the USSR receives consumer and some manufactured goods for which it does not have to pay hard currency.

As for Albania, Moscow has made it clear that, since the change in leadership there, it would like very much to normalize relations.[16] But despite the change and notwithstanding Albania's evident willingness to improve and establish relations with many other states, the USSR is still not among its preferred partners. Under Gorbachev, the Soviet Union can be expected to continue to try to renew the relationship. Even more significantly, Moscow will be sure to react negatively to any developments that might change Albania's current status outside the alliance system, say, to one that brought it closer to Soviet adversaries in the West. Although such a development is, to say the least, very unlikely, given the strategic location of the country, any movement to warm up to the West, to the extent that it allows military advantage to NATO, is likely to alarm Moscow.

A critical factor in all scenarios is the domestic political situation in the USSR. The foregoing scenarios—except for number 3—presume the continued viability of the Gorbachev leadership team. But Gorbachev must begin to show some success for his efforts. Internationally, his actions have borne fruit: the INF treaty, the withdrawal from Afghanistan, and the high international standing he enjoys. Domestically, however, the fruits of *perestroika* are scarce and expensive. Domestic economic restructuring is, after all, just beginning, and many of the policies, such as taxes on independent enterprises, are being made up as they go along. The situation for consumers is worse than it has been for a long time with roughly two-thirds of all consumables officially "in deficit." Although the population seems generally to support the aims of the top leadership, they also resent the growing cooperative sector and are increasingly weary from trying to make ends meet. However the March 1989 elections to the Congress of People's Deputies are interpreted, the party cannot interpret away the overwhelming popular rejection of the current situation which the results represented. Residual opposition at the top is personified by Yigor Ligachev, and even more deleterious opposition exists throughout the apparatus and state bureaucracy. Here a huge number of people clearly perceive that their role in *perestroika* is to move aside and that their "gain" may be unemployment. Hence, their incentive to make the new system work is minimal, and many suggest that they are undermining reform in order to build support for junking *perestroika*. Into this mix are added the extremely volatile nationalities issues, about which the regime has yet to produce an effective response.

Should a combination of these factors coalesce to remove Gorbachev or to weaken his commitment or ability to continue to pursue *perestroika* or its external component, new thinking, we might expect a return to business as usual in Eastern Europe. Such a return would probably take place preemptively, as elites there moved to get back in line with what they perceived to be new—or, in this case, old—realities in Moscow.

The dynamics could also work the other way, that is, that upheaval in Eastern Europe, say, scenario 3 above, would provoke a harsh reaction from Moscow and then the removal or weakening of Gorbachev and the petering out of *perestroika* at home. However they operate, the dynamics of Soviet interest in and involvement with this region will continue to demonstrate the region's significance for intra-European relations and overall East-West relations.

NOTES

The author wishes to acknowledge the support of the National Council for Soviet and East European Research, the Kennan Institute for Advanced Russian Studies of the Woodrow Wilson International Center for Scholars, and the International Research and Exchanges Board, whose support made possible the research and drafting of this chapter.

1. Paul Marer, "Has Eastern Europe Become a Liability to the Soviet Union? The Economic Aspect," in Charles Gati, ed., *The International Politics of Eastern Europe* (New York: Praeger, 1976), 59–81.

2. Michael Marrese and Jan Vanous, *Soviet Subsidization of Trade with Eastern Europe: A Soviet Perspective* (Berkeley: University of California, Institute of International Studies, 1983).

3. Iu. Shiriaev, "SEV: Kurs na perestroiku mekhanisma mnogostroennovo sotrudinchestva" [CMEA: The Way to Restructure the Mechanism of Multilateral Collaboration], *Mezhdunarodnaia Zhizn*, No. 12 (1987), pp. 21–29; L. Yagodovsky, "Reforms call for more reforms," *New Times* No. 3, January 17–23, 1989.

4. S. Kovalev, "Suverinitet i internatsional'nye obiazannosti sotsialisticheckikh stran" ["Sovereignty and the International Obligations of Socialist Countries"], *Pravda*, September 26, 1968, p. 4.

5. This was revealed by the Solidarity newspaper *Gazeta Wyborcza* and confirmed by the head of the Department of Foreign Affairs of the Hungarian party. See Radio Warsaw Domestic Service, September 29, 1989; Radio Budapest Domestic Service, October 2, 1989.

6. During the 1956 Hungarian revolution one dramatic illustration of this concern was Khrushchev's remark to Tito just before the Soviet invasion: "They are cutting Communists' throats there," he said. Reported by Veljko Micunovic in his *Moscow Diary* (Garden City, N.Y.: Doubleday, 1980) cited in Brian McCauley, "Hungary and Suez, 1956: The Limits of Soviet and American Power," in Bela Kiraly, Barbara

Lotze and Nandor Dreisziger, eds., *The First War Between Socialist States: The Hungarian Revolution of 1956 and Its Impact* (New York: Brooklyn College Press, 1984), 306.

7. See Ronald H. Linden, *Communist States and International Change* (Winchester, Mass.: Allen & Unwin, 1987), 28–32, 54–60, 76–84; and Ronald H. Linden, "Romanian Foreign Policy in the 1980's: Domestic-Foreign Policy Linkages," in Michael J. Sodaro and Sharon L. Wolchik, eds., *Foreign and Domestic Policy in Eastern Europe in the 1980s* (London: Macmillan Press, 1983), 47–80.

8. See the discussion in Michael Shafir, "Soviet Reaction to Polish Developments: Widened Limits of Tolerated Change" *Radio Free Europe Research*, September 20, 1989, esp. pp. 6–7.

9. See the remarks by Soviet Premier Nikolai Ryzhkov at the 44th CMEA session; "Osnova Sotsialisticheskoi ekonomicheskoi integratsii" ["The Basis for Socialist Economic Integration"] *Izvestia*, July 7, 1988, p. 4. See also Iu. C. Shirayev, "Mekhanizm sotrudinchestva: Novyie kriterii" ["Mechanism of Collaboration: New Criteria"], *Ekonomicheskaia Gazeta* 30 (July 1986): 20.

10. See, for example, Gorbachev's statement in Prague, Soviet TV, April 10, 1987 [*Summary of World Broadcasts*, April 13, 1987, p. EE/8541/C10]. Gorbachev voiced a similar sentiment to Karoly Grosz when the Hungarian leader visited Moscow in July 1988; *Pravda*, July 6, 1988, p. 2. Compare the comments of Aleksandr Yakovlev in Hungary, *Pravda*, November 13, 1988, p. 4.

11. Aleksandr Kondrashov, "Ob antichekhoslovatskoi kampanii na Zapade" ["About the Anti-Czechoslovak Campaign in the West"], *Izvestia*, August 22, 1988, p. 3; *Tass*, August 19, 1988 [FBIS, August 22, 1988, p. 41].

12. See, for example, E. Fadeev, "Edinstvennyi put' " ["The only path"] *Pravda*, April 10, 1989, p. 6.

13. Soviet Deputy Foreign Minister Vladimir Petrovsky explicitly compared the Transylvania and Nagorno-Karabakh conflicts in Budapest in August 1988. See *Radio Liberty*, August 5, 1988, p. 12.

14. Medvedev's comments were reported in ibid. The Moscow demonstration was reported by Budapest Domestic Service, November 16, 1988 [FBIS, November 21, 1988, p. 35].

15. I am indebted to Paul Shoup for adding this last qualifier.

16. "SSSR—Albaniia: v chem raznoglaciia," ["USSR—Albania: On What Are Their Disagreements"] *Pravda*, March 20, 1989, p. 4; G. Mitkevich, "Albaniia: Pamiati bovyshikh bortsov" ["Albania: Memories of Higher Struggles"] May 4, 1986, p. 4.

11

CHALLENGED PREMISES OF U.S. POLICY IN SOUTHEASTERN EUROPE

Dennison Rusinow

At the end of the 1980s Eastern Europe has become, in Charles Gati's words, a "frequently surprising, fast-changing and ultimately ambiguous world," concerning which "no easy generalizations, and certainly none that are conclusive, can be offered"—apparently except for his own later generalization that "today, too, Eastern Europe is the 'sick man of Europe,'" where "upheavals in the 1990s are likely."[1] The Communist-ruled countries of Southeastern Europe, including non-bloc Yugoslavia and Albania as well as Romania and Bulgaria within the Soviet bloc, are part of that world of change and ambiguity.

This situation is challenging, in whole or in part, almost all the premises on which U.S. policies toward these countries and others throughout the region have been based since Stalin's last years or, in the Romanian case, since about 1964. Challenged premises are challenged policies.

U.S. POLICY IN HISTORICAL PERSPECTIVE

If retrospectively incidental and contingent fluctuations in U.S. policies toward Communist-ruled Southeastern Europe are "flattened out," these policies reveal a remarkable consistency that is generally in conformity with a hitherto generally valid set of assumptions.

These policies have usually functioned as a subspecies of U.S. policy toward Communist-ruled Eastern Europe in general. This fact is understandable in the context of the cold war, but it has had two deleterious consequences: First, especially when U.S. attitudes and policies have been influenced by popular perceptions or formulated outside the executive branch, they have not always recognized that Southeastern Europe includes two countries that are under Communist rule but have been outside and wholly or partly opposed to the "Soviet bloc" since 1948 (Yugoslavia) and 1960 (Albania). If many Americans (in this writer's experience including people interested and influential in foreign-policy matters) describe even non-Communist Austria as "behind the Iron Curtain," the same mistake is predictably far more common with regard to Yugoslavia, where it has sometimes run the risk of becoming a self-fulfilling prophecy. Second, U.S. policies have not always recognized the specifically Balkan or Mediterranean dimensions of the region. When they have taken these dimensions into account, they have done so in the direction of a particularly pronounced and pragmatic emphasis on geostrategic and geopolitical considerations—such as the importance of the loss to the Soviet Union of its access to the Mediterranean, Italy, and Greece through the defections of Yugoslavia and then Albania. More commonly, U.S. policy in the region has been subordinated to purely U.S.-Soviet considerations that have attempted to disregard the distracting subtleties of Greek-Turkish disputes over the Aegean and Cyprus (as was discussed in Chapter 8 of this volume).

In common with U.S. policies toward Eastern (and Western) Europe as a whole, policies toward the area also reflect the relative strengths and weaknesses and political preferences of domestic "ethnic lobbies" of Americans with an interest in the lands of their own or their ancestors' origins, particularly Greek, Croatian, and Serbian.

The assumptions that have determined or influenced U.S. policies in the region for up to forty years, and that are now wholly or partly challengeable, include the following, in rough chronological order of their establishment and evolution:

1. The division of Europe along lines established by about 1949—when Yugoslavia was newly outside the Soviet bloc and when only the fates of Austria and Germany (and, in some views, Yugoslavia) were still uncertain and potentially "up for grabs"—has been a given of world politics, reacknowledged in the Helsinki Final Act of 1975. Calls for the "rollback" of Communist domination and "liberation" of "captive nations" have been a mixture of wishful thinking, rhetoric, and primarily domestic partisan political calculations, although such calls have occasionally been taken seriously by some people in Eastern Europe as well as in the United States.

2. Yugoslavia's separation from the Soviet bloc in 1948 and subsequent deviation from the Soviet "model" constituted an important

geostrategic, geopolitical, and later ideological gain for the West. It follows that support for "Titoist" Yugoslavia *as is*—united, one-party Communist, maverick "socialist," and nonaligned but independent of the Soviet bloc and a potentially infectious example of non-Soviet "socialism"—is in the national interest of the United States. Despite periodic "blips" in U.S.-Yugoslav relations and more consistent doubts voiced in the U.S. Congress and by Yugoslav-American communities and others, this understanding of U.S. interest in Yugoslavia has remained one of the most significant constants in U.S. foreign policy, through Democratic and Republican administrations, from 1949 to the present.[2] By the 1960s, acceptance by *both* superpowers of Yugoslavia's nonalignment and its pugnaciously independent Communist regime's heterodox (and, in Soviet eyes, still heretical) definition and practice of "socialism" was solid enough to survive periodic irritants: a spate of "anti-American" positions on Vietnam and other issues in the mid–1960s, outspoken criticism of Soviet military interventions in Czechoslovakia and Afghanistan, demonstrable or supposed Yugoslav "tilts" toward one side or the other in the nonaligned movement, and others. Washington and Moscow competed in listening respectfully to Tito's views and in tendering recognition to Yugoslavia's contribution, which each had earlier regarded as a "Trojan horse" for the other, to the nonaligned movement that both had earlier regarded with utmost suspicion.

3. For U.S. policy it follows that if and when another East European Communist regime *successfully* asserts and maintains some independence from the Soviet Union, it should ipso facto be considered eligible for U.S. approval and support. Two countries have fulfilled this requirement since then, but in different forms and with different effects on U.S. policy:

First, Albania's transformation from a Soviet into a Chinese ally and protégé in 1960–1 constituted a modest military and geopolitical "plus" for the United States and NATO, if only because Saseno Island in the Adriatic was no longer available to the Soviet Union as a submarine base. However, there was nothing else in Albania's new foreign alignment or domestic policies that invited or would accept U.S. or other Western support. U.S.-Albanian relations continued to be nonexistent, and Albania remained a footnote in U.S. foreign policy.

Second, Romania's "declaration of independence" of April 1964, preceded and facilitated by changes in foreign economic relations to reduce dependence on the Soviet Union and CMEA, was exciting and engendered (retrospectively) exaggerated expectations. It would be many years before U.S. policymakers would seriously question the morality or the international and domestic political wisdom of ignoring Nicolae Ceausescu's despotic abuse of his country and its people, as a cost of continuing support for Ceausescu's qualified defiance of the Soviet Union.

Of the four Communist-ruled states in Southeastern Europe, only Bulgaria has failed to qualify for special attention by some form of dramatic defiance of the Soviet Union. Virtually written off the agenda of U.S. foreign policy after efforts to forestall the consolidation of Communist rule before the signing of peace treaties with Germany's wartime allies eliminated the last potentially effective Western leverage in Sofia, Bulgaria has never been written on again.

4. In the past ten years, multiplying dimensions of Eastern Europe's "return to diversity,"[3] which have reinforced the delayed recognition that there had always been more diversity than was suggested by "bloc" images of the region, have fostered an extension and sophistication of the preceding premises—a codicil lately codified as "differentiation." In earlier days Yugoslavia and then Romania were accorded different and preferential treatment in U.S. foreign policy, when Yugoslavia's defection from the Soviet bloc and Romania's deviation from (some of) Moscow's foreign policy and military and economic prescriptions seemed to merit support. Now the definition of differences that U.S. administrations might actively approve or disapprove, with corresponding support or sanctions, has been expanded to include the *domestic* policies of East European regimes.[4] Initially focused on "human rights" (a particular and worldwide concern of the Carter administration), this expansion currently also encompasses economic and other political reforms that seem to be commensurate with U.S. government values and preferences—that is, reforms favoring market forces and the private sector in the economy and "pluralization" of the polity.

Speaking in the Habsburgs' Hofburg Palace in Vienna after visiting Hungary, Romania, and Yugoslavia in September 1983, Vice-President George Bush described his understanding of this codicil in principle and with reference to specific countries in Eastern and Southeastern Europe:

> Our policy is one of differentiation—that is, we look to what degree countries pursue autonomous foreign policies, independent of Moscow's direction; and to what degree they foster domestic liberalization—politically, economically, and in their respect for human rights. The United States will engage in

closer political, economic, and cultural relations with those countries such as Hungary and Romania which assert greater openness or independence. . . . We will not, however, reward closed societies and belligerent foreign policies—countries such as Bulgaria and Czechoslovakia, which continue to flagrantly violate the most fundamental human rights; and countries such as East Germany and, again, Bulgaria, which act as proxies to the Soviets in the training, funding, and arming of terrorists, and which supply advisors and military and technical assistance to armed movements seeking to destabilize governments in the developing world. . . . But we are not about to write off a single country. We are ready to respond to each to the extent that they are meeting their own people's aspirations, are pursuing their own, independent foreign policy, and are willing to open up to the rest of the world.[5]

5. Perceptions of a U.S. interest in the maintenance of civil peace in Eastern Europe—a region where lack of civil peace has often led to wars between outside and greater powers, especially in and over the "Balkan powderkeg"—provide a less frequently articulated counterpoint that is potentially in conflict with all but the first of the other assumptions underlying U.S. policy in Eastern Europe. U.S. interest also corresponds significantly, if with less intensity and fewer consequences, to the third of the major Soviet concerns in the same region and subregion described in Chapter 10 of this volume. Thus the so-called Sonnenfeldt Doctrine of 1975 (suggesting an American as well as a Soviet interest in "a more organic relationship"—whatever that means—between the Soviet Union and its European allies) seemed sufficiently analogous to the so-called Brezhnev Doctrine of 1968 (strictly limiting the extent to which East European regimes might deviate from Soviet prescriptions) to invoke Yugoslav descriptions of the two together as "the Brezhfeldt Doctrine"—two sides of a single superpower coin, which might apply to Yugoslavia as well as the bloc.

CHALLENGES TO THE PREMISES

The multiple challenges from and to Gorbachev throughout Southeastern Europe and the concurrent turmoil in Yugoslavia are described in other contributions to this volume. Collateral challenges that these developments pose to the premises underlying U.S. policies in Southeastern Europe, as already listed, include the following:

1. The tidy division of Southeastern Europe that was established by 1950 (Soviet allies and client Communist regimes in Romania, Bul-

garia, and Albania; NATO-aligned Greece and Turkey; Communist-ruled but nonaligned Yugoslavia) and amended in 1960–61 (Albania) and 1964 (a "Gaullist" Romania in the Soviet bloc) is in question in each of its constituent parts. Portents of change include the Gorbachev phenomenon (a direct or indirect factor in all the rest), the prospective departure of aging and hated or unpopular leaders in Romania and Bulgaria, turmoil in Yugoslavia, and mixed signals about the future orientation of Albanian domestic and foreign policies. They also include the potential effects of diminishing perceptions of "the Soviet threat" on Greek and Turkish attitudes and U.S. policies toward Greece and Turkey. All are in various ways "reopening the Eastern Question," as is argued later.

2. Yugoslav "scenarios" suggested in other contributions to this volume include disintegration, civil war, a military-or Serbian-dominated civilian dictatorship, a "one state with two systems" solution on the Chinese—Hong Kong model, an apparently diminishing likelihood of successful "muddling through," or a progression through the first three of these. With the possible exception of successful "muddling through," any of these outcomes will invalidate a forty-year-old U.S. policy of supporting the independence and territorial integrity of Yugoslavia *as it is*, because it will no longer be what it has been. Yugoslavia either will no longer exist or may no longer be a Yugoslavia that the United States can or should want to support, as it has been wont to do. There are two obvious reasons to conduct the "agonizing reappraisal" before the event: if there is a preference for one of the prospective outcomes, and if time still permits, there may be ways of strengthening the odds in its favor; and it is normally a good idea to have alternative policies ready for every contingency when a triggering change may occur suddenly.

If the political profile ascribed to Slobodan Milosevic and his Serbian party and its allies by their domestic opponents and foreign critics is to a significant degree accurate, the Yugoslavia they would seek to create were they to achieve a countrywide predominance would be at least as centralized, Serbian, and authoritarian as King Alexander's was in the early 1930s. (Its other hypothetical attributes are harder to describe in advance and are a matter of currently disputed views about the political and economic mechanisms and goals these forces "really" favor.) Whether such a regime and country would be more durable than Alexander's, and whether a benign U.S. reaction would be in the U.S. national interest and consonant with the values that putatively also influence U.S. foreign policy, are both open to question. The principal argument in favor of cultivating these forces in anticipation of their success, and taking a benign attitude toward what they do afterward, is that failure to do so will "drive them into the arms of the Soviets," and that this possibility takes priority over other considerations.

The same set of considerations also apply, ceteris paribus, to American attitudes, before and after the hypothetical event, toward those who might impose martial law or a military dictatorship. Here the consequences of similar events in the recent histories of Greece, Turkey, and Poland, and of U.S. policies in the first two of these cases, may be instructive.

The disintegration of Yugoslavia would pose even more difficult questions for U.S. (and Soviet) foreign policies, especially because it is highly likely that disintegration into what could rarely be called "pure" ethno-national units would be consummated or annulled by civil war over the boundaries of the successor states.

It is also still possible that none of the scenarios listed above will come to pass—that the race between effective economic reforms and a political explosion may after all be won by the former. To facilitate this outcome and sustain it, the attitudes of the Yugoslavs and of other Europeans toward Yugoslavia's integration into "Europe" are likely to be more important than any policy Washington adopts. In this instance, as with the Hungarians' similar hopes and aspirations, "Europe" includes the European Free Trade Association (EFTA) as well as the European Community (EC). The Yugoslavs only recently seem to have absorbed the implications of their economic isolation as the only European country that is not a member of any of the Continent's multistate economic associations and markets: EC, EFTA, and CMEA. If they do not want the third and the first will not have them, an enlarged EFTA (collectively, the EC's most important trading partner) with Yugoslavia and Hungary as additional members is an intriguing possibility for the Yugoslavs and Hungarians, for EFTA, and for the future shape of Europe and East-West relations.

3. Albanian isolationism (with an assumption that nothing can or needs to be done about it) and the putative benefits for the United States of Romanian stability (with a likeable foreign policy and debt-repayment record marred by a thoroughly unlikable domestic regime) have been the premises underlying U.S. policy toward Romania and apparent lack of one with regard to Albania. Both premises are currently in doubt, but so are the ultimate direction and extent of Albania's still tentative emergence from isolation and the answer to when and how Ceausescu's reign will end and what will follow it. It is quite likely, however, that further developments will recommend an

inversion of traditional American foreign policy interest in Romania and disinterest in Albania—i.e., that the United States will find that it can do little to influence the outcome in Romania but can and should pursue a cautiously activist policy of encouraging current trends toward economic and political rapprochement between Albania and Western Europe.

4. U.S. policy based on "differentiation" among the countries of the Soviet Union's quondam bloc in Eastern Europe, including Romania and Bulgaria in the Balkans, may paradoxically be more rather than less constrained by Gorbachev's "new thinking," with its liberalized, but in most interpretations less than laissez-faire, attitude to diversity and autonomy. As Trond Gilberg notes in Chapter 3, Soviet military intervention now seems likely "only if other actors (especially the major powers of Western Europe or the United States) attempt to take advantage of current or future problems of the region to expand Western control (as opposed to influence) into part of the former bloc." That this might be seen to be happening would ultimately be a matter of perception, still through lenses of suspicion made in and for the Cold War. That no one, presumably including the Soviet leadership, knows the precise height of the new threshold of Soviet tolerance for diversity and Western "influence" inhibits Western (including U.S.) as well as East European boldness.

THE EASTERN QUESTION REVISITED

Once upon a time, which ended with World War I, the weakening grip of the Ottoman Empire on Southeastern Europe confronted the Great Powers of that day, particularly the rulers of the Russian and Habsburg empires, with a choice of three answers to what was known as "the Eastern Question": (1) They could collaborate, or tolerate one another's share, in partitioning the decaying empire's European possessions. (2) They could compete for the inheritance, with a strong probability that this course would lead to war or a series of wars between them. Or (3) they could cooperate in attempting to impose reforms on the Ottoman Empire that would inhibit revolts by improving conditions for its subject Orthodox and Catholic peoples, who tended to draw their coreligionists and protectors from the two Christian empires into their struggles, again raising the specter of conflict between them over spheres of influence if not of annexations. The first and third were conflict-avoidance strategies. The second was not.

The first answer worked in the eighteenth century, before the thrusts of Habsburg and Russian conquests and annexations in Pannonia and north of the Black Sea began to intersect. Thereafter the Habsburg and Russian courts usually showed a preference for the third, in which they were joined by other powers, with reasons of their own for wanting to deny domination in the Balkans or the Turkish Straits to a strong actual or potential rival. It did not work—the Ottoman court and Ottoman institutions turned out to be unwilling or unable to carry out the requisite reforms—but Vienna and St. Petersburg continued to try periodically (making a final joint attempt over Macedonia in 1903) while the Ottoman Empire in Europe dwindled to a Thracian glacis west of Constantinople-Istanbul. It was replaced in the rest of the Balkans by a patchwork of successor-states that were intensely nationalistic, prone to conflict over irredentist claims, and self-interestedly fickle in their allegiance to Austria-Hungary or Russia as rival Great Power patrons. Thus, the empires eventually went to war over Serbia and for hegemony in the lands of the Eastern Question, dragging in most of the rest of the world.

Parables, including those that oversimplify or distort history to this end, usually have a moral. This one also has a sequel. After sixteen post–1918 years of illusory genuine independence for these and the other "lands between" of Eastern Europe, followed by ten years of a "German solution" and forty-five years of a "Soviet solution," the apparent faltering of the Soviet will to empire in the region recalls the faltering of Ottoman power that posed the Eastern Question in the first place. If Soviet will genuinely falters, which is still in doubt, the Eastern Question will have been reopened. The three historic answers will then be on the agenda again—this time the United States (and its allies?) and the Soviet Union will be cast in the Habsburg and Romanov roles of cooperating or contending Great Power players whose best-laid plans, including conflict-avoidance strategies, can be confounded by local actors and events.

Several indicators of current thinking in the Soviet Union (see the previous chapter in this volume) and in the United States suggest an awareness that these are in fact the current agenda and its attendant risks, and that pursuit of the second historic answer—competitive efforts to possess or repossess the pieces of a decaying empire—would put neo-détente and peace in Europe at grave risk. Suggestions that Washington and Moscow should "talk about Eastern Europe" in the context of Moscow's "new thinking" provide a case in point.

The debate in the United States engendered by these suggestions has revealed a difference of view over whether such talks, were they to take place, would in practice (or should in principle) correspond to the first or the third of the Eastern Question's historic answers—the conflict-avoidance ones.

The first historic answer is implicit in descriptions of the ideas as a proposal for "a revision of Yalta" (tendentiously assuming that "Yalta" countenanced the East-West division of Europe). These descriptions clearly envisage, without necessarily approving (indeed, the contrary is usually the case), a U.S.-Soviet spheres-of-interest agreement to lower the risk of conflict between them over who in Eastern Europe can "get away with" how many changes in domestic and foreign policy. So does speculation about an agreed division of Yugoslavia into "Western" and "Eastern" spheres of interest after (or even without) that country's putative further disintegration.

Other commentaries on the proposal for direct U.S.-Soviet talks about Eastern Europe conjure images, whether approved or disapproved by the commentators, of a different kind: of an agreement to "prop up the Sick Man of Europe," now its quondam Soviet bloc rather than the Ottoman Empire, for the same reasons that led most of the nineteenth century's Great Powers to the same policy preference, most of the time, vis à vis that earlier patient. Would this not be the effect of talks about the kinds of reforms that would simultaneously satisfy the U.S. side's principal concerns (already defined under the rubric of "differentiation"), thereby triggering U.S. measures to assist ailing economies in the name of encouraging economic and political liberalization, and the Soviet side's key priorities (defined in Chapter 10)?

There are two important differences between the original version and draft scenarios for its revival in modern dress, as The Return of the Eastern Question. The first is that the Soviet Union would be playing both the Russian and the Ottoman empires in the revival, a contender for its own succession in some form. The second is that the states created or reaffirmed in the peace settlement after World War I can now be regarded as permanent features of the political map of Eastern Europe, although some of their present borders and the unity of the most multinational of them (Yugoslavia) are hypothetically subject to challenge.

The latter difference is ultimately a consequence of the power and universal European acceptance in principle of the idea that nations have a "right" to nation-states of their own ("national self-determination"), which the outcome of World War I had seemed to vindicate. Even Hitler and Stalin felt obliged to give it lipservice, when they wiped entire "artificial Versailles states" off the map, through devices like the Protectorate of Bohemia-Moravia and Government-general around Warsaw for the core Czech and Polish lands and Soviet Socialist Republics for the former Baltic states. Today it is almost (literally) unthinkable that Poland, Czechoslovakia, and Albania could again disappear from the map. By the same token, some observers are finding it thinkable that the Baltic republics might reappear, or that the nations of Yugoslavia might exercise their right to selfdetermination by choosing a confederation or even separate states. Irredentist claims to lands in neighboring states with majorities or large minorities comprising members of one's own nation have similarly become thinkable again.

The aspirations of Southeastern Europe's nations or their elites for national independence and completeness did as much as Ottoman (and Habsburg) inability to solve the national and social questions of their empires to foil the best-laid plans for reforms that would maintain the minimum of civil peace and order through which a wider conflict would be avoided. Possibilities for interference by local agents in the plans of outside great powers, if the pax Sovietica in the bloc and the pax Tito in Yugoslavia are suspended, are legion.

Historical analogies always run a grave risk of being more misleading than instructive. However, the fate of attempts to program the answers of Great Powers to an earlier version of the Eastern Question may be worth recalling.

NOTES

1. Charles Gati, "Eastern Europe on Its Own," *Foreign Affairs* 68, no. 1 (1989): 99 and 117.
2. John R. Lampe and Lorraine Lees, eds., *Yugoslav-American Relations* (forthcoming), provides an "update" but few pre–1966 amendments or additions to John C. Campbell, *Tito's Separate Road* (New York: Harper & Row for the Council on Foreign Relations, 1967).
3. The title of Joseph Rothschild's useful survey of the region's postwar history (Oxford and New York: Oxford University Press, 1969), which Gati seems to have in mind when he described the present situation as "beyond diversity," in "Eastern Europe on Its Own," 101.
4. A development anticipated in debates in the American media and Congress over support for Tito's Yugoslavia since the 1950s (see Campbell *Tito's Separate Road*, and Lampe and Lees, *Yugoslavia-American Relations* passim.)
5. "Address of Vice President George Bush Before the Austrian Association for Foreign Policy and International Relations at the Hofburg, Vienna, September 21, 1983," (official text courtesy USIA, the U.S. Embassy in Vienna). The speech also included praise for Austria, Yugoslavia, and the idea of "*Mitteleuropa*" (*sic*). It was apparently intended as a major policy statement (according to officials accompanying the vice president), but received little media notice.

12

THE UNITED STATES AND SOUTHEASTERN EUROPE IN THE 1990s

Paul S. Shoup

Before World War II, Southeastern Europe was a region about which the United States was largely ignorant. As Walter Roberts suggests in Chapter 2 of this volume, U.S. policy between the two world wars was ill-prepared to deal with the national passions and the great-power politics historically associated with the region. Only when the looming confrontation with the Soviet Union compelled the United States to take responsibility for shaping Allied policy in Southeastern Europe— a process that Roberts shows began with the disputes over Churchill's interest, and Roosevelt's disinterest, in Allied wartime operations on the Balkan Peninsula—did U.S. policymakers begin to come to grips with the complexities of the region.

At that point the United States found itself plunged into the problems and the politics of one of the most volatile regions in the world. Although a part of Europe, Southeastern Europe had, in fact, long been a place apart, thanks to its centuries-long occupation by the Turks, its long and often fruitless efforts to modernize, and its diverse ethnic makeup. For most of the nineteenth and the first half of the twentieth century, the region had been the scene of continuous conflict, into which the Great Powers of Europe had been, to their own ill-fortune, inevitably drawn.

The confrontation between the United States and the Soviet Union in Southeastern Europe after World War II was both a continuation of these earlier struggles and a historic turning point. The emergence of U.S. and Soviet spheres of influence, facilitated by a mutual interest in restoring the boundaries established after World War I, created conditions under which the countries of Southeastern Europe could focus on domestic development. The United States, for its part, developed fairly close ties with all but two of the six countries of the region—Albania and Bulgaria—ties that have survived more or less intact to the present day.

From 1947 (the year of the Truman Doctrine) to roughly the mid-1980s, U.S. policy toward Southeastern Europe focused almost exclusively on the Soviet threat. At the risk of oversimplification, this policy can be said to have been concerned with three tasks: containing Soviet expansion through extending military and economic aid to those countries willing to receive it; encouraging the Communist states of the Balkans to assert their independence of the Soviet Union; and acting as a mediator in disputes between Turkey and Greece, two allies of the United States in NATO.

Recent developments have challenged the relevance of the first two of these policies for the 1990s. As the contributors to this volume note, the threat of Soviet intervention in Southeastern Europe has diminished. Concomitantly, the Communist states of the region are experiencing an economic slowdown that is aggravating other systemic weaknesses. Whereas Greece and Turkey anticipate closer ties with Western Europe and continued economic growth, the Communist Balkan states appear to be entering a critical decade in which they must either reform or risk becoming a backwater in an otherwise prosperous Europe.

For the United States, the period of spectacular diplomatic triumphs is over. More and more, the United States will have to draw on its capital of goodwill to act as a stabilizing force in the region, hoping to contain conflict and to encourage modernization and reform. In the 1990s, those who formulate and carry out U.S. policy in the region may come to view the period of cold war diplomacy with nostalgia.

U.S. policymakers will also have to confront the growing perception that in the absence of a Soviet threat the region should not be high on the U.S. agenda. This perception finds justification in the argument that the crumbling of the Soviet empire will result in democratization of the Communist systems of Eastern Europe. There are echoes of the rollback policy of the 1950s in this view, which assumed that the ultimate objective of removing the Soviet Union from Eastern Europe and reincorporating the region into the rest of Europe (perhaps through "Finlandization") would occur more or less spontaneously—accompanied by economic reforms and renewed economic growth as soon as the Soviets withdraw.

The contributors to this volume cast serious doubt on the validity of this set of assumptions for Southeastern Europe. The authors suggest that outside Greece and Turkey, the region will modernize itself slowly and only with the greatest difficulty. The outcome may not be democracy but new forms of authoritarianism, as yet difficult to describe in their particulars. Instability in the region, if it becomes endemic, will, in turn, rekindle U.S. and Soviet rivalries. Addressing the problem as a historian, Dennison Rusinow speaks in Chapter 11 of the reemergence in Romania, Bulgaria, Yugoslavia, and Albania of the "Eastern Question" of the nineteenth century.

If Rusinow is correct, U.S. policy toward Southeastern Europe must be reassessed. On the one hand, U.S. policymakers cannot be under any illusion that the problems of the region are caused primarily by Soviet efforts to place Eastern Europe under its hegemony, and that, left to their own devices, the Yugoslavs, Romanians, and the rest will devise a homegrown form of communism suitable to their own needs, stabilized and legitimated to a large degree by the Soviet threat. The evidence in this volume is overwhelming that this set of assumptions, which for so long has guided the U.S. perceptions of the region, is no longer valid.

On the other hand, it is equally unrealistic to expect that U.S.-Soviet competition in Southeastern Europe will end, primarily because both sides have important conflicting interests and obligations in the region. But the United States and the Soviet Union have important common interests as well—above all, the maintenance of peace and stability in the region. Yet such common interests no more rule out rivalry between the superpowers than common interests within the Western alliance preclude competition over issues of trade. Regardless of how it is packaged for local consumption in the countries of the region, U.S. policy will continue to be driven to a greater or lesser degree by the Soviet factor when dealing with the region.

As a result, we foresee a continuing U.S. involvement in Southeastern Europe. Although elsewhere in Eastern Europe (notably in Poland and Hungary) the systemic crisis of communism is leading to new arrangements that constitute the partial Finlandization of Communist states, this process has yet to begin in Southeastern Europe, and indeed, as we argue later, might easily self-destruct once it gets under way. Whereas Central and Northern Europe may be the stage for large-scale moves meant to end the cold war, the Communist portion of Southeastern Europe is potentially a theater for renewed great-power rivalries, not over cold war issues, but over a power vacuum in a region where the United States and the Soviet Union have long-established interests and concerns.

Yugoslavia provides dramatic evidence for this thesis. It is no longer possible to assert, as U.S. policymakers have done until recently, that the forces for change now at work in the country represent minor adjustments to the Titoist system, that Yugoslavia is making progress toward economic and political reform, and that national passions will cool once economic growth resumes. Christopher Cviic, in Chapter 5, describes a country in the throes of a systemic crisis, the outcome of which is extremely difficult to predict. More and more, Yugoslavia seems unable to function as a viable nation-state.

The chief conclusion we draw from this picture is that this region is on the verge of rapid and perhaps destructive change. The short-term objective of U.S. policy must be to act as a stabilizing force, vigorously opposing the use of violence and repression (especially toward minorities) and the emergence of new forms of authoritarianism. The long-term objective must be to facilitate the transition from state-run economies to market-driven economies, supported by pluralistic institutions. Working toward this objective need not mean a vast commitment of American resources, but should be a highly visible element in U.S. policy. It must encompass long-term projects in countries not yet ready for reform as well as more blunt assessments of failure in those countries that are now engaged in efforts to marketize their economies.

The primary reason for pursuing such a policy lies in the need to forestall a loss of hope among the nations of Southeastern Europe in their ability to modernize, to draw closer to Europe and the United States, and, ultimately, to democratize. The alternative is a region that has no stake in peace—and that situation could prove dangerously destabilizing. Another rationale lies in the challenge facing the United States over the next decade in dealing with the Soviet Union. If the United States is to counter the spread of Soviet influence in Southeastern Europe, which may very well follow the growing dependency of these countries on the Soviet Union economically and in other ways, U.S. policy must give a higher priority to encouraging economic and political reforms in Southeastern Europe.

In this context it is important for the United States to realize that the policy of supporting "national communism" is now largely outdated. In the 1960s, the United States was able to appeal to self-confident maverick Communist states, whose economies were robust, to oppose Soviet hegemonistic designs. Today neither the Soviet threat nor the economic dynamism of the 1960s, is present. In their place, disguised by the new freedoms won by *perestroika* and *glasnost,* is a pervasive weakness.

Considerations such as these raise the question of what is to replace a policy of supporting national communism. Our authors favor the notion of selective rewards and penalties to encourage Communist countries to engage in reform—what U.S. policymakers choose to call differentiation. There can be little argument with the notion of differentiation, that is, of encouraging East European countries to engage in reform. The question is whether such an approach remains tainted by association with the policy of supporting any and all national Communist regimes—as has clearly been the case in Southeastern Europe in the past—or whether it denotes a new, realistic appraisal of the importance of making progress toward reforms that, in the end, will strengthen the economy and contribute to democracy, while forestalling any future tendencies toward a "coalition of weakness" in the Communist world.

This U.S. policy has important implications for the shorter term. If economic and political reforms are to have a chance of success, nations such as Yugoslavia must have safety nets—loans from international agencies, emergency credits from the United States, and special privileges with the European Community. At the same time, the United States must give more thought to long-term programs that can be launched even before basic reforms are adopted, to lay the groundwork for a successful transition to a market economy. (Such programs would be appropriate in the case of Bulgaria.) Moreover, U.S. policymakers must constantly shun mere verbal commitments by countries in the region to reform while encouraging steps to marketize.

The tremendous obstacles to the implementation of such policies are evident in the largely failed efforts of the United States up to now to persuade the countries of Southeastern Europe to undertake reforms. Yet the United States has many assets on which to draw. First and most important, the Soviet Union is not in principle opposed. Second, Europe is poised to make a major contribution if the countries in the region initiate real reforms. Third, there is a palpable "Eurofever" sweeping over Eastern Europe—a hope and a desire for a better life in closer association with the European Community. This Eurofever could subside into passivity and despair if the nations of the region do not take concrete steps soon to improve conditions there.

These recommendations, if implemented, would meet their greatest test in Yugoslavia, where the United States has invested the greatest diplomatic capital. It is in Yugoslavia that U.S. criticism of the pace of reform and of actions on the human-rights front runs the risk of weakening bonds that, as Walter Roberts points out, have grown, despite setbacks, since the 1960s. It should be clear that our ties with Yugoslavia are indeed an asset not to be squandered, and that Yugoslav sensitivities over the national question and over the pace of reform are very great. Yet it should be possible to convey to the Yugoslavs the fact that U.S. policies in support of reform are not contrary to Yugoslavia's long-term interests. Indeed, the notion of encouraging national renewal could be viewed as building on earlier U.S. efforts in support of national communism. Even at the risk of appearing to criticize, the United States should not be reluctant to express its own views about how such national renewal can be achieved.

In the rest of this chapter, we examine these policies in terms of problems dealt with by the contributors to this volume. We turn first to the need to limit regional conflicts in Southeastern Europe, and then deal with the problems associated with encouraging economic reform. Then we consider problems of domestic stability and conclude with a look at the Soviet role in Southeastern Europe, especially in respect to Yugoslavia.

THE AVOIDANCE OF CONFLICT IN SOUTHEASTERN EUROPE

The 1990s will be a period in which declining superpower influence in Southeastern Europe will combine with rising nationalism to increase the likelihood of regional conflicts. Containing these conflicts will test the maturity of the countries of the region. U.S. policymakers will be challenged to assure that the United States is not drawn into these disputes if they do occur.

Our contributors agree that the greatest potential for conflict at present lies in disputes over minorities: tensions over the status of the Hungarian minority in Romania; the controversy over the status of the Albanian minority in Kosovo; concern about the treatment of the Turkish minority in Bulgaria; the Macedonian issue; and the Cyprus dispute, stemming from the Turkish invasion of Cyprus in 1974. Although both superpowers seek to restrain these conflicts, especially among their allies, neither NATO nor the Warsaw Pact has been successful in preventing these regional disputes from disrupting intraalliance relations. F. Stephen Larrabee in Chapter 8 notes that the Greeks and the Turks are no nearer to a solution of the Cyprus conflict than they were when the dispute began. The controversy between Romania and Hungary, for its part, has grown so intense that the two Warsaw Pact powers have all but broken off diplomatic relations.

The most important limit on these disputes appears to be psychological. The countries of the region simply do not wish to go to war. Memories of World War II must play some role in this attitude, as well as a fear that the region might become another Middle East, rife with terrorism. As Cviic notes, Kosovo has not, contrary to the fears of some following the Yugoslavs' repression of the uprising by the Albanians there, turned into another Lebanon (although it still could do so). A second factor limiting the spread of disputes in the region is the universal support in the region for the territorial status quo, given concrete expression in the Conference on Security and Cooperation in Europe (CSCE) process. Finally, as Roberts and Zachary Irwin (Chapter 7) point out, recent years have seen attempts to foster Balkan cooperation. The role of the United States must be to uphold this framework of peace by encouraging Balkan cooperation and the broadening of the CSCE process, with the ultimate goal of applying human-rights standards to the minority disputes of the region.

Cautious optimism is in order, therefore, that nationality disputes in the region will not threaten peace and support for the territorial status quo. Yet U.S. policymakers still have reason for concern. There is the danger that psychological constraints against violence, if breached, can never be restored. The danger that the rules of civilized behavior will fall into abeyance is acute in the case of Yugoslavia, for whose citizens the question of minimizing communal and national violence is literally one of physical and national survival. It need hardly be added that a Yugoslavia built on repression, rather than on consensus, would be a major destabilizing force in the region.

Even if military conflict is unlikely in Southeastern Europe in the coming decade, U.S. policymakers must contend with the possibility that the nations of Southeastern Europe will shift their attention away from external threats (primarily the Soviet Union) toward regional concerns—a change in perceptions that might itself aggravate tensions. As Larrabee notes, Greece already defines its security in terms of a possible conflict with Turkey. Yugoslavia, as Irwin points out, has long felt that the geographical proximity of Albania to Bulgaria was a threat to southern Yugoslavia. At the same time, as Irwin notes, the Yugoslavs have developed a doctrine of "special war," which defines the threat to the country's security in terms of a linkup between unspecified foreign forces and domestic opponents of the regime.

This doctrine of special war reflects the growing fixation of the Yugoslav military on the internal crisis in Yugoslavia.

The situation in Bulgaria is quite different. As Daniel Nelson points out in Chapter 6, Bulgaria, in response to Soviet pressures, has long maintained a military establishment that is, relative to the country's population, one of the largest in Eastern Europe. A reevaluation of security priorities in Bulgaria might lead to a cutback in military spending and set the stage for successful economic restructuring.

PROGRESS TOWARD ECONOMIC REFORM

The absence of conflict in Southeastern Europe is a precondition for progress in the region. The realization of that progress must, meanwhile, come through economic reform. Whereas Greece and Turkey have been strengthening their economies in preparation for the Europe of 1992, the Communist states of the Balkans have allowed their economies to stagnate or, in the Yugoslav and Romanian cases, have experienced a sharp decline in living standards and economic performance. The stage has been set for efforts in the 1990s to inject new life into the economies of the region through market reforms.

As the contributors to this volume note, each country faces special problems, reflecting its level of economic development, burden of debt, and relationship with the Soviet Union. Albania, which is still underdeveloped, might put off market reforms altogether and might continue to develop economically by investing more in agriculture while permitting a limited amount of foreign capital. (Whether economic growth would keep up with the population increase is another question.) At the other extreme, Yugoslavia's experiments in partial reform from the 1960s onward have virtually compelled that country to take the course of complete marketization, combined with some form of political pluralization, if it is to revitalize its economy.

Individual cases aside, the assessment by our contributors of the prospects for economic reform are, to say the least, gloomy. John Lampe, in his introductory chapter dealing with the historical forces that have shaped modernization in Southeastern Europe, stresses the traditional barriers to economic progress that would presumably quash attempts at reform. Roland Schönfeld's account, in Chapter 4, of the mismanagement of the economies of Yugoslavia and Romania and the obstacles that face reform elsewhere is pessimistic in the extreme.

U.S. policymakers must therefore reconcile themselves to the fact that the Communist states of Southeastern Europe will achieve economic reform, which is the basis for long-term stability, only with the greatest difficulty. If the experience of Yugoslavia (and other Communist countries that have initiated reforms) is any guide, reform efforts will be accompanied by serious dislocations and possibly more, not less, U.S. involvement in domestic economic decisions (supporting debt relief schemes of international agencies and the like). To adapt Samuel Johnson's aphorism about certain second marriages, advocating a policy of reform for the state-run economies of Southeastern Europe requires "the triumph of hope over experience."

Yet there is little alternative for these countries, over the longer term, other than to "marketize" their economies and to introduce some political pluralization. It is toward these goals—short term in the Yugoslav case, longer term in the rest of the region—that U.S. efforts must be directed.

Even in cases where reform is not immediately contemplated, U.S. policy should encourage steps that will prepare the ground for economic reform, political conditions permitting. The Yugoslav experience in introducing decentralization in a society not ready to accommodate to even "semimarket" conditions suggests how important it is to educate a developing society in the ways of a market economy well before reform gets under way.

What is essential under present conditions is to keep alive the hope of economic reform (and closer relationships with Europe and the United States)—even if to do so requires something of an act of faith. Nothing would be more destructive to U.S. interests than to take the attitude that reform is bound to fail. Amid all the passivity and despair in Eastern Europe, hope exists for a better future through closer ties with Europe and the United States. By advocating reform the United States signals its recognition of, and sympathy with, these fragile hopes.

THREATS TO DOMESTIC STABILITY AND THE CRISES IN YUGOSLAVIA AND ROMANIA

The contributors to this volume agree that the Communist states of Southeastern Europe are experiencing a deep systemic crisis that could undermine their stability and legitimacy. This has been dramatically evident in the case of Yugoslavia since the demonstrations in Serbia, Slovenia, and Montenegro in the summer and fall of 1988. Trond Gilberg warns, in Chapter 3, that if other Communist states delay reform, they may face irresistible demands for change at some future date. Schönfeld supports this view of the gravity of the situation in his analysis of the obstacles to economic reform. Lampe warns that if reforms do fail, populist authoritarian leaders could emerge, compromising hopes for greater democracy in the region in the future.

The picture this volume presents, therefore, is sobering. Without domestic stability it may prove impossible to engage in economic reform. Yet the economic situation may have to deteriorate still further before the governments of the region are convinced of the necessity of introducing basic political reforms. At this point, however, a backlash could occur, encouraging new authoritarian leaders to emerge.

The threat to domestic stability varies throughout Southeastern Europe. Greece and Turkey do not face a systemic challenge at present. Larrabee notes that the political systems of both countries are more broadly based and stable than a decade ago. Albania and Bulgaria are encountering growing economic difficulties, yet neither country faces any immediate threat to its political stability, and market reforms in Albania could be delayed for the remainder of the decade without disastrous consequences.

But Romania and Yugoslavia face serious, indeed grave, problems. The excesses of Ceausescu's rule in Romania cast their shadow over the entire region. Nelson and Gilberg agree that there will be no change in Romania until Ceausescu dies, but that the ensuing struggle for power might lead to the release of pressures that have been building in the country over the past thirty years. The fate of Romania after Ceausescu passes from the scene is therefore veiled in uncertainty; a "Romania 1956" is possible if the struggle for power were to be prolonged.

The Yugoslav crisis has steadily worsened since the economic downturn began in the early 1980s. Today, the country is in political turmoil; drastic economic reforms have been promised but, as Schönfeld points out, not yet implemented. Populist currents have emerged in Serbia and in Montenegro (the latter more progressive than the former). Yugoslavia's ability to survive in its present form is questionable, with incalculable consequences should violence become the order of the day.

As Rusinow points out, these developments have rendered invalid many of the assumptions on which U.S. policy toward Yugoslavia has been based in the past. Yet the rapidly developing crisis makes policy recommendations difficult. Cviic, in his analysis of the situation, suggests that basic political changes may be in the offing in Yugoslavia, leading to the emergence of a government and party dominated by

Slobodan Milosevic, but Cviic is skeptical that Milosevic is an advocate of economic reform. Cviic also believes that the struggle for reform and democratization will not cease, regardless of the outcome of the struggle for power. He therefore suggests that the United States should keep its distance from Milosevic, in effect applying the same criteria to a Milosevic-dominated regime as to other East European governments—support and rewards for the implementation of market reforms but active disapproval for violation of human rights. Yet it could be argued that U.S. policy must go still further. It is of the greatest importance that the United States support a federal system in Yugoslavia based on consensus, not the domination of one group or nationality, lest the dark shadow of repression and national conflict fall permanently over that country.

THE ROLE OF THE SOVIET UNION IN SOUTHEASTERN EUROPE

The evidence presented in this volume suggests that two historic changes are taking place in Soviet thinking toward Eastern Europe, and therefore toward the Communist nations of the Balkans.

The first of these changes can be summarized as one of changing perceptions. The Soviet Union no longer views Eastern Europe, along with Southeastern Europe, as a "bloc" unified by a commitment to a common view of socialism and fealty to the Soviet Union. Rather, the Soviet leadership envisages a future Eastern Europe of socialist-oriented states with friendly ties to the Soviet Union capable of maintaining social and economic stability within their own borders. One might call it, in J. F. Brown's words, the triumph of the concept of viability over cohesion in Soviet thinking about Eastern Europe. This shift in perceptions may not be complete, and it may to some extent be reversible. It nevertheless seems to be very much on the minds of our contributors, who take the position that Soviet intervention aimed at reasserting Soviet control over the Communist nations of Southeastern Europe is highly unlikely.

The second change in the Soviet position toward the region lies in Soviet support for reform. For the first time since the 1960s, the Soviet Union is the facilitator, not the inhibitor, of change. The effects of this new policy have yet to be fully felt, but the policy could profoundly influence the evolution of the Communist systems of Eastern Europe in the coming decade.

The point that Soviet support of reforms can be withdrawn is not a convincing argument against U.S. initiatives designed to take advantage of the opportunity offered by Gorbachev's proreform position. In the past the United States has been able to pursue a successful policy toward Southeastern Europe by taking advantage of windows of opportunity, such as the one that opened in 1948 when the Soviet-Yugoslav dispute broke out. The present window of opportunity offers the United States the chance to contribute to the democratization of Southeastern Europe in a reform atmosphere unparalleled in the postwar history of Eastern Europe.

Our study also points to a long history of Russian and Soviet involvement in Southeastern Europe based on treaty obligations, security concerns, and economic ties. As a result of these commitments and interests, the Soviet Union should play an active role in the affairs of Southeastern Europe in the decade ahead, especially with respect to the two Warsaw Pact allies, Bulgaria and Romania.

In the case of Yugoslavia, another option has emerged for Soviet diplomacy: playing the Slavic card. That such a possibility exists has become evident in the past year. Gorbachev spoke of a "genetic" tie between the Russians and the Serbs in his conversations with Slobodan Milosevic when visiting Belgrade in the spring of 1988. Soviet policy has supported the repression of the Albanian uprising in Kosovo in March 1989; as Irwin points out, Moscow has accepted the view that the uprising in Kosovo was the work of a conspiracy. The Soviet position on Kosovo is undoubtedly influenced by Soviet concerns over the national question in the Soviet Union, especially with regard to the dangers of centrifugal forces developing in Soviet Central Asia. Whatever the reasons, Soviet support for Yugoslavia on the Kosovo issue projects the Soviet Union into Yugoslav domestic politics, on the side of the Serbs.

Bulgaria has reacted with greater caution than the Soviet Union, yet there is evidence that Bulgaria also supports the Serbs on the Kosovo issue. Moreover, the Bulgarians have shown an interest in discussing Balkan questions with the Serbs—perhaps with the intent of reopening the Macedonian question. U.S. policymakers need not take such undercurrents of Balkan intrigue too seriously, yet they illustrate the forces at work attracting certain of the Slavic people of the Balkans to one another and to Moscow, in a period of rising nationalism and social and political unrest.

The greatest imponderable in judging future Soviet behavior in Southeastern Europe concerns possible unilateral Soviet intervention, military or otherwise, in the region. The United States must try to anticipate and, to the extent possible, forestall such Soviet actions.

The evidence in this volume on this point is ambiguous. We have suggested that Soviet perceptions of Eastern Europe have fundamentally changed in recent years. Phillip Petersen and Joshua Spero point out in Chapter 9 on the Soviet military view of Southeaster Europe, that Soviet military intervention in Southeastern Europe is unlikely in the decade ahead. Yet both Nelson and Ronald Linden (in Chapter 10) note that the Soviet Union would probably not hesitate to use force if its basic interests were challenged in either Bulgaria or Romania. Linden speaks of certain limits that the Soviet Union continues to place on political change in Eastern Europe, limits that greatly resemble those of the Brezhnev Doctrine. And Gilberg notes that although unilateral and unprovoked Soviet intervention is probably a thing of the past, the Soviet Union might still feel compelled to take preemptive action against what it perceives as aggressive moves to extend U.S. influence in the region.

The problem requires more thorough analysis than we can offer here. It appears that a new "Gorbachev Doctrine" is emerging in central and northern Europe which justifies the Soviets' turning a blind eye toward power-sharing arrangements in Hungary and Poland, arrangements that in the past would have been considered violations of the Brezhnev Doctrine. Two considerations seem to govern this change in attitude. The first is the Soviet desire to see social stability in Eastern Europe. (Linden also alludes to this desire as a criterion for judging the Soviet propensity to intervene unilaterally in Eastern Europe.) The second consideration is that Hungary and Poland remain locked into a strategic relationship with Moscow that cannot be easily changed without express Soviet approval.

The application of this "Gorbachev Doctrine" to Southeastern Europe would seem, at first glance, to rule out any Soviet intervention in the region. Of the six Warsaw Pact members in Eastern Europe, Bulgaria and Romania would be of least strategic importance to the Soviet Union if war were to break out in Europe. But, it could be argued that any threat to the Soviet presence in Southeastern Europe would be sudden and destabilizing—the opposite of what is evolving (or what it is hoped will evolve) in Central Europe. In the Romanian case, furthermore, Moscow would have to reckon with a neighbor whose behavior not only over the past twenty years but ever since the Bolshevik Revolution has been in many respects hostile to the Soviet Union. For these and a variety of reasons relating to the cultural traditions of Southeastern Europe, the Soviet Union might find it extremely difficult, faced with a situation in which a Communist regime in Southeastern Europe was in jeopardy, to stand to one side.

To summarize, we suggest that a more pragmatic view on the part of the Soviet Union toward relations with Eastern Europe, and a desire in principle not to employ force, opens up new opportunities for U.S. foreign policy to encourage political and economic reform in the region. Such a policy need not conflict with basic Soviet interests. However, events could trigger a harsh Soviet response that policymakers could not have anticipated by analyzing current Soviet statements relating to the Brezhnev Doctrine or recent Soviet toleration of power-sharing arrangements in Poland and Hungary.

Among the uncertainties surrounding Soviet policy toward the Communist states of Southeastern Europe in the upcoming decade, one looms above all others: What effect will the growing instability in the region have on the region's relations with the Soviet Union? Will this instability reinforce centrifugal tendencies or increase the region's dependence on Moscow? An opaque crystal ball suggests an ambiguous answer, at best. The continued growth of nationalism, in the case of Romania, for example, would seem to attenuate Soviet influence and control. Bulgaria might cautiously follow in Romania's footsteps after changes in its aging leadership. Yet a new "coalition of weakness" could emerge between the Soviet Union and the former national-Communist states of the region, characterized not so much by Soviet control, but by the dependence of these countries on one another.

THE FUTURE OF SOUTHEASTERN EUROPE

It is appropriate to end this volume with a word about the peoples of Southeastern Europe—the Yugoslavs, Romanians, Bulgarians, Albanians, Greeks, and Turks—whose presence has given the region its uniqueness, distinctive nationalism, and fierce love of freedom. These qualities have, from time immemorial, inspired these diverse peoples to search for independence, national self-affirmation, and economic betterment.

The struggle is now entering in a new phase. From the U.S. point of view, it is the post-cold war era. For the peoples of Southeastern Europe, however, this new chapter in their history is part of a long and continuing battle for security and progress. It is a struggle that often seems unending. New obstacles appear as soon as existing ones are overcome.

It is a struggle that the peoples of the region themselves must win or lose. If there are setbacks, the United States will, however, be seen as bearing part of the responsibility (as will the Soviet Union, the other superpower). To avoid such a backlash, and at the same time to hold out hope for basic changes, it is important that the United States demonstrate restraint in dealing with regional problems and concerns. We cannot shape the future of Southeastern Europe; that is the task of the peoples of the region themselves. We can inject a passion of our own, however, in the task of showing how reform is to be achieved. In the last analysis, the problem is a state of mind, not a particular policy. In the decade ahead, U.S. policymakers diplomacy must demonstrate an unwavering commitment to the process of reform. Only in this way can the United States hope to reverse the negative trends now evident in the region.

U.S. policymakers must also reassess their understanding of, and policy toward, national communism. In the past, support for national communism resulted in U.S. backing for any Communist country that would declare its independence of the Soviet Union and accept U.S. aid. In the event, Southeastern Europe proved to be chockablock with maverick Communist states, and a successful proving ground for the policy of support of national communism. Today, putative independence of the Soviet Union may conceal long-term contrary trends, while serving as an excuse for putting off desperately needed reforms. National communism must become synonymous with national renewal, or it will be devoid of content in the Eastern Europe of the 1990s.

The new U.S. policy toward Eastern Europe appears to be that of "differentiation." As we have suggested, the policy appears reasonable, as long as its content is appropriate to the countries and regions in which it is supposed to be applied. In Hungary and Poland it seems to necessitate that a country, in order to win U.S. favor, engage in democratic reforms up to and including power sharing with the opposition.

In Southeastern Europe, however, the goal of democratization and political pluralization must be viewed as the end result of a process the beginnings of which include a focus on modernization, practical steps towards economic reform, and the search for democratic forms of legitimation in the broadest sense. There is no reason why this goal cannot be achieved within a one-party structure, because this is indeed the form of government that is most firmly established in most of the Communist countries of the region. Yugoslavia is a special case, for it embraces both republics in which political development cannot be halted short of real democracy and those in which the one-party system is still firmly entrenched. Given the country's rapid economic decline, free elections and the formation of opposition parties may well be preconditions for reconstituting a government that can govern.

We believe that "differentiation" in Southeastern Europe implies a pragmatic choice of programs that will have some chance of success, will maintain momentum toward reform, and will divert energies toward constructive national renewal and away from destructive nationalist vendettas. Differentiation also means that those countries that wish to join Europe should be helped to do so, to the extent that they are able. In this context, the effort of Albania to end its economic isolation becomes as important in U.S. thinking about the region as the need to liberalize the autocratic system in Romania. As we suggested earlier, it may be that programs can be initiated to prepare the ground for a market economy well before reforms are introduced. In this fashion some of the mistakes of rapid decentralization in Yugoslavia could be avoided elsewhere in the Balkans.

The Soviet threat no longer lies in expansion but in its opposite, a weakness that is attractive to conservative forces in the region and breeds economic dependence. Because the Soviet Union is not deliberately trying to make the planned economies of Southeastern Europe dependent on the Soviet Union—for example, by encouraging the export to the Soviet Union of substandard goods that cannot be sold in the West—the issue is not subject to negotiation with the Soviets. Yet growing economic dependence on the Soviet Union—a trend that these countries are attempting to resist—could become a conscious policy in the countries of the region if reforms do not succeed. This is not the direction the peoples of Southeastern Europe wish to go. The United States, in its relations with the proud peoples of the region, must work to persuade them that the European alternative, with U.S. backing, is where their future lies.

ABOUT THE AUTHORS

Editor

Paul S. Shoup is Professor of Government at the University of Virginia. He holds a Ph.D. from Columbia University. He held a Fulbright-Hayes Fellowship for Yugoslavia and Switzerland in 1969–70 and IREX grants for study in Yugoslavia, Poland, and Slovenia in 1981 and 1988. He was Director of the Center for Russian and East European Studies, 1983–1986, at the University of Virginia. Dr. Shoup is author of *Communism and the Yugoslav National Question* (1968) and *The East European and Soviet Data Handbook: Political, Social, and Development Indicators* (1981), and is a frequent contributor to professional journals.

Project Director

George W. Hoffman is Professor emeritus of the University of Texas at Austin and Research Professor at the Institute for Sino-Soviet Studies of the Elliott School of International Affairs, George Washington University. A former Secretary of the East European Program, the Woodrow Wilson International Centers for Scholars, he holds a Ph.D. from the University of Michigan. Dr. Hoffman was a Fulbright Professor at Munich in 1962 and in Heidelberg in 1972. He holds membership in numerous professional societies. His awards include the following: Honors Award, the Association of American Geographers; Member d'honneur, Serbian Geographical Society; Jiricek Gold Medal of the Southeast European Society, Munich; and awards from the governments of the Federal Republic of Germany, Austria, and Yugoslavia. He was a member of first Academic Advisory Council, Kennan Institute for Advanced Russian Studies; The Woodrow Wilson Center; Chairman of the Committee on Research and Development, American Association for Advancement of Slavic Studies; Council of Learned Societies/Social Science Research; a member, Committee on East European Studies, American Council of Learned Societies/Social Science Research Council; and Senior Councillor, Atlantic Council of the United States. His publications include *Europe in the 1990s, A Geographical Analysis*, (sixth. ed., 1989); *The Energy Challenge, East and West*

(1985); *The Balkans in Transition* (1963, reprint 1983); *The Common Market* (1976); *Regional Development Strategy in Southeast Europe* (1972); "Political Geography and Foreign Relations," in *Earth '88: Changing Geographic Perspectives* (National Geographic Society, 1988) (with F. W. Neal); *Yugoslavia and the New Communism* (1962), and also numerous contributions to books. He has been editor of several volumes, and has published more than one hundred professional articles.

Contributors

Christopher Cviic is East European correspondent of *The Economist* and Editor of *The World Today*, Royal Institute of International Affairs, London. Formerly an editor with BBC External Services in London, Mr. Cviic is the author of numerous articles and studies on Eastern Europe.

Trond Gilberg is Professor of Political Science, the Pennsylvania State University. Since 1988, he has also been Director of the Slavic and Soviet Language and Area Center at Pennsylvania State, having been Associate Director since 1977. He received a Ph.D. from the University of Wisconsin. He was previously Research Professor, Strategic Studies Institute, U.S. Army War College, Carlisle, Pennsylvania, Visiting Professor of Political Science at the U.S. Military Academy 1980–83, and Visiting Professor, University of Kiel, West Germany. Dr. Gilberg is the author of *The Soviet Communist Party and Scandinavian Communism: The Norwegian Case* (1973), *Modernization in Romania since World War II* (1975), and *Coalition Strategies of Marxist Parties* (1988) and editor (with Jeffrey Simon) of *Security Implications of Nationalism in Eastern Europe* (1985).

Zachary T. Irwin is Associate Professor of Political Science at Pennsylvania State University-Erie, the Behrend College. He holds a Ph.D. from Pennsylvania State University. He held a Fulbright-Hayes fellowship in Yugoslavia and summer research grant at Kennan Institute fir Advanced Russian Studies at the Woodrow Wilson International Center for Scholars. Dr. Irwin has written of numerous articles on communism and Islam in the Balkans; he was also the coauthor of *Introduction in Political Science* (with J.K. Gamble) (1987).

John R. Lampe is Professor of History at the University of Maryland and Director of the East European Program at the Woodrow

International Center for Scholars. He holds a Ph.D. from the University of Wisconsin. Dr. Lampe held a Fulbright Distinguished Professor Grant in Yugoslavia in 1983, a research grant to Bulgaria in 1981, and a Fulbright research grant to Romania in 1979. He was a U.S. Foreign Service Officer, 1964–1967. Dr. Lampe is author of *The Bulgarian Economy in the Twentieth Century* (1986). He also edited (with Marvin R. Jackson) *Balkan Economic History, 1550– 1950: From Imperial Borderlands to Developing Nations* (1982).

F. Stephen Larrabee is Distinguished Scholar-in-Residence at the Institute for East-West Security Studies in New York, where he was Vice-President and Director of Studies from 1983 to 1989. His Ph.D. is from Columbia University. In 1966–67 he was a Teaching Fellow at Athens College in Greece. Between 1978 and 1981 he served on the U.S. National Security Council Staff, where he was responsible for Soviet-East European Affairs and East-West Security relations. Dr. Larrabee is the author of many articles on East-West political relations, including "Gorbachev and the Soviet Military," *Foreign Affairs* (Summer 1988) and "Eastern Europe: A Generation Change," *Foreign Policy* (Spring 1988). His most recent publications are *The Two German States and European Security* (1989) and (with Robert D. Balckwill) *Conventional Arms Control and East-West Relations* (1989).

Ronald H. Linden is Director of Research, Radio Free Europe, Munich, and Associate Professor of Political Science, University of Pittsburgh. His Ph.D. is from from Princeton University. He has held IREX and Fulbright fellowships and was a Research scholar at the Kennan Institute for Advanced Russian Studies, The Woodrow Wilson Center. Dr. Linden is the author of "Romania: The Search for Economic Sovereignty," in *East Europe* (Joint Economic Committee of Congress, forthcoming); *Communist States and International Change* (1987).

Daniel N. Nelson is Senior Associate at the Carnegie Endowment in Washington, D.C., and Professor of Political Science at the University of Kentucky. He has a Ph.D. from Johns Hopkins University. He was Hoover Institution Senior Research Fellow, a Kellogg Foundation National Fellow, has held an IREX Exchange grant with Poland and Romania, and has been Fulbright Fellow in Romania. Dr. Nelson is the author of *Elite-Mass Relations in Communist States* (1988) and *Romanian Politics in the Ceausescu Era* (1989). He was the editor (with R. Menon) of *Limits to Soviet Power* (1989) and (with R. B. Anderson) of *Soviet-American Relations* (1988).

Phillip A. Petersen is Assistant for Europe and the Soviet Union on the Policy Support staff in the Office of the Deputy Under Secretary of Defense for Policy. His Ph.D. is from the University of Illinois. He was formerly a Research Analyst at the Federal Research Division of the Library of Congress and at the Defense Intelligence Agency. Dr. Petersen has contributed to numerous journals, including *Air Forces Magazine, Air University Review, Armées Socialistes* (Paris), *Dis Politika* (Ankara), *International Defense Review* (Rome), *NATO's Sixteen Nations, Naval War College Review, ORBIS, Slavic Review, The Washington Quarterly,* and to eleven books.

Walter R. Roberts is currently Diplomat in Residence at the Elliott School of International Affairs, the George Washington University. His Ph.D. is from Cambridge University. A retired government official, Dr. Roberts had several stateside and overseas assignments in the State Department and the U.S. Information Agency, including Counselor of the American Embassy in Belgrade, Yugoslavia, and Associate Director of the U.S. Information Agency. He is author of *Tito, Mihailovic and the Allies, 1941–1945* (1973; reprint 1987) and several other publications.

Dennison I. Rusinow is Research Professor in East European Studies and Adjunct Professor of History at the University of Pittsburgh. His Ph.D. is from Oxford University. Dr. Rusinov has been associated with Universities Field Staff International, 1963–1988. He was Visiting Professor at Dartmouth College, California Institute of Technology, and Michigan State University, and was the Balkans correspondent for the *Washington Star-News* and the *Chicago Daily News*. He is the author of *The Yugoslav Experiment* (1976), *Italy's Austrian Heritage 1919–1946* (1969), and numerous articles on Yugoslavia. He was editor of *Yugoslavia: A Fractured Federalism* (The Wilson Center Press, 1988).

Roland Schönfeld is Executive Director of the Südosteuropa-Gesellschaft, Munich. He has a Dr. oec. from University of Munich. Dr. Schönfeld was head of the Department of Contemporary Research and Deputy Director, Südost-Institut, Munich. He was also the Editor of the monthly journal *Südosteuropa*. He is a Lecturer at the College of Political Science, University of Munich. Dr. Schönfeld is also President of the German Association for Central and East European Studies and a Member of the Executive Committee of the Advisory Council for East-West Relations in the Federal Ministry for Foreign Affairs. Among his many publications are (with Werner Gumpel) *Southeastern Europe: Politics and Economics* (1986); "Foreign Economic Relations," in *Southeast Europe Handbook V: Hungary* (1987); "Romania: High Price of Autonomy," in *Aus Politik und Zeitgeschichte, Das Parlament* (1987); "Old and New Conflicts in the Balkans," *Die Internationale Politik 1985–1986* (1988); and *The CMEA: State and Prospects* (forthcoming).

Joshua Spero is Deputy Assistant for Europe and the Soviet Union in the Policy Support Programs Office, Deputy Under Secretary of Defense for Policy, Office of the Secretary of Defense, and the Pentagon Liaison Officer/Foreign Military Affairs Analyst with the Soviet Army Studies Office, Fort Leavenworth, Kansas. Formerly he was a Research Analyst of Soviet Defense Economics at the Federal Research Division of the Library of Congress. He has an M.A. from the Center for Russian and East European Studies, University of Michigan.

COMMENTATORS AND VISITORS

Commentators

Dr. Franz-Lothar Altmann, Deputy Director, Südost-Institut, Munich; and a former Fellow, The Woodrow Wilson Center.

P. Nikiforos Diamandouros, Director, Greek Institute for International Security Studies, Athens.

Dr. Gyorgy Enyedi, Professor of Geography and Deputy Director of the Geographical Institute, Hungarian Academy of Science, Budapest; Director, Research Center for Regional Studies; and a former Fellow, The Woodrow Wilson Center.

Dr. Wolfgang Höpken, Senior Fellow, Südost-Institut, Munich.

Dr. Raymond Hutchings, Editor for Soviet and East European Abstracts Series, Croyden, England.

Dr. Ali L. Karaosmanoglu, Professor of International Relations Bilken University, Ankara, Turkey; member, Board of Directors, Foreign Policy Institute, Ankara.

Dr. Hans Thalberg, Ambassador and past Director, Austrian Institute for International Affairs, Vienna; Ambassador to the People's Republic of China, Switzerland, Mexico, and Cuba and Central American Republics; Head, Austrian Mission to Berlin.

Dr. Radovan Vukadinović, University of Zagreb, Yugoslavia; Director, Postgraduate Program in International Affairs and Professor of International Affairs; chairman, UN Association of Yugoslavia.

Visitors Attending the Various Meetings

Nicholas G. Andrews, retired Foreign Service Officer, Washington, D.C.

David J. Fischer, U.S. Consul General, Munich.

Anneli Ute Gabanyi, Senior Fellow, Südost-Institut, Munich.

Dr. Anton Goslar, Lecturer in Geography, University of Ljubljana, Yugoslavia.

Hermann Gross, Professor emeritus, University of Munich.

Klaus Hausmann, Siemens A.G., Munich.

Dr. Guenther Hedtkamp, Professor of Economics, University of Munich.

A. Michael Hoffman, Managing Director, E. M. Warburg, Pincus, Ltd., London.

Dr. Ross Johnson, Director, Radio Free Europe, Munich.

Dr. William R. Johnson, Professor of Political Science and International Affairs, Institute for Sino-Soviet Studies and Elliott School of International Affairs, George Washington University.

Katheryn L. Koob, Public Affairs Officer, Amerika-Haus, Munich.

Dr. Carl Linden, Professor of Political Science and International Affairs, Institute for Sino-Soviet Studies and Elliott School of International Affairs, George Washington University.

William W. Marsh, Executive Vice President, Radio Free Europe/Radio Liberty, Munich.

Dr. Lawrence D. Orton, Chair, Soviet and East European Studies, Foreign Service Institute, U. S. Department of State.

Dr. Jens Reuter, Senior Fellow, Südost Institut, Munich.

Dr. Irena Reuter-Hendrichs, Senior Fellow, Stiftung Wissenchaft und Politik, Ebenhausen.

The Hon. John D. Scanlan, former U.S. Ambassador, Belgrade, Yugoslavia.

Professor Wilfried Schulz, Professor of Economics, University of the Bundeswehr, Munich.

Jack Seymour, former Deputy Director, Office of Eastern Europe and Yugoslav Affairs, U. S. Department of State.

Dr. William L. Stearman, Special Consultant, National Security Council.

Günther Wagenlehner, Studiengesellschaft für Zeitprobleme, Bonn.